COLLEGE OUTLINE SERIES

PRINCIPLES OF
SOCIOLOGY

ALFRED McCLUNG LEE, Editor

INTRODUCTION BY SAMUEL SMITH

CO-AUTHORS

HERBERT BLUMER
University of California at Berkeley

AUGUST B. HOLLINGSHEAD
Yale University

EVERETT C. HUGHES
Boston College

ALFRED McCLUNG LEE
Brooklyn College of The City University of New York

EDWARD B. REUTER
Late of Fisk University

BARNES & NOBLE, INC. • NEW YORK

PUBLISHERS BOOKSELLERS SINCE 1873

To the Memory of

ROBERT EZRA PARK

Great Teacher and Inspiring Stimulator
of Sociological Research

PREFACE TO THE THIRD EDITION

To be helpful to students of sociology in a wide range of colleges and universities, an outline of sociological principles must grow in many hands and in terms of many points of view. Under the editorship of the late Professor Robert E. Park of the University of Chicago, the first edition of this volume had the benefit of such a broad conception in his inspiration and guidance and in the work of the co-authors. It has been the purpose of the present editor and co-authors to carry on this conception in the various revisions through which this work has gone. In doing so, each co-author has had sole responsibility for his own section.

The present edition not only contains an entirely new section on "Social Problems," but the co-authors have also revised and substantially rewritten their respective sections on "Collective Behavior," "Human Ecology," "Institutions," and "Socialization of the Individual."

The following related titles in the Barnes & Noble College Outline Series and the companion series of Everyday Handbooks will be helpful to the student of sociology: *Sociology: An Introduction to the Science of Society; General Anthropology; Readings in General Psychology; Marriage and the Family; Dictionary of Economics; Political Science; Dictionary of American Politics.*

The co-authors and Dr. Samuel Smith, Editor-in-Chief, and Miss Nancy Cone of the Editorial Department, Barnes & Noble, Inc., have generously given of their time and effort, and their co-operation is appreciated. In addition, Dr. Elizabeth Briant Lee has contributed numerous helpful criticisms and necessary encouragement.

A. McC. L.

ABOUT THE AUTHORS

ALFRED McCLUNG LEE is Professor of Sociology at Brooklyn College and The Graduate Center of The City University of New York. In recent years, as visiting professor, he also served UNESCO at Milan, the Fulbright program at the University of Rome, and the American specialist program in Pakistan, India, the Middle East, Europe, and Iceland. In 1951, he organized the Society for the Study of Social Problems and later served as its second president. His books include *Marriage and the Family* (a College Outline), *The Daily Newspaper in America, Race Riot, Social Problems in America, How to Understand Propaganda, Fraternities Without Brotherhood*, and *Multivalent Man*.

HERBERT BLUMER was on the faculty of the University of Chicago for many years and is now Professor of Sociology at the University of California, Berkeley. Among his many public services, he has been liaison officer between the Office of War Information and the Board of Economic Warfare, permanent arbitrator for Armour & Co., and chairman of the board of arbitration of the U.S. Steel Corporation. He has been editor of the *American Journal of Sociology* and president of the American Sociological Association and the Society for the Study of Social Problems.

AUGUST B. HOLLINGSHEAD is the William Graham Sumner Professor of Sociology at Yale University. He is consultant in mental health to the U.S. Public Health Service and to the Committee on Behavioral Sciences of the World Health Organization. His books include *Principles of Human Ecology, Elmtown's Youth, Social Class and Mental Illness, Trapped: Families and Schizophrenia*, and *Sickness and Society*.

EVERETT C. HUGHES is Professor of Sociology at Boston College. He was formerly chairman of the department at the University of Chicago, editor of the *American Journal of Sociology*, president of the American Sociological Association, and professor at Brandeis University. He has written *French Canada in Transition, Men and Their Work, Where Peoples Meet*, and *Twenty Thousand Nurses Tell Their Story*.

EDWARD B. REUTER (1880–1946) taught at the University of Illinois, Goucher College, the University of Iowa, and Fisk University. He wrote a number of books and articles for professional journals on race and race mixture, subjects on which he became a well-known authority.

CONTENTS

Contents

INTRODUCTION

By SAMUEL SMITH

Sociology, the scientific study of society, deals with the behavior of men in group situations, with activities, customs, and institutions essential to the perpetuation and functioning of society, with the principles governing the reciprocal relationships of men, and with the factors entering into and ensuing from social interaction. Wherever an individual is in communication with others, wherever direct or indirect contacts with others recur, that individual is an interacting member of the social order. The elements, patterns, and consequences of this process of interaction among individuals and between groups is the chief subject matter of sociology.

SCOPE OF SOCIOLOGY

The scope of sociology is much broader than that of any of the other social sciences, for it encompasses all interactions among individuals and groups in their community setting. Economics deals principally with activities related to the production, distribution, and consumption of wealth; government, with the special province of political and civic experiences; history, with the chronological record of man's enterprises and achievements. Sociology synthesizes data from these and other social sciences as a basis for its generalizations. Thus, sociology is concerned with historical events insofar as they shed light upon the continuous process of group life, that is to say, upon the forces common to many events in the history of the group. The history of an institution, for example, may be studied in order to disclose the factors, principles, and types of group relationships involved in the genesis and career of such institutions. (The history of sociology is a specialized area of study employing the methods and techniques of historical scholarship, although its subject matter is of particular interest and value to students of the various social sciences.)

Sociology considers the total environment and the nature of man insofar as these forces influence the experiences shared by human beings and the processes of their group life. During group life, more or less clearly defined forms, ways, standards, mechanisms, problems, and group characteristics develop. All these facts affect the relationships among men and constitute major aspects of sociological analysis.

Introduction

SOCIOLOGY AS A SCIENCE

Science is a systematic search for the facts about the world. Sociology reveals many facts about human beings and their social environment. Problems common to many recurring situations are defined. Data relating to these problems are assembled, recorded, classified, and organized. Theories to explain observed phenomena are constructed. Observation, experience, analysis, and experimentation are utilized to test the accuracy of theories. In other words, sociology emphasizes the same quest for the truth about the universe and the same scientific method of inquiry that are characteristic of all the sciences. This field of knowledge deals with events from a sociological point of view, just as other sciences do from a biological point of view or a psychological point of view, etc. Its ethical neutrality and scientific validity are well established owing to the use of scientific procedures of investigation and to the verified results of sociological research.

The sociologist studies the structures and processes of social life as a whole, and therefore utilizes a somewhat different approach from that of the other social sciences which are concerned primarily with one or another limited aspect of social life. From psychology, he secures important data concerning human behavior, motives, stimuli, responses, and growth. From biology and related natural sciences, he obtains fundamental contributions, such as the laws of heredity, descriptions of the physiological processes of animal life, and the like. In other words, for its purposes and in dealing with its characteristic subject matter, sociology makes liberal use of information supplied by numerous other fields of knowledge.

DIVISIONS OF SOCIOLOGY

Sociology may be divided into the following broad subdivisions, corresponding to the six sections of this Outline, which collectively give consideration to the three main phases of sociological study, namely, human nature and growth, human interaction and communication, and collective adjustment to the environment:

Socialization of the Individual relates the person to society. It shows what society does to the individual and what the person can do with society. It analyzes the nature and nurture of his changing personality, his roles as a self and as a member of his group, as a transmitter of culture through family and other institutions, as a conformist or nonconformist to behavior patterns of his group, as a participant in the stabilization or reconstruction of society. Man is portrayed as the creature, carrier, creator, and manipulator of culture.

Collective Behavior is concerned with the rise of new societies and new social units, insofar as they are formed in the efforts of societies and social groups to act collectively. Collective behavior studies social movements and the tentative organizations by which they carry on before they have become fully institutionalized. Most social movements tend in the long run to terminate in institutions.

Introduction

Social Institutions have been regarded by some as the only proper subject of a sociological science. A sociology so conceived tends to be identified with social anthropology or ethnology. Ethnology seeks to study institutions from the point of view of their evolution, while sociology studies them in the light of their contemporary functions.

Race and Culture looks at society from the point of view of the ethnologist, that is, as an association of individuals whose distinctive physical characteristics have subdivided them into various socially distant majority and minority groups. Certain cultural instruments, such as traditions and customs used by individual groups, contribute to the perpetuation of social distance among them. As human association and civilization expand within a society, these long-established forces of separatism or isolation, which have formed the basis for national, caste, and class distinctions, tend to impede desired changes in the organization and structure of the society.

Human Ecology is concerned with man in the physical, as distinguished from the cultural or institutional environment. The ecological order grows up as a result of competition and the coincident co-operation which inevitably arise among individuals and peoples living together in a common habitat. Ecology looks at society from the point of view of population, its growth and decline, its dispersion and settlement. From this point of view society appears primarily as a biological rather than a civic or moral order.

Social Problems, or what is also called Applied Sociology, seeks to diagnose and deal in a practical way with current social problems. To do this effectively requires the prior appreciation of the basic social factors which bring these problems into existence. The section on Social Problems therefore constitutes the natural culmination to the more theoretical considerations that precede it in the book.

It should be noted that the divisions in this classification of subject matter are not independent of one another, but are closely interdependent and overlapping. For example, social problems may arise from the distribution of people in slum areas (an ecological factor) where an ethnic minority may be subjected to class or caste distinctions (a factor of race and culture) requiring or stimulating new social movements (collective behavior) and transformed social agencies (social institutions), all of which have an impact upon the character and social behavior of individuals as members of their group (socialization of the individual).

PRACTICAL VALUES OF SOCIOLOGY

The science of sociology has demonstrated its practical values in assisting the individual and the community to improve their interrelationships for sake of mutual benefit and social progress.

For the Individual. Knowledge improves understanding and increases the power of action. Adequate comprehension of sociological processes is essential for those who wish to adjust their intelligence and abilities most effectively to the world of man and nature. This

Introduction

science should substantially assist the individual to understand himself, his resources and limitations, his potentialities and his role in society.

As Community Resources. Like the individual, the community of individuals has need of a constantly increasing fund of shared knowledge concerning the life-processes of its members and groups. Individuals, singly or in association, are enabled to draw upon this common fund of facts. With accelerated progress, in recent years, in the scientific contributions of our "science of society," the facts of sociology provide a storehouse of resources for the extension of knowledge and the advancement of civilization.

As Applied to Social Problems. Contemporary society is beset by numerous maladjustments and crucial problems challenging the best powers of scientists and social idealists. Just as the facts of chemistry and other natural sciences have proved eminently useful to the art of medicine, so too we look to the future in the hope and faith that men will use the contributions of sociology for the solution of their common problems and the betterment of society. These contributions have been made and are constantly being augmented. The social scientist discloses truths; society can use or misuse these truths as it sees fit. As a scientist, the sociologist is loyal exclusively to the cause of factual research. As a constituent member of the human community, his interest and expectation are that the results of research will be applied to the benefit of mankind.

Part One

Socialization
of the
Individual

By

Alfred McClung Lee
Brooklyn College of the City University of New York

Chapter One

INDIVIDUAL AND ENVIRONMENT

Sociology provides two major perspectives upon human affairs and contributes significantly to two others. These viewpoints focus upon social relationships in terms of (1) *society,* (2) *the group,* (3) the overt social creature, *the individual as person,* and (4) the covert product of heredity, maturation, and socialization, *the individual as self.* Each is a different point of departure and emphasis for the study of the structure, functionings, and changes in the patterns of interrelationship among men, groups, and classes in tribe, nation, country, and the "great society" of mankind. Each in turn treats society, the group, the person, and the self as the central configuration to be considered.

Other sections of this book place more stress upon the societal and group perspectives but not to the exclusion of the individual. While not at all excluding the societal and group, the present section concentrates more upon such questions as: What about *me?* How am *I* related to society? What has society done to *me?* What can *I* do to and with society? In grappling with these questions, sociologists and psychologists have begun to work out more useful knowledge about the person and the self.

INDIVIDUAL AND SOCIETY

An individual is born with an organism so equipped genetically as to set for him general possibilities and limits for growth and accomplishment. As he matures physically and mentally in relationship to his environment, he accumulates attitudes, sentiments, practices, and habits that canalize his drives and help him to cope with his needs and wishes. He thus comes to behave in due course as an adult person. He is a product and a continuing illustration of physical, mental, and social processes at work.

He is thus a creature of his biological descent and of his physical and human environment. He carries, can manipulate somewhat, and occasionally creates or borrows and introduces some small or great variation in his group or societal culture.

Psychologists and psychiatrists as well as sociologists study this gradual conversion of a generalized organism into an adult personality with a complex mechanism for thought and communication. The fields investigated by these specialists overlap, but their contributions provide invaluable cross-stimulation obtainable only through such overlapping from different starting points. The psychologists, in their researches, approach the socialization processes from what, for the sake of simplicity, may be called the psychic or neural viewpoint, from within the subjects' skins, as it were. Sociologists, on the other hand, begin with the societal aggregate and stress interpersonal rather than individual aspects. Social psychologists, who may regard themselves as either sociologists or psychologists, have done much to bring together such contributions by working in the overlapping area. And psychiatrists find that their clinical needs bring them more and more to the utilization of a synthesis of both approaches.

"ORIGINAL NATURE"

The late Russell Gordon Smith liked to remind his Columbia undergraduates that each had arrived in this world "a polymorphous-perverse little ape with a billion years of biological evolution precipitated, so to speak, in your dimpled organism." Other than such generalized equipment, with potentialities for maturation that depend in part upon the influences of physical and human environment, each had little else—no clothes, modesty, language, food tastes, or dexterities, and certainly no notions about aesthetics, morality, religion, and science. "You came with no higher desires than to have your capacious belly filled with milk and your somatic and visceral itches scratched by loving hands. . . . Think of yourself as a bawling and puking brat with your nose and bladder in perennial flux, and then look at yourself now."

The term individual as used technically is a biopsychological conception. As Charles Horton Cooley wrote in 1902 in *Human Nature and the Social Order,* "A separate individual is an abstraction unknown to experience, and so likewise is society when regarded as something apart from individuals."

Heredity. A socialized individual cannot be sliced up, like a cadaver, and have any great meaning for purposes of social psychological investigation. Neither can one select out factors or traits and label some products of "original nature" and some the results exclusively of "environment" or "nurture." From inception the physical environment and from birth the physical and social environment constantly interact with the individual's existing potentialities and characteristics. Hereditary factors can only be developed in response to an evocative environment. Acquired factors can only result from modification of already existing structure. This is to deny old wives' tales concerning the transmission of acquired characteristics and the role of "prenatal influences" in the postnatal life of a child, how little Johnnie became a physician because his mother nursed a sick aunt while carrying him.

To a sociologist, an individual's or mankind's biological background is significant in three particular ways: (1) to provide, in relation to typical human environments, definitions of *typical mental characteristics;* (2) to elucidate the nature of *race differences;* and (3) to contribute to an understanding of *individual differences.* In all of these areas, the physiologists, physical anthropologists, and psychologists have offered useful orientation to the sociologists, and the sociologists in turn have contributed substantially to our knowledge of typical psychological equipment through life-history studies, observations of group behavior, and cross-cultural analyses and comparisons. These findings are outlined quite briefly in the following chapters.

Typical Mental Characteristics. A variety of efforts have been made to reduce to compact proportions the salient aspects of the human being's psychic outfit. The proliferation of lists of "instincts" early in this century, stimulated by William McDougall's *Introduction to Social Psychology* (1908), brought sharp criticism and deflation from a number of investigators but most substantially from L. L. Bernard in his *Instinct* (1924). In place of such atomizations of human motives and drives, John Dewey, George H. Mead, and Charles H. Cooley among social psychologists and sociologists and Sigmund Freud and his followers among psychologists gave emphasis to a more organic or "whole" view of human urges, drives, motives, or whatever the aspects of the libido or vital force might be labeled. "Mental" is used here as a shorthand term for the conscious and subconscious aspects of the psyche or mind.

Psychological Conclusions. Recognizing the basic fact of the irritability of all living matter, more recent "whole" views of drives begin with a pleasure-pain theory which may be elaborated in the manner of Freud into one of frustration and aggression. Man, like other organisms, seeks to prolong or repeat pleasure-giving experiences and to avoid painful ones. Painful stimuli make for frustrations that turn the organism toward overt aggressions or, where that is not possible or expedient, toward "boiling inwardly." With this background, Freud then related the canalizations of the individual's libido to his life-history. Through the conditioning of response mechanisms by experiences of pleasure and pain, the libido becomes canalized in different directions during successive stages of maturation. These stages, he indicated, begin with the infantile (oral and anal-urethral) and end with the adult (heterosexual). He ascribed colorations of motivation and personality in the adult to the "normal" and "deviant" patterns of maturational experience as these are defined for a given society and culture.

Sociological Conclusions. That such a theory touches upon "shameful" matters should not prevent us from understanding it. As Cooley noted in his *Human Nature and the Social Order,* "The human mind is indeed a cave swarming with strange forms of life, most of them unconscious and unilluminated. Unless we can understand something as to how the motives that issue from this obscurity are generated, we can hardly hope to foresee or control them."

Cross-cultural comparisons, in showing the possibilities of cultural variability and their relations with human needs and desires and with available environments, give new dimensions to our knowledge of the nature of typical mental characteristics. *Life-history studies* by sociologists and anthropologists have helped us to relate our conceptions of the individual more perceptively to his evolving social environment. *Observations of group behavior,* carried out in many types of group, have provided data for delineating behavioral possibilities, spontaneities, and more precise conceptions of conformity to and deviance from cultural patterns.

Other drive and wish theories are also influential. With a pleasure-pain theory similar to that of Freud, but on the basis of cross-cultural sociological analyses rather than of the consideration of psychiatric clinical data, W. G. Sumner and A. G. Keller concluded that for sociological purposes the generalized vital drive may be thought of as being canalized by maturation under the influence of environmental conditions into hunger, sex-love, ghost-fear (anxiety in the presence of the unknown), and vanity (related to Freud's narcissism), as they indicate in their *Science of Society* (1927). Of a somewhat more derived sort is W. I. Thomas's list of four wishes, originally set forth in H. S. Jennings and others, *Suggestions of Modern Science Concerning Education* (1917). His four wishes are: (1) for new experience, (2) for security, (3) for recognition, and (4) for response. He related these to "original emotional reactions"—fear, rage or anger, joy or love, and curiosity. In using any such suggestive list, we must realize that the labels are given to rather arbitrary abstractions derived from the complex processes of life.

Race Differences. The teachings of scientists concerning psychological differences among men of diverse racial stocks are useful chiefly in deflating popular allegations of differences. Such popular claims are based upon *ethnocentrism* (self-flattery through overevaluating the qualities of one's own people). *Existing evidence points to no significant inborn neurological differences, either in character or capacities, among the major racial stocks of mankind.*

Individual Differences. The fact that individual men and women in all tribes, peoples, and nations range, for reasons of "original nature" and nurture, between rather wide extremes in terms of any set of psychological criteria, has considerable sociological significance. In capacities of one sort or another, in interests, in normality, the large bulk of a group usually falls into an "average" category, with smaller numbers ranging off towards various extremes.

The sources of such variability are deeply imbedded in the intertwined nature-nurture situation. More gifted children may be found in the homes of professionals than of unskilled laborers. Why is this? Extreme eugenists claim that this is due to the superior hereditary endowment of the professional families and to the "poor human stock" of the unskilled. Without becoming

environmental extremists, sociologists point to the home, economic, and social advantages and opportunities of the children
of professionals. In this, too, the roles of "contacts" and of the
encouragement provided by successful and familiar models should
not be overlooked. A similar analysis can be made of the fact
that more juvenile delinquents *become a matter of police record*
from slum homes than from homes in the better neighborhoods.
Not only should deprivation be mentioned in this connection, but
it also is pertinent that the "better" families are more often given
opportunities to keep their delinquencies out of police records.
In both these illustrations, above all, both nature and nurture
make contributions.

Sociologists are interested in individual variations in capacity
and character because such deviations from accepted norms
figure in theories of leadership, genius, agitation, group and class
structure, mental defects and abnormalities, crime, criminals,
susceptibility to illness, and social change.

ENVIRONMENT AND NURTURE

From inception, as it is noted above, the human being is
subject to influences other than those carried within its cell walls.
These influences are at first physical and chemical and then,
following birth, come to include in addition geographical (climate, fauna, and flora), interpersonal, and cultural factors.
Studies of unsocialized children and of identical twins, as well as
of psychopathic cases and of diverse tribes and cultures, have
shed more and more light upon these postnatal environmental
influences. At any rate, it is impossible to segregate the results of
environmental influences from those called biological.

Unsocialized children have been found who grew in isolation
or with few socializing influences. The few well described cases
help to dramatize the tremendous role of culture and interpersonal relationships in human behavior and especially in the
growth and definition of personality. One girl found and studied
by Kingsley Davis lived in isolation with her deaf-mute mother
in a dark room for six and one-half years. Although she appeared
to be mentally defective when discovered, she reacted so rapidly
to intensive training that in two years she could converse well
and had an I.Q. score three times as high as in the beginning. By

fourteen, she had finished the sixth grade and appeared normal.

Identical twins, especially those reared under dissimilar conditions or conditions dissimilar in well-indicated respects, provide examples of the manner in which biologically similar beings react to disparate environmental influences. Such studies indicate that certain personality tendencies, as well as intelligence, appear to be in some degree heritable genetically, but in any event environment constantly influences such tendencies both positively and negatively.

Life-histories of psychopathic cases, neurotics and psychotics, especially when verifiably reconstructed, offer help for the understanding of "normal" or average people. Such accounts provide descriptions of biologically and/or environmentally stimulated deviations from the "normal." Cooperative subjects for such detailed probings are more available from among the mentally ill and the imprisoned than from among the rest of the population, and descriptions of their deviant lives help to highlight by comparison characteristics of "normal" people.

Cross-cultural investigations have yielded, from observations of many and diverse tribes, conclusions regarding psychological and sociological elements entering into (1) all cultures known or (2) cultures existing under given geographical and historical conditions. They have also enriched (3) our knowledge of the ranges of variability in patterned feeling and behavior.

Environment: Physical and Symbolic. Unlike other animals, man matures and functions in a developed symbolic environment as well as in a physical environment. A symbol is a sound, gesture, sign, other object, or person with which people have learned to associate a meaning and a value. The communication of meaning and value through symbols elicits reactions which, in a given social situation, are often those anticipated. The value of a symbol is its relative worth to those who share a version of its significance. A symbol thus stands for an aspect of a society's or a group's shared understandings, its culture, in other words for all or part of a learned pattern of thought, emotion, and action. Through symbols, man can summarize and communicate not only his own personal experiences and thoughts but also those of his group and society. He can also stimulate and manipulate the thoughts, feelings, and actions of his fellows.

Societal Culture. Edward B. Tylor, in his *Primitive Culture* (1871), provided a general definition for societal culture still widely accepted among social scientists. He characterized it as "that complex whole which includes knowledge, belief, art, morals, law, custom, and other capabilities and habits acquired by man as a member of society." Russell Gordon Smith (*Fugitive Papers*, 1930) told his students that "nine-tenths of all you do or say or think or feel from the time you get up in the morning until the time you go to bed at night is done and said and thought and felt, not in independent self-expression, but in uncritical, unconscious conformity with rules, regulations, group habits, standards, codes, styles, and sanctions that were in existence long before you were born." The "nine-tenths" is a rough guess; the fraction would vary and might be larger.

Tylor defined societal culture, the general patterns common to a society as a whole. A part of them would be the verbal conventions—words and definitions—set forth in a small pocket dictionary of its language.

Group-Cultures. Teen-age slang, occupational jargon, professional terminology, and standing family jokes are all evidences of group-cultures. Sometimes we speak a language resembling that of a pocket dictionary, but many times we talk in the more familiar verbal short-cuts of the group in which we find ourselves. Smith's students conformed to cultural patterns a large share of their waking hours but not necessarily to those of societal culture. They deviated from such general patterns in their thoughts, feelings, and actions even though in doing so they could still be considered conformists. Like students and other young people of all periods, they were conforming to group cultures which differed in many respects from the over-all culture of their time and place. They also did not behave the same way in all of the social situations into which they entered. At home, in student play groups, in classroom situations, while doing a part-time job, at church, they sensed the requirements of the social situation and either behaved in terms of the appropriate group-culture's patterns or defied them by flaunting inappropriate behavior. In other words, they and certainly their parents performed a variety of social roles as they went through each day's activities, roles prescribed by societal and group usage. For all their struggles with culture's inconsistencies and its conflicting role prescriptions, students are in the process at their age in our society of becoming more comfortable with their own conflicting values, or to introduce the term used in this book, with their own multivalence [1]; their "square" parents have usually already made that adjustment.

Conflicts of Values Leading to Multivalent Conditioning. Thus, man matures in a complex, multivalent or many-valued culture. In becoming conditioned for "normal" behavior in such a society, he becomes "many-minded," able to function in terms of the values and behavior patterns of each social group of which he is a member. From childhood, he is assimilated into group after group, and he takes on membership roles in each group as he learns how to participate in it. Man and his contrasting and even conflicting roles are treated in more detail in the next chapter.

Conventions, Folkways, Practices, and Attitudes. When culture is viewed in terms of separate trait models, it is well to bear in mind that each such trait is an integral part of larger patterns or complexes, patterns of personal behavior (roles) and of social structure (institutions and associations, classes and groups). With this in mind, the terms conventions, folkways, practices, and attitudes are defined respectively as the societal, group, personal, and self versions of cultural patterns that are related to similar interests, wishes, needs.

Conventions are traditional abstractions or models which are overtly exemplified by ourselves and others and which we take to be typical of our society. As we express ourselves in our behavior in ways resembling our society's conventions, we assume that we know how other people typically think and feel about such patterns, and we find it appropriate to do likewise. We have come to such assumptions through experience with the reactions of others during our assimilation into our social environments. Conventions thus influence our behavior directly and our thoughts and emotions indirectly. Conventions also provide norms for group folkways as well as individual practices and attitudes.

The *folkways* of a group may or may not resemble corresponding societal conventions, but in any given society the two sets of patterns are in each case usually given some arbitrary or rationalized relationship even though they may be in sharp con-

---

1 A term introduced by A. McC. Lee in "A Sociological Discussion of Consistency and Inconsistency in Intergroup Relations," *Journal of Social Issues,* V, No. 3 (1949), 12–18. See also "Attitudinal Multivalence in Relation to Culture and Personality," *American Journal of Sociology,* LX (1954–55), 294–299, and *Multivalent Man* (New York: George Braziller, 1966).

trast. Folkways are thus patterns of behavior, more or less modeled after the conventions, which have become common and customary in a group, association, or class. They are regarded as typical of a group at a given time and place. They have stability, but they are also caught up in the processes of social change. Like conventions, folkways may be seen in a variety of contexts: They are parts of a group-culture, of the group's definition of one or more roles, and of the group's prescription for the operation of a given association (a group manifestation of a social institution). Folkways find expression in individual thought, emotion, and action, again when the individual is in a suitable "frame of mind," that is, when he is functioning as a group member in a suitable group context or situation.

Practices are socially exemplified behavior patterns as adapted and taken on by individuals. They are personal counterparts of folkways and conventions plus the results of peculiar individual experiences and the somewhat unique or variant inferences and interpretations he makes of these. They are more or less permanent elements of personality. The similarities and differences between "dictionary language," a given group's ways of saying things, and a given person's mannerisms of speech illustrate the relation of practices to conventions and folkways.

Attitudes are accustomed states of mental readiness, patterned largely after societal conventions and group folkways, which offer formulas or channels for drive, motivation, or reaction by a person in response to classes of objects, situations, objectives, or persons. The individual differs from societal and group norms to the extent to which the self is an imperfect creature and carrier of culture and to which the self has deviant faculties and experiences, fantasies and inferences. This naturally implies that attitudes are multivalent. The attitude or valence which is operative in a given social action becomes so in response to cues presumed to indicate the societal, group, or personal context of the situation.

Each of our attitudes functions as a facet of an attitude complex, which is like saying that an attitude is one side of a many-sided die. We have many such dice in our minds ready for us to relate them to stimuli as the stimuli arise, and each side of each of them is related to a group-situation context. When we enter into such a situation, we recognize the type of group context from available cues, and this brings into play the side of our dice (attitude complexes) appropriate to the situation in hand. If all goes "normally," all the different dice turn up sides which correspond to the group context (as we understand it) and with one another. These upturned dice faces (attitudes or valences) are collectively our definition of our proper behavior under the circumstances.

Morals, Mores, Habits, and Sentiments. To certain of the four types of trait patterns—conventions, folkways, practices, and attitudes—society, social groups, individuals as persons, and individuals as selves attach a greater degree of compulsion. These more imperative societal, group and class, personal, and self patterns are named respectively morals, mores, habits, and sentiments.

Morals are conventions to which have been given a judgment of societal welfare. They are traditional generalities concerning right, wrong, duties, rights, and taboos handed down in a society and frequently formalized into sets of commandments, codes of ethics, or canons of ethical principles. They contain large elements of asceticism, humanitarianism, and formalism or ritualism. They dominate the teachings of societal surrogates—parents, ministers, teachers—even though they are frequently at odds with the group mores of such surrogates and of the groups served by them: "Do as I say, not as I do!" Morals represent crystallizations of a society's traditional aspirations as vaguely defined and somewhat colored by dominant group and class mores, but with significant rationalistic concessions to the dominated. They are chiefly useful in shaping the superegos of the young and in providing the main staples for propagandists—glittering generalities and name-calling symbols, righteous justifications and condemnations, suitably and variously interpreted, for social institutions, functionaries, roles, and courses of action. Morals have no necessary congruity with mores of constituent groups or with habits of individuals. Such subjects as theology, ethics, and traditional—but not scientific—social science concern themselves to a great measure with working out rationalizations between morals and group mores.

Mores are folkways that have had added to them, as Sumner stated in *Folkways* (1906), "a judgment that they are conducive to societal welfare." R. E. Park and E. W. Burgess, in their *Introduction to the Science of Sociology* (1924), note that "Under the influence of the mores men act typically, and so representatively, not as individuals but as members of a group." Folkways and especially mores define the characteristics of social roles and institutions as they are acted out. They are crystallizations of the expediencies of group experience. Conventions and morals provide façades for social institutions and cloaks for social roles, about as influential "internally" as façades and cloaks usually are.

Habits are practices the taking on of which has been accomplished by some form of real or fancied, actual or potential, societal and group compulsion. They are the personalized counterparts of mores and morals, the corresponding group and societal patterns. They include the results of peculiar individual experiences and somewhat unique or variant inferences.

Sentiments are central attitudes or valences of a sentiment complex. They have functions on the self level corresponding to those of morals and mores on the societal and group levels. They are products of the internalization of morals and mores in such multivalence configurations as have just been listed. Sentiments are among the more enduring, integrating, consistent, and stable aspects of a self. They are freighted with emotion. People do not like to reveal many of their sentiment valences accurately, especially the fact that their sentiments are multivalent. Psychiatrists have discovered that people's sentiments are often contradictory but that they are not so regarded by their owners, that sentiment valences change very slowly and more in detail and in effectiveness than in basic character, and that they are difficult to ferret out, characterize, and assess. Psychiatrists know that our sentiments toward others frequently contain both affection and hate, sympathy and detestation, and they ordinarily speak of this as ambivalence. Now they are beginning to recognize sentiment multivalence and its significant relations with social structures.

The motto, "Honesty is the best policy," is a useful illustration of these four terms. As stated, it is a part of the morals of our society. Modified to "Honesty is the best policy, but business is business" or to "Honesty is the best policy, but labor [management] has to look out for labor [management]," one has a *mos* (singular of *mores*), an example of group adaptation of a moral. Further modifications in either mos formula through the addition of such words as these, "but in *this* case I've got a higher loyalty to myself," supplies a typical sentiment pattern that the self uses to rationalize to himself and to others his overt habit pattern.

The latter may be interpreted by others in any given instance as shrewd, expected, peculiar, or criminal.[1]

PERSONALITY AND PERSONALITY CHANGE

The sociologist needs to know as much as he can about both aspects of the individual—self and person—even though his research concern is with the overtly social, the behaving person, group, and society.

Basic Aspects of Personality. The *self* is of concern to sociologists as in part a social product, but it is investigated chiefly by psychologists, psychiatrists, and social psychologists. The self is a somatic and a psychic as well as a social product. It is the covert and internal entity corresponding to the individual's overt entity, the *person*.

The *individual's conception of self* is derived chiefly from the reflection he perceives of his personal behavior in the reactions of others, his looking-glass selves (to adapt C. H. Cooley's term). Cooley noted that the self is always a social self, and in his *Human Nature and the Social Order* he assigned it "three principal elements: the imagination of our appearance to the other person; the imagination of his judgment of that appearance; and some sort of self-feeling, such as pride or mortification." George H. Mead, in his *Mind, Self & Society,* concluded that self-consciousness arises through "taking the role of the other" and related the social compulsions behind morals and mores to the psychological influence of a "generalized other," a conception resembling somewhat Freud's superego. An individual strives to integrate his conception of his self, but, like the varied social reflections of the person, the self is many-faceted. Behind the individual's social roles and social personalities, the self is a complex socio-psycho-somatic entity. The self becomes reified, rationalized, and in part loosely integrated out of the individual's maturing neural equipment, reflected selves, and other experiences.

In his elaboration of the conception of the self, Mead differentiated between the "I" and the "me." He defined the "I" as

---

1 Digested from A. McC. Lee, "Levels of Culture as Levels of Social Generalization," *American Sociological Review,* X (1945), 485–495, and "Attitudinal Multivalence in Relation to Culture and Personality," *American Journal of Sociology,* XL (1954–55), 294–299. See also Lee, *Multivalent Man* (New York: George Braziller, 1966).

"the response of the organism to the attitudes of the others; the 'me' is the organized set of attitudes of others which one himself assumes." Freud, on the other hand, perceived three phases of self which he called superego, ego, and id. The superego is roughly equivalent to that which is ordinarily labeled conscience, formed especially through early training in the morals. The superego is partly conscious, partly sunk in the subconscious. The ego is the conscious phase of self, the part of the self which attempts to understand and cope with external and internal realities and phantasms. The id is the subconscious, that to which Cooley chiefly referred when he spoke of "a cave swarming with strange forms of life, most of them unconscious and unilluminated." Here are elements of the superego, past experiences, old fears, submerged temporarily or permanently beneath the level of consciousness but still operative in motivation.

The *person* is the overt, acting, social entity through which the self functions in relation to others and to physical environment. We see, hear, touch, and come to know the person. The organization of action, emotion, thought, and physical characteristics which the behaving person manifests to others is what we call personality, but each person has many social personalities. In other words, his personal organization is seen differently in terms of his different roles and his diverse group contexts. Except as a matter of emphasis, self and person cannot be separated; they must be understood together.

The *individual* thus consists of a self and a person. He develops both of these aspects as a result of gradually expanding participation in social interaction during childhood and youth. This comes with assuming, and functioning in, statuses and roles in groups and in society.

How Do Personalities Change? Social situations that may modify personalities include (1) drastic societal change, (2) rapid or violent intergroup readjustment, (3) migration, (4) personal mobility within a society, (5) intermarriage, (6) conversion, (7) psychotherapy or group therapy, (8) education, and (9) personal crisis.[1] Culture change in a society may affect certain groups and classes more than others. The form of the conventions and morals—especially their symbolic descriptions in words and otherwise—may give the appearance of permanence while the

---

1 Lee, *Multivalent Man, op. cit.,* pp. 7–9, 285–297.

"content" or the functioning folkways and mores of constituent groups may have changed, and this makes for subtle and continuous changes in social personalities. Personal crises should be thought of as including the personality adaptations necessitated during any typical life-history as a person leaves and enters groups or statuses in groups. As changes take place in a person's social personalities, concomitant internal or covert changes proceed in the multivalent self.

CHAPTER TWO

ROLES

We have each a number of more or less related roles that we assume and put off, store in our minds for future use, revise, or permit to retire into our subconscious, perhaps to be brought forth again. Roles are associated with statuses or social positions which either we have been assigned or we have acquired. As the preceding chapter suggests, roles are defined and expressed in four major ways: societal, group (including class and caste), personal, and self.

SOCIETAL ROLES

Societal roles are prescribed by the conventions and morals of a society. Just as societal institutions represent configurations of conventions and morals in terms of broadly felt needs, interests, and wishes, so societal roles are configurations of conventions and morals in terms of the man-as-he-should-be in some area of social life. There are societal role prescriptions for a great many social statuses, for example, bride and groom, mother and father, professional people, governmental officials. They include chiefly functionary and member roles in societal institutions.

Societal roles, like the morals giving them their principal substance, tend to be absolute in statement or form, albeit vague and open to interpretation and rationalization in performance. They contain large elements of promise and aspiration, asceticism and humanitarianism. To the extent that societal functionary roles are believed in popularly as influencing the behavior of those performing them, they provide valuable crystallizations of status and power for those publicly granted legitimately to possess them, for example, government officials, physicians, clergymen, teachers.

Ambivalent Attitudes Toward Functionaries. The roles of societal functionaries of considerable prestige arouse ambivalent sentiments in the minds of their publics, the members of groups with which they are in contact. A mother or father, fulfilling the role of a societal surrogate, is both loved and hated by his or her offspring. Individuals who have reached the intimate and trusted status achieved by the medical profession are similarly subject, personally and as members of a group, to feelings both of gratitude and high expectation on the one hand and of distrust and rejection on the other. Illustrations of such attitudes toward governmental officials readily come to mind.

Roles in a Changing Society. Especially as society changes, human beings can seldom measure up to the idealizations current concerning how they as societal functionaries should behave. Regardless of the brightness and shininess of their tunics, the creatures within them are forced to reveal themselves, at least to those who prod, as what they are, human beings with feet of clay. But supported as they are in their necessary shortcomings by their group's mores, societal functionaries in a changing culture do what they can to combat efforts to undermine their prestige by frantic or noble efforts to re-establish popular acceptance of the weakened moral patterns. A part of this is frequently the drafting and promulgation of codes of ethics.

Although it may be far from fair, the public which helps to create impossible idealizations also seldom excuses its idols for failing to appear to live up to these idealizations. News stories or unprinted rumors of fee-splitting by physicians, of the unfairness of "company" doctors to employees, founded or unfounded gossip concerning irresponsibility by practitioners in times of private crisis, even misrepresentations of a physician's natural weariness at the end of a hard day as callousness—all these are very real problems to the medical profession. And in our changing culture, other societal functionaries have similar problems more or less as pressing.

Member Roles. Societal roles prescribe both how the man-as-he-should-be behaves as a functionary in places of responsibility, prestige, or leadership, and also how he acts as a member, a part of the rank-and-file of institutions and associations. Such societal member roles define what the citizen, the consumer, the soldier, the businessman, the trade-unionist, the parent ought to be like. They are useful in social control and, like uniforms, in giving otherwise insecure persons the security that comes through a sense of identification with something taken to be much larger or more important than themselves.

GROUP ROLES

Group versions of roles are prescribed in each group's folkways and mores. They represent integrations of a group's traditional experiences and expediencies that set the *intragroup* patterns for the man-as-he-has-to-be in social interactions which are within the group or of concern to its members. Group roles usually contrast in many respects with the *intergroup* or societal patterns, those prescribed for the moral man-as-he-should-be. Social distance obscures such contrasts to outsiders, and appropriate rationalizations make them tenable or unnoticeable to insiders. A group and its roles exist to satisfy one or more common interests, needs, or wishes of its members. It may be a clique, an association, a class or stratum, an ethnic or ethnoid segment, a caste, or one of the more dynamic and transitory types mentioned by Blumer in Part II of this outline. The child, marriage, and family roles outlined in the two succeeding chapters illustrate further what is meant by group roles as well as by societal roles.

Roles and Societal Structure. Social status groups tend to form within these three larger types of cross-hatching group in our society: (1) ethnic or ethnoid (ethnic-like) segments, (2) social classes or strata, and (3) occupational status-ladder social segments. Each social status group thus tends to fall within one ethnic or ethnoid segment, one social stratum, and one occupational status-ladder social segment. In consequence, its membership and individual role patterns tend to be a composite of those prescribed in the group-cultures of the larger groups. Our chief evolving ethnoid segments are labeled by their members and others as the Protestant, Roman Catholic, Colored, and Jewish even though in each case these are arbitrary social designations rather than descriptive terms. "Social class" is a term with which a social scientist can refer to a stratum or layer of social groups which are popularly treated as being roughly equal. They are roughly equal in social prestige and influence or lack thereof. Recognizable groups holding similar social status—made up of families and family connections and related to vocational groups, neighborhood groups, and many others—are popularly created and used, but they are not often named or otherwise identified with social class except in a very vague manner. Our major occupational status-ladder social segments, cutting across all social strata and ethnoid segments, can be characterized as being those of (1) entrepreneurs, those absorbed in some version of what they often call "the game," (2) bureaucrats, those absorbed in affairs related to "the organization," whatever their organization may be, as well as the status-ladders associated with that organization, (3) artisans and technicians, those absorbed in the merchandising and utilizing of their techniques, skills, status, reputation, and related wisdom, and (4) innovators, those absorbed in searching for novelty under whatever conditions they find available and involving.

Caste Roles. The division between the three white and the one colored ethnoid segments is so extreme in our society that it is often called castelike. Separating the country into all-too-segregated communities is something that might be called the "Bandana Curtain." Through it, which is less opaque for them, the nonwhites see little that endears the white community to them. Even the gestures of liberals and humanitarians so lack persistence, consistency, and decisiveness that they tend chiefly to provide still other stimulations to frustration. Through the Bandana Curtain, even when torn by riot reports, whites see little, and what they see is distorted. The Bandana Curtain is a barrier of myth, fantasy, wishful thinking, and social distance that sharply separates the white and colored communities. It makes accurate communication from one to the other exceedingly difficult.

Types of Group Role. Group membership and individual roles correspond to their societal cloaks, societal membership and functionary roles. Group membership roles are the intragroup prescriptions common in strata, ethnic and ethnoid segments vocational, family, and age groups. An individual role is one that only one or a few persons in any given group perform. It is such as leader, storyteller, good Joe, butt of jokes, playboy, bully, schemer, intermediary, hard worker. A physician or a clergyman has a membership role in a group of his fellow specialists as well as a corresponding individualized role elsewhere; the behavior prescribed for each version of either role is different. When a physician becomes a member of a group of non-physicians, he finds himself functioning in the group in part in terms of his societal physician role and in part in terms of a membership role prescribed by the group, probably a specialized one to reflect his status as a physician.

Roles and Group Identity. Our first experiences with roles, as we outline in the next chapter, are especially vivid ones, ones so vivid as to make those roles prototypical ones influential throughout the rest of our lives. Those *prototypical roles*—child, mother, father, sibling, nonsibling peer, stranger—become models for *successor roles*. These are group-membership roles, at first of very small and intimate groups of two and then of larger ones. Some of these groups are *frame-of-reference groups* in the sense that they provide us with a membership role, a partial orientation to life, a group-culture, which is typical of the group. Others of our prototypical groups (for example, those of parents and of strangers) are out-groups which become significant *point-of-reference groups*. Groups which are important to us as points of reference in our thinking include both frame-of-reference in-groups and also certain out-groups. These are sometimes called simply "reference groups," but the use of frame-of-reference and point-of-reference appears to us to be useful and to have validity. Point-of-reference groups are either in-groups which are important to an individual or group, or out-groups standing in a relation of conflict or competition with one or more groups of the individual. Certain point-of-reference out-groups are sufficiently attractive and penetrable to encourage individuals to find ways to move as individuals into them or to merge as groups with them. They then become frame-of-reference groups. Identity with groups is thus a comparative matter. It can be characterized by the terms: full group identity or fully assimilated membership and participation; marginal identity or some form of partial assimilation into membership; aspired identity, such as some have for membership in point-of-reference out-groups; and repressed or rejected identity, such as a person continues to hold willy-nilly in a group he hopes he has left behind.[1]

---

1 For more extensive discussions of prototypical roles and groups, and successor roles and groups, see A. McC. and E. B. Lee, *Marriage and the Family* (2nd ed.; New York: Barnes & Noble, 1967), chap. 8, and A. McC. Lee, *Multivalent Man* (New York: George Braziller, 1966), chap. 12. On frame-of-reference and point-of-reference groups, see the latter, chap. 9.

PERSONAL ROLES

The personalized versions of societal and group roles that are performed socially are routinized for individuals in their practices and habits. Except for permissible mannerisms, as for example personal variants in speech, personal roles resemble quite closely the group and societal role types the supposed audience supposedly anticipates.

In role-taking, role-assumption, role-enactment, or role-playing, roles have personal definitions for a given social situation which are usually within the limits of tolerance of societal culture or of a group-culture and of individual perception and willingness to comply. Quite briefly but not with too much violence to the senses given them by their formulators, *role-taking* and *role-assumption* refer to the habituation of an individual to his perception of a role; *role-enactment* and *role-playing* refer to behavior suggested or dictated by that perception and taken by others to be typical of the given role when it is socially stereotyped.

The number of short stories and novels written about the theme of the tyranny of social roles, especially by unadjusted writers in such periods of flux as that following World War I in the 1920's on through the other wars into the 1960's, testifies to a fact not usually bothersome or even recognized, namely, the tyranny of social roles over our behavior. It takes a maladjusted or unadjusted person—a beatnik or a hippie—to detect this tyranny, and it takes an unadjusted period to give such writings a vogue.

Lincoln Steffens sums up the popular attitude toward the deviation of group and personal roles from those of the societal man-as-he-should-be in a passage in his *Autobiography* (1931). "I have told how," he notes, "as the boy chum of a page in the Legislature of California, I had seen from below the machinery and bribery of politics; as a New York reporter I had seen police, political, legislative, and judicial corruption; but I did with these observations what other people do with such disturbing knowledge: I put them off in a separate compartment of the brain. I did not let them alter my conception of life." It was for this reason, he said, that for many years he was an acceptable newspaper reporter and editor. "You may beat the public to the news, not to the truth." Many men and women, even under a yoke as bitter as that of Nazism, forego opportunities for heroic social service and give themselves and their families "protective coloration" by appearing to adhere to societal and group role patterns then ascendent.

SELF ROLES

The self is the multivalent internal or covert aspect of the individual. It has, as we have seen, its subjective constituent, the ego or "I," and its objective constituent, the superego or "generalized other" or "me." The subjective self is what consciously reacts to stimuli. It is the integration of the individual's consciousness. It is the element of the self which reacts to what it perceives in "looking glasses," or in the responses of other people to its behaving person, to use Cooley's conception. In G. H. Mead's terms, what the "I" is doing is patterned by the "me," directly or indirectly, positively or negatively. The "I" reacts to the behavior of others. The "me" contains sets of attitudes related to roles and keyed to appropriate social situations. The multivalent "me" or objective self is the sum of social experiences with others, an extended conception of the conscience. It includes an awareness of the behavior traits of others, both specifically (practices) and in generalized or typical forms (folkways and conventions).

Self roles are roles of the "I" taken on from the "me" and from fantasies as reactions to internal and external events. They are self-dramatizations for the benefit of the self, either kept in the realm of fantasy or permitted to color the person's social behavior. To give the "I" some stability and security in the face of the frustrations and uncertainties of life, the "I" dramatizes itself in terms of various roles which are accurate or distorted counterparts of the roles performed by admired, envied, or detested people plus those recounted in historical and imaginative writings. Genealogies, lodge rituals, religious personages and roles, cults, and imagination all aid in the substantiation and proliferation of such self or "I" roles.

ROLES IN SOCIAL MOVEMENTS

Social movements, as Blumer points out in Section II of this outline, can be seen as collective efforts to modify aspects or all of society. Member roles in such movements in part derive from the role types prescribed by societal and group culture and in part represent novel and experimental adaptations in such types. The roles of functionaries in movements, however, include certain well-recognized models.

Types of roles in social movements include (1) leaders, (2) promoters, (3) manipulators, (4) sponsors, (5) bureaucrats, (6) rank-and-file volunteer workers, (7) "just members," and (8) "fellow travelers." These are not mutually exclusive categories. They are rough role types. Like other more or less specialized roles, they draw to their performance different emotional and intellectual personality types.

Leaders of a movement's doctrine usually partake of what Max Weber has called the charismatic. They feel they have been given some special grace. They have a mission. Whether paid or volunteer, they are the agitators and preachers who furnish the emotional drive, the personal symbolism, the unflinching zeal, the really dogmatic and uncompromising fanaticism that serves as the spearhead of a movement's campaigns and program.

Promoters, because of the technical problems confronting a successful agitation, tend to be professionals who know the arts of speech-writing, of influencing the mass media, of arranging public meetings, and of penetrating the programs of other organizations. They usually sell their services upon the basis of their competence in one or more areas necessary to the movement. They tend to have an objectivity less mixed with emotionalism than do the leaders, and they thus help to stabilize and direct a movement towards realizable goals.

Manipulators or power-brokers are often looked upon by leaders and promoters as "necessary evils" in an agitational effort. They are privy to the sources of available funds and to the terms under which such funds may be obtained. Often lawyers or experienced politicians, they work themselves into quiet but powerful positions in successful movements.

Sponsors or "fronts" are people connected with the movement who possess statuses with high prestige but whose participation is minimal. When they accept a tenuous identification with a movement, for example as board member of an organization, some of their prestige is hopefully transferred to the movement.

Bureaucrats trail behind the leaders, promoters, and manipulators into any movement. They are those with small talents and narrow aspirations who see opportunities for jobs as such and little more. They know the arts of memo-passing, protective coloration, and self-preservation and care for little else than the comparative security thus provided.

Rank-and-file volunteer workers and *"just members"* are the bulk of any movement. The workers are the more faithful and helpful soldiers of the army. "Just members" are the casual contributors of funds, the members of audiences, the bulk of mailing lists of "interested people," the persons who "think it's a good thing" and "want to be identified with it."

Fellow travelers are those who perform the role of carrying a movement's message to other groups without being identified with the movement's organizations and perhaps without even knowing of their function in the movement.

From the foregoing, it is apparent that all participants bring strengths and weaknesses to a movement through the roles they have in more established groups. The leader role represents a tentative new integration or a variant interpretation of aspirations that have been embedded in the morals for many generations. In addition, the movement-preacher portrays other roles (class, caste, ethnic, vocational, religious), possibly exaggerated, which bring him into relation with other groups of people not directly concerned in his cause. Thus, many were attracted to the antiwar agitations of Dr. Benjamin Spock because of his authorship of the best-selling book, *Baby and Child Care.* The status of the Rev. Martin Luther King, Jr. as a Christian clergyman gave added dimension to his agitation for interracial equality.

ROLE CHANGE THROUGH HORIZONTAL AND VERTICAL MOBILITY

To go from one social stratum to another, either up or down in a prestige scale, requires the acquisition of a new class role, a decided shift in personality. This type of circulation is referred to as *vertical mobility.* To move from one ethnic or ethnoid segment or from one occupation to another may require similarly difficult changes in role; these are examples of what is called *horizontal mobility.*

Individuals in any social status group (stratum, ethnoid segment, and similar occupational status-ladder area) have great difficulty in learning accurately the precise behavior patterns appropriate for full and unexceptional participation in another social status group, especially when it involves a change in either social stratum or ethnoid segment. Only under conditions such as were outlined at the end of the previous chapter, conditions making for social and individual marginality, can people undergo the disturbing and lengthy learning experiences necessary for a basic role shift. Even then, it is likely to be perceptibly imperfect. Even entering a new intraclass or two-class group, whether of age or interest, and in which a change of class is not necessary, presents problems. But these problems are rendered less difficult in such cases by initiation arrangements of a formal and informal nature. To "pass," to go from one caste to another, granted skin color suitable for the purpose, requires decided and rather fundamental adjustments.

Influences opposing both horizontal and vertical mobility include both the centripetal ones that build group solidarity and also centrifugal ones that work against those who attempt to invade the group without adequate and acceptable identification. Both groups of forces are strengthened in the United States by the fact that immigrant ethnic group members, and also the native nonwhites, are usually obliged to "start at the bottom and work up." The price for being permitted to "work up" frequently becomes that of assimilation, loss of previous identity.

CHAPTER THREE

CHILD AND FAMILY

The socialization of the individual typically begins in the family, as that institution may be defined by a given culture, and it continues largely under family domination during the individual's most impressionable years. Mother, father, and siblings, or substitutes for any or all of them, provide the most decisive molds for the individual's personality and social personalities, the consequences of which persist throughout life. Family members accomplish this in these six principal ways: 1. They provide a *prototypical microcosm of society*. 2. They exemplify in it their versions of customary societal and group interaction patterns in the context of their family drama rituals. 3. They furnish the most significant "looking glasses" by means of which the individual develops his "looking-glass selves." 4. They establish the "right" models for generalized and specific societal and group roles, the *prototypical roles* which influence an individual's fulfilling or reacting to successor roles later in life. 5. They set prototypical models for basic social groups, and these *prototypical groups* influence an individual's participation in and reaction to successor groups later in life. 6. They serve as surrogates of society and of various groups who attempt to initiate the new person into the complex of cultural series represented by the family's members.

As the child matures, the child's nonsibling peer associates and the family's network of relatives and friends, especially in the neighborhood of the family home, help to expand and give more detail to the family microcosm of society. The nonsibling peers of the child's playgroups usually provide his first and most influential steps outside his family-dominated sphere.

Since the cultural definition of family drama differs from society to society, among a society's social status groups, and through time, it will be useful to touch briefly first upon the nature of the family as a social institution. The discussion will then turn to the functioning of the family and the significance of the family drama, then to sociological aspects of childhood and adolescence.

This chapter emphasizes the person as the *creature* of society, the product of the *family of orientation* (one's parents, siblings, and self).

THE PERSON IN AN EVOLVING INSTITUTION

Society's basic life-conditions change, and its institutions adjust to them with more or less delay, after more or less painful or pleasant lack of adjustment. Elements more closely related to individual existence—matters of sustenance and domination—change most immediately to meet the tests of efficiency and workability in terms of new conditions of social contact, invention, and physical environment. Religious elements, on the other hand, come down to us with comparatively gradual modification from a remote past. The family as procreator and orientor has a rate of change somewhere between the extremes of economics and religion, with both of which it is interrelated. Rates of cultural evolution or adaptation differ, too, for various classes and groups in a society, and for the moral and moretic versions of culture.

Consanguine and Conjugal Family Organization. The historical foundations of the American family institution may be found in the folk culture of western Europe and its antecedents. The tribes Julius Caesar found and the more recent peasantry from whom Americans more directly have sprung emphasized patriarchal controls, childbearing, and child rearing. In addition, their family organization performed important economic, educational, religious, recreational, and more broadly societal functions. When Christianity succeeded earlier forms of worship, it at first continued to stress a strong moral-religious interpretation of the family's role, and this included doctrines of otherworldliness, sexual sin, and low status for women. Under such conditions, the consanguine family ("blood" kin) organization played a highly important part in locating the conjugal unit (parents and children) in the social structure and in assuring it some degree of stability.

As better methods of transportation and agriculture developed, the consanguine family changed in character and began to diminish in cohesiveness and extensiveness. The conjugal family became the predominant and characteristic unit, with increasingly important economic, political, religious, and other social ties outside consanguine limits.

The Modern Family. With the rise of industrialism, urbanism, and gadgetism, even more drastic changes in family organization appeared. The husband's work locus moved away from the family home or farm, sometimes many miles away to a factory or office building. The extensive primary group controls of the ancient consanguine family and of the more recent farm and village modifications thereof gave way to urban anonymity at first, to new types of less immediate and compulsive social relationships. As we have become more adapted to urban living, neighborhood-based networks of kin and friends have become our new urban communities which give a growing child some sense of family and community controls. Such networks are social-psychological rather than geographical entities.

Rise of Competing Institutions. Many educational, religious, recreational, and other social functions have drifted rapidly into the hands of specialists and are carried on to a great extent or exclusively outside of the home. Even births and deaths are arranged to take place, when possible, in hospitals, with burials from "funeral homes." With the appearance of modern birth control techniques and rises in the proportionate cost per child for delivery, care, and rearing, the conjugal family unit has continued to decrease in size. These factors as well as the prolongation of parental lives have resulted in only about one-half of modern families having children living at home. In this "stripped down" type of family, affectional elements in family relationships are being emphasized and the status of women has risen rapidly. The latter has also been stimulated by the increasing ease of women in obtaining remunerative employment and, because of the mechanization of the home and the pre-preparation of foods, by their ability to be absent from their homes.

Personality-Forming Functions Still Significant. Even though much of the formal educational function has been shifted from the family, the functions of the modern family in the formation of personality still remain its most important ones. In the smaller families of today, children spend more time during their most impressionable years with parents and less with siblings and playmates than did their parents or grandparents, and the responsibility thus placed on the parents has become very great.

In the family institution, as it has evolved, its member persons have gradually developed rather different personalities. The clashes between grandmother's and mother's ideas on raising the baby dramatize somewhat, among other considerations, the rate of change, as well as the greater susceptibility of youth to the modifying influences of changed life-conditions. The ever-present generation gap between parents and teen-agers, a favorite topic for newspaper and television sensationalism, further illustrates the point.

THE FAMILY DRAMA

In view of the wide range of conditions of family organization to be found in the United States among rural, suburban, and urban areas and among Americans of various ethnic and racial backgrounds, it is difficult to generalize about the patterning of family drama routines and roles. And when one takes into consideration the even greater differences in other parts of the world, the difficulty becomes extreme. Even in the United States, examples of the patriarchal father and the matriarchal mother, of the closely integrated consanguine extended family and of tiny two- and three-member conjugal units may be found. In an outline way, however, some tenable generalizations may be offered about socialization processes in the human family and concerning its examples in the United States.

Family Member Roles. As a child grows up in a family, he sees his mother and father and to a less extent his siblings, or their substitutes, as stock players in a drama. The mother and father, as he perceives and understands them, furnish prototypical conceptions of woman and man, wife and husband. Typically both mother and father in our society attempt to give the child an idealistic moral rather than a moretic picture of their roles, but they succeed in doing both. The interaction patterns that they follow day after day sink into the child's mind, with all their pleasures and frustrations, anxieties and opportunities for expression. These patterns of affection and struggle, co-operation, competition, and conflict come to characterize his thinking about interpersonal relationships. Extra-familial characters—especially nonsibling peer playmates—also figure in these mental formulations. In later life, the person tends to place new associates into successors to the old prototypical family drama roles and then to attempt to carry out old and familiar interaction patterns with them, more or less adapted, modified, and rationalized for the occasion. If such a new associate as a wife or husband does not perform the role "properly," her or his failures may become a source of friction, the causes of which may be quite mysterious to the spouse.

Roles of Family Members in Other Institutions. To change the metaphor slightly, the members of the family "stock company" present themselves upon the family "stage" in roles of other institutions and groups as well as in their basic ones as family members. These roles are largely defined for their performer in terms of group folkways and mores, but the father or mother or sibling usually attempts to present them to the other family members as they are defined by conventions and morals, in terms of the societal cloaks of the roles. A specific mother, therefore, may exemplify for her family *the* clubwoman, artist, community or church leader, professional woman. A specific father may illustrate *the* bricklayer, boxer, professional man, lodge potentate, postage stamp collector, soldier, political leader, church dignitary. These models aid in the moral training of the child's superego, the direction of ambition, and the assurance of a degree of invidious distinction and identity and thus something of what passes for psychological security.

Societal Surrogates. Especially in their ambivalent attitudes toward their social roles, parents serve automatically to make themselves societal surrogates, instructional representatives of society. The contrasts between moral and moretic roles, outlined more fully in the preceding chapter, arouse sufficiently the guilt feelings of parents (based upon their own morals-dominated superegos) to make them want to present their roles and many other ideas about society in moral terms. It has been as a part of this whole moralistic (ascetic and idealistic) situation that parents in our society so long disliked to tell their children facts of sex, even of sex hygiene. Such revelations went behind and, they apparently thought, tended to debase the societal façade or moral cloak of the roles of motherhood and fatherhood. This also explains why teen-agers so often rebel against what they tend to see as the hypocritical contrasts between moral and moretic role patterns.

Group Surrogates. As children gradually mature, facts present themselves to them for which they demand explanation, facts the morals do not recognize. Thus mothers eventually find themselves compelled to "have a heart-to-heart talk with daughter." Fathers eventually find it wise to pass along to their sons bits of expedient wisdom, the folkways and mores of masculine groups, of their trade or profession, of political and social life. In such efforts to usher the child from the moral absolutes of childhood into group mores, parents are acting as group surrogates, self-appointed educational representatives of groups to which they belong. Because of the social distance morals help to interpose in certain areas between parents and children, group surrogates may more effectively be persons other than parents or even other than professional teachers. The latter, except in trade and professional schools, are likely to perform chiefly as societal surrogates. Nonsibling peer playmates and their successors in later life are among our most influential group surrogates.

From the foregoing, it is not to be inferred that children learn little but idealized patterns from their parents, but what parents formally try to teach them is usually presented in a moral context. In addition, the child identifies with and emulates the patterns of behavior of those whom he loves or whose power and prestige he envies. Such identification and emulation, plus careful perception of what others do as well as what they say, are significant clues to cultural reproduction. This taking on of culture may be in the sense of preparing a predisposition, not in all cases of a complete assimilation of a pattern. It constitutes many times an emotional conditioning rather than the acceptance of specific cultural detail as such. The cultural detail then later fits into the general configuration.

CHILDHOOD

Through cross-cultural comparisons, anthropologists have learned from their data what psychiatrists concluded from theirs: Differences in the feeding and cleanliness training given children are powerful determinants of intercultural differences in personality formation. Customs concerning breast feeding and weaning, regarding the control of defecation and urination vary widely. Some apparently stimulate tendencies toward dependence, revolt against maternal or paternal authority, competitiveness, co-operativeness, self-expression in accumulative or in oral activity.

In our own society, the casualness with which many responsible medical practitioners ignore the personality consequences of early child-training is rather shocking at times. The hospitalization of childbirth, for example, has many times introduced routines based upon institutional and professional convenience rather than with a view to personality consequences for the child. A physician of the New York University College of Medicine, Dr. Harry Bakwin, put it thus: "Separating the baby from its mother at birth, instead of allowing it to be cuddled and breastfed, is a bad beginning. . . . The crime is compounded when the baby is put on a clock-ruled feeding schedule."

The search for dependable guidance in child-rearing in this century has been fraught with the appearance and disappearance of many fads and a general uncertainty as to who is an "expert" in this area. Even when the counsel of a grandmother or old family friend is available to recite and apply traditional folk procedures, the anxious young mother often doubts the utility of such "old-fashioned" ideas. Fortunately, under the leadership of the U.S. Children's Bureau and of academic specialists, practical handbooks for the day-to-day counseling and reassurance of mothers and fathers are now abundantly available. The most dependable and also the most popular of these are booklets of the U.S. Children's Bureau for each age level, Public Affairs Pamphlets on each phase of the subject, and the all-time secular best-selling book, Dr. Benjamin Spock's *Baby and Child Care*.

Growth. The mental growth of a child is regarded as a long process of learning through imitation and rejection, through unfolding experiences in symbolic interaction, of ego-reinforcement, of autonomy development. From birth onward, there are innumerable gross and subtle differences in the ways of satisfying and shaping an infant's needs. These differences in experience combine with a wide range of biological heredities to supply the diversity of personalities needed in each new generation. The differences in physical and social environment often vary along ethnic, class, and occupational lines. They help to lay deep roots of contrast among such groups. There are also, it needs to be added, the individual divergences that enrich life within all sorts of groups.

The Course of Personality Development. Like the physical organism, this is never a straight line. There are spurts, plateaus, and even regressions. A. L. Gesell concludes that, "even in the prodigiously complicated field of personality formation, growth factors are primarily determining." On the other hand, Kurt Lewin, Erik H. Erikson, and others have demonstrated the effects of frustration in retarding and even lowering the level of a child's achievements, and they have also attested to the value of favorable stimuli. At any rate, the basic training period (oral and anal-urethral), the family drama with its prototypical roles and groups, and the fact of growth join with the emotional experiences of certain transitional periods ("little adolescence" and adolescence) as crucial aspects of the person's life-history.

Sequence of Age-Roles. Between the ages of two and four, the child begins to get around more freely, to function more independently. His critical abilities develop more rapidly than his dexterities, and a certain amount of floundering and frustration results. This is the age of the "little adolescence," as it has been called, the period of transition from the child's first role, that of being a baby, to a role labeled enticingly by parents as that of "big girl" or "big boy." Unless parents have great patience and understanding, this is a period of considerable strain for the child.

As children mature, they proceed through a series of ill-defined age-roles, roles that identify them with children of a similar age level and sex and that provide them with invidious distinctions from the age-roles now behind them. This sequence of age-roles, this quest and struggle for greater maturational status, plays a significant part in sibling rivalry and in the formation of nonsibling play groups, gangs, and friendships.

Prototypical Groups and Roles. More significant than age-groups and age-roles as continuing influences in personality development are the prototypical groups and roles and their successors. The principal prototypical groups are (1a) the maternal: son and mother; (1b) maternal: daughter and mother; (2a) paternal: son and father; (2b) paternal: daughter and father; (3) sibling; (4) nonsibling peer; and (5) stranger.[1] With each of his prototypical groups the child works out one or several kinds of identification, and each participant in the group takes

---

1 For a more comprehensive list and discussion, see A. McC. Lee, *Multivalent Man* (New York: George Braziller, 1966), esp. chaps. 12–13.

on related roles. He also learns how to adjust to other people and to society at large in ways that he later discovers to be similar to the customary ways of successor groups, i.e., of groups which he joins when, in due time, he outgrows the early prototypical groups. Successors to sibling prototypical groups are such as school classroom groups and the formal aspects of bureaucratic work situations. Successors to nonsibling peer prototypical groups are college social fraternities, ward political organizations, poker clubs, and sales organizations.

Multivalence. The various prototypical groups require of their participants different attitudes and practices. As children are assimilated and develop within these crucial socializing groups, they literally become of "many minds." They become "multivalent" in the sense that they learn to operate in terms of several different systems of value and of behavior. They acquire different social personalities for each of their basic prototypical groups.

The reader may recall the development of multivalence in his own experience. He may try to date his first awareness that his parents had a different community of interest with each other or a different type of identification with other adults than with him. He may recollect his first discovery that he could discuss some things more readily and freely with other children, with members of a play group, than with parent or sibling. He may remember when his mother or father first showed surprise at reports of how differently he acted with some of his peers than he did in the presence of his parents. It is not easy to recall consciously such events of early life experience. Much of our ease as adults in slipping from one role (one set of attitudinal valences, one social personality) into another comes from our long habituation to the etiquette of group identities, to behavior keyed to group referents. This "division of man into several selves," as the psychologist William James discerned it, "may be a discordant splitting, as where one is afraid to let one set of his acquaintances know him as he is elsewhere; or it may be a perfectly harmonious division of labor, as where one tender to his children is stern to the soldiers or prisoners under his command."

ADOLESCENCE

Cross-cultural students of society do not find in certain other families the tensions and strains, the sharp contrasts between childhood and maturity, which characterize adolescence in our society. Because of the morals-mores contrasts in our culture, coupled with our competitiveness and emphasis upon individuality and personality, the transitional period known as adolescence is indeed a difficult one among us.

In our society, the "generation gap" or social distance between the generations and the moralistic rather than moretic preparation for adulthood leave children nearing sexual maturity to work out many personal problems alone or with inadequate or damaging peer-group guidance. Symptoms of the period are a boy's regressive unkemptness and crude manners, a girl's regressive silliness and irresponsibility, contrasting sharply with periodic efforts at mature appearance, responsibility, and behavior. Major developments towards which such evolving personalities strive are: emotional emancipation from parents; secure initiation into the mores of adult groups; and satisfactory heterosexual adjustment.

CHAPTER FOUR

COURTSHIP, MARRIAGE, DIVORCE

Marriage is the public joining together, under socially specified regulations, of a man and woman as husband and wife. In marriage, the couple enters into a publicly recognized agreement to adhere to the rules and regulations of their society concerning their rights, duties, and privileges toward each other and toward their children, other kin, and other people.

The marriage ceremony may be a very simple act or the occasion for elaborate celebrations lasting for many days, but throughout the world its essential characteristic is that it is a public contract. Premarital and extramarital sexual arrangements are not to be confused with marriage, a morally, legally, and moretically defined social agreement.

Marriage gives social recognition to the formation of a new family of procreation. It may or may not initiate cohabitation. The new conjugal unit may take its place within a large and cohesive consanguineal family organization, or it may be separate.

What is a family? [1] Only in the broadest sense can one give a single meaning to the term family throughout the world. In common American usage, a "family" is: (1) the group which lives in a house under a single head or couple; (2) a group of immediate kinsmen, especially of parents and children, whether living together or not; and (3) the descendants of a common forebear, whether immediate or remote. These three meanings are also found in other societies, but they are not accepted universally. About as universal a definition of "family" as we can come to is to regard it as a group, membership in which depends upon real or assumed biological relationships.

---

[1] A more extended discussion of the material in this chapter and the previous one may be found in A. McC. Lee and E. B. Lee, *Marriage and the Family* (2nd ed., New York: Barnes and Noble, 1967).

THE FAMILY UNIT

In discussing the family, it is necessary to avoid confusion between the biological phenomenon, the "basic reproductive unit," and the societal phenomenon, the "basic family unit." The basic reproductive unit is composed of a man and a woman, who have a fertile sexual relationship, and whatever offspring they may have. The basic family unit, on the other hand, is a culturally specified relationship which those constituting it down through many generations have elaborated and adapted. It is a group of two or more persons, bound together by marriage, blood, or adoption, who are distinguished socially as making up a single household or subhousehold. Such a unit need not include more than one person serving actively in the principal maternal or paternal role. It may lack either. It rarely lacks both. If a single parent or parent-substitute does not head the unit, it may consist only of siblings. Usually a basic family unit is initiated by marriage. It may eventually include children. Grandchildren would usually be members of other basic family units.

A basic family unit may at a given time consist of only one generation or of any of the other types of membership mentioned, but it has certain similarities wherever it is found. It is publicly recognized and sanctioned as an arrangement for dwelling together in relatively intimate face-to-face association, and it has the ability to assimilate new members, especially the young, into it and thus into society.

The type of household most commonly found in the United States today is the single basic family unit with ethnic, class, and regional variations or colorations. However, some multi-unit or extended families are still to be found, and even polygamous families are occasionally discovered. As a rule, each person is, during his lifetime, a member of at least two basic family units: the family into which he is born or adopted, and the family which he helps by marriage to form and in which he may become a parent. These two types are called, respectively, the *family of orientation* and the *family of procreation*.

TYPES OF MARRIAGE

Two millenniums ago in the Western World, the most common type of marriage specified by societal morals was the *monogynous* (one husband, one full status or ranking wife, with the possibility of one or more socially sanctioned concubines). The most common type of marriage actually practiced then, for numerical and economic reasons, amounted to monogamy. At the present time, the morals and laws most commonly specify *monogamy* (one husband and one wife at a time).

The world's peoples have sanctioned many other types of marriage and with them, many bases for the organization of multi-unit as well as single-unit families. In fact, all mathematical possibilities in formalizing relationships between men and women have been tried in the world's multiplicity of cultures. Other types of marriage have included *monandry* (one de facto husband at a time, recognized societally as not necessarily a permanent or a sexually exclusive relationship with a wife), *polyandry* (one wife and two or more husbands who are usually brothers), *polygyny* (one husband and two or more full-status wives), and *group marriage* (two or more husbands, two or more wives).

All of these forms are far from comparable in prevalence and persistence to the two major types, monogyny and monogamy. All except monogamy are properly referred to as forms of *polygamy* (permitting many marriages to be in force at once).

Functions of Marriage Types. *Multiple wives* (especially in monogyny and polygyny) are associated with conditions under which they can perform valuable economic functions or serve as means to obtain or demonstrate heightened status and prestige. *Multiple husbands* (polyandry) may be an adjustment to female infanticide or to arduous economic conditions. Examples of polyandry are found among the Todas of southern India (fraternal) and among the Marquesans of Polynesia (nonfraternal). Group marriage appears among the Kaingang of Brazil; it is quite a rare form. It was tried in the experimental Oneida Community established in 1848 in New York State, but there the group was community wide, and perhaps its form should be called *communal marriage*.

Significance of Marriage Types. The mere fact that "everything has been tried" in marriage forms is not an argument for claiming that "everything" might well be attempted in our society. Each of the marriage forms mentioned is or has been part of the culture of a number of peoples. Each was taken seriously, believed in, and lived by. Each fit into the economic, political, and religious aspects of that people's culture. Any notion that they have been or should be treated casually or experimentally is without supporting evidence.

Endogamy and Exogamy. Groups, classes, castes, and peoples in all societies define, with more or less precision, the groups from which their young people may and may not obtain spouses or into which they may be taken in marriage. They typically specify both endogamy ("in-marriage") and exogamy ("out-marriage"). They require endogamy within preferred groups similar to their own and place an exogamic taboo on marriage within certain degrees of relationship. Examples in our society of endogamy are the social pressures brought to bear upon a person to make a "suitable" marriage, that is to say a marriage with someone within certain prescribed groups, defined ethnically, racially, economically, religiously, and educationally. Examples of exogamy are indicated by the moral and legal prohibitions against marriage between close relations.

Sociologically, exogamy has its greatest significance as a facilitator of cultural borrowing and assimilation, especially when out-marriage involves people from quite different ethnic groups. On the other hand, endogamy promotes relative cultural isolation and stability. Regardless of what might be true physiologically, too close inbreeding in a class, caste, or society makes for *cultural* sterility. Intermarriage within broad limits, especially between spouses with diverse ethnic backgrounds, makes for cultural stimulation through the intimate intermingling of diverse customs. It also helps to nurture the kinds of marginal offspring which swell the ranks of the disaffected and delinquent as well as of the ambitious and creative.

COURTSHIP CUSTOMS

Courtship customs vary throughout the world at least as much as do marriage customs. They include conventions ranging from those calling for force, music, dancing, games, or the exchange of presents to those involving periods of trial sexual intercourse, "bundling," a marriage broker, or parental arrangement. The highly romantic coloration of courtship and even the prevalence of kissing in our culture are far from universal. Whatever the customs may be, however, they are geared to family interests, marriage morals, and the provision of care for the possible offspring. Exceptions are not morally sanctioned even though they may occur and may even have the moretic sanction of a group or groups in a society. Our various "free love" cults down through the years are examples of the latter.

Courtship, U.S.A. In this country, the playful and bargaining process which may result in engagement and marriage does not usually follow a straight line of development. It includes principally the phases: (1) rating, (2) dating, (3) sexual stimulation, (4) selection, (5) accommodation, (6) getting serious, maturation, (7) engagement, and (8) marriage. These phases may be variously arranged and repeated; some may be omitted entirely. Whether courtship begins with rating and dating or with the selection of a potential mate depends on whether wooing is taking as starting with youthful play or narrowly defined as a heterosexual bargaining process aimed specifically at obtaining a mate. The former conception appears to us to be the more tenable. Let us look briefly at each of these possible phases.

Rating refers to the relative desirability with which the unmarried in a given social situation regard available members of the other sex and the nature of the criteria employed. It is most frequently discussed as it occurs among students in one of those great heterosexual market places, a co-educational university campus. Some have assumed that students over-evaluate smoothness in appearance, heroic campus roles, fraternity and sorority memberships, dancing skills, good clothes, and access to a car and overlook sterling virtues of a more durable sort. Some probably do. Actually, students—like the young unmarried elsewhere —have many sets of criteria in our multivalent society for evaluating each other. They want many different types of person either for a playmate or a marriage mate. *Social rating* is a kind of crude preliminary screening or grading process largely for the purpose of selecting desirable people to date. The intimacies of dating may then replace social rating with the more *personal rating* procedure.

Dating is a more or less serious game with which young people spice their lives between sexual maturity and the time at which they can consider marriage. To a certain point, it takes the form of having fun and avoiding involvement of an enduring sort. Interpersonal attraction and sexual stimulation sooner or later turn dating into a more serious pursuit.

Sexual stimulation may lead to necking and then to petting. Premarital coitus becomes more likely the longer marriage is delayed. The extent to which premarital coitus leads to pregnancy and precipitated marriage is not clear in available studies, but some element of panic or force is not rare in formal mating in our society.

Selection of a potential mate rather than just a date arises in our society chiefly out of the rating and dating process. Just how much choice goes into such selection and the significance of such ability to choose among many possibilities are difficult problems. The obtaining of adequate knowledge for selection requires considerable time, a high degree of mutual acceptance and even intimacy, and opportunities to interact with one another in many different situations and in terms of many different problems. Men especially try to use a different set of criteria for selecting a woman who is merely a good "date" and for choosing a woman to court, but in our society this differentiation may break down. Many a person has become deeply enmeshed and willingly so with another who was at first just a possible companion for an evening. An "ideal mate" is rarely very far from a cultural model, with its oversimplifying mandates. Even when it represents a revolt against group standards, the ideal is influenced by the standards against which it is a revolt.

Accommodation of one potential spouse to another is a complex process. Many others besides Shakespeare have observed that the "course of true love never did run smooth." Misunderstandings and even quarrels are the "zigs" in the zigzag relations between a couple, and more and more intimate and tender makings-up can be the "zags"—when there is not a permanent break. Granted an accepted basis for the beginning of a relationship and for its continuation, a great many different types of persons can arrive at a sufficiently strong and deep desire or understanding or "love" to wish to marry and to stay married. The couple who first meet are not the couple who get married days, weeks, months, or years later; they change each other. Rarely are matings ideal "fits." A person who delays marriage in his search for an ideal mate may make a poor compromise in the end or, as often happens, remain unmarried.

Getting serious, maturation of the relationship, can result from a combination of the preceding phases. It comes with a rejection of whatever purely fun-centered or exploitative goals either of a couple may once have had and involves the development of an interpersonal sense of resonsibility and affection.

Engagement takes some four recognized forms among high school and college students, but only the fourth is generally accepted as more than "quasi-engagement." Marriage can follow any one of the four. The forms are: (i) "going together," (ii) "going steady," (iii) "formally tagged" or "formally pinned" through the man giving the woman a school ring, club or fraternity pin, or some other recognizably masculine piece of jewelry, and (iv) "formally engaged" with all the ritual of ring and announcement party. Even "going together" somewhat regularly once constituted at least informal betrothal, and it is quite binding today in certain parts of Europe and the Americas.

Marriage is pictured in romantic dramas many times as the culmination of a story. Boy finally gets girl, and all is well. Even though about one marriage in four in the United States ends in divorce, many remarriages are successful. At any rate, we are a much married country. About two-thirds of those over 13 years of age are currently married, and some nine of ten Americans eventually marry.

Courtship Problems. A basic courtship problem is that, in the marriageable ages of our population, there are about four percent more females than males. In addition, shy people and especially those in certain vocational and professional groups have difficulty in meeting possible suitable mates under propitious conditions. Dating bureau schemes, marriage agents, marriage advertisements, special dances, weekends, and vacations for the unmarried, get-acquainted bars and coffee houses, and even social lectures and night-school classes are offered as solutions, but there remain a number of apparently eligible isolates interested in marriage. Our various wars further aggravate this problem by removing so many men from the United States for periods of years, some of whom marry in other countries.

The period of possible courtship may be lonely, tense, and frightening or a happy prelude to marriage. With courtship so often based upon illusions, bargaining, and compromise rather than upon accurate mutual perceptions of a range of possible mates, the probable compatibility of a couple remains a gamble somewhat hedged by the processes of habituation.

AMERICAN MARRIAGE PATTERNS

For all the segregative tendencies of American life especially as expressed in residential arrangements, intermarriage among members of the principal ethnoid segments of our society continues at a high rate. Studies of Jewish communities indicate a rising percentage of intermarriage with non-Jews as generation succeeds generation in the American environment; third and subsequent generation members find almost 1 in 5 of their mates outside the Jewish ethnoid segment. Among Roman Catholics, studies place church-sanctioned marriages with non-Catholics at 25 to 30 percent of the total; non-sanctioned marriages have not been adequately studied, but they would take the percentage higher. Comprehensive studies of interracial marriage are not available. Available data indicate a minute percentage of white-nonwhite marriages.

Family Law. Much of American marriage and family law is within the jurisdiction of the states, and there is thus considerable variation in it. On the other hand, the similarity of the heritage of our states has tended to limit this diversity. Popular pressures for the standardization of domestic legislation and the increasing mobility of our population are very slowly eroding state differences. A growing number of states now refuse to accept divorces or annulments obtained by their residents elsewhere. To get around such laws, a state's resident has to establish a legally valid residence in the other state where the action is to take place. A Uniform Reciprocal Enforcement of Support Act is now in effect throughout all United States jurisdictions. Under this statute, a person liable for the support of a mate or child may be made to furnish such support wherever he may be.

Working Wives. Time was when women worked outside their conjugal homes only when they *had to.* Husband, children, and house were primary considerations. With the rise of gadgetry, bakeries, canned and deep-frozen prepared foods, laundries, corner restaurants, nursery schools, and school restaurants, not to mention modern birth-control techniques, in many groups it is now a matter of whether or not wives can get outside employment. They dislike the routines of small homes, the anonymity of urban living or the "goldfish bowl" existence of the suburbanite, and want to get out and meet new situations. In 1900, 1 in 18 married women was gainfully employed; by 1940, about 1 in 6; by 1950, 1 in 4; by 1960, almost 1 in 3; and the proportion has continued to climb since. Each of the wartime periods of this century stimulated this trend, and afterwards only a part gave up outside work. Such working and also prolonged education are frequently associated, but not necessarily, with delayed child-bearing and the estimate that the United States has almost as many "criminal" abortions as live births. Modern conditions of shared responsibilities, the spacing of births, and better educational opportunities for both men and women have encouraged and permitted more of the population to be married as well as for more married women to work.

SEPARATION

Marriages may be temporarily broken by war, migration, hospitalization, imprisonment, or employment conditions, or permanently broken by desertion, divorce, hospitalization, imprisonment, or death. If the separation is more than a brief one, it can create far-reaching problems.

War Separations. War becomes a great major premise in private discussions and arguments, a reason or a rationalization for many private courses of action. It stimulates the abbreviation of courtship. It provides a way for husband or wife to solve temporarily an irritating family situation by enlisting or, in the case of the husband, more plausibly, by being drafted. It is a heart-rending period of anxiety for wives who got on well with their husbands and who want and need them back. The breaking up of a crystallized relationship, the working out by each party of new wartime adjustments which may come to appear more desirable than the old, the need for making new postwar adaptations between spouses with somewhat changed personalities— these are crucial problems for husbands and wives to face in wartime separations. Children may have to confront, possibly during their most formative years, the consequences of the absence of father or mother, of makeshift living conditions, of a broken home with all that that implies.

Other Temporary Separations. The migrant husband, with newly gained sophistication, may be shocked by the extent to which he has "grown away" from his family. He may also anticipate this, not send for them to come to the new home, and "disappear." Long-term hospitalization raises humanitarian and sentimental considerations that may make the sacrifices entailed much easier to bear than in other cases. But the shame of imprisonment makes a permanent break the more likely.

Bereavement. Of those widowed and not remarried at any time, four-fifths are women, and one-fifth, men. To meet the shock of death and also of divorce, routines are invaluable during the time needed for a reintegration of the survivors' perspectives and relationships. Some cultures prohibit remarriage of a widow and others make remarriage for widow or widower difficult, but in our society an intelligent attitude by associates can prevent handicaps. The prolongation of life is delaying widowhood and is making remarriage more possible.

DESERTION AND DIVORCE

Most cultures provide some method or methods for handling marital frauds, misunderstandings, and errors. Methods range from the return of a bride price or dowry with some form of public renunciation or cancellation of vows to legal proceedings looking toward annulment, separation, or divorce. Causes depend upon the character of marriage standards and upon the status of women. They may be restricted to one or a few, such as barrenness, disloyalty, and disabling mental and physical diseases, or they may include such broad categories as "incompatibility."

Desertion. Because of social pressures, legal recourses available to the deserted, and the costliness of severing professional and business ties, desertion is relatively rare among middle- and upper-class families. It is more common among low-wage-earning groups, both skilled and semiskilled, and among such underprivileged people as the northern urban Negroes. Estimates of desertions are only approximate. There are probably at least 50,000 a year in the United States, more during war periods and depressions. Desertion differs from separation in that separation involves some arrangement or understanding, some "agreement to disagree." The separation arrangement may be voluntary or compulsory, and it often includes provision for support. In both desertion and separation, Thomas D. Eliot observes, "there may be hope or fear of return on either side." Desertion, most often by the husband, results chiefly from emotional, even neurotic problems. It is a way out for those who cannot bring themselves to use more regular procedures and who lack the imagination, resources, or luck to engineer an "unavoidable" separation.

Types of Desertion. Five types of deserters are frequently listed: (1) the *spurious,* prompted by requirements of public relief laws or interested in dodging or helping his family dodge some financial responsibility; (2) the *gradual,* an outgrowth of enforced absences from home, found especially among immigrants and discharged soldiers; (3) the *intermittent,* the chronic but temporary deserter; (4) the *panicky* deserter who takes leave from an ill-advised or forced marriage, also referred to as getting a "poor man's annulment"; and (5) the *"fed up"* or *last-resort* deserter who departs from what has long appeared to him to be a family situation with no other solution, also called getting a "poor man's divorce."

Divorce in Our Culture. St. Paul and other early church fathers had little enthusiasm for marriage and less for divorce. In I Corinthians, St. Paul advised, "If they cannot contain, let them marry. For it is better to marry than to burn." He was strongly opposed to divorce. "Let not the wife depart from her husband," he wrote, "but and if she depart, let her remain unmarried, or be reconciled to her husband and let not the husband put away his wife." Jesus, according to St. Matthew, recognized fornication as a basis for a man putting away his wife, with the stipulation that anyone marrying such a woman committed adultery. As a result of these positions and of revolts against them in personal behavior and in the mores, a constant struggle between Christian fundamentalists and advocates of a more socialized doctrine covering marital relationships has been in progress for many generations.

Divorce in the United States. Divorce—like marriage—laws differ in the states of the United States, as well as from country to country in what we are pleased to call our Western Civilization. But the variations in divorce law create striking problems, because a person may be married to one spouse in terms of the law of one state, to none in another, and to several in a third. Acceptable causes range widely, but actual causes probably have much more in common. Actual causes are irritations and tensions, misunderstandings and incompatibilities, that drive husband and wife apart. Because of the artificialities of the law, the causes stated and argued in court may have little in common with the actual psychological ones, which as a matter of fact the principals might not even recognize themselves. Current morals demand that the wife should sue for divorce and that the husband, regardless of the situation unless the wife is too notorious, should provide proper and tenable legal grounds for divorce. In other words, collusion to mitigate the harshness of the divorce morals is relatively common. Wives initiate three in four divorce suits.

Adultery is accepted throughout the United States as a ground for divorce. Bigamy has similar status with respect to annulment, and it may be grounds for divorce in one-fourth of the states. Most states also recognize conviction of a crime, cruelty, desertion, fraud, impotency, insanity, and nonsupport as justifiable grounds for divorce action.

Two major types of divorce exist: (1) *absolute,* which returns the parties to the status of single persons; and (2) *partial,* or legal separation from "bed and board." Decrees *nisi* may provide the latter type for a trial period, perhaps a year, before the divorce is declared "absolute." Alimony, usually payable to the wife but occasionally as in Illinois to a needy husband, is provided for in all states. It is intended as a way of effecting equitable adjustments in financial arrangements, especially to cover the costs of child-care.

Divorce and Family Disorganization. Just short of a half-million divorces are granted in the United States each year. Even though the people of this country have tended to be more and more married, the rising tide of divorces has brought talk about marriage being an "outmoded institution." Children of divorced parents suffer psychic damages such as one expects from broken homes, but the children of incompatible parents who are "fighting it out" may suffer even greater mental wear and tear. Some say that it "builds character" to face a marital maladjustment judiciously and continue to live with it and work it out. In general, however, taking into consideration as many handicaps and problems as possible, the weight of evidence seems to indicate that the frank and wise use of divorce as an instrument of social adjustment has made of marriage a more workable human institution.

Divorce has become more acceptable socially as it has become more common. In consequence, more couples are inclined to legal unions with the idea that they can end them at not too great a social cost if they find they have to. This same opinion makes second marriages easier to contract even after harrowing first experiences. In commenting upon these developments, Elizabeth Briant Lee concludes, "Our high marriage and divorce rates are indicative (1) of our idealization of family life, (2) of our not unsuccessful efforts to adjust laws to suit life conditions, and (3) of the preference of Americans for legally sanctioned unions rather than under-cover affairs such as are more common in other countries."

CHAPTER FIVE

DEVIANTS

A society has within it tremendous forces making for conformity, for the persistence of trait, personality, and institution types, for the preservation of the *status quo*. Its rewards and punishments stimulate overwhelming drives toward accepting and adhering to its norms of behavior and toward finding self-expression in terms of them. At the same time, in society—as throughout the known universe—is the pervasive and disturbing force of change. Reproduction is always at least a slightly imperfect process. In addition, conditions change and help to select cultural variations that appear to adapt to them. The pressure for change, especially when resisted, may bring breaks in established structures, breaks which may assume the proportions of a revolution or of annihilation.

THE NATURE OF DEVIATION

Individual deviations of a genetic or experiential sort and personal, group, and societal deviations in cultural patterns are constantly appearing in human society. Some personal deviants become symbols or spearheads of social change. Others have limited utility for a time and then yield to social pressure. Many others fail, and society ignores them or places them in institutions for the segregative care of criminals and mental patients.

In Part VI of this outline, we treat social deviants as social problems. In the present chapter, we interpret salient phenomena of social deviation in terms of the socialization of the individual.

Deviants are taken to be persons who, for any complex of reasons, do not conform to social norms sufficiently to keep from being regarded as different, eccentric, superior, inferior, unusually virtuous, or unusually evil. In some one or more of these respects, they go beyond the ordinary limits of social tolerance for difference in one or more groups or in society. Because of their social significance, famous or notorious deviants considered individually and problem deviants considered as groups or types are of more interest to sociologists than minor deviations.

Cross-cultural studies indicate that a type of mental deviant that is outcast, hospitalized, exploited, or imprisoned in one society may be accorded special status, honor, and authority in another. Whether or not a deviant is a social problem, a social asset, or just another person depends upon the whole cultural situation—group, class, caste, and societal. Here as elsewhere in society the principle of *societal or cultural relativity* has application and significance. Every person and every cultural element depends for what it is upon the other persons and cultural elements in the society and upon the society's general relationships among its parts.

THE DEFICIENT AND THE DERANGED

Feeblemindedness, mental deficiency, or amentia refers to a mental incapacity from birth or from the early months of life. On the other hand, dementia or derangement refers to consequences of organic brain damage through infection, injury, or other physiological disorder, or to a functional aberration.

Feeblemindedness. This may be due to malformation, malnutrition, lack of adequate socializing experiences, injury, disease, or a combination of two or more of these afflictions. Some, not as amented as others, are called subnormals or borderline defectives. The various I.Q. (intelligence quotient) measures are only a rough guide. They test current evidences of intelligence and not innate intellectual ability. Regarded as more satisfactory now are measurements of mental "profiles" which test aptitudes, talents, dexterities, and, to a certain extent, potentialities along a number of different lines. They are called "profile" tests because the scores are not averaged but are given separately for each aspect, and a person's series of scores may then be compared with available norms. In such tests, too, as in all psychological considerations, the influences of heredity and environment are inseparable. Potentialities remain discoverable chiefly through hopeful experimentation.

Because of the hereditary factors in some feeblemindedness,

sterilization plans have been advanced as ways of decreasing its incidence. On the contrary, a large share of feeblemindedness is not hereditary but caused or augmented by other factors beginning with intra-uterine conditions. Situational therapy, special educational techniques, and kindly understanding are said to yield useful improvements.

The Mentally Deranged. Because of the strangeness of mental derangements, the demented have often been treated throughout history with extremes of superstition and brutality. Dementia may be functional or organic; it may be a mild derangement, a neurosis, or a more serious one, a psychosis. Neither broad, general division of the field is too satisfactory, but both are used. The three organic mental disorders most commonly found among admissions to state hospitals are the arteriosclerotic senile psychoses, paresis (dementia paralytica, an aftermath of syphilis), and the psychoses deriving from alcoholism. Sociologists are concerned with these and other organic mental disorders as social problems, but the functional disorders or those without an organic basis also interest the sociologist as significant failures in socializing processes. The latter are commonly termed the neuroses, schizophrenia, the manic depressive psychoses, and paranoia.

The Deranged as Failures in Socialization. Except for those abnormal at birth or through organic damage or disease, mental disorder represents either a failure of the processes of socialization in which the person has taken part or a maturation of innate deranging elements in the person's make-up. The failure may result, not from the deprivation of ordinary social and cultural contacts, but from aberrations in them either continually or at certain critical life-history periods. The latter may be situational or be linked more specifically to what are called traumatic experiences.

Therapies for the Deranged. One of the great problems in the treatment of mental disorder is the lack of understanding of the person by others. Close relatives and friends are frequently fearful or unable to accept the fact that the patient is mentally ill. Popular education is doing much to overcome this obstacle to treatment, and it is also helping to cope with mental disease through nurturing a more rational attitude towards it.

The therapeutic techniques used to treat mental problems vary widely. Medical psychiatrists use a range of drugs, shock treatments, sedatives, rest, occupational procedures, music, hyp-

nosis, situational modifications, and physical devices. Psycho-
analysts try to help their patients make the facts of their
life-histories conscious for the purpose of re-examining, "reliving," and thus understanding and adjusting to them. This is
done to allay old anxieties and fantasms and to enable the patient
to live more sensibly with his background experiences, his subconscious self, and his superego. J. L. Moreno, through his
psychodrama or spontaneity theater, encourages his patients to
re-enact traumatic and other possibly significant incidents with
the help of auxiliaries who take the part of others in incidents.
Others, for example Fritz Redl, have developed what are known
as clinical group-work techniques; carefully designed interacting
groups, with appropriate activities, are used for therapeutic purposes. Such group work has been used especially with delinquent
and deranged juveniles. Unfortunately, the techniques available
for curing or readjusting the deranged are expensive, and trained
workers are few in number.

Under the impact of high-speed modern life, with our cultural elements in a flux that confuses many, with strains that make
for growing anxieties, figures for the mentally ill continue to
mount, especially in urban areas. In the past generation, the rate
of admission of mental patients to hospitals has doubled, and the
use of outpatient psychiatric clinics has grown rapidly. Great
strides have been made in effecting practical adjustments for
patients, by educating them in classes, through publications and
other visual materials. We are also instructing the families of
patients and the American public at large in the nature of psy-
choneurotic discharges from the armed forces and of mental
illnesses in general. In this, certain regular commercial motion
pictures have been quite helpful. The improvement and broadening of such efforts can do much to promote human mental health.

THE CRIMINAL

As ordinarily conceived, a criminal is a person who has
broken a criminal law, has been caught and arraigned, and has
been convicted. Many social scientists would broaden the scope
of the definition. They would say that a criminal is a person
whose conduct has been adjudged antisocial in a respect covered
by the criminal laws or even that he is one who has committed
such an act whether so adjudged or not.

The Difficulty of Defining Criminality. In his startling 1939 presidential address before the American Sociological Society, Edwin H. Sutherland pointed to the narrowness of such definitions in an analysis of white-collar criminality. He noted that relatively few so-called criminals are members of the dominant upper and upper-middle classes, that crime and criminology are defined largely in terms of lower-class convictions, but that even those investment swindlers, stock waterers, unpatriotic cartel manipulators, and others who are caught cost society far more than all lower-class criminals combined.

What makes people violate criminal statutes? What makes people engage in antisocial behavior? How do criminals become such at any given time and place?

John Steinbeck suggests the pervasiveness of such questions in his novel, *Cannery Row* (1945). He makes a lovable character say to a friend, "It has always seemed strange to me. . . . The things we admire in men, kindness and generosity, openness, honesty, understanding and feeling are the concomitants of failure in our system. And those traits we detest, sharpness, greed, acquisitiveness, meanness, egotism and self-interest are the traits of success. And while men admire the quality of the first they love the produce of the second." It is perhaps an oversimplification, but it is a probing suggestion, and it is not something to be found only in our own culture.

Criminals and the Socialization Processes. Generally speaking, antisocal persons are products of (1) individual deviation, (2) group deviation, or, most commonly, (3) a mixture of both. Juvenile sexual perverts are usually more of the first type. Juvenile thieves and gangsters are frequently quite "normal" members of groups whose folkways and mores are regarded by "society" as delinquent. Since individual deviants tend to find and join deviant groups and are thus stimulated in their deviation, mixtures of both rather than "pure types" are usually found.

From a causal standpoint, this is a highly significant typification. In the first group are persons who are psychologically maladjusted, mentally ill, and should be treated as such. Upon them, for personal, family, and other reasons, the ordinary processes of socialization failed to produce the usual degree of conformity to societal norms. A deviant family drama, traumatic experiences at critical periods in life-history, or some physiological problem may have initiated the situation. In the second group, the group deviants, are persons who took on the membership characteristics or roles of social groups whose folkways and mores specified behavior regarded by organized society as criminal. Here one has a problem of adjusting the person to new group cultures and of changing group cultures that make for lower-class or white-collar criminality. Such students of man and law as Judge Ben Lindsey, Clarence Darrow, Lincoln Steffens, and many sociologists have taken the position that, in many criminal cases, society might well be convicted of permitting such group culture and conditions to persist but that the person in custody only did what might have been anticipated.

THE FAMOUS

In his book on the type of deviation called genius, Wilhelm Lange-Eichbaum concludes that the appearance of famous and notorious deviants in general depends upon "nothing absolute" and results from "not a being but a working." Acclaim, he goes on to say, may arise from "a favorable concatenation of circumstances," from "the concentration of fame upon one individual instead of upon the real multiplicity of producers," from "the might of psychopathological delusion," or from "the outcome of supreme talent." And he adds, "Almost everywhere, and especially in the subjective fields of imaginative writing, religion, and music, gifted 'insanity' gains the victory over simple, healthy talent."

Studies of inventors, political and business leaders, scientists, artists, and criminals come to similar conclusions. To become famous or notorious, such persons must have been (1) born at a suitable time and place or precipitated in some other way into a suitable combination of circumstances, (2) given credit due as well to many others, (3) opportune in the psychic delusion that drives them, or (4), probably not nearly as often as one might expect, except in combination with the others, possessed of a "supreme talent." Most commonly, one finds mixtures of such factors have been at work.

Individual Basis for Eminence. In *The Way of All Flesh*, Samuel Butler differentiates the ordinarily successful man from other deviants by saying, "The successful man will see just so much more than his neighbors, as they will be able to see too when it is shown them, but not enough to puzzle them. It is far safer to know too little than too much. People will condemn the one, though they will resent being called upon to exert themselves to follow the other." It is because of social pressure toward conformity that it takes an unusually aggressive, persistent, heedless, or fortunate person to scale the heights of popular acclaim or esteem that are labeled eminence or fame. It is thus little wonder that in so many cases, "gifted 'insanity' gains the victory over simple, healthy talent."

Factors Making for Fame. After investigating the life-histories of 628 eminent American women, Elizabeth Briant Lee in her *Eminent Women* concludes that her subjects achieved fame, on the whole, because of (1) need, especially economic need frequently precipitated by the death of the male breadwinner, (2) a combination of social and cultural factors, and (3), but not nearly as frequently or importantly as the two preceding, superior mental endowment. Subjects "were found whose capacities appear not to have been especially extraordinary yet who chanced through a fortunate combination of circumstances ultimately to have become famous." She listed the following social and cultural factors as being especially propitious, granted the drive furnished by need: (1) born into a small family; (2) a high standard of living but not too great wealth, enough to provide formal schooling and other means to develop abilities but not enough to prevent the growth of self-reliance and economic independence; (3) childhood in or very near a large urban center; (4) a professional father and an active mother who share their lives and interests with their few offspring; (5) familiar early association with outstanding characters, either as relatives or family friends; (6) liberal religious training; (7) available educational opportunities; and (8) available economic or career opportunities. With so many different careers represented by the 628 women, this is naturally a very generalized summary.

The situation for men requires only a few obvious modifications. Need, in the form of economic need, is more prevalent, and the need can probably be satisfied more readily by men than by women. This is where extra drive, opportunity, or luck plays its part. Liberal religious training, point (6) above, probably has more significance for women than for men because of the taboos on female deviation in many fundamentalist beliefs. The last two points may be broadened and illustrated with some "as ifs." If Charles Darwin had become as an infant a member of the primitive Todas of southern India, he might have been something of a leader, but he would not have been enshrined in biology textbooks and Westminster Abbey. Similarly transferred at birth, Abraham Lincoln would not have become President of the United States or even of India, and he would not have been likely to free any slaves.

LEADERS AND SOCIAL CAUSATION

A leader is a person (1) who occupies a leadership status, a culturally set position of dominance or control, in a group or society, (2) who is the symbol of a movement and understands its personnel well enough to be its internal and external spokesman, or (3) who has few or no immediate followers but who charts courses later taken up and followed. Illustrations are respectively (1) a hereditary kingship, (2) the headship of a new trade-union, and (3) a writer "ahead of his time."

What can a leader do? Extreme answers to this question are common. With a contempt for the common man that led him into pro-Nazi sympathies, Alexis Carrel in *Man the Unknown* asserted, "Humanity has never gained anything from the efforts of the crowd. It is driven onward by the passion of a few abnormal individuals, by the flame of their intelligence, by their ideal of science, of charity, and of beauty." A far more measured conclusion is that of A. G. Keller in his *Societal Evolution* when he says, "The great man is the product of his time and place, and his greatness consists in his insight, or luck, in producing a variation—in anticipating some massive movement that is about to take place anyhow. He is the protagonist in adjustment to existing . . . and to altered life-conditions of society, not the dictator or challenger of either. This is no derogation from his greatness. . . . But the determining social cause is something very different from the human agency; the latter is always secondary and relatively incidental, and wholly ineffective by itself. . . . The effective cause lies in the unpremeditated movement of the masses of men. The great man interprets them to themselves."

CHAPTER SIX

THE PERSON AND SOCIAL POLICY

How free should the individual be to pursue his own goals? How much control of individual lives should be vested in those in positions of leadership? Under what safeguards? How does society benefit from the stimulation of individual freedom and at the same time preserve the sense of security many find in stability and continuity?

These are questions social thinkers and leaders have pondered down through the centuries. Sometimes they state them more in these terms: What relationship should the individual have to social policy? How responsive can social decision-makers be to current popular demands?

A stable society, embedded in ancient traditions, may give the impression of relative harmony among pursuits satisfying to the individual and pursuits fulfilling society's collective needs. In the face of changing social conditions, however, individual freedom to innovate is stimulated and comes into conflict with social pressures to conform, to resist change.

How individuals see themselves in the societal context influences their image of society. Conversely, how societies react to mounting pressure for change determines limits within which they will tolerate individual freedom of action and expression.

SOCIETY'S MANY GUISES

Society is pictured to us popularly in many guises. Some are terrifying and encourage us to depend for security upon some great and good source of authority. Others give the person a challenge and self-reliance.

Society as a Super-Monster. To some, society is a monster crashing its way down through the forests of time. Each of us, like a cell in the monster's body, has his day in the huge functioning organism and then disappears. Management—the definition and execution of social policy—is an automatic affair dictated by the nature of the beast and of other beasts (societies) and the exigencies of the jungle. That is a caricature of the nineteenth-century perspective of such social philosophers as Herbert Spencer. It still has adherents from among those whose cells are well placed and who thus believe that change might be disastrous to the lumbering superorganism.

Society as a Mechanism Guided by Wise Men. To others, society is or should be like the mechanism of a huge corporation or of a gigantic governmental bureaucracy. Each person works or should work in an office or plant at understood tasks and had best leave problems of policy to the wise men at the helm, the financiers, skilled management technicians, and possibly labor union leaders of a "responsible" sort. The degree to which the "wise men" are left alone depends upon the extent to which the society has relatively a loose or a definite class system. The more definite and accepted the class system may be, the greater will be the power of rationalizations that the "wise men" know what is "best" for the rest of us. The basis for this "wisdom" may be divine revelation, personal age, hereditary status, conquest, or scholarship. But whatever the basis, so long as popular compulsion upon those in control is lacking, it is an aristocratic or pseudoaristocratic conception, with all the limitations that that implies.

Society as All of Us. To still others, society consists of and depends upon the activities, experiences, and thoughts of all of us. This conception is well illustrated by the way in which scientific advancements take place. Such gains result from constant testings of existing explanations by thousands of small men, the "hod carriers" and "bricklayers" of science. Their work slowly brings more or less extensive parts of existing theory into question. The "flashes of genius" of occasional "great men" of science help crystallize changing theory in such a way as to aid in clearing away outworn formulations, as Thomas S. Kuhn has shown in *The Structure of Scientific Revolutions*. As Kuhn indicates, both the creation of a crisis in existing knowledge and the assimilation of a major modification in theory are social movements. Such change "requires the reconstruction of prior theory and the re-evaluation of prior fact, an intrinsically revolutionary process that is seldom completed by a single man and never overnight. No wonder historians have had difficulty in dating precisely this extended process."

Thus, as among fine artists, outstanding scientists show their heads and shoulders *among* their fellows in a movement. As a kind of shorthand and in recognition of relative leadership, the names of the more prominent formulators of a scientific theory and exemplars of an artistic style or conception become milestones in a movement. So, too, changes in social policy frequently come to be known by their facilitators even though they result most significantly from a rising tide of gradually accumulating experience and conviction by thousands and even millions of people. Despite tremendous opposition, "open-shop" cities and industries have become unionized, sometimes by unions with meager resources of a financial sort. Despite tremendous vested power, too, outworn governments have crashed before the onward sweep of new and popular political movements.

THE UNDISTINGUISHED AND THE UNREASONABLE

Sociologists tend to favor the latter view of society, society as all of us. They know the utility of leaders and great men as symbols, as crystallizers of sentiment. They know that leaders can sense the direction being taken and can rush out ahead and say, "Follow me!" And this may at times save some wear and tear on the body politic by facilitating social change. But sociologists are even more aware of the contributions to social policy and social change by the rest of us, *the undistinguished,* and those who goad us, *the unreasonable.*

Tolerating "the Unreasonable." In this whole situation, the chief problem sociologists see is this: When there is orderly and gradual change, the fewest people are hurt by change, the most gain by it, and society remains most healthy. The prevention of well-indicated changes stores up periods of tension and suffering. But the way-breakers for social change, whether gradual or drastic, are social deviants. They are those sufficiently aggressive and heedless to defy the overwhelming social forces making for uniformity and the maintenance of the *status quo.* They are the social manipulators of change just as the successful dominators of society are the social manipulators of stability or against change. And the chief characteristic of such manipulators or agitators of change is that they are—to established and satisfied members of society—unreasonable.

In *Free Speech in the United States,* Zechariah Chafee, Jr., presents quite clearly the social need for tolerating the "unreasonable." He cogently observes, "Too often we assume that such persistent trouble-makers are the only persons injured by a censorship or a sedition law, and conclude from the indiscreet and unreasonable qualities of their speech and writing that after all the loss to the world of thought has been very slight. Too often we forget the multitude of cautious and sensitive men, men with wives and children dependent upon them, men who abhor publicity, who prefer to keep silent in the hope of better days. We cannot know what is lost through the effect upon them of repression, for it is simply left unsaid." And he adds that the "agitator's effort is made on behalf of those thoughtful men as well as for his own sake; and if he wins, the gain to truth comes, not perhaps from his ideas, but from theirs."

A SOCIETY OF FREE MEN

The problem of encouraging the undistinguished through tolerating the unreasonable poses, stated otherwise, the problem of stimulating freedom, of maintaining a constantly rejuvenating society through making it a society of free men.

What Is a Free Man? In a novel of Italian life under the Fascist dictatorship, *Bread and Wine,* Ignazio Silone has an anti-Fascist give his impression of what it means to be a free man. "Liberty isn't a thing you are given as a present," the man asserts. "You can be a free man under a dictatorship. It is sufficient if you struggle against it. He who thinks with his own head is a free man. He who struggles for what he believes to be right is a free man. Even if you live in the freest country in the world and are lazy, callous, apathetic, irresolute, you are not free but a slave, though there be no coercion and no oppression. Liberty is something you have to take for yourself. It's no use begging it from others." But the hero of Sinclair Lewis's *Gideon Planish* had a more typical reaction. "All the rest of his life, in crises, Gideon Planish was to say, 'But this isn't the time for it,'" relates Lewis. "It is the slogan of discreet Liberalism."

Now vs. Not Now. All are not freedom-loving deviants like Silone's anti-Fascist who suffer and die for human privileges. All are not self-centered puppets like Lewis's Planish who do nothing and do it in a valiant and dramatic fashion. The problem is to maintain sufficient freedom of discussion, sufficient access to the facts, and sufficient means of translating opinions into expressions of social policy for all significant minorities to make their actual impression upon social policy without recourse to extreme measures. As Marshall Field concludes, in *Freedom Is More than a Word,* "The greatest good can only be arrived at by discussion, conflict of opinion, and group decision. It cannot be planned nor can it be imposed from above. Anyone who labors under the delusion that it can is either a prospective tyrant or is in danger of throwing away his freedom to a demagogue. Discipline, yes— the survival of democracy depends on discipline. But it must be a self-discipline imposed by ourselves and for objectives we mutually decide upon. It must never be a discipline imposed from above by any person or group."

The Role of Sociology. The struggle to keep our society reasonably in adjustment to changing life-conditions, reasonably rejuvenated, Robert E. Park said should take the form of a "revolution absolute," a continual rather than a spasmodic series of adaptations. And he regarded as the essential element in that "revolutionary" process, the acquiring and disseminating of accurate knowledge about society, both accurate facts and accurate theoretical formulations. The critics and guides in this process are the general social scientists, the sociologists, and their fellows in the segments of social science, especially the economists and political scientists.

From sociology, as Franklin H. Giddings put it, the practical man wants to know the range of possible choices or lines of activity, and the scientist furnishes such a conception by portraying as precisely as he can the nature of social order. "To the scientific mind the universe is order; to the practical mind it is possibility," Giddings observed in his *Studies in the Theory of Human Society.* "Both minds, however, know that order and possibility are compatible; it is only the mind that is neither practical nor scientific which imagines that they are not."

As our scientific knowledge of sociology increases, practical men will have more confidence in it and come to base their decisions perforce more and more upon it. Within the framework of order and possibility thus described, the "undistinguished" multitudes—goaded by "unreasonable" deviants—will exert their

Part Two

Collective Behavior

By

HERBERT BLUMER
University of California at Berkeley

CHAPTER SEVEN

THE FIELD OF
COLLECTIVE BEHAVIOR

The nature of collective behavior is suggested by consideration of such topics as crowds, mobs, panics, manias, dancing crazes, stampedes, mass behavior, public opinion, propaganda, fashion, fads, social movements, revolutions, and reforms. The sociologist has always been interested in such topics, but it is only in recent years that efforts have been made to group them in a single division of sociological concern and to regard them as different expressions of the same generic factors. The term *collective behavior* is used to label this area of sociological interest.

THE BASIS OF COLLECTIVE BEHAVIOR

From one point of view practically all group activity can be thought of as collective behavior. Group activity means that individuals are acting *together* in some fashion; that there is some division of labor among them; and that there is some fitting together of the different lines of individual conduct. In this sense, group activity is a collective matter. In the classroom, for example, there is a division of labor between the teacher and the students. The students act in expected ways and the teacher, likewise, has a different kind of activity which is expected of him. The activities of the different students and of the teacher fit together to form orderly and concerted group conduct. This conduct is collective in character.

In the example which has just been used, the collective behavior occurs because students and teachers have common understandings or traditions as to how they are to behave in the classroom. The students are expected to act in certain ways and they are aware of such expectations; the teacher, likewise, is expected to act in a certain way, and he understands that expectation. This guidance of behavior by common expectations always marks group activity that is under the influence of custom, tradition, conventions, rules, or institutional regulations. Thus, two things may be said: *First*, that the great bulk of collective behavior among human beings occurs because people have common understandings and expectations. *Second*, that the major portion of the field of sociology is devoted to the study of such collective behavior. When the sociologist studies customs, traditions, folkways, mores, institutions, and social organization, he is dealing with the social rules and social definitions through which collective behavior is organized.

COLLECTIVE BEHAVIOR AS A DIVISION OF SOCIOLOGY

If practically all sociology is concerned with collective behavior, in what sense can one speak of the study of *collective behavior* as a separate division of sociology? The answer to this question will enable us to state a little more clearly what the study of collective behavior deals with.

Elementary Forms of Collective Behavior. While most of the collective behavior of human beings exists in the form of regulated group activity, there is a great deal which is not under the influence of rules or understandings. A highly excited mob, a business panic, a state of war hysteria, a condition of social unrest represent instances of collective behavior which are of this character. In these instances, the collective behavior arises spontaneously and is not due to pre-established understandings or traditions. It is the study of just such elementary and spontaneous forms that constitutes one of the major interests in the field of collective behavior.

Organized Forms of Collective Behavior. The other major interest in the study of collective behavior is tracing the way in which the elementary and spontaneous forms develop into organized forms. Customs, conventions, institutions, and the social organization have a career, represented by the passage from a fluid and unorganized condition to a set and organized status. To determine the lines and manner of such development becomes a matter of important concern in the study of collective behavior.

Definition of Collective Behavior. Stated in the most general form, these remarks suggest that the student of collective behavior seeks to understand the way in which a social order arises, for the emergence of a new social order is equivalent to the emergence of new forms of collective behavior. This way of stating the matter permits one to distinguish the field of collective behavior from the rest of sociology. One may say that sociology in general is interested in studying the social order and its constituents (customs, rules, institutions, etc.) as they are; collective behavior is concerned in studying the ways by which the social order comes into existence, in the sense of the emergence and solidification of new forms of collective behavior.

CHAPTER EIGHT

ELEMENTARY COLLECTIVE BEHAVIOR

We use the term "elementary collective behavior" to refer to the incipient and primitive forms of human interaction that underlie and operate through all instances of collective behavior. They are an antecedent condition to crowd behavior, social unrest, collective excitement, crazes and manias, public discussion, mass behavior and social movements; and they may come into play at any point in the career of such instances of collective behavior. They represent basic forms of group interaction that are natural and indigenous in human association. They constitute the basic mechanisms whereby people are led to act collectively in breaking through established rules and routines of group life.

CIRCULAR REACTION AND SOCIAL UNREST

One gets a clue to the nature of elementary collective behavior by recognizing the form of social interaction that has been called *circular reaction.* This refers to a type of interstimulation wherein the response of one individual reproduces the stimulation that has come from another individual and in being reflected back to this individual reinforces the stimulation. Thus the interstimulation assumes a circular form in which individuals reflect one another's states of feeling and in so doing intensify this feeling. It is well evidenced in the transmission of feelings and moods among people who are in a state of excitement. One sees the process clearly at work amidst cattle in a state of alarm. The expression of fear through bellowing, breathing, and movements of the body, induces the same feeling in the case of other cattle who, as they in turn express their alarm, intensify this emotional state in one another. It is through such a process of circular reaction that there arises among cattle a general condition of intense fear and excitement, as in the case of a stampede.

The nature of circular reaction can be further helpfully understood by contrasting it with *interpretative interaction,* which is the form chiefly to be found among human beings who are in association. Ordinarily, human beings respond to one another, as in carrying on a conversation, by interpreting one another's actions or remarks and then reacting on the basis of the interpretation. Responses, consequently, are not made directly to the stimulation, but follow, rather, upon interpretation; further, they are likely to be different in nature from the stimulating acts, being essentially adjustments to these acts. Thus interpretative interaction might be likened to a game of tennis and has the character of a shuttle-like process instead of a circular process. It tends, in degree, to make people different; circular reaction tends to make people alike.

Circular Reaction in Collective Behavior. Circular reaction is very common among human beings. It is the chief form of interstimulation present in spontaneous and elementary collective behavior. Its role in this respect will be seen in the discussion of social unrest, collective excitement, social contagion, and in the instance of crowd activity. Here it may be pointed out that it gives rise to collective, or shared behavior, which is not based on the adherence to common understandings or rules. It is for this reason that circular reaction is the natural mechanism of elementary collective behavior.

The Genesis of Elementary Collective Behavior. Under what conditions does spontaneous and elementary collective behavior arise? Seemingly, under conditions of unrest or disturbance in the usual forms of living or routines of life. Where group life is carried on satisfactorily in accordance with rules or cultural definitions, there is clearly no occasion for the emergence of any new forms of collective behavior. The wishes, needs, and dispositions of people are satisfied through the ordinary cultural activities of their groups. In the event, however, of some disturbance of these established ways of acting, or in the event of the appearance of new dispositions which cannot be satisfied by the existing cultural definitions, elementary collective behavior is likely to arise.

The Factor of Restlessness. When people have impulses, desires, or dispositions which cannot be satisfied by the existing forms of living they are in a state of unrest. Their experience is one of feeling an urge to act but of being balked in doing so;

consequently the experience is one of discomfort, frustration, insecurity, and usually of alienation or loneliness. This inner tension, in the absence of regulated means for its release, will express itself usually through random and unco-ordinated activity. This is a mark of restlessness. Externally, the activity is likely to be erratic, lacking in consistency, and rather similar to a sort of indefinite prowling; internally, it is likely to take the form of disordered imagination and disturbed feelings. In its more acute forms it is characteristic of neurotic behavior.

The Development of Social Unrest. The presence of restlessness among many individuals need not mean, however, the existence of a state of social unrest. It is only when restlessness is involved in circular reaction, or becomes contagious, that social unrest exists. One may view social unrest as the socialization of restlessness. Unless the restlessness of individuals has a reciprocally stimulating and reinforcing effect, it is neither shared nor collective. Such a condition seems to be true of modern neurotic restlessness. The neurotic individual can be regarded as isolated and socially apart—one who finds it difficult to be free, easy, and spontaneous in his association with other people. His disturbed feelings arise as a reaction against other individuals, rather than as a sympathetic sharing of their feelings. The display of neurotic restlessness is likely to irritate others and to alienate them. By contrast, in the instance of social unrest, restlessness has a reciprocal character, i.e., its display awakens a similar condition of restlessness on the part of others, and there occurs mutual reinforcement of this state as the individuals interact with each other. It follows that social unrest is most likely to exist where people are sensitized to one another, or prepared to enter readily into rapport, and also where they undergo together the derangement of their routines of living. These conditions are met in such instances of social unrest as revolutionary unrest, agrarian unrest, the unrest of women, religious and moral unrest, labor unrest—to mention but a few of the many forms. These instances bespeak fundamental disturbances in the feelings, thoughts, and behavior of people due to significant changes in their ways of living.

The Extent and Intensity of Social Unrest. Social unrest may range both in extent and in intensity. It may be confined to a small community as in a case of a small mining community at the time of a strike, or it may extend to a larger dispersed population as in the instance of present-day unrest of youth.

It may be mild and general, as in the case of much of current moral unrest, or be specific and acute as in the revolutionary unrest immediately preceding the Russian Revolution of 1917. Whether narrowly confined or extensive, subdued or acute, social unrest has certain common characteristics which should be designated.

Characteristics of Social Unrest. One of the most interesting of these traits of social unrest is the random character of behavior. People are likely to move around in an erratic and aimless way, as if seeking to find or avoid something, but without knowing what it is that they are trying to find or avoid. Indeed, it is just this lack of understood objectives that explains restless behavior. People are in a state of tension and uneasiness, and feel a strong urge to act. This urge to act, in the absence of goals, necessarily leads to aimless and random behavior.

Another significant mark of social unrest is excited feeling, usually in the form of vague apprehensions, alarm, fears, insecurity, eagerness, or aroused pugnacity. Such excited feeling is conducive to rumors and to exaggerated views and perceptions.

A third important characteristic of social unrest is the irritability and increased suggestibility of people. In a state of social unrest, people are psychologically unstable, suffering from disturbed impulses and feelings. Their attention is likely to be variable and shifting, and lacking in usual continuity. Their condition makes them much more sensitive to others, but also less constant and stable in their make-up and in their conduct. To recognize this increased instability and restlessness is to understand why people in a state of social unrest are suggestible, responsive to new stimulations and ideas, and also more malleable.

Types of Social Unrest. Little scholarly attention has been given to analyzing types of social unrest. It is possible to discern at least five significant types. One is in the nature of a state of general uneasiness. People feel insecure in a vague and indefinite manner, sense that normal life is out of gear, and view the imminent future as uncertain and fraught with dire possibilities. A second type of social unrest is marked by feelings of frustration and protest over an existing mode of life and a consequent readiness to lash out in violent forms of attack on targets symbolizing that mode of life. A third kind of social unrest takes the form of a flight from the existing world; it is likely to show itself in such ways as a yearning for an utopian existence, or a seeking for new forms of sensual gratification, or a cultivating of new philosophies, phantasies, and cultish doctrines. A fourth general type of social unrest has an outgoing expansive character, marked by strong feelings of eagerness, enthusiasm, and avidity to do things, although with great uncertainty as to what should be done. Finally, in contrast, a fifth type of social unrest is characterized by a sense of despair, feelings of apathy, and expressions of lamentation.

These types of social unrest signify that despite its fluid and malleable character social unrest may lay down different general directions to the activities that may develop. The significant alternative directions are: (1) to change the external world of institutional life; (2) to leave the world intact and to seek, instead, a moral transformation of individuals; (3) to flee from the existing world into some refuge of detached cultish or philosophical life; and (4) to dissipate unrest inside of the existing world by engaging in frivolity, fun-seeking, or gratification of the senses.

The Role of Social Unrest. These remarks indicate the important role of social unrest. On one hand, social unrest is a symptom of disruption or breaking down of the order of living. On the other hand, it signifies incipient preparation for new forms of collective behavior. In a metaphorical sense, social unrest can be thought of as a condition which is unorganized, unregulated, fluid, and active. Social unrest may be regarded as the crucible out of which emerge new forms of organized activity —such as social movements, reforms, revolutions, religious cults, spiritual awakenings, and new moral orders. In itself, it may be thought of as having the potentiality of many diverse expressions; that is to say that the alternative forms of newly organized activity into which social unrest may resolve itself are many. We shall be interested in seeing how social unrest develops and expresses itself in new ways of behavior.

MECHANISMS OF ELEMENTARY COLLECTIVE BEHAVIOR

The behavior of people who are in a state of social unrest shows a number of typical forms of interaction which we can designate as the elementary mechanisms of collective behavior.

They are elementary because they appear spontaneously and naturally, they are the simplest and earliest ways in which people interact in order to act together, and they usually lead to more advanced and complicated forms.

Milling. The basic type of such elementary forms is that of *milling*. Milling can be thought of as a pure instance of circular reaction. In milling, individuals move around amongst one another in an aimless and random fashion, such as in the interweaving of cattle and sheep who are in a state of excitement. The primary effect of milling is to make the individuals more sensitive and responsive to one another, so that they become increasingly preoccupied with one another and decreasingly responsive to ordinary objects of stimulation. It is such a condition to which the term *rapport* refers. We observe this state in a magnified form in the instance of hypnosis. The hypnotic subject becomes increasingly preoccupied with the hypnotist, in such a way that his attention becomes riveted upon the hypnotist and correspondingly he develops an immunity to most other types of stimulation to which he would ordinarily respond. Milling tends to induce this condition among people. Their attention becomes increasingly focused on one another and less on objects and events which would ordinarily concern them. Being preoccupied with each other they are inclined to respond to one another quickly, directly, and unwittingly. Because milling induces this preoccupation and this readiness to quick response, it clearly makes for collective behavior. People in this state are much more disposed to act together, under the influence of a common impulse or mood, than they are to act separately, under the influence of feelings that are not common to them. Viewed in this way, milling can be regarded as an elementary and natural means by which people are prepared to act together in a spontaneous way.

Collective Excitement. We may single out collective excitement as a more intense form of milling and treat it as a separate elementary mechanism conducive to collective behavior. While it may be regarded as a speeding up of the milling process and hence as having the general features of circular reaction, it has certain specific marks that deserve attention. First, one should appreciate the power of excited behavior in catching and riveting the attention of observers. In all societies, animal as well as human, individuals are particularly sensitive to the display of excitement upon the part of one another. It is difficult to ignore such excited behavior; to do so one must remove himself from the scene of action or force his attention to some other object by the aid of some verbal formulae. His natural tendency is to pay attention to the excited behavior and to take an interest in it. This power of excited behavior in compelling attention is of particular interest, for to the extent which one becomes preoccupied with an object, to that extent one comes under its control. A human being controls himself in the face of an object of attention to the extent that he is able to call up images which he can oppose to such an object. Yet excited behavior, as an object of attention, interferes with this process of directed imagery. Where people are collectively excited, as a result of some form of milling, this loss of normal control becomes pronounced, setting the stage for contagious behavior.

Another interesting feature of collective excitement is that under its influence people become more emotionally aroused and more likely to be carried away by impulses and feelings; hence rendered more unstable and irresponsible. In collective excitement, ordinary commitments and routine activities are more readily broken; the stage is set for the formation of new forms of behavior and for the reorganization of the individual. In collective excitement, individuals may embark on lines of conduct which previously they would not likely have thought of, much less dared to undertake. Likewise, under its stress, and with opportunities for the release of tension, individuals may incur significant reorganization in their sentiments, habits, and traits of personality.

These remarks suggest how influential collective excitement may be in bringing people together into new forms of collective association and in laying the basis for new forms of collective behavior.

Social Contagion. Where collective excitement is intense and widespread, there is every likelihood for some kind of social contagion to take place. Social contagion refers to the relatively rapid, unwitting, and nonrational dissemination of a mood, impulse, or form of conduct; it is well exemplified by the spread of crazes, manias, and fads. In its more extreme forms it has the character of a social epidemic, as in the instance of the tulip mania in Holland in the eighteenth century or of the dancing mania of the Middle Ages. In modern times, we see it clearly

pronounced in the development of war hysteria or in the operation of financial panics.

Social contagion may be regarded as an intense form of milling and collective excitement; in it the development of rapport
and unreflective responsiveness of individuals to one another
becomes pronounced. What is most interesting and spectacular
about social contagion is that it attracts and infects individuals,
many of whom originally are merely detached and indifferent
spectators and bystanders. At first, people may be merely curious
about the given behavior, or mildly interested in it. As they catch
the spirit of excitement and become more attentive to the behavior, they become more inclined to engage in it. This may be
viewed as a lowering of social resistance brought about by the
fact that they suffer some loss of self-consciousness and, accordingly, of ability to interpret the activity of others. Self-consciousness is a means of barricading oneself against the influence of
others, for with it the individual checks his immediate, natural
responses and impulses, and makes judgments before acting.
Consequently, when people are under the stress of collective
excitement, becoming more and more preoccupied with a given
type of behavior, they are more likely to be subject to the impulses awakened in them. Where people already have a common
disposition to act in a certain way, such as to seek gain, to flee
from danger, or to express hatred, the display of such behavior
under conditions of collective excitement easily releases the
corresponding impulses on their part. Under such conditions the
given kind of behavior will "spread like wildfire," as one sees it
in the case of a speculative orgy, a financial panic, or a wave of
patriotic hysteria.

CHAPTER NINE

ELEMENTARY COLLECTIVE GROUPINGS

Our discussion so far has sought to show briefly the nature of collective behavior in its most elementary and spontaneous form and to explain the nature of the mechanisms by which it operates. Our next task is to discuss the different types of elementary collective groups. Four important types of elementary collective groups can be isolated: the acting crowd, the expressive crowd, the mass, and the public. These social groupings can be regarded as elementary since they arise spontaneously and their action is not set or determined by existing cultural patterns. Each has a distinctive character and each arises under a special set of conditions.

THE CROWD

Much of the initial interest of sociologists in the field of collective behavior has centered on the study of the crowd. This interest was lively particularly towards the end of the last century, especially among French scholars. It gained its most vivid expression in the classical work, *The Crowd*, by Gustave Le Bon. This work and others have provided us with much insight into the nature and behavior of the crowd, although much still remains unknown.

Types of Crowds. It is convenient to identify four types of crowds. The first can be called a *casual* crowd, as in the instance of a street crowd watching a performer in a store window. The casual crowd usually has a momentary existence; more important, it has a very loose organization and scarcely any unity. Its members come and go, giving but temporary attention to the object which has awakened the interest of the crowd, and entering into only feeble association with one another. While the chief mechanisms of crowd formation are present in the casual crowd, they are so reduced in scope and weak in operation, that we need not concern ourselves further with this type of crowd. A second type may be designated as the *conventionalized* crowd, such as the spectators at an exciting baseball game. Their behavior is essentially like that of casual crowds, except that it is expressed in established and regularized ways. It is this regularized activity that marks off the conventional crowd as a distinct type. The third type of crowd is the *acting,* aggressive crowd, best represented by a revolutionary crowd or a lynching mob. The outstanding mark of this type of crowd is the presence of an aim or objective toward which the activity of the crowd is directed. It is this type of crowd which is the object of concern in practically all studies of the crowd. The remaining type is the *expressive* or "dancing" crowd, such as one sees in the case of carnivals or in the beginning stage of many religious sects. Its distinguishing trait is that excitement is expressed in physical movement primarily as a form of release instead of being directed toward some objective. We shall consider the acting crowd, and then the expressive crowd.

Formation of Crowds. The essential steps in the formation of a crowd seem to be quite clear. First is the occurrence of some exciting event which catches the attention and arouses the interest of people. In becoming preoccupied with this event and stirred by its excitatory character, an individual is already likely to lose some of his ordinary self-control and to be dominated by the exciting object. Further, this kind of experience, by arousing impulses and feelings, establishes a condition of tension which, in turn, presses the individual on to action. Thus, a number of people stimulated by the same exciting event are disposed by that very fact to behave like a crowd.

This becomes clear in the second step—the beginning of the milling process. The tension of individuals who are aroused by some stimulating event, leads them to move around and to talk to one another; in this milling the incipient excitement becomes greater. The excitement of each is conveyed to others, and, as we have indicated above, in being reflected back to each, is intensified. The most obvious effect of this milling is to disseminate a common mood, feeling, or emotional impulse, and also to increase its intensity. This leads to a state of marked rapport wherein individuals become sensitive and responsive to one another and where, consequently, all are more disposed to act together as a collective unit.

Another important result may come from the milling process, and may be regarded as the third important step in the formation of the acting crowd. This step is the emergence of a common object of attention on which the impulses, feelings, and imagery of the people become focused. Usually the common object is the exciting event which has aroused the people; much more frequently, however, it is an image which has been built up and fixed through the talking and acting of people as they mill. This image, or object, like the excitement, is common and shared. Its importance is that it gives a common orientation to the people, and so provides a common objective to their activity. With such a common objective, the crowd is in a position to act with unity, purpose, and consistency.

The last step may be thought of as the stimulation and fostering of the impulses that correspond to the crowd objective, up to the point where the members are ready to act on them. This nurturing and crystallizing of impulses is a result of the interstimulation that takes place in milling and in response to leadership. It occurs primarily as a result of images that are aroused through the process of suggestion and imitation, and reinforced through mutual acceptance. When the members of a crowd have a common impulse oriented toward a fixed image and supported by an intense collective feeling, they are ready to act in the aggressive fashion typical of the acting crowd.

THE ACTING CROWD

It should be noted, first, that such a group is spontaneous and lives in the momentary present. As such it is not a society or a cultural group. Its action is not preset by accepted conventions, established expectations, or rules. It lacks other important marks of a society such as an established social organization, an established division of labor, a structure of established roles, a recognized leadership, a set of norms, a set of moral regulations, an awareness of its own identity, or a recognized "we-consciousness." Instead of acting, then, on the basis of established rule, it acts on the basis of aroused impulse. Just as it is, in this sense, a noncultural group, so likewise it tends to be a nonmoral group. In the light of this fact it is not difficult to understand that crowd actions may be strange, forbidding, and at times atrocious. Not having a body of definitions or rules to guide its behavior and, instead, acting on the basis of impulse, the crowd is fickle, suggestible, and irresponsible.

This character of the crowd can be appreciated better by understanding the condition of the typical member. Such an individual loses ordinary critical understanding and self-control as he enters into rapport with other crowd members and becomes infused by the collective excitement which dominates them. He responds immediately and directly to the remarks and actions of others instead of interpreting these gestures, as he would do in ordinary conduct. His inability to survey the actions of others before responding to them carries over to his own tendencies to act. Consequently, the impulses aroused in him by his sympathetic sharing of the collective excitement are likely to gain immediate expression instead of being submitted to his own judgment. This explains why suggestion is so pronounced in the crowd. It should be noted, however, that this suggestibility exists only along the line of the aroused impulses; suggestions made contrary to them are ignored. This limiting of the area of suggestibility, but with an intensification of the suggestibility inside of these limits, is a point which is frequently overlooked by students of crowd behavior.

The loss of customary critical interpretation and the arousing of impulses and excited feelings explain the queer, vehement, and surprising behavior so frequent among members of a genuine crowd. Impulses which ordinarily would be subject to a severe check by the individual's judgment and control of himself now have a free passage to expression. That many of these impulses should have an atavistic character is not strange, nor, consequently, is it surprising that much of the actual behavior should be violent, cruel, and destructive. Further, the release of impulses and feelings which encounter no restraint, which come to possess the individual, and which acquire a quasi-sanction through the support of other people, gives the individual a sense of power, of ego-expansion, and of rectitude. Thus, he is likely to experience a sense of invincibility and of conviction in his actions.

It should be borne in mind that this state of the members of the crowd is due to their extreme rapport and mutual excitement; and, in turn, that this rapport in the acting crowd has become

organized around a common objective of activity. Common
focusing of attention, rapport, and individual submergence—these
exist as different phases of one another, and explain the unity
of the crowd and the general character of its behavior. We
should note that individuals may be physically present in a crowd
yet not participate sympathetically in its process of shared excitement; such individuals are not true members of the crowd.

To prevent the formation of a mob or to break up a mob it is
necessary to disrupt the milling process so that attention ceases
to be focused collectively on one object. This is the theoretical
principle underlying crowd control. Insofar as the attention of
the members is directed toward different objects, they form an
aggregation of individuals instead of a crowd united by intimate
rapport. Thus, to throw people into a state of panic, or to get
them interested in other objects, or to get them engaged in discussion or argumentation represents different ways in which a
crowd can be broken up.

Our discussion of the crowd has presented the psychological
bond of the crowd, or the spirit, that may be called "crowd-
mindedness" to use a felicitous phrase of E. A. Ross.[1] If we think
in terms of crowd-mindedness, it is clear that many groups may
take on the character of a crowd without having to be as small in
size as in the instance of a lynching mob. Under certain conditions, a nation may come to be like a crowd. If the people become
preoccupied with the same stirring event or object, if they develop a high state of mutual excitement marked by no disagreement, and if they have strong impulses to act toward the object
with which they are preoccupied, their action will be like that
of the crowd. We are familiar with such behavior on a huge
scale in the case of social contagion, like that of patriotic hysteria.

THE EXPRESSIVE CROWD

The distinguishing feature of the acting crowd, as we have
seen, is the direction of the attention toward some common objective or goal; the action of the crowd is the behavior gone
through to reach that objective. In contrast, the expressive crowd
has no goal or objective—its impulses and feelings are spent in

1 E. A. Ross, *Social Psychology* (New York: Macmillan Co., 1908).

mere expressive actions, usually in unrestrained physical movements, which give release to tension without having any other
purpose. We see such behavior in a marked form in the saturna-
lia, the carnival, and the dancing crowds of primitive sects.

Comparisons with the Acting Crowd. In explaining the nature
of the expressive crowd we should note that in formation and
fundamental character it is very much like the acting crowd. It
consists of people who are excited, who mill, and who in doing
so, spread and intensify the excitement. There develops among
them the same condition of rapport marked by quick and unwitting mutual responsiveness. Individuals lose awareness of themselves. Impulses and feelings are aroused, and are no longer
subject to the constraint and control which an individual usually
exercises over them. In these respects the expressive crowd is
essentially like the acting crowd.

The fundamental difference is that the expressive crowd does
not develop any image of a goal or objective, and, consequently,
suggestion does not operate to build up a plan of action. Without
having an objective toward which it might act, the crowd can
release its aroused tension and excitement only in physical movement. Stated tersely, the crowd has to act, but it has nothing
toward which it can act, and so it merely engages in excited
movements. The excitement of the crowd stimulates further excitement which does not, however, become organized around
some purposive act which the crowd seeks to carry out. In such
a situation the expression of excited feeling becomes an end in
itself; the behavior, therefore, may take the form of laughing,
weeping, shouting, leaping, and dancing. In a more extreme
expression, it may be in the form of uttering gibberish or having
violent physical spasms.

Rhythmic Expression. Perhaps the most interesting feature of
this expressive behavior, as it is carried on collectively, is that
it tends to become rhythmical; so that with sufficient repetition
and with the existence of sufficient rapport, it takes on the form
of people's acting in unison. In more advanced form it comes to
be like a collective dance; it is this aspect that leads one to
designate the expressive crowd as a dancing crowd. It may be
said that just as an acting crowd develops its unity through the
formation of a common objective, the expressive crowd forms its
unity through the rhythmical expression of its tension.

This feature is of outstanding significance, for it throws considerable light on the interesting association between "dancing" behavior and primitive religious sentiment. To illustrate this point, let us consider the experience of the individual in such a crowd.

The Individual in the Expressive Crowd. The stimulation that the individual receives from those with whom he is in rapport lessens his ordinary self-control and evokes and incites impulsive feelings which take possession of him. He feels carried away by a spirit whose source is unknown, but whose effect is acutely appreciated. There are two conditions which are likely to make this experience one of ecstasy and exaltation, and to seal it with a sacred or divine stamp. The first is that the experience is cathartic in nature. The individual who has been in a state of tension, discomfort, and perhaps anxiety, suddenly gains full release and experiences the joy and fullness that come with such relief. This organic satisfaction unquestionably yields a pleasure and exhilaration that makes the experience momentous. The fact that this mood has such complete and unobstructed control over the individual easily leads him to feel that he is possessed or pervaded by a kind of transcendental spirit. The other condition which gives the experience a religious character is the approval and sanction implied in the support coming from those with whom he is in rapport. The fact that others are sharing the same experience rids it of suspicion and enables its unqualified acceptance. When an experience gives complete and full satisfaction, when it is socially stimulated, approved, and sustained, and when it comes in the form of a mysterious possession from the outside, it easily acquires a religious character.

The Development of Collective Ecstasy. When an expressive crowd reaches the height of such collective ecstasy, the tendency is for this feeling to be projected upon objects which are sensed as having some intimate connection with it. Thereupon such objects become sacred to the members of the crowd. These objects may vary; they may include persons (such as a religious prophet), the dance, a song, or physical objects which are felt to be linked with the ecstatic experience. The appearance of such sacred objects lays the basis for the formation of a cult, sect, or primitive religion.

Not all expressive crowds attain this stage of development. Most of them do not pass beyond the early milling or excited stage. But implicitly, they have the potentiality of doing so, and they have most of the characteristic features, even though they be in a subdued form.

Like the acting crowd, the expressive crowd need not be confined to a small compact group whose members are in immediate physical proximity of one another. The behavior which is characteristic of it may be found on occasion in a large group, such as the nation-wide public.

Evaluation. A brief evaluation of the acting crowd and the expressive crowd can be made here. Both of them are spontaneous groupings. Both of them represent elementary collectivities. Their form and structure are not traceable to any body of culture or set of rules; instead, such structures as they have, arise indigenously out of the milling of excited individuals. The acting crowd focuses its tension on an objective and so becomes organized around a plan of action; the expressive crowd merely releases its tension in expressive movement which tends to become rhythmical and establishes unity in this fashion. In both crowds the individual is stripped of much of his conscious, ordinary behavior, and is rendered malleable by the crucible of collective excitement. With the breakdown of his previous personal organization, he is in a position to develop new forms of conduct and to crystallize a new personal organization along new and different lines. In this sense, crowd behavior is a means by which the breakup of the social organization and personal structure is brought about, and at the same time is a potential device for the emergence of new forms of conduct and personality. The acting crowd presents one of the alternative lines for such reorganization—the development of aggressive behavior in the direction of purposive social change. We shall view this line of reorganization as giving rise to a political order. The expressive crowd stands for the other alternative—the release of inner tension in conduct which tends to become sacred and marked by deep sentiment. This might be regarded as giving rise to a religious order of behavior.

THE MASS

We are selecting the term *mass* to denote another elementary and spontaneous collective grouping which, in some respects, is like the crowd but is fundamentally different from it in other ways. The mass is represented by people who participate in mass behavior, such as those who are excited by some national event, those who share in a land boom, those who are interested in a murder trial which is reported in the press, or those who participate in some large migration.

Distinguishable Features of the Mass. So conceived, the mass has a number of distinguishable features. *First,* its membership may come from all walks of life, and from all distinguishable social strata; it may include people of different class position, of different vocation, of different cultural attainment, and of different wealth. One can recognize this in the case of the mass of people who follow a murder trial. *Second,* the mass is an anonymous group, or more exactly, is composed of anonymous individuals. *Third,* there exists little interaction or exchange of experience between the members of the mass. They are usually physically separated from one another, and, being anonymous, do not have the opportunity to mill as do the members of the crowd. *Fourth,* the mass is very loosely organized and is not able to act with the concertedness or unity that marks the crowd.

The Role of Individuals in the Mass. The fact that the mass consists of individuals belonging to a wide variety of local groups and cultures is important. For it signifies that the object of interest which gains the attention of those who form the mass is something which lies on the outside of the local cultures and groups; and therefore, that this object of interest is not defined or explained in terms of the understandings or rules of these local groups. The object of mass interest can be thought of as attracting the attention of people away from their local cultures and spheres of life and turning it toward a wider universe, toward areas which are not defined or covered by rules, regulations, or expectations. In this sense the mass can be viewed as constituted by detached and alienated individuals who face objects or areas of life which are interesting, but which are also puzzling and not easy to understand and order. Consequently, before such objects, the members of the mass are likely to be confused and uncertain in their actions. Further, in not being able to communicate with one another, except in limited and imperfect ways, the members of the mass are forced to act separately, as individuals.

Society and the Mass. From this brief characterization it can be seen that the mass is devoid of the features of a society or a community. It has no social organization, no body of custom and tradition, no established set of rules or rituals, no organized group of sentiments, no structure of status roles, and no established leadership. It merely consists of an aggregation of individuals who are separate, detached, anonymous, and thus, homogeneous as far as mass behavior is concerned. It can be seen, further, that the behavior of the mass, just because it is not made by pre-established rule or expectation, is spontaneous, indigenous, and elementary. In these respects, the mass is a great deal like the crowd.

In other respects, there is an important difference. It has already been noted that the mass does not mill or interact as the crowd does. Instead, the individuals are separated from one another and unknown to one another. This fact means that the individual in the mass, instead of being stripped of his self-awareness is, on the other hand, apt to be rather acutely self-conscious. Instead of acting in response to the suggestions and excited stimulation of those with whom he is in rapport, he acts in response to the object that has gained his attention and on the basis of the impulses that are aroused by it.

Nature of Mass Behavior. This raises the question as to how the mass behaves. The answer is in terms of each individual's seeking to answer his own needs. The form of mass behavior, paradoxically, is laid down by individual lines of activity and not by concerted action. These individual activities are primarily in the form of selections—such as the selection of a new dentifrice, a book, a play, a party platform, a new fashion, a philosophy, or a gospel—selections which are made in response to the vague impulses and feelings which are awakened by the object of mass interest. Mass behavior, even though a congeries of individual lines of action, may become a momentous significance. If these lines converge, the influence of the mass may be enormous, as is shown by the far-reaching effects on institutions ensuing from shifts in the selective interest of the mass. A political party may be disorganized or a commercial institution wrecked by such shifts in interest or taste.

When mass behavior becomes organized, as into a movement, it ceases to be mass behavior, but becomes societal in nature. Its whole nature changes in acquiring a structure, a program, a defining culture, traditions, prescribed rules, an in-group attitude, and a we-consciousness. It is for this reason that we have appropriately limited it to the forms of behavior which have been described.

Increasing Importance of Mass Behavior. Under conditions of modern urban and industrial life, mass behavior has emerged in increasing magnitude and importance. This is due primarily to the operation of factors which have detached people from their local cultures and local group settings. Migration, changes of residence, newspapers, motion pictures, the radio, education—all have operated to detach individuals from customary moorings and thrust them into a new and wider world. In the face of this world, individuals have had to make adjustments on the basis of largely unaided selections. The convergence of their selections has made the mass a potent influence. At times, its behavior comes to approximate that of a crowd, especially under conditions of excitement. At such times it is likely to be influenced by excited appeals as these appear in the press or over the radio—appeals that play upon primitive impulses, antipathies, and traditional hatreds. This should not obscure the fact that the mass may behave without such crowdlike frenzy. It may be much more influenced by an artist or a writer who happens to sense the vague feelings of the mass and to give expression and articulation to them.

Instances of Mass Behavior. In order to make clearer the nature of the mass and of mass behavior, a brief consideration can be given to a few instances. Gold rushes and land rushes illustrate many of the features of mass behavior. The people who participate in them usually come from a wide variety of backgrounds; together they constitute a heterogeneous assemblage. Thus, those who engaged in the Klondike Rush or the Oklahoma Land Boom came from different localities and areas. In the rush, each individual (or at best, family) had his own goal or objective, so that between the participants there was a minimum of cooperation and very little feeling of allegiance or loyalty. Each was trying to get ahead of the other, and each had to take care of himself. Once the rush is under way, there is little discipline, and no organization to enforce order. Under such conditions it is easy to see how a rush turns in to a stampede or a panic.

Mass Advertising. Some further appreciation of the nature of mass behavior is yielded by a brief treatment of mass advertising. In such advertising, the appeal has to be addressed to the anonymous individual. The relation between the advertisement and the prospective purchaser is a direct one—there is no organization or leadership which can deliver, so to speak, the body of purchasers to the seller. Instead, each individual acts upon the basis of his own selection. The purchasers are a heterogeneous group coming from many communities and walks of life; as members of the mass, however, because of their anonymity, they are homogeneous or essentially alike.

Proletarian Masses. What are sometimes spoken of as the proletarian masses illustrate other features of the mass. They represent a large population with little organization or effective communication. Such people usually have been wrested loose from a stable group life. They are usually disturbed, even though it be only in the form of vague hopes or new tastes and interests. Consequently, there is a lot of groping in their behavior—an uncertain process of selection among objects and ideas that come to their attention.

THE PUBLIC

We shall consider the public as the remaining elementary collective grouping. The term *public* is used to refer to a group of people (*a*) who are confronted by an issue, (*b*) who are divided in their ideas as to how to meet the issue, and (*c*) who engage in discussion over the issue. As such, it is to be distinguished from a public in the sense of a national people, as when one speaks of the public of the United States, and also from a *following*, as in the instance of the "public" of a motion-picture star. The presence of an issue, of discussion, and of a collective opinion is the mark of the public.

The Public as a Group. We refer to the public as an elementary and spontaneous collective grouping because it comes into existence not as a result of design, but as a natural response to a certain kind of situation. That the public does not exist as an established group and that its behavior is not prescribed by traditions or cultural patterns is indicated by the very fact that its existence centers on the presence of an issue. As issues vary, so do the corresponding publics. And the fact that an issue exists signifies the presence of a situation which cannot be met on the basis of a cultural rule but which must be met by a collective decision arrived at through a process of discussion. In this sense, the public is a grouping that is spontaneous and not pre-established.

Characteristic Features of the Public. This elementary and spontaneous character of the public can be better appreciated by noticing that the public, like the crowd and the mass, is lacking in the characteristic features of a society. The existence of an issue means that the group has to act; yet there are no understandings, definitions, or rules prescribing what that action should be. If there were, there would be, of course, no issue. It is in this sense that we can speak of the public as having no culture—no traditions to dictate what its action shall be. Further, since a public comes into existence only with an issue it does not have the form or organization of a society. In it, people do not have fixed status roles. Nor does the public have any we-feeling or consciousness of its identity. Instead, the public is a kind of amorphous group whose size and membership varies with the issue; instead of having its activity prescribed, it is engaged in an effort to arrive at an act, and therefore forced to *create* its action.

The peculiarity of the public is that it is marked by disagreement and hence by *discussion* as to what should be done. This fact has a number of implications. For one thing, it indicates that the interaction that occurs in the public is markedly different from that which takes place in the crowd. A crowd mills, develops rapport, and reaches a unanimity unmarred by disagreement. The public interacts on the basis of interpretation, enters into dispute, and consequently is characterized by conflict relations. Correspondingly, individuals in the public are likely to have their self-consciousness intensified and their critical powers heightened instead of losing self-awareness and critical ability as occurs in the crowd. In the public, arguments are advanced, are criticized, and are met by counterarguments. The interaction, therefore, makes for opposition instead of the mutual support and unanimity that mark the crowd.

Another point of interest is that this discussion, which is based on difference, places some premium on facts and makes for rational consideration. While, as we shall see, the interaction may fall short by far of realizing these characteristics, the tendency is in their direction. The crowd means that rumor and spectacular suggestion predominate; but the presence of opposition and disagreement in the public means that contentions are challenged and become subject to criticism. In the face of attack that threatens to undermine their character, such contentions have to be bolstered or revised in the face of criticisms that cannot be ignored. Since facts can maintain their validity, they come to be valued; and since the discussion is argumentative, rational considerations come to occupy a role of some importance.

Behavior Patterns of the Public. Now we can consider the question as to how a public acts. This question is interesting, particularly because the public does not act like a society, a crowd, or the mass. A society manages to act by following a prescribed rule or consensus; a crowd, by developing rapport; and the mass, by the convergence of individual selections. But the public faces, in a sense, the dilemma of how to become a unit when it is actually divided, of how to act concertedly when there is a disagreement as to what the action should be. The public acquires its particular type of unity and manages to act by arriving at a collective decision or by developing a collective opinion. It becomes necessary to consider now the nature of public opinion and the manner of its formation.

PUBLIC OPINION

Public opinion should be viewed as a collective product. As such, it is not a unanimous opinion with which everyone in the public agrees, nor is it necessarily the opinion of a majority. Being a collective opinion it may be (and usually is) different from the opinion of any of the groups in the public. It can be thought of, perhaps, as a composite opinion formed out of the several opinions that are held in the public; or better, as the central tendency set by the striving among these separate opinions and, consequently, as being shaped by the relative strength and play of opposition among them. In this process, the opinion of some minority group may exert a much greater influence in the shaping of the collective opinion than does the view of a majority group. Being a collective product, public opinion does represent the entire public as it is being mobilized to act on the issue, and as such, does enable concerted action which is not necessarily based on consensus, rapport, or chance alignment of individual choices. Public opinion is always moving toward a decision even though it never is unanimous.

The Universe of Discourse. The formation of public opinion occurs through the give and take of discussion. Argument and counterargument become the means by which it is shaped. For this process of discussion to go on, it is essential for the public to have what has been called a "universe of discourse"—the possession of a common language or the ability to agree on the meaning of fundamental terms. Unless they can understand one another, discussion and argumentation are not only fruitless, but impossible. Public discussion today, particularly on certain national issues, is likely to be hampered by the absence of a universe of discourse. Further, if the groups or parties in the public adopt dogmatic and sectarian positions, public discussion comes to a standstill; for such sectarian attitudes are tantamount to a refusal to adopt the point of view of one another and to alter one's own position in the face of attack or criticism. The formation of public opinion implies that people share one another's experience and are willing to make compromises and concessions. It is only in this way that the public, divided as it is, can come to act as a unit.

Interest Groups. The public, ordinarily, is made up of interest groups and a more detached and disinterested spectator-like body. The issue which creates the public is usually set by contesting interest groups. These interest groups have an immediate private concern in the way the issue is met and, therefore, they endeavor to win to their position the support and allegiance of the outside disinterested group. This puts the disinterested group, as Lippmann has pointed out, in the position of arbiter and judge. It is their alignment which determines, usually, which of the competing schemes is likely to enter most freely into the final action. This strategic and decisive place held by those not identified with the immediate interest groups means that public discussion is carried on primarily among them. The interest groups endeavor to shape and set the opinions of these relatively disinterested people.

Viewed in this way, one can understand the varying quality of public opinion, and also the use of means of influence such as propaganda, which subvert intelligent public discussion. A given public opinion is likely to be anywhere between a highly emotional and prejudiced point of view and a highly intelligent and thoughtful opinion. In other words, public discussion may be carried on different levels, with different degrees of thoroughness and limitation. The efforts made by interest groups to shape public opinion may be primarily attempts to arouse or set emotional attitudes and to provide misinformation. It is this feature which had led many students of public opinion to deny its rational character and to emphasize instead, its emotional and unreasoned nature. One must recognize, however, that the very process of controversial discussion forces a certain amount of rational consideration and that, consequently, the resulting collective opinion has a certain rational character. The fact that contentions have to be defended and justified and opposing contentions criticized and shown to be untenable, involves evaluation, weighing, and judgment. Perhaps it would be accurate to say that public opinion is rational, but need not be intelligent.

The Role of Public Discussion. It is clear that the quality of public opinion depends to a large extent on the effectiveness of public discussion. In turn, this effectiveness depends on the availability and flexibility of the agencies of public communication, such as the press, television, and public meetings. Basic to their effective use is the possibility of free discussion. If certain of the contending views are barred from gaining presentation to the disinterested public or suffer some discrimination as to the possibility of being argued before them, then, correspondingly, there is interference with effective public discussion.

As mentioned above, the concerns of interest groups readily lead them to efforts to manipulate public opinion. This is particularly true today, when public issues are many and the opportunities for thorough discussion are limited. This setting has been conducive to the employment, in increasing degree, of "propaganda"; today most students of public opinion find that their chief concern is the study of propaganda.

PROPAGANDA

Propaganda can be thought of as a deliberately evoked and guided campaign to induce people to accept a given view, sentiment, or value. Its peculiarity is that in seeking to attain this end it does not give fair consideration to opposing views. The end is dominant and the means are subservient to this end. Hence, we find that a primary characteristic of propaganda is the effort to gain the acceptance of a view not on the basis of the merits of that view but, instead, by appealing to other motives. It is this feature that has made propaganda suspect. In the area of public discussion and public consideration, propaganda operates to mold opinions and judgments not on the basis of the merits of an issue, but chiefly by playing upon emotional attitudes and feelings. Its aim is to implant an attitude or value which comes to be felt by people as natural, true, and proper, and, therefore, as one which expresses itself spontaneously and without coercion.

Collective Action through Propaganda. It is important to realize that propaganda seeks to bring about collective action rather than mere individual action. In this sense it should be distinguished from advertising, since advertising tries to influence individual action. In propaganda, by contrast, there is the effort to create a conviction and to get action in accordance with this conviction. Those who share a conviction are more easily disposed to act together and to give one another support. From this point of view, everyone who preaches a doctrine or who seeks to propagate a faith is a propagandist, for his ultimate purpose is not to discuss the merits of an issue, but instead to implant a given conviction. With this character, it is clear that propaganda operates to end discussion and reflection.

Practical Rules of Propaganda. There are a few simple rules which are generally recognized to apply to propaganda. *First*, of course, to implant a desired view or attitude, it is necessary to attract the attention of people. *Next*, the object in which it is desired that they become interested should be given a favorable and appealing setting, as in the instance of advertising. *Third*, the images which are used to influence them should be simple and clean-cut. *Fourth*, there should be continuous repetition of the slogans or catchwords or of the presented images. *Fifth*, it is best never to argue, but simply to persist in assertion and reassertion. Such simple techniques are held to be particularly effective in the case of the bulk of people whose attention is ordinarily easily diverted and whose interest easily flags.

The Chief Procedures of Propaganda. The chief lines along which propaganda may operate, however, are broader and deserve more thorough consideration. We can distinguish three primary ways by which propaganda is likely to achieve its ends. The first is by simply misrepresenting facts and by providing false information. Judgments and opinions of people are obviously shaped by such data as are available to them. By manipulating the facts, concealing some and misrepresenting others, the propagandist can do much to induce the formation of a given attitude.

Another favorite means of propaganda is to make use of in-group–out-group attitudes. It is well known by sociologists that when two groups develop a keen sense of opposition, strong and unreasonable feelings are released. Each group tends to foster attitudes of loyalty and altruism among the members and to inculcate bitter feelings of hatred and enmity toward the outsiders. The ability to use this in-group–out-group pattern is a primary desideratum to the propagandist. He endeavors to get people to identify his views with their in-group feelings, and opposing views with out-group attitudes. It is the presence of this in-group–out-group setting that explains the extreme effectiveness of propaganda during times of war.

Perhaps the outstanding method of the propagandist is to utilize the emotional attitudes and prejudices which people already have. His purpose here is to build up an association between them and his propagandistic message. Thus, if he can link his views to certain favorable attitudes which people already have, these views will gain acceptance. Also, if opposing views can be associated with unfavorable attitudes, they are likely to be rejected. We see a great deal of this device in current discussions. Efforts are made to identify contentions with such beneficently toned stereotypes as "democracy," "save the Constitution," and "individual liberty," and opposing contentions with such stereotypes as "communism" and "anti-American." It is by playing upon the feelings and prejudices which people already have, that propaganda primarly operates.

The Ingenuity of Propagandists. While it is possible to indicate the simple rules which propaganda follows and the psychological mechanisms which it employs, it is important to realize that it depends primarily upon ingenuity. Each situation has to be met in terms of its peculiarities; a device which may be very successful in one situation may be of no value in another. In this sense, propaganda is like persuasion in face-to-face situations; much depends on intuitive impression and artful ingenuity.

Conflicting Propagandas. Without doubt, there is an increasing use of propaganda at the present time in the public arena, and undoubtedly, this factor has influenced both the nature of public opinion and the manner of its information. This consequence has led to despair on the part of many as to the serviceability of democratic machinery. However, it is important to realize that the presence of propaganda and counter-propaganda sets, again, an issue and ushers in the discussional process which we have spoken of above. For when there are conflicting and opposing propagandas at work, the stage is set for a logical duel, where facts have a premium and rational considerations enter. From this point of view one may understand the remark that propaganda is harmful and dangerous only when there is *one* propaganda.

Steps in the Public Opinion Process. The possibilities for controlling or manipulating public opinion become clear when one recognizes the steps in the public opinion process. This process involves six discernible stages: (1) the emergence of an issue; (2) the initial definition of the issue; (3) the entrance of different groups of protagonists; (4) public discussion of the issue; (5) use of different lines of access to decision makers; and (6) assessment by decision makers of proposals brought to their attention. The process of forming and expressing effective public opinion can be influenced mightily at any one of these six steps. The media of communication may prevent issues of potential significance from entering the arena of public discussion; there are hosts of important issues that never get the opportunity of a public hearing. The initial manner of defining or characterizing an issue that does appear on the scene may profoundly determine what is going to be its fate. In the third stage the ability or inability to induce powerful and especially respectable groups to enter the fray in support of a given proposal may be decisive in setting the prospects of that proposal. The fourth step is peculiarly the stage in which propaganda operates to affect the shaping of opinion. The availability and use of lines of access to those (like congressmen) who cast the ultimate decision on the issue makes the fifth step of crucial significance. If proponents of given proposals cannot get their views effectively before the decision makers their views, irrespective of merit, may wither on the vine. Finally, decision makers have to formulate their position on an issue by assessing the different views that get into the area of their concern and reflection; the outcome of the public opinion process may be profoundly affected by influence exerted on such assessment. It should be clear from this brief sketch of the steps followed in the formation of *effective* public opinion that the points at which the process may be manipulated are many. The sketch also suggests that public opinion polling is inadequate in foretelling the outcome of public opinion; the results of the polling are only one of the elements that enter into the assessment by decision makers and may be overshadowed by other presentations that are pressed on them.

THE PUBLIC, THE CROWD, AND THE MASS

Before concluding the discussion of the public, it should be pointed out that under certain conditions the public may be changed into a crowd. Most propaganda tends to do this, anyway. When the people in the public are aroused by an appeal to a sentiment which is common to them, they begin to mill and to develop rapport. Then, their expression is in the form of public sentiment and not public opinion. In modern life, however, there seems to be less tendency for the public to become the crowd than for it to be displaced by the mass. The increasing detachment of people from local life, the multiplication of public issues, the expansion of agencies of mass communication, together with other factors, have led people to act increasingly by individual selection rather than by participating in public discussion. So true is this, that in many ways the public and the mass are likely to exist intermingled with one another. This fact adds confusion to the scene of contemporary collective behavior and renders analysis by the student difficult.

COLLECTIVE GROUPINGS AND SOCIAL CHANGE

In the discussion of elementary collective groupings we have considered the acting crowd, the expressive crowd, the mass, and the public. There are other primitive groupings which we can mention here only briefly, such as the panic, the stampede, the strike, the riot, the "popular justice" vigilante committee, the procession, the cult, the mutiny, and the revolt. Most of these groupings represent variations of the crowd; each of them operates through the primitive mechanisms of collective behavior which we have described. Like the four major types which we have considered, they are not societies, but operate outside of a governing framework of rules and culture. They are elementary, natural, and spontaneous, arising under certain fit circumstances.

The appearance of elementary collective groupings is indicative of a process of social change. They have the dual character of implying the disintegration of the old and the appearance of the new. They play an important part in the development of new collective behavior and of new forms of social life. More accurately, the typical mechanisms of primitive association which they show have a significant role in the formation of a new social order.

It is to this problem of the formation of a new social order, that we shall now devote ourselves. Our task will be to consider primarily the social movements by which new kinds of collective behavior are built up and crystallized into fixed social forms.

CHAPTER TEN

SOCIAL MOVEMENTS

Social movements can be viewed as collective enterprises seeking to establish a new order of life. They have their inception in a condition of unrest, and derive their motive power on one hand from dissatisfaction with the current form of life, and on the other hand, from wishes and hopes for a new scheme or system of living. The career of a social movement depicts the emergence of a new order of life. In its beginning, a social movement is amorphous, poorly organized, and without form; the collective behavior is on the primitive level that we have already discussed, and the mechanisms of interaction are the elementary, spontaneous mechanisms of which we have spoken. As a social movement develops, it takes on the character of a society. It acquires organization and form, a body of customs and traditions, established leadership, an enduring division of labor, social rules and social values—in short, a culture, a social organization, and a new scheme of life.

Our treatment of social movements will deal with three kinds —general social movements, specific social movements, and expressive social movements.[1]

GENERAL SOCIAL MOVEMENTS

By general social movements we have in mind movements such as the labor movement, the youth movement, the women's

---

[1] Attention is called, in passing, to spatial movements, such as nomadic movements, barbaric invasions, crusades, pilgrimages, colonization, and migrations. Such movements may be carried on as societies, as in the case of tribal migrations; as diverse peoples with a common goal, as in the case of the religious crusades of the Middle Ages; or as individuals with similar goals, as in most of the immigration into the United States. Mechanisms of their collective operation will be dealt with in the following discussion of social movements. In themselves, such movements are too complicated and diversified to be dealt with adequately here.

movement, and the peace movement. Their background is constituted by gradual and pervasive changes in the values of people—changes which can be called cultural drifts. Such cultural drifts stand for a general shifting in the ideas of people, particularly along the line of the conceptions which people have of themselves, and of their rights and privileges. Over a period of time many people may develop a new view of what they believe they are entitled to—a view largely made up of desires and hopes. It signifies the emergence of a new set of values, which influence people in the way in which they look upon their own lives. Examples of such cultural drifts in our own recent history are the increased value of health, the belief in free education, the extension of the franchise, the emancipation of women, the increasing regard for children, and the increasing prestige of science.

Indefinite Images and Behavior. The development of the new values which such cultural drifts bring forth involve some interesting psychological changes which provide the motivation for general social movements. They mean, in a general sense, that people have come to form new conceptions of themselves which do not conform to the actual positions which they occupy in their life. They acquire new dispositions and interests and, accordingly, become sensitized in new directions; and, conversely, they come to experience dissatisfaction where before they had none. These new images of themselves, which people begin to develop in response to cultural drifts, are vague and indefinite; and correspondingly, the behavior in response to such images is uncertain and without definite aim. It is this feature which provides a clue for the understanding of general social movements.

Characteristics of General Social Movements. General social movements take the form of groping and unco-ordinated efforts. They have only a general direction, toward which they move in a slow, halting, erratic yet persistent fashion. As movements they are unorganized, with neither established leadership nor recognized membership, and little guidance and control. Such a movement as the women's movement, which has the general and vague aim of the emancipation of women, suggests these features of a general social movement. The women's movement, like all general social movements, operates over a wide range—in the home, in marriage, in education, in industry, in politics, in travel —in each area of which it represents a search for an arrangement which will answer to the new idea of status being formed by women. Such a movement is episodic in its career, with very scattered manifestations of activity. It may show considerable enthusiasm at one point and reluctance and inertia at another; it may experience success in one area, and abortive effort in another. In general, it may be said that its progress is very uneven with setbacks, reverses, and frequent retreading of the same ground. At one time the impetus to the movement may come from people in one place, at another time in another place. On the whole the movement is likely to be carried on by many unknown and obscure people who struggle in different areas without their striving and achievements becoming generally known.

A general social movement usually is characterized by a literature, but the literature is as varied and ill-defined as is the movement itself. It is likely to be an expression of protest, with a general depiction of a kind of utopian existence. As such, it vaguely outlines a philosophy based on new values and self-conceptions. Such a literature is of great importance in spreading a message or view, however imprecise it may be, and so in implanting suggestions, awakening hopes, and arousing dissatisfactions. Similarly, the "leaders" of a general social movement play an important part—not in the sense of exercising directive control over the movement, but in the sense of being pace-makers. Such leaders are likely to be "voices in the wilderness," pioneers without any solid following, and frequently not very clear about their own goals. However, their example helps to develop sensitivities, arouse hopes, and break down resistances. From these traits one can easily realize that the general social movement develops primarily in an informal, inconspicuous, and largely subterranean fashion. Its media of interaction are primarily reading, conversations, talks, discussions, and the perception of examples. Its achievements and operations are likely to be made primarily in the realm of individual experience rather than by noticeable concerted action of groups. It seems evident that the general social movement is dominated to a large extent by the mechanisms of mass behavior, such as we have described in our treatment of the mass. Especially in its earlier stages, general social movements are likely to be merely an aggregation of individual lines of action based on individual decisions and selections. As is characteristic of the mass and of mass behavior, general social movements are rather formless in organization and inarticulate in expression.

The Basis for Specific Social Movements. Just as cultural drifts provide the background out of which emerge general social movements, so the general social movement constitutes the setting out of which develop specific social movements. Indeed, a specific social movement is usually a crystallization of much of the motivation of dissatisfaction, hope, and desire awakened by the general social movement and the focusing of this motivation on some specific objective. A convenient illustration is the anti-slavery movement, which was, to a considerable degree, an individual expression of the widespread humanitarian movement of the nineteenth century. With this recognition of the relation between general and specific social movements, we can turn to a consideration of the latter.

SPECIFIC SOCIAL MOVEMENTS

The outstanding instances of this type of movement are re-form movements and revolutionary movements. A specific social movement is one which has a well-defined objective or goal which it seeks to reach. In this effort it develops an organization and structure, making it essentially a society. It develops a recognized and accepted leadership and a definite membership characterized by a "we-consciousness." It forms a body of traditions, a guiding set of values, a philosophy, sets of rules, and a general body of expectations. Its members form allegiances and loyalties. Within it there develops a division of labor, particularly in the form of a social structure in which individuals occupy status positions. Thus, individuals develop personalities and conceptions of themselves, representing the individual counterpart of a social structure.

A social movement, of the specific sort, does not come into existence with such a structure and organization already established. Instead, its organization and its culture are developed in the course of its career. It is necessary to view social movements from this temporal and developmental perspective. In the beginning a social movement is loosely organized and characterized by impulsive behavior. It has no clear objective; its behavior and thinking are largely under the dominance of restlessness and collective excitement. As a social movement develops, however, its behavior, which was originally dispersed, tends to become organized, solidified, and persistent. It is possible to delineate stages roughly in the career of a social movement which represent this increasing organization. One scheme of four stages has been suggested by Dawson and Gettys.[1] These are the stage of social unrest, the stage of popular excitement, the stage of formalization, and the stage of institutionalization.

Stages of Development. In the first of these four stages people are restless, uneasy, and act in the random fashion that we have considered. They are susceptible to appeals and suggestions that tap their discontent, and hence, in this stage, the agitator is likely to play an important role. The random and erratic behavior is significant in sensitizing people to one another and so makes possible the focusing of their restlessness on certain objects. The stage of popular excitement is marked even more by milling, but it is not quite so random and aimless. More definite notions emerge as to the cause of their condition and as to what should be done in the way of social change. So there is a sharpening of objectives. In this stage the leader is likely to be a prophet or a reformer. In the stage of formalization the movement becomes more clearly organized with rules, policies, tactics, and discipline. Here the leader is likely to be in the nature of a statesman. In the institutional stage, the movement has crystallized into a fixed organization with a definite personnel and structure to carry into execution the purposes of the movement. Here the leader is likely to be an administrator. In considering the development of the specific social movement our interest is less in considering the stages through which it passes than in discussing the mechanisms and means through which such a movement is able to grow and become organized. It is convenient to group these mechanisms under five heads: (1) agitation, (2) development of *esprit de corps*, (3) development of morale, (4) the formation of an ideology, and (5) the development of operating tactics.

The Role of Agitation. Agitation is of primary importance in a social movement. It plays its most significant role in the beginning and early stages of a movement, although it may persist in minor form in the later portions of the life-cycle of the movement. As the term suggests, agitation operates to arouse people and so make them possible recruits for the movement. It is essen-

---

1 C. A. Dawson and W. E. Gettys, *Introduction to Sociology* (Rev. ed.; New York: Ronald Press Co., 1935, chap. 19).

tially a means of exciting people and of awakening within them new impulses and ideas which make them restless and dissatisfied. Consequently, it acts to loosen the hold on them of their previous attachments, and to break down their previous ways of thinking and acting. For a movement to begin and gain impetus, it is necessary for people to be jarred loose from their customary ways of thinking and believing, and to have aroused within them new impulses and wishes. This is what agitation seeks to do. To be successful, it must first gain the attention of people; second, it must excite them, and arouse feelings and impulses; and third, it must give some direction to these impulses and feelings through ideas, suggestions, criticisms, and promises.

Agitation operates in two kinds of situations. One is a situation marked by abuse, unfair discrimination, and injustice, but a situation wherein people take this mode of life for granted and do not raise questions about it. Thus, while the situation is potentially fraught with suffering and protest, the people are marked by inertia. Their views of their situation incline them to accept it; hence the function of the agitation is to lead them to challenge and question their own modes of living. It is in such a situation that agitation may create social unrest where none existed previously. The other situation is one wherein people are already aroused, restless, and discontented, but where they either are too timid to act or else do not know what to do. In this situation the function of agitation is not so much to implant the seeds of unrest, as to intensify, release, and direct the tensions which people already have.

Agitators seem to fall into two types corresponding roughly to these two situations. One type of agitator is an excitable, restless, and aggressive individual. His dynamic and energetic behavior attracts the attention of people to him; and the excitement and restlessness of his behavior tends to infect them. He is likely to act with dramatic gesture and to talk in terms of spectacular imagery. His appearance and behavior foster the contagion of unrest and excitement. This type of agitator is likely to be most successful in the situation where people are already disturbed and unsettled; in such a situation his own excited and energetic activity can easily arouse other people who are sensitized to such behavior and already disposed to excitability.

The second type of agitator is more calm, quiet, and dignified. He stirs people not by what he does, but what he says.

He is likely to be a man sparing in his words, but capable of saying very caustic, incisive, and biting things—things which get "under the skin" of people and force them to view things in a new light. This type of agitator is more suited to the first of the social situations discussed—the situation where people endure hardships or discrimination without developing attitudes of resentment. In this situation, his function is to make people aware of their own position and of the inequalities, deficiencies, and injustices that seem to mark their lot. He leads them to raise questions about what they have previously taken for granted and to form new wishes, inclinations, and hopes.

The function of agitation, as stated above, is in part to dislodge and stir up people and so liberate them for movement in new directions. More specifically, it operates to change the conceptions which people have of themselves, and the notions which they have of their rights and dues. Such new conceptions involving beliefs that one is justly entitled to privileges from which he is excluded, provide the dominant motive force for the social movement. Agitation, as the means of implanting these new conceptions among people, becomes, in this way, of basic importance to the success of asocial movement.

A brief remark relative to the tactics of agitation may be made here. It is sufficient to say that the tactics of agitation vary with the situation, the people, and the culture. A procedure which may be highly successful in one situation may turn out to be ludicrous in another situation. This suggests the problem of identifying different types of situations and correlating with each the appropriate form of agitation. Practically no study has been conducted on this problem. Here, one can merely state the truism that the agitator, to be successful, must sense the thoughts, interests, and values of his listeners.

The Development of *Esprit de Corps*. Agitation is merely the means of arousing the interest of people and thus getting them to participate in a movement. While it serves to recruit members, to give initial impetus, and to give some direction, by itself it could never organize or sustain a movement. Collective activities based on mere agitation would be sporadic, disconnected, and short-lived. Other mechanisms have to enter to give solidity and persistency to a social movement. One of these is the development of *esprit de corps*.

Esprit de corps might be thought of as the organizing of feelings on behalf of the movement. In itself, it is the sense which people have of belonging together and of being identified with one another in a common undertaking. Its basis is constituted by a condition of rapport. In developing feelings of intimacy and closeness, people have the sense of sharing a common experience and of forming a select group. In one another's presence they feel at ease and as comrades. Personal reserve breaks down and feelings of strangeness, difference, and alienation disappear. Under such conditions, relations tend to be of co-operation instead of personal competition. The behavior of one tends to facilitate the release of behavior on the part of others, instead of tending to inhibit or check that behavior; in this sense each person tends to inspire others. Such conditions of mutual sympathy and responsiveness obviously make for concerted behavior.

Esprit de corps is of importance to a social movement in other ways. Very significant is the fact that it serves to reinforce the new conception of himself that the individual has formed as a result of the movement and of his participation in it. His feeling of belonging with others, and they with him, yields him a sense of collective support. In this way his views of himself and of the aims of the movement are maintained and invigorated. It follows that the development of *esprit de corps* helps to foster an attachment of people to a movement. Each individual has his sentiments focused on, and intertwined with, the objectives of the movement. The resulting feeling of expansion which he experiences is in the direction of greater allegiance to the movement. It should be clear that *esprit de corps* is an important means of developing solidarity and so of giving solidity to a movement.

How is *esprit de corps* developed in a social movement? It would seem chiefly in three ways: the development of an in-group–out-group relation, the formation of informal fellowship association, and the participation in formal ceremonial behavior.

THE IN-GROUP–OUT-GROUP RELATION. The nature of the in-group–out-group relation should be familiar to the student. It exists when two groups come to identify each other as enemies. In such a situation each group regards itself as the upholder of virtue and develops among its members feelings of altruism, loyalty, and fidelity. The out-group is regarded as unscrupulous and vicious, and is felt to be attacking the values which the in-group holds dear. Before the out-group the members of the in-group not only feel that they are right and correct, but believe they have a common responsibility to defend and preserve their values.

The value of these in-group–out-group attitudes in developing solidarity in a social movement is quite clear. The belief on the part of its members that the movement is being opposed unjustly and unfairly by vicious and unscrupulous groups serves to rally the members around their aims and values. To have an enemy, in this sense, is very important for imparting solidarity to the movement. In addition, the "enemy" plays the important role of a scapegoat. It is advantageous to a movement to develop an enemy; this development is usually in itself spontaneous. Once made, it functions to establish *esprit de corps*.

INFORMAL FELLOWSHIP. *Esprit de corps* is formed also in a very significant way by the development of informal association on the basis of fellowship. Where people can come together informally in this way they have the opportunity of coming to know one another as human beings instead of as institutional symbols. They are then in a much better position to take one another's roles and, unwittingly, to share one another's experience. It seems that in such a relationship, people unconsciously import and assimilate into themselves the gestures, attitudes, values, and philosophy of life of one another. The net result is to develop a common sympathy and sense of intimacy which contributes much to solidarity. Thus, we find in social movements the emergence and use of many kinds of informal and communal association. Singing, dancing, picnics, joking, having fun, and friendly informal conversation are important devices of this sort in a social movement. Through them, the individual gets a sense of status and a sense of social acceptance and support, in place of prior loneliness and personal alienation.

CEREMONIAL BEHAVIOR. The third important way in which social movements develop *esprit de corps* is through the use of formal ceremonial behavior and of ritual. The value of mass meetings, rallies, parades, huge demonstrations, and commemorative ceremonies has always been apparent to those entrusted with the development of a social movement; the value is one that comes from large assemblages, in the form of the sense of vast support that is experienced by the participant. The psychology that is involved here is the psychology of being on parade. The individual participant experiences the feeling of considerable personal expansion and therefore has the sense of being somebody distinctly important. Since this feeling of personal expansion comes to be identified with the movement as such, it makes for *esprit de corps*. Likewise, the paraphernalia of ritual possessed by every movement serves to foster feelings of common identity and sympathy. This paraphernalia consists of a set of sentimental symbols, such as slogans, songs, cheers, poems, hymns, expressive gestures, and uniforms. Every movement has some of these. Since they acquire a sentimental significance symbolizing the common feelings about the movement, their use serves as a constant reliving and re-enforcement of these mutual feelings.

Esprit de corps may be regarded, then, as an organization of group feeling and essentially as a form of group enthusiasm. It is what imparts life to a movement. Yet just as agitation is inadequate for the development of a movement, so is mere reliance on *esprit de corps* insufficient. A movement which depends entirely on *esprit de corps* is usually like a boom and is likely to collapse in the face of a serious crisis. Since the allegiance which it commands is based merely on heightened enthusiasm, it is likely to vanish with the collapse of such enthusiasm. Thus, to succeed, especially in the face of adversity, a movement must command a more persistent and fixed loyalty. This is yielded by the development of morale.

The Development of Morale. As we have seen, *esprit de corps* is a collective feeling which gives life, enthusiasm, and vigor to a movement. Morale can be thought of as giving persistency and determination to a movement; its test is whether solidarity can be maintained in the face of adversity. In this sense, morale can be thought of as a group will or an enduring collective purpose.

Morale seems to be based on, and yielded by, a set of convictions. In the case of a social movement these seem to be of three kinds. First is a conviction of the rectitude of the purpose of the movement. This is accompanied by the belief that the attainment of the objectives of the movement will usher in something approaching a millennial state. What is evil, unjust, improper, and wrong will be eradicated with the success of the movement. In this sense, the goal is always overvalued. Yet these beliefs yield to the members of a movement a marked confidence in themselves. A second conviction closely identified with these beliefs is a faith in the ultimate attainment, by the movement, of its goal. There is believed to be a certain inevitability about this. Since the movement is felt to be a necessary agent for the regeneration of the world, it is regarded as being in line with the higher moral values of the universe, and in this sense as divinely favored. Hence, there arises the belief that success is inevitable, even though it be only after a hard struggle. Finally, as part of this complex of convictions, there is the belief that the movement is charged with a sacred mission. Together, these convictions serve to give an enduring and unchangeable character to the goal of a movement and a tenacity to its effort. Obstructions, checks, and reversals are occasions for renewed effort instead of for disheartenment and despair, since they do not seriously impair the faith in the rectitude of the movement nor in the inevitability of its success.

It is clear from this explanation that the development of morale in a movement is essentially a matter of developing a sectarian attitude and a religious faith. This provides a cue to the more prominent means by which morale is built up in a movement. One of these is found in the emergence of a saint cult which is to be discerned in every enduring and persisting social movement. There is usually a major saint and a series of minor saints, chosen from the popular leaders of the movement. Hitler, Lenin, Marx, Mary Baker Eddy, and Sun Yat-sen will serve as convenient examples of major saints. Such leaders become essentially deified and endowed with miraculous power. They are regarded as grossly superior, intelligent, and infallible. People develop toward them attitudes of reverence and awe, and resent efforts to depict them as ordinary human beings. The pictures or other mementos of such individuals come to have the character of religious idols. Allied with the saints of a movement are its heroes and its martyrs. They also come to be regarded as sacred figures. The development of this whole saint cult is an important means of imparting essentially a religious faith to the movement and of helping to build up the kind of convictions spoken of above.

Similar in function is the emergence in the movement of a creed and of a sacred literature. These, again, are to be found in all persisting social movements. Thus, as has been said frequently, *Das Kapital* and *Mein Kampf* have been the bibles respectively of the communist movement and of the National

Socialist movement. The role of a creed and literature of this sort in imparting religious conviction to a movement should be clear.

Finally, great importance must be attached to myths in the development of morale in a social movement. Such myths may be varied. They may be myths of being a select group or a chosen people; myths of the inhumanity of one's opponents; myths about the destiny of the movement; myths depicting a glorious and millennial society to be realized by the movement. Such myths usually grow out of, and in response to, the desires and hopes of the people in the movement and acquire by virtue of their collective character a solidity, a permanency, and an unquestioned acceptance. It is primarily through them that the members of the movement achieve the dogmatic fixity of their convictions, and seek to justify their actions to the rest of the world.

The Development of Group Ideology. Without an ideology a social movement would grope along in an uncertain fashion and could scarcely maintain itself in the face of pointed opposition from outside groups. Hence, the ideology plays a significant role in the life of a movement; it is a mechanism essential to the persistency and development of a movement. The ideology of a movement consists of a body of doctrine, beliefs, and myths. More specifically, it seems to consist of the following: *first,* a statement of the objective, purpose, and premises of the movement; *second,* a body of criticism and condemnation of the existing structure which the movement is attacking and seeking to change; *third,* a body of defense doctrine which serves as a justification of the movement and of its objectives; *fourth,* a body of belief dealing with policies, tactics, and practical operation of the movement; and, *fifth,* the myths of the movement.

This ideology is almost certain to be of a twofold character. In the first place, much of it is erudite and scholarly. This is the form in which it is developed by the intellectuals of the movement. It is likely to consist of elaborate treatises of an abstract and highly logical character. It grows up usually in response to the criticism of outside intellectuals, and seeks to gain for its tenets a respectable and defensible position in this world of higher learning and higher intellectual values. The ideology has another character, however—a popular character. In this guise, it seeks to appeal to the uneducated and to the masses. In its popular character, the ideology takes the form of emotional symbols, shibboleths, stereotypes, smooth and graphic phrases, and folk arguments. It deals, also, with the tenets of the movement, but presents them in a form that makes for their ready comprehension and consumption.

The ideology of a movement may be thought of as providing a movement with its philosophy and its psychology. It gives a set of values, a set of convictions, a set of criticisms, a set of arguments, and a set of defenses. As such, it furnishes to a movement (*a*) direction, (*b*) justification, (*c*) weapons of attack, (*d*) weapons of defense, and (*e*) inspiration and hope. To be effective in these respects, the ideology must carry respectability and prestige—a character that is provided primarily by the intelligentsia of the movement. More important than this, however, is the need of the ideology to answer to the distress, wishes, and hopes of the people. Unless it has this popular appeal, it will be of no value to the movement.

The Role of Tactics. We have referred to tactics as the fifth major mechanism essential to the development of a social movement. Obviously the tactics are evolved along three lines: gaining adherents, holding adherents, and reaching objectives. Little more can be said than this, unless one deals with specific kinds of movements in specific kinds of situations. For, tactics are always dependent on the nature of the situation in which a movement is operating and always with reference to the cultural background of the movement. This functional dependency of tactics on the peculiarity of the situation helps to explain the ludicrous failures that frequently attend the application of certain tactics to one situation even though they may have been successful in other situations. To attempt revolutionary tactics these days in terms of the tactics of two centuries ago would be palpably foolish. Similarly, to seek to develop a movement in this country in terms of tactics employed in a similar movement in some different cultural setting would probably bring very discouraging results. In general, it may be said that tactics are almost by definition flexible and variable, taking their form from the nature of the situation, the exigencies of the circumstances, and the ingenuity of the people.

We can conclude this discussion of the five mechanisms considered merely by reiterating that the successful development of a movement is dependent on them. It is these mechanisms which establish a program, set policies, develop and maintain discipline, and evoke allegiance.

Reform and Revolution. Mention has been made of the fact that specific social movements are primarily of two sorts: reform and revolutionary movements. Both seek to effect changes in the social order and in existing institutions. Their life-cycles are somewhat similar, and the development of both is dependent on the mechanisms which we have just discussed. However, noteworthy differences exist between the two; some of these differences will now be indicated.

The two movements differ in the *scope of their objectives.* A reform movement seeks to change some specific phase or limited area of the existing social order; it may seek, for example, to abolish child labor or to prohibit the consumption of alcohol. A revolutionary movement has a broader aim; it seeks to reconstruct the entire social order.

This difference in objective is linked with a *different vantage point of attack.* In endeavoring to change just a portion of the prevailing social order, the reform movement accepts the basic tenets of that social order. More precisely, the reform movement accepts the existing mores; indeed, it uses them to criticize the social defects which it is attacking. The reform movement starts with the prevailing code of ethics, and derives much of its support because it is so well grounded on the ethical side. This makes its position rather unassailable. It is difficult to attack a reform movement or reformers on the basis of their moral aims; the attack is usually more in the form of caricature and ridicule, and in characterizing reformers as visionary and impractical. By contrast, a revolutionary movement always challenges the existing mores and proposes a new scheme of moral values. Hence, it lays itself open to vigorous attack from the standpoint of existing mores.

A third difference between the two movements follows from the points which have been made. A reform movement has *respectability.* By virtue of accepting the existing social order and of orienting itself around the ideal code, it has a claim on existing institutions. Consequently, it makes use of these institutions such as the school, the church, the press, established clubs, and the government. Here again the revolutionary movement stands in marked contrast. In attacking the social order and in rejecting its mores, the revolutionary movement is blocked by existing institutions and its use of them is forbidden. Thus, the revolutionary movement is usually and finally driven underground; whatever use is made of existing institutions has to be carefully disguised. In general, whatever agitation, proselytizing, and maneuvers are carried on by revolutionary movements have to be done outside the fold of existing institutions. In the event that a reform movement is felt as challenging too seriously some powerful class or vested interests, it is likely to have closed to it the use of existing institutions. This tends to change a reform movement into a revolutionary movement; its objectives broaden to include the reorganization of the institutions which are now blocking its progress.

The differences in position between reform and revolutionary movements bring in an important distinction in their *general procedure and tactics*. A reform movement endeavors to proceed by developing a public opinion favorable to its aims; consequently, it seeks to establish a public issue and to make use of the discussion process which we have already considered. The reform party can be viewed as a conflict group, opposed by interest groups and surrounded by a large inert population. The reform movement addresses its message to this indifferent or disinterested public in the effort to gain its support. In contradistinction, the revolutionary movement does not seek primarily to influence public opinion, but instead tries to make converts. In this sense it operates more like a religion.

This means some difference as to the groups among which the two movements respectively conduct their agitation and seek their adherents. The reform movement, while usually existing on behalf of some distressed or exploited group, does little to establish its strength among them. Instead, it tries to enlist the allegiance of a middle-class public on the outside and to awaken within them a vicarious sympathy for the oppressed group. Hence, generally, it is infrequent that the leadership or membership of of a reform movement comes from the group whose rights are being espoused. In this sense a revolutionary movement differs. Its agitation is carried on among those who are regarded as in a state of distress or exploitation. It endeavors to establish its strength by bringing these people inside of its ranks. Hence, the revolutionary movement is usually a lower-class movement operating among the underprivileged.

Finally, by virtue of these characteristic differences, the two movements diverge in their functions. The primary function of the reform movement is probably not so much the bringing about of social change, as it is to reaffirm the ideal values of a given society. In the case of a revolutionary movement, the tendency to dichotomize the world between those who have and those who have not, and to develop a strong, cohesive, and uncompromising group out of the latter, makes its function that of introducing a new set of essentially religious values.

A concluding remark may be made about specific social movements. They can be viewed as societies in miniature, and as such, represent the building up of organized and formalized collective behavior out of what was originally amorphous and undefined. In their growth a social organization is developed, new values are formed, and new personalities are organized. These, indeed, constitute their residue. They leave behind an institutional structure and a body of functionaries, new objects and views, and a new set of self-conceptions.

EXPRESSIVE MOVEMENTS

The characteristic feature of expressive movements is that they do not seek to change the institutions of the social order or its objective character. The tension and unrest out of which they emerge are not focused upon some objective of social change which the movement seeks collectively to achieve. Instead, they are released in some type of expressive behavior which, however, in becoming crystallized, may have profound effects on the personalities of individuals and on the character of the social order. We shall consider two kinds of expressive movements: religious movements and fashion movements.

Religious Movements. Genuine religious movements are to be distinguished from reform movements and factional splits that take place inside of an established religious body. Religious movements begin essentially as cults; they have their setting in a situation which, psychologically, is like that of the dancing crowd. They represent an inward direction of unrest and tension in the form of disturbed feelings which ultimately express themselves in movement designed to release the tension. The tension does not then go over into purposive action but into expression. This characteristic suggests the nature of the situation from which religious movements emerge. It is a situation wherein people are upset and disturbed, but wherein they cannot act; in other words, a situation of frustration. The inability to release their tension in the direction of some actual change in the social order leaves as the alternative mere expressive behavior.

It is well to recall here the most prominent features of the dancing crowd. One of these is a feeling of *intense intimacy* and *esprit de corps*. Another is a heightened feeling of *exaltation* and ecstasy which leads individuals to experience personal expansion and to have a sense of being possessed by some transcendental spirit. Individuals feel inspired and are likely to engage in prophetic utterances. A third mark is the *projection of the collective feelings on outside objects*—persons, behavior, songs, words, phrases, and material objects—which thereby take on a sacred character. With the recurrence and repetition of this crowd behavior, the *esprit de corps* becomes strengthened, the dancing behavior formalized and ritualized, and the sacred objects reinforced. It is at this stage that the sect or cult appears. Since the growth of a religious movement is patterned after that of the sect, let us consider some of the important features of the sect.

First it should be noted that the members of a sect may be recruited from a heterogeneous background, showing differences in wealth, rank, education, and social background. These differences and distinctions have no significance in the sect. In the milling and in the development of rapport everyone is reduced to a common level of brotherhood. This fact is shown not only by the feelings and attitudes which the members have for one another, but also by the manner in which they refer to one another and the way in which they address one another.

Around the feelings of exaltation and the sacred symbols in which these feelings become crystallized, there grow up a series of beliefs and rites which become the *creed and the ritual of the sect*. The whole life of the sect becomes centered around this creed and ritual which, in themselves, come to acquire a sacred character. Since they symbolize the intense feelings of the group, they become absolute and imperative. The prophet plays an important role here. He is a sacred personage and he tends to symbolize in himself the creed and ritual of the group. Also, he is the primary guardian of this creed and ritual.

The creed of the group becomes elaborated into an extensive body of doctrine as the sect becomes cognizant of criticisms made by outsiders and as it seeks to justify its views. It is in this way that a *theology* arises; a large part of it is in the form of an apologia. Accompanying this is some change in the ritual. Those features of its practices and modes of living which subject the sect to criticism and even persecution at the hands of outsiders are likely to be cherished by the sect as the marks of its own identity and thus acquire a special significance.

Another important feature of the sect that arises from its peculiar experience and sacred character is the belief that it is divinely favored, and that it consists of a *select group of sacred souls*. The personal transformation experienced by members of the sect and the new moral and communal vistas that it yields, readily lead them to this conviction. People on the outside of the sect are regarded as lost souls; they have not been blessed with this rectifying experience.

The feeling which the sect has of itself as a community of saved souls easily disposes it to aggressive proselyting of outsiders. Frequently, it feels it has a divine mission to save others and to "show them the light." Hence it seeks *converts*. In order to become a member, an outsider has to have a conversion experience—a moral transformation similar in character to that of the original members. The public confession is a testimonial of such an experience, and is a sign that the individual is a member of the select. These remarks point to a particularly significant characteristic of the sect—the intense conflict relation in which the sect stands with reference to the outside world. The sect may be said to be at war with the outside world, yet it is a peculiar kind of conflict relation, in that the sect is not concerned with seeking to change the institutions or the objective social order, but instead seeks the moral regeneration of the world. It aims, at least orginally, not to change the outside existence, but to change the inner life. In this sense, the sect might be thought of as profoundly revolutionary, in that it endeavors to inculcate a new conception of the universe instead of merely seeking to remake institutions or the objective structure of a social order.

A religious movement tends to share these features of the sect. Its program represents a new way of living and it aims at a moral regeneration of the world. As it develops from the amorphous state that it is likely to have in the situation of the dancing crowd, it tends to acquire a structure like that of the sect, and so develops into a society. In this way it becomes analogous to specific social movements except that its aims are of a profoundly different nature.[1]

Fashion Movements. While fashion is thought of usually in relation to clothing, it is important to realize that it covers a much wider domain. It is to be found in manners, the arts, literature, and philosophy, and may even reach into certain areas of science. In fact, it may operate in any field of group life, apart from the technological and utilitarian area and the area of the sacred. Its operation requires a class society, for in its essential character it does not occur either in a homogeneous society like a primitive group, or in a caste society.

Fashion behaves as a movement, and on this basis it is different from custom which, by comparison, is static. This is due to the fact that fashion is based fundamentally on differentiation and emulation. In a class society, the upper classes or so-called social elite are not able to differentiate themselves by *fixed* symbols or badges. Hence the more external features of their life and behavior are likely to be imitated by classes immediately subjacent to them, who, in turn, are imitated by groups immediately below them in the social structure. This process gives to fashion a vertical descent. However, the elite class finds that it is no longer distinguishable, by reason of the imitation made by others, and hence is led to adopt new differentiating criteria, only to displace these as they in turn are imitated. It is primarily this feature that makes fashion into a movement and which has led one writer to remark that a fashion, once launched, moves to its doom.

As a movement, fashion shows little resemblance to any of the other movements which we have considered. While it occurs spontaneously and moves along in a characteristic cycle, it involves little in the way of crowd behavior and it is not dependent upon the discussion process and the resulting public opinion. It does not depend upon the mechanisms of which we have spoken. The participants are not recruited through agitation or proselyting. No *esprit de corps* or morale is built up among them. Nor does the fashion movement have, or require, an ideology. Further, since it does not have a leadership imparting *conscious*

---

1 There are political as well as religious sects. The difference is that the political sect seeks to bring about political revolution as well as change in the fundamental philosophy of life.

direction to the movement, it does not build up a set of tactics.[1] People participate in the fashion movement voluntarily and in response to the interesting and powerful kind of control which fashion imposes on them.

Not only is the fashion movement unique in terms of its character, but it differs from other movements in that it does not develop into a society. It does not build up a social organization; it has no personnel or functionaries; it does not develop a division of labor among its participants with each being assigned a given status; it does not construct a set of symbols, myths, values, philosophy, or set of practices, and in this sense does not form a culture; and finally, it does not develop a set of loyalties or form a we-consciousness.

Nevertheless, the movement of fashion is an important form of collective behavior with very significant results for the social order. First, it should be noted that the fashion movement is a genuine expressive movement. It does not have a conscious goal which people are trying to reach through collective action, as is true in the case of the specific social movements. Nor does it represent the release of excitement and tension generated in a dancing crowd situation. It is expressive, however, of certain fundamental impulses and tendencies, such as an inclination toward novel experience, a desire of distinction, and an urge to conform. Fashion is important especially in providing a means for the expression of developing tastes and dispositions; this feature establishes it as a form of expressive behavior.

The latter remark provides a cue for understanding the role of fashion and the way in which it contributes to the formation of a new social order. In a changing society, such as is necessarily presupposed for the operation of fashion, people are continually having their subjective lives upset; they experience new dispositions and tastes which, however, are vague and ill-defined. It seems quite clear that fashion, by providing an opportunity for the expression of dispositions and tastes, serves to make them definite and to channelize them and, consequently, to fix and solidify them. To understand this, one should appreciate the fact that the movement and success of fashion are dependent upon the acceptance of the given style or pattern. In turn, this ac-

---

1 This discussion may appear to be contradicted in the area of clothes fashions by the existence of a large fashion industry which depends heavily on massive, well-organized promotional campaigns. The appearance is delusory. Tastes may be manipulated but only within limits. The fashion industry serves the process; it does not create it.

ceptance is based not merely upon the prestige attached to the style but also upon whether the style meets and answers to the dispositions and developing tastes of people. (The notorious failures that attend efforts to make styles fashionable upon the basis of mere prestige provide some support for this point.) From this point of view, we can regard fashion as arising and flourishing in response to new subjective demands. In providing means for the expression of these dispositions and tastes, fashion acts, as suggested before, to shape and crystallize these tastes. In the long run fashion aids, in this manner, to construct a *Zeitgeist* or a common subjective life, and in doing so, helps to lay the foundation for a new social order.

REVIVAL MOVEMENTS AND
NATIONALIST MOVEMENTS

In our discussion so far, we have been treating separately specific social movements, religious movements, and fashion movements. Yet it should be clear that they can be merged, even though in very different degrees. Thus a revolutionary movement may have many of the features of a religious movement, with its success dependent to some extent upon the movement's becoming fashionable.

Revival Movements. Revival movements and nationalist movements are particularly likely to have this mixed character. We shall devote a few remarks to them. In revival movements people idealize the past, venerate the ideal picture that they have, and seek to mold contemporary life in terms of this ideal picture. Such movements are explainable, apparently, as a response to a situation of frustration. In this situation people are experiencing a loss of self-respect. Since the future holds no promise for them to form a new respectful conception of themselves, they turn to the past in an effort to do so. By recalling past glories and achievements they can regain a modicum of self-respect and satisfaction. That such movements should have a strong religious character is to be expected. Nationalist movements are very similar in these respects.

Nationalist Movements. Movements of nationalism are exceedingly pronounced in our current epoch. They represent efforts of a given people sharing some sense of common identity and historical lineage to gain independent status inside of an international order of sovereign bodies. They seek to guide their own destiny in place of being subservient to the control of an alien group. "Liberty" and "freedom" thus become both the goal and the inspiring clarion calls of nationalist movements. This type of movement has its source in distressing personal experiences in which individuals are made to feel inferior because of the subordinate status of the people to which they belong. They seek, accordingly, to raise the status of their group. While usually beginning as reform movements nationalist movements generally become revolutionary in character. Barred from the institutions and channels of the dominant group they resort to the use of revolutionary tactics, carrying on their agitation and planning inside of their own separate institutions, frequently their native church. At the same time, like a reform movement, they solicit the favorable opinion of outside peoples. Thus, nationalist movements rely on the use of the mechanisms previously discussed in the case of specific social movements. One should note, in addition, the strong revivalistic slant that nationalist movements usually take; such movements seek to glorify the past of the people and eulogize the distinctive culture of the people, particularly their language. Where there is no sense of a common past or the sharing of a common language, as in the case of many recent nationalist movements in present-day Africa, a nationalist movement has to depend primarily on cultivating and using the in-group–out-group mechanism as the means of developing unity and persistence.

CHAPTER ELEVEN

CONCLUSIONS CONCERNING
COLLECTIVE BEHAVIOR

A social order can be regarded as consisting of the following elements, among others. *First,* a body of common expectations, upon the basis of which people are able to co-operate and regulate their activities to one another. This procedure yields them customs, traditions, rules, and norms. *Second,* a set of values which are attached to these expectations and which determine how important they are, and how readily people will adhere to them. *Third,* the conceptions which people have of themselves in relation to one another and to their groups. And, *fourth,* a common subjective orientation in the form of dispositions and moods.

This conception of a social order enables one to understand more readily the statement made at the beginning of the discussion that in studying collective behavior we were concerned with the process of building up a social order. In the early stages of this process, collective behavior is uncertain in character and relatively unorganized. The elementary and spontaneous types appear. In them, one sees most clearly the primary mechanisms of association. As the interaction between people continues, collective behavior secures form and organization. There appear new expectations, new values, new conceptions of rights and obligations, and new tastes and moods. We have sought to show in this process the role of collective behavior mechanisms and the function of social movements. In general, we can say that movements centering around the mechanisms of the public give rise to the political phase of the social order; those using primarily the mechanisms of the crowd and of rapport give rise to a moral order and a sacred order; and those, like fashion, which stress the mechanisms of the mass, yield subjective orientations in the form of common tastes and inclinations.

Part Three

—

Institutions

By

Everett Cherrington Hughes
Boston College

CHAPTER TWELVE

INSTITUTIONS INTRODUCED
AND DEFINED

Institutions are defined in two rather contradictory ways. The term may be applied to features of particular societies which have outlasted many biological generations and have survived many catastrophes and changes, as to the festivals of the turning of the seasons, known to us as Easter and Christmas. Institutions thus last and last, and outlast. On the other hand, institutions may be considered as universal and timeless, springing up wherever humans live in communities: kinship and marriage, control over production and distribution of goods and services, performance of sacred rites, regulation of conflict, provision of sanctions for the breaking of rules, and assignment of persons by sex, age, or other characteristics to categories which define duties and privileges toward others. Institutions, in this sense, since they spring up anew in various forms, are generic rather than historical.

Of more interest than these broad definitions are the particular ways in which societies, especially our own, are organized; how institutions are established and maintained, and how they change. Every society and time has its particular ways of doing all the things that humans do; it has its own "going concerns" or organized enterprises which mobilize people for action or expression, and its own customs for meeting a wide variety of situations if and when they arise. We live in a time in which many new kinds of going concerns are being initiated to meet new problems and in which older ones are undergoing great change. It is also a time in which there are many changes in older organizations and customs. We shall emphasize these processes rather than tell in detail the facts about particular institutions.

THE CONCEPT IN OTHER FIELDS OF STUDY

All of the social sciences study social institutions. Anthropologists, sociologists, and historians tend to study whole societies, regions, or periods; hence, they may study institutions of any kind. Other branches of study tend to specialize in some given kind of institution. The economists study the institutions of production, exchange, and distribution of goods and services; they also construct theories about economic behavior. Political science is the study of political institutions; it appears, however, to be moving somewhat from the study of history and formal constitutions to the study of political behavior by methods commonly employed in other social sciences. The field of education is, in fact, the study of schools, which are numerous and elaborate in our time; but it also shares with psychology the study of the processes of learning and teaching. Psychology itself, although in part devoted to physiology, is deeply involved in the study of institutions, since they are the settings in which human behavior occurs. Philosophers yearn to discuss logic and ethics in the abstract, but a good deal of their effort is put into considering these matters in actual human, institutional settings.

THE VIEWS OF SOCIOLOGISTS

Among the earlier American sociologists who defined institutions and distinguished them from other social phenomena are Charles H. Cooley and William G. Sumner. In his book *Folkways* Sumner considered a body of folkways to be the elementary social phenomenon. These popular usages are at once the product of past collective behavior and the mold for acceptable present and future behavior. In following them, the individual acts under a constraint which is so internalized that he may not be aware of it. Sumner distinguishes institutions from folkways; the institutions require a more conscious and formal co-operation. An institution, he says, consists of a concept (idea, doctrine, interest) and a structure. At its simplest, the structure is only a "number of functionaries set to cooperate in prescribed ways at a certain conjuncture."

Robert Merton has invented the convenient term *role-set* for this phenomenon. If some North American boys decide to play with a ball and bat, there is a known set of offices, or established roles for them to assume, including that of umpire. The game would be baseball. English boys would make it cricket. When each has been assigned to and accepted his role, together they form a role-set and know what is expected of them so long as they are cast in those offices, roles, or positions. The structure may be much more complicated, as in the raising of money for charities in a large city, but there is always a role-set of those undertaking the leadership and a wider mobilization of large elements of the population in less well defined roles or offices.

In *Social Organization,* C. H. Cooley, writing at about the same time as Sumner, took as his elementary phenomenon the *primary group.* The primary group, matrix in which the human nature of individuals is nurtured, has no formal rules, thus no functionaries or offices; but the individual in it becomes sensitive to the gestures and opinions of others. Sensitivity to the regard of others is the basis of that social constraint which becomes set in the folkways. George H. Mead, the pragmatic philosopher of the same period, also based his study of social behavior on sensitivity to the regard of others. Primary groups, says Cooley, "are the springs of life not only for the individual, but for social institutions." The latter are "mature, specialized and comparatively rigid parts of the social structure." Ellsworth Faris says that in the institution, unlike the primary group, a person acts in an office.

More recent sociological work has had to do not with the definition of institutions, but with the operating organization of society, as for example in recent books on formal organization and on social systems. Studies have been and are being made of a great variety of institutions, such as hospitals, corporations and social agencies, as well as of families, religious institutions, and schools. Sociologists themselves have become engaged in the study of an extremely wide variety of institutions. In this way they obtain knowledge of the operation of our society and at the same time assemble material for comparative and theoretic study.

DEVELOPMENT OF INSTITUTIONS

Marginal to social institutions are those phenomena of collective behavior which occur contrary to, or outside of, accepted and expected social usage. These marginal forms are crucial for an understanding of institutional processes, for every established form of collective behavior was once not so. Our interest is in precisely those processes by which collective behavior which begins outside formal offices and without formal rules, engaged in by unconventional groups of people, in unexpected situations, or in ways contrary to use and wont, develop formal offices, organized groups, defined situations, and a new body of sanctioned use and wont. Institutions do not spring full-formed from the head of Zeus. They take form from such diverse collective behavior as celebrations, festivals; social movements such as revolutions, strikes, and protests; from reform movements and business enterprises; and from voluntary efforts to achieve some particular end, such as the prevention of infantile paralysis, the reduction of taxes, or the cleaning up of the water supply.

Before considering how institutions arise and change in our society, it is well to have in mind the elementary form of institutions as found in simple, stable societies such as have generally been studied by anthropologists. "The real component units of culture which have a considerable degree of permanence, universality and independence are the organized systems of human activities called institutions. Every institution centers around a fundamental need, permanently unites a group of people in a cooperative task and has its particular body of doctrine and its techniques or craft. Institutions are not correlated simply and directly to their functions; one need does not receive one satisfaction in one institution. But institutions show a pronounced amalgamation of functions and have a synthetic character." [1] Elementary institutions, as described by Malinowski, do not show that singleness of function which is the ideal of so many people in an efficiency-minded society. Each of them satisfies a variety of needs.

Examples of elementary institutions are the *fiesta* of Mayan villages in Yucatan, as described by Redfield; the *kula,* as described by Malinowski; and the town meeting which still survives in New England. These institutions occurred in simple communities. Everyone in the community had some part in them. The moral consensus was so complete that no one was violently opposed to their operation. Their operation was taken for granted.

Such distinctions of social status as existed in the community

1 B. Malinowski, "Culture," *Encyclopaedia of the Social Sciences* (1931), Vol. 4, p. 626.

determined the parts played by various persons in these institutions. The accepted leaders of the community expected in turn to assume the burdens and to enjoy the honors of office. It was their moral and civic right and duty to do so. The offices involved both the performance of ritual and the effective exercise of authority and initiative.

The procedures and rituals of these elementary institutions were known, in a general way, to all adult members of the community. They knew what to expect. This does not mean that any member of the community could have carried them out or that there was no mystery about them, but simply that they knew when to expect them and how to react to each part of the procedure. This was true, not only of the people of a given village, or parish, but of all the people of the region. For these institutions were common to an area, although each community had its own officers and participants as well as its own peculiarities of tradition and practice.

It would be difficult to say what the purposes of these institutions were, for they were so well established in tradition as to be unquestioned. Purposes occur *within* human behavior and are but an aspect of it. Institutions which are established are not subject to a single purpose. They may perform many functions, but the functions are implicit, rather than explicit.

The voluntary and conscious assumption of offices by persons of appropriate status is a feature of a well-established institution. The criteria and mechanisms by which the succeeding incumbents of the offices in the role-sets are chosen, trained and legitimately charged may be much more complicated. Sometimes great mobilizations of people for expression or action are led by prophets, upstarts, adventurers, or promoters whose authority is not sanctioned by tradition or law. They operate on their own charism; their successors appeal to the authority of the founding master. That is the beginning of an institution.

As civilization proceeds, social organization becomes much more complicated. Institutions multiply; some arise whose workings are mysterious to the general mass of people. Their mechanisms are elaborated. Social sanctions become confused. But wherever institutions are found, the features mentioned are present, although not always in the complete yet simple form here described.

CHAPTER THIRTEEN

KINDS OF INSTITUTIONS

Institutions are generally classified according to a supposed central function of each. The nineteenth century sociologist Herbert Spencer used the following categories: domestic, ceremonial, political, ecclesiastical, professional, and industrial. Some sociologists reserve the term institutions for such general categories, and use the term association for a particular instance,—an army, a corporation, a college. But most of our modern organizations are rather too complicated to be called simply associations. It is, moreover, difficult, if not impossible, to study the general category except by studying the particular cases. Furthermore, there are many particular "associations" in this sense which do not clearly belong in one of the conventional categories. Yet there are a number of such categories which are commonly used in our society; family, school, state, church, corporation, prison, hospital, social agency, library. And to these are constantly added new ones, such as shopping center, discothèque, labor union, senior citizens' club, mutual funds. It is easier to get a list of names of such instances operating in society at a given time than it is to arrive at a systematic classification of them. In this section "institution" will refer to both individual instance and to general category.

INSTITUTIONAL FUNCTIONS

It must not be assumed that an institution performs but one function. Families look after children; the members aid each other and provide mutual affection and protection. Families often perform economic functions and carry out religious ritual. If children fail in school the failure is often blamed on the short-

130

comings of parents as teachers. The church has often been in charge of education, the social services, and care of the sick. Trade unions sometimes engage in sports and run night schools as well as bargain with employers.

Functions are shared among institutions. It cannot be assumed that a given social function is performed exclusively by any one institution. If we conceive education as all the activities by which children learn or are taught the techniques, customs, and sentiments of the society in which they live, it is obvious that the school has no monopoly upon education. Indeed, some societies produce leaders for their enterprises, experts in their arts, and masters of their folklore, ritual, and custom without any schools at all. In our own society, certain types of knowledge such as the hippie culture, sex lore, the technique of professional stealing, and even religion, persist in spite of their exclusion from school curricula, although the school may provide a setting where these things may be learned.

Advertising, news and informal conversation are influential sources of knowledge and belief, often contradicting what is taught in school. The schools, said Sumner, teach the current orthodoxy of whoever controls the school, rather than all of the knowledge and beliefs on which a society really rests. It is even more obvious that not all playing is done in playgrounds, nor all the charity given by social agencies.

Certain functions are performed by elaborate systems of interconnected institutions. The traditional doctor's office, which once served as clinic, medical school, surgery, and laboratory, is today but one among many institutions concerned with health and disease. In addition to those already named there are hospitals for particular kinds of people and certain ailments, the schools and professional associations of various auxiliary occupations, the associations and examining boards of special branches of medicine, as well as the governmental, philanthropic, and private institutions for distributing medical care and protecting the health of the public. As knowledge of health and disease advances, as environmental influences upon health are better understood, and as people expect an ever higher standard of medical service, the health system becomes more and more elaborate. People now speak of the health industry. To say that the function of any part of this system is healing is a truism; one must look further to discover the actual part played by any institution within the system. It may be that some parts of the system actually impede progress toward good health.

The discovery of the specific functions of given institutions in the social system is a chief aim of sociological study. A. R. Radcliffe-Brown gave us a definition of function useful for this purpose:

By the function of an institution I mean the part it plays in the total system of social integration of which it is a part. By using that phrase, social integration, I am assuming that the function of culture as a whole is to unite individual human beings into more or less stable social structures; i.e., stable systems of groups determining and regulating the relation of those individuals to one another, and providing such adaptation to the physical environment, and such internal adaptation between the component individuals or groups, as to make possible an ordered social life.[1]

Social Interrelations. A society is an integrated system which can continue to exist only under certain conditions. There must be replacement of the member individuals by others. There must be provision and distribution of the means of life. The incoming members must learn and carry on the techniques and rules of the society. These conditions all depend upon another; viz., some measure of consensus with respect to a body of beliefs or sentiments. These are but bare bones. Actually, society consists of people doing all these things in particular ways. The functions of an institution are its part in such a system.

It follows that no institution, however classified, may be understood in isolation. The church, for instance, depends not only upon the religious beliefs of people, but also upon other institutions and informal parts of culture and society. Religious attitudes often include beliefs concerning the economic order, the political system, and the family. A celibate priesthood is unthinkable without pious families in which sons are encouraged to listen to the call. Indeed, there is something of a crisis in the recruitment of young people to religious professions in many countries; the crisis is occurring in a variety of religions at the same time. The ordinary participants or laymen of a religious body have other interests; they give only some part of their time,

1 A. R. Radcliffe-Brown, "The Present Position of Anthropological Studies," *British Association for the Advancement of Science, Centenary Meeting* (London, 1931), Section H., p. 13.

attention, money, and loyalty to the church. A church, or a synagogue, may in fact be an item of conspicuous consumption for its members. The functions of the church, as those of any institution, are to be understood only by analyzing its many relations with the other aspects of society.

Claims of Participants. Institutions may be classified according to the nature and limits of the claims of the institution upon the various kinds of people associated with it and of the participants upon each other. At one pole one might put those institutions which claim complete control over all aspects of the lives of all participants. A religious order or a sect will demand that its members both think and act at all times in accordance with the role they play; to keep them firmly in role the members may be required to wear a special costume so that no one ever sees them, and they never see themselves in the company of others, without clear identification. Cooley said, "an institution . . . is made up of persons, but not of whole persons; each one enters into it with a trained and specialized part of himself." The sect and the religious order seek to specialize the whole life and nature of the individual. Erving Goffman has given the name "total institution" to one which controls the whole life and around-the-clock activity of an individual. He thus characterizes asylums, which impose an identity and a routine upon the patient, even to the point of taking away his false teeth, rings, and all those small things which he has with him wherever he goes, alone and in company. The army also takes full external control of a person, and demands complete obedience; but a soldier who obeys to the letter grudgingly makes his officers unhappy. An institution is even more "total" when it demands full commitment of thought and intent as well as external conformity. It is most "total" if it demands commitment for life and control over all the details of thought, life, and action.

At the opposite pole stand certain action structures in which individuals rather coolly band together voluntarily to attain some clearly defined common aim. They ask naught of each other but cooperation on the matter in hand. Trade associations ask no one to bleed and die for them, although perhaps their members may feel pressure and may in effect wear clothing that tells what kind of men they are. If, however, people continue to act together for a long time, even with regard to some limited and secular goal, they develop claims on each other. Personal and moral claims may arise in a business enterprise. They may, in fact, be its undoing.

The measure and nature of claims is subject to change in the course of the life of an institution. Large and established institutions usually involve a number of categories of participants, some of whom are more deeply and fully committed and controlled than are others. It is not necessarily true that those most totally committed will have great power in the operation.

Our aim here is to call attention to the fact that one may describe an institution as a system of claims of the participants on the institution and its claims upon them.

Type of Organization. Another way of classifying institutions is by type of organization, that is, by the configurations of officers, leaders, and participants of various kinds. In the family, members have various functions to perform and various claims upon each other according to age, sex, and kinship. In the *collegium*, or guild, a group of equals who have been subjected to common specialized training co-operate on a democratic basis within, but are sharply differentiated from other types of persons of the society to which they belong. Many of the institutions of our time are organized around one or more professions. The typical form of organization seen in extreme form in hospitals, is that of a dominant *collegium* of a leading profession (medicine), aided by one or more less dominant professions who carry on a great deal of the central activity (nurses), and filled out by a number of professional and non-professional people who administer, keep house, advise on various technical matters, and help keep relations with the clients and the public smooth. One enters such an institution in a certain role and cannot easily change to another; there are strata with little or no movement from one to another.

Another system with a central profession is the legal system with its judges, lawyers, bailiffs, parole officers, and so on. It has become very complicated, and has many connections with other systems.

In the modern business enterprise, generally a corporation, a group of stockholders, who are legally owners of shares, are called together from time to time by the officers, who carry on the business and make the major decisions; the officers ask and generally get support from the stockholders. Most of the officers are also employees. Then there are large number of employees, some organized into unions whose officers deal with the employing officers of the corporation. Finally, there are customers who buy the product of the business from time to time. The relations between these categories of people change periodically; at one time one category is powerful, later power may pass to another.

Whatever the peculiarities of each form, there are certain features shared by many institutions. In our urban and mass society most institutions operate with a corps of people who are concerned with its affairs day in, day out; others are mobilized from time to time either routinely or by some intermittent need or occasional emergency.

We have here been noting likenesses not in the supposed ends or aims of institutions, but rather in the manner in which they mobilize people for their operations. Such distinctions are, like others, useful only insofar as they aid us in understanding how institutions work within the framework of a society.

INSTITUTIONAL CHANGES IN OUR SOCIETY

Not only do we have many new institutions, but some of our older ones are taking on new forms.

Changes in the Family. The most familiar operating family in our society is the nuclear family household: a married couple with, at appropriate stages in their life-cycle, children under the same roof, eating from the same pot, and watched over and provided for out of a common income gained by participation in the economy. Fewer and fewer of these units operate a farm or other enterprise; more and more of them gain their living by cash earnings of the husband-father and, in an increasing proportion of families, of the wife-mother. A very high proportion of all children born live to adulthood; they are expected to leave the parental household as young adults. They generally do leave, and the leaving coincides with marriage, some turning point in their education, or perhaps just the desire to get away. They remain bound to the parental family by sentiment and perhaps by property interests. The period in which the family has sole responsibility for and control over the child in very short, as all must attend school at a certain age and many continue beyond high school and even into universities and professional training until the mid-twenties of their lives. Since people live longer than they used to and since women bear their last child at an earlier age, there is a large number of married couples with no children in the house. The biological composition of the family is subject to greater control than in the past, since both the time and number of births can be planned.

At various points, nuclear families may join with other kin for celebrations or to meet crises of one kind or another. The prevailing patterns of family life and enterprise with respect to all of these matters may vary from social class to class, and according to religion, ethnic group, race, region, and as between country and city. In certain circumstances, the state or various social agencies may intervene in family control; if a family cannot make its living, if a mother is not wed, if a child is caught breaking some law or violating the prevailing code of behavior, some authority may take over some of the family functions.

As do other enterprises, the family shows a division of labor among its members. As more women work, as household machinery takes over the heavier work, and as more functions are performed for the family by outside organizations, the division of labor in the family changes.

Sociological study of the family is devoted to analyzing changes in all of these matters. It is of special interest to know what circumstances favor continuance of the marriage of a couple and the fiscal and social success of the household and of the partners to the marriage.

The Impact of Economic Institutions. A particular feature of our society has been the great increase in the number of professional and other services, and the great variety and amounts of goods which are distributed to the public. We are a consumers' society, and an affluent one. Institutions which produce and distribute goods and services are a major part of our operating social structure. New systems of consumer credit have been developed. Insurance schemes, public and private, aim to guarantee ability to consume goods and services through thick and thin to an increasing proportion of the population. Our communications system—radio, television, press—is part of the complex that influences the choice and distribution of consumer goods. Often those who have goods to sell—drugs and cigarettes, for example —use these systems of public communication to offer products which scientists, teachers, and physicians advise people not to use.

In order to have personnel trained to do the new kinds of

work demanded in this kind of society, we keep our children in school longer than has any society in history. This results in a great burgeoning of educational enterprises, and in changing of functions of many of those already in existence. Study of educational institutions has become itself a major part of research in psychology, sociology, economics, and politics.

Although some argue that ours is not a very religious society, it includes many churches and affiliated institutions. Established churches are usually organized into territorial parishes or congregations in which the families live grouped around their church. In this country this pattern has been broken up by diversity of religion and of the ethnic groups in many neighborhoods. Nowadays mobility is so common and diversity so great that the territorial form of religious organization is being questioned even by members of its stoutest defender, the Roman Catholic church. Something of the same crisis is occurring in schools, which were traditionally neighborhood affairs in the elementary grades, but with larger territorial base at the upper levels. This whole philosophy is now being called into question in order to mix children more randomly by race and social class. Thus, two contending forces are at work in both churches and schools, the forces in favor of organizing internally homogeneous operating units while allowing the various units (in different areas) to be different from each other, and the forces in favor of making the operant units internally heterogeneous while each is more or less like others (in other neighborhoods). Some such stress is found in many of our institutions.

CHAPTER FOURTEEN

INSTITUTIONS IN PROCESS

Institutions, no matter how stable and unchanged they appear, are ongoing things. They consist of the complementary activity of the several categories of participating persons. When an institution is in a stable condition some of the people may take its operation so for granted that they give it little attention while participating in a routine way. They count on the various functionaries and leaders to do their part when the occasion arises. Mothers wash their children's faces and send them to school at the appointed hour. The teachers, for their part, expect the chidren to turn up, not perhaps with enthusiasm, but without undue fuss. But the day comes when the expected does not happen and the unexpected does. A crisis occurs in which, to quote W. I. Thomas—". . . the attention is aroused and explores the situation with a view to reconstructing modes of activity."

CRISES AND THE RISE OF NEW INSTITUTIONS

In crises old institutional forms are questioned and sometimes broken up. If the crisis is severe, the livelier forms of collective behavior, described by Herbert Blumer in Part II take the place of ordered institutional conduct. Some category of people may become so discontent with the institution that they cease to participate at all, participate so actively that they threaten the whole operation, or act in some concerted obstructive way. The class, the congregation, the audience, or the working force becomes a crowd; they act collectively but in an excited way and not within the bounds of their expected roles, that is, they "forget who they are." They become dangerous to the established institutional order.

A crisis in the life of an individual is not usually a crisis for an institution in which he participates, which fulfills some of his needs or controls some part of his life. In fact, institutions regularly take care of the crises of individuals; that is their function and their nature. His crises are their daily routine. To the individual, his marriage, illnesses, sins and guilt, and fear of death are unique and critical; the church has a way of dealing with all of them and supplies roughly the number of functionaries to do so for the given population of adherents. Other institutions are there when one has children to educate, feels ill, or wants to borrow money to buy a house.

But a new situation may come in which some whole category of people is no longer content with their part in an institution and with what they get from it. They reject the bargain concerning exchange of services implict in the operation of the institution. Then the institution itself is in a critical state.

There are crises which threaten particular operating units of some type of institution but which do not constitute a crisis for the type itself as such and do not presage any great change in it. Early death of the wage-earning father may cut short the life-cycle of his family. The congregation of a church may move away and be replaced by people of some other religion, class, or ethnic group. A factory may lose its market through new technology, or its labor force through competition with industries which can pay more. In these and other cases, particular units may go out of existence, while the type persists. New similar units are constantly established and exist for longer or shorter periods of time depending upon their success in meeting their particular crises.

The Formation of New Units. Although the foundation of new units of an institution may be provided for in an orderly way, they do not get under way without crises, and without bringing to attention many matters which ordinarily lie buried in routine and tradition. A new family is established by marriage, but whether the couple will settle near one parent or the other, the style of life they will lead, when and how many children they will have, and many other things are decided by the couple, not always without some interference from kinfolk, friends, and even clergy and public authorities. Choice of marriage mates is a matter of much discussion, conflict, and of some regulation by law.

A Roman Catholic parish is considered more or less indestructible. New parishes are founded when the population be-

comes too great for existing parishes or when Catholics move
into new territory. The initiative may be taken by the hierarchy.
But Roman Catholics of some new nationality or language who
move into the territory may, by popular movement, practically
force the establishment of a special parish manned by priests of
their own nationality, and under the patronage of one of their
favorite saints. Even when the parish is established because of
growth or movement of population, as to the suburbs, the new
unit must find its place in the class and financial structure of the
community. It has to attach to itself the loyalty of the parishioners
whose first love may still be their native parish somewhere in
the city. When Protestant churches move to the suburbs, they
lose many members to other denominations and gain new people
who, in moving to the suburbs, may seek religious company
among their new neighbors even if that requires change of
denomination.

Conditions for Formation of New Units. We are a society
with great freedom to establish new organizations and enterprises. Yet there are many limits on the process. Many institutions
require a great deal of capital. Hospitals require capital goods
that usually is raised by some communal effort, with an increasing amount of subsidy from the government. Certain government
regulations must be met. Often the new enterprise will require
a staff of professional people, who will not come unless conditions set by the licensing and accrediting bodies of the profession
and appropriate government agencies are also met. Accrediting
is itself an American institution, carried on by nominally voluntary associations of schools, hospitals, social agencies, even of
athletic clubs, community charity campaigns, and social clubs.
Anybody who would establish, say, a school or college must
reckon with the licensing and accrediting authorities and with
the sources of capital for the enterprise. Potential adherents,
customers, and clients will likely have some sophistication about
these matters and will withhold support unless satisfied as to
what league the new institution is likely to get into. There are,
of course, some people who want some new kind of service (a
new kind of education, a new treatment of disease, new experiments) not offered by the orthodox and accredited institutions.
New institutions may be established to provide these new things,
sometimes as a protest against 'the establishment.'

Frontiers of Settlement. In newly populated areas the entire institutional structure may be lacking. Even where, as in New England, the first settlers were of one language and religion, the functionaries and material appurtenances were lacking. No one had either the manifest authority or the knowledge necessary to reconstruct there what they had left in England. They didn't want to. There followed a period of great inventiveness with regard to law, tenure of land, and other things. It took self-conscious effort to make a social order. Something similar to this happened all across this continent. The character of the particular frontier determined in some measure the kind of institutions which were established. A turning point comes when women get to the frontier in sufficient number to have some influence; if women come, children will not be far behind. The age and sex structure will in time approach that of older settlements, and so will the institutional structure.

What new frontiers now remain are outposts of industry or the military. Canada has a new frontier as a result of finding valuable ores and earths in the far north. The resulting communities are usually planned by the government or large companies. Unlike the company towns of earlier times, these are usually planned for families and appropriate religious, educational, and recreational facilities are provided; these facilities may not fully satisfy the adult male population who come there to work.

Another feature of the American frontier was a large number of communities established by religious sects who sought to establish their own peculiar social order in isolation from "the world." Eventually the world caught up with most of them, causing them to modify somewhat their cherished "kingdom of heaven on earth." But they have left many peculiar institutions in their wake, and sometimes retain control of the general organization of society over a large area, as do the Mormons. Others have been remarkably persistent in keeping their institutions intact even in smaller areas; such are the Amish and other Mennonite communities, and some of the Hutterites in the northwest and in western Canada.

The more common kinds of new community nowadays are the suburb on the rim of large cities, and the planned housing development. The suburb may grow where there was once a small town with its school, government, churches, clubs, and the like. The new suburban people try to take over these institutions, or they may simply found new ones in fields where that is possible and fight with the natives over the control of schools, government, hospitals which of necessity concern everyone. In other cases, the suburb may be entirely new. In that case, the institutions are new and may be of a new type. There is a literature on the suburban church, the suburban improvement societies and social clubs, and on the suburban schools. People in a new suburb may be rather alike in age, income, and in aspirations, if not in social background. Their institutions reflect these aspirations, at least at the beginning. As time goes on, not all achieve their aspirations. The high school they are so proud of may become a burden. Poorer people, Blacks or others who do not fit their conception of themselves, may try to move into the neighborhood. Among the most interesting sites for observation of the founding and change of institutions are these new communities of various kinds.

Still more dramatic are the institutions which arise in parts of the world where people come into cities from much simpler societies than any who come to North American cities. The modification of kin, tribal, religious, and economic institutions in African cities is a new focus of interest for social scientists of all disciplines.

CULTURAL FRONTIERS

At various places in the world two or more cultures are in contact. The people of the several cultures live in the same city or region, exchange goods, perform services for each other, must use the same public utilities and somehow settle disputes across cultural lines as well as within each group. In modern times, such contact has often been a result of European economic and political expansion, and of European migration.

In such cases, the institutions of the several cultures involved are likely to be modified. One society may be so powerful it can impose its economic and legal institutions upon the other, but usually it cannot completely destroy native institutions, even if it wishes. The two or more peoples in contact may preserve many of their institutions, and even exclude the others from them.

Some new institutions may be established. The plantation, so typical of semi-tropical regions which produced sugar, tobacco, and other commodities for a world market was rather a new development. The European entrepreneurs used labor from non-European countries to work under complete control of the employer. The founders of plantations often claimed to believe in free wage labor, but nevertheless used contract and forced labor, even slaves, to get their product and put it on the market. The plantation was, in effect, a total institution, for the employer was also landlord, banker, policeman, and judge to his employees and their families.

Industrial Revolutions. The invasion of a foreign culture into a region is likely to bring an industrial revolution to the native peoples of the region. New kinds of economic enterprise, using capital goods and expensive machinery, require different laws of property and exchange. New kinds of occupations require new skills and new schools. A new system of classes and new vested interests arise at the expense of the old. Old institutional claims are threatened—those of family, tribe, and guild. In adjusting to or resisting the new institutions of the invader, the natives will establish new institutions; some of them will be initiated by free, individualistic natives or marginal men. Even if an attempt is made to establish foreign institutions in a new setting, they generally undergo a good deal of change as may be seen in the effort to take the English classical tradition to Africa. The native elite created by the university eventually use the university for their purposes, not those of the empire.

Empire and Missions as Cultural Frontiers. On colonial and quasi-colonial frontiers, where a dominant society invades weaker peoples, the religion of the dominant group has often been carried to the colony. Zealous missionaries attempt to convert natives to their religion. Converts are usually found in certain classes of the native population, generally among the poor and deprived. The resulting religious institutions may be led by the missionaries for some time, and may influence many aspects of native life, such as medicine, education, and the family. In due time, however, they may be taken over by natives, change their form and become instruments of native nationalism. Christianity and Mohammedanism have run this cycle in much of the modern world. Of course, missionaries from the colonial counties may also, if permitted, make converts in the dominant countries, and the converts may use the religion again as a political weapon.

New ideologies are thus introduced in both dominant and colonial countries.

Immigration. A cultural frontier more familiar to Americans is created by immigration of people of alien culture into a world which they do not dominate, but in which they seek a place. The resulting immigrant institutions are of two kinds. Some are new units designed according to old forms, to give comfort to the immigrant by furnishing a *cadre* within which he may live according to his traditions. Others are established to meet crises peculiar to the immigrant, to enhance his status, to help him get on in the new world. Foreign churches are of the first sort; mutual-aid societies, the immigrant press, and nationalist organizations are of the second sort. They received classic treatment by W. I. Thomas and Florian Znaniecki in *The Polish Peasant in Europe and America,* and by R. E. Park in *The Immigrant Press* at about the time of the First World War when immigration to the United States had seen its peak.

Immigrant institutions are never quite the same in structure and function as those which they are designed to replace. The role of the layman, in bringing about the establishment of a Roman Catholic church for people of his own nationality within the bounds of already existing parishes, gives him a new sense of his importance. A change in the balance of power between priest and people may result.

A Roman Catholic parish in the United States has generally been founded by the enterprise of some small group of laymen or of some priest or religious order. To hold their children in a society with a strong public school system and a strong tradition of separation of church and state, the parishes established schools of their own. Later on, they established high schools, which required a larger base than a single parish. In due time they established colleges, not merely to train priests, but also to give higher education to laymen. Eventually, some of the colleges developed into universities with graduate and professional schools. Other religious groups have developed a special set of institutions in this country. In every case, if the institutions grow, they become like other American institutions in general pattern, although somewhat separate from them. Jewish institutions in this country—the congregation with its large array of clubs and classes, organizations for defense from anti-Semitism and in support of Israel, and even universities—are distinctly American in style and form.

The rate and degree of assimilation of immigrant groups varies greatly, and there is corresponding variety in the development and fate of immigrant institutions.

The City as a Frontier. New elements of culture—fashions, practices, inventions, and ideas—tend to gather in cities and to move out from there to surrounding regions and even to remote places. The population of cities is recruited more by migration than by excess of births over deaths. Internal mobility, especially great in growing cities, breaks up accustomed aggregations of people. Institutions are constantly threatened by change of fashion and taste for various kinds of goods and amusements, by the moving away of their clientele, by changes in the means of transport and hence of the movements of people, as well as by changes in belief and sentiment which may weaken institutional claims.

As new occupations and commodities arise, new interest groups, organized about them, become part of the working structure of cities. A particular new development is increase in what economists call the tertiary part of the economy, a complex of services, communication, and technical operations and occupations. Research institutes are a part of this complex. They tend to center in cities, but to decentralize many of their activities to suburbs and outlying centers.

At the same time, the nature of city slums is changing in North America and to some extent in Europe. In North America the slums are no longer occupied by recent immigrants from Europe seeking unskilled work in industry; the new slum-dwellers come from our own poorest rural areas, released by the decline of demand for stoop-labor in agriculture and the abandoning of marginal lands. They have little hope of finding unskilled industrial labor, for there is no demand for that. They either remain unemployed or find irregular employment on the margins of the new service economy. Similar immigrants from non-industrial regions and colonies are coming into the cities of England and western Europe. They form restless masses who appear likely to question many of the established institutions—the schools, local government, trade unions, political organizations, the parish churches, and the social agencies.

Concurrently, much of the white-collar population of cities is moving to the suburbs. There are characteristic complexes of institutions to be found in suburbs. Sometimes the whole suburb is planned by a real estate firm, which will try to see to it that only people who are thought to be compatible with each other settle there, and develop an institutional complex accordingly. Other suburbs simply grow up; even so, there is great activity in building up a system of schools, churches, clubs, and the like,— as we mentioned earlier.

Crises in the City. The city is a place of crises for many persons. There may be enough people who share one peculiarity to allow them to join together to make a cult of it. Esoteric cults burgeon. But so do organizations of alcoholics, of parents of retarded children, of fatties who play at getting thin. Older people form Golden Years clubs, which become matrimonial bureaus. The reorganization of life in the city proceeds in part by the rise of peculiar institutions which resolve personal crises. Park discussed these aspects of city life in his well-known article on *The City,* in 1915; since then study of city problems has become an ever larger part of sociological work. It had its start in the survey movement in England in the late 19th century, and was continued here. Charles Booth's *Study of the Life and Labour of the People of London* (1892, 1902) had first shown in detail how many institutions change their form and functioning according to the classes of people who live or circulate in the various areas of the city.

Emancipation. Emancipation is a feature of secular change. It may be either physical or mental. A change in industrial techniques may give some group of people a freer disposition of their time. This is physical emancipation. Many women have been physically emancipated by easier, more rapid ways of doing housework, as well as by transfer of many industrial processes from the household to outside enterprises.

Emancipation from domestic drudgery has been accompanied by great increase in the number of married women, many of them mothers, who go to work in their early 30's and who resume study to bring their training up to date.

Educational institutions have adapted themselves to this new clientele, and many organizations have changed working hours and policies in order to make use of this element of the labor force.

Intellectual emancipation from beliefs and moral emancipation from claims may also accompany secular changes. Since beliefs and claims are so important a part of institutions, emancipation affects their functioning. Every secular change is a potential moral crisis. It is notorious that an industrial revolution begets moral issues. Prophets and other agitators seek to bring about changes in the social order to meet such issues.

TYPICAL CYCLES OF INSTITUTIONALIZATION

We will now consider some of the typical processes involved in the establishment of institutions. We postulate typical life-cycles, or courses of change, by which institutions take form. Much of what is here said can be understood only by reference to the section on Collective Behavior.

From Expressive Behavior to Ritual. Some institutions have their origins in expressive behavior, as in a religious revival. Such behavior, if repeated, does not long remain purely expressive. Wesley and his aides of the Methodist Awakening soon undertook to discipline those who saw the great light. Little patience was shown those whose ecstasy of repentance was not followed by good works and methodical recourse to the means of grace. Ecstasy soon becomes interpreted as a sign of conversion, and tests are set up to determine whether the latter is genuine. At this point an element of consistency has already been introduced; consistency implies authority. Expressive behavior brought under discipline is on the way to becoming established ritual. So long as the rightness of this recurrent ritual is recognized only by the participants, and is contested by the surrounding community, it is not fully instituted. The group may be at war with the prevailing mores, and is thus sectarian. If and when it is acknowledged by the larger society, known as "the world," it becomes instituted in a fuller sense.

Social Acceptance. From this point expressive behavior, now ritual, may come to have a generally accepted moral connotation. It may become a sign of acceptance of the sacred sentiments of a society, and the person who refrains from participating in it is then suspect. Meanwhile the ritual will have been rationalized so that people do not question its relation to the accepted moral values and legitimate pursuits of the society.

By this time, regulative and even political activities are likely to have overshadowed the original elements of expressive be-havior: an institution will have developed which, having vested interests in the social system, will make certain compromises with other forces. This is the familiar cycle by which religious sects become established denominations. The political sect, in like fashion, may succeed in gaining a measure of political power and become a responsible party at the cost of its original militant fervor. Responsibility, in this sense, means that the leaders of the party now feel bound by promises made to leaders of other parties; this is called revisionism by the more doctrinaire mem-bers of the movement. Such a cycle may also be run by move-ments whose aim is to change the social, economic and legal status of a group of people. In the United States various or-ganizations have sought to improve the place of people who are defined in custom or law as Negroes. Some have sought to elimi-nate the race line entirely; that is one possible goal of radical change. Others have sought some particular kinds of change, such as elimination of residential or school segregation. But, as time goes on, and the ultimate goal is not achieved, new organizations accuse the old ones of having settled for limited goals and themselves set new and more radical goals, and perhaps advocate new methods of attaining their goals. Similar processes occur in other minorities in this and other countries.

A similar cycle begins in spontaneous celebration, which develops into recurrent and expected festivity led by proper functionaries and conducted in a traditional way. The second celebration of a great event is not the same as that which broke out at the time of the event itself: the second occasion may be planned, more formal, and less violent. In time, leadership of the celebrations may be monopolized by the recognized leaders of the society. It would be impertinent of a communist leader to ask for a place in a Fourth of July parade. The celebrated event itself finally is rationalized into something more than an event; it becomes a symbol—of man's salvation from sin, of the freedom of the country, or of democracy. Being so rationalized, it will be associated with the currently dominant sentiments of the society; it acquires a conventional meaning somewhat different from that attached to the original event by the people who actually par-ticipated in it. Again and again "debunking" historians have failed to shake an established festival and its conventional mean-ing by telling "what really happened."

From Strike to Trade-Union. In a strike, one of the classes of persons participating in an institution collectively refrains from expected routine. Strong collective discontent is a condition necessary to the beginning of a strike; morale is necessary to its maintenance, for a strike is a form of conflict. The early leaders must be agitators. But the successful strike ends in negotiation; negotiation, in turn, depends upon the leaders' ability to have the terms of settlement accepted by the strikers. The development of labor unions turns about these two contradictory functions of leadership.

The cycle runs from bitter conflict led by agitators, to the armed truce of an organized group ready for conflict but refraining from it in their own interest, and then to an established organization run by administrators who may begin to fear conflict. At this point, the workers may begin to suspect their leaders of having sold out, and "outlaw unions" led by "rank-and-file" leaders may start unauthorized strikes. These may run through the same cycle. Meantime the strike, as such, has become a recognized way of gaining the ends of labor, and of having the labor union accepted as a proper institution. Any given strike and any given union may still be suspect, because of the role which conflict plays in their origin and successful maintenance, and because of their threat to the authority of employers.

To the extent that labor unions become institutions with the sanctions of contracts and law, as well as the support of the workers, they bring about a constitutional change in industrial and business institutions. They provide a new body of defined rights, new classes of recognized functionaries, and new sanctioned ways of action. For the student of institutions, these changes are of more significance than the economic question of the effects of strikes and unions upon wages and production.

Reform. Another cycle of institutional development common in America begins in a reform movement. Self-appointed enthusiasts set about to change some aspect of the mores; failing in that they seek change through legislation. If successful in this, they may try to take on the role of enforcing the law. At this point, their organization may change character, or even pass out of existence. Other reformers seek to stir the population and public authorities to effective action on some matter to which all nominally agree. They may make an issue of infant mortality, which everyone admits ought to be reduced. They propose means of remedy. Such a movement, although no one opposes its sentiment, is an attack on institutions already operating. They are accused, by implication, of but half doing their duty. The movement to help victims of infantile paralysis was very successful; when immunization reduced the incidence of that disease, the now established organization broadened its objective to include rehabilitation from other diseases. The specific aim is generalized and, thus, institutionalized. The juvenile court, the settlement house, playgrounds, libraries, night schools for adults, all are institutions which were brought into being by reform movements. The agitating leaders are succeeded by administrators with full legitimacy. In course of becoming legitimate, however, much of the fervor of the movement may be lost. After a period of trying to be more like a social agency than a court, it appears that the juvenile court is becoming more and more like other courts in its procedures. It may, however, have had its effects on other courts in the process.

One product of reform movements is new institutions. A problem for study is the amount of net change in the operation of institutions with respect to the matter in question,—health, delinquency, education, etc.

Revolutions. A revolutionary movement aims to change the entire institutional order. The French revolutionaries of the 18th century sought to establish a new calendar, for old sentiments and practices come to special expression on certain dates. The early leaders of the communist movement attacked marriage and the family as instruments of capitalist exploitation; furthermore, traditions are transmitted in the family. However, after a period of attack on these institutions, the new Soviet state began to support the family quite strongly. When a revolutionary movement has been successful in establishing a new state, it still has the problem of establishing a new order. This raises many problems, some of which may be solved by reinforcing some older institutions, perhaps giving them new names. Decorated evergreen trees are set up in the great halls of the Kremlin on the Russian New Year's day, and Father Frost—who looks just like Santa Claus—hands out gifts to school children who are brought in for great parties. Bears dance, acrobats tumble, tales are told, and songs are sung. But the word Christmas is not used. One of the most interesting problems concerning revolutions is just this matter of what new institutions are in fact established, which are

destroyed or die out, and of the extent to which the structure of
the whole society and certain of its customs continue. In this lies
the more general question of the extent to which the institutional
structure of a society depends upon the social doctrines.

Voluntary Secular Co-operation. The institutional cycles just
discussed all commence in the more lively forms of collective
behavior. Discontent, enthusiasm, even ecstatic crowd behavior
and violence may have occurred. The development, if it continues long enough, moves toward a cooler rule of precedent and
even expediency, elaboration of a rationale, increasing formality
of structure, and an accepted place in the existing social order.
Another type of cycle begins with conscious and rational co-
operation, by which each participating individual hopes to gain
some advantage not otherwise to be attained. The individuals
experience little or no excitement, and each enters into co-operation voluntarily and critically. The collectivity, regarded as a
means to an end, may be dissolved without pain to any one. A
familiar example is the trade association in which the co-operating
individuals are competitors in some line of business. Real-estate
agents may co-operate to protect themselves against tenants who
don't pay rent, landlords who don't pay commissions, and even
against agents who steal clients. If such conscious co-operative
collective action continues, the ends sought are given a more
general statement; new common problems are discovered, some
of which inhere in the social system and are therefore not capable
of definitive and final solution. With respect to these problems,
precedents arise and a long-time policy is elaborated. Meanwhile
the co-operating members become aware that their collective
body has become a recognized instrument, and they consider it
as having a place in the order of things. Outsiders likewise may
eventually accept it as the right and proper body to appeal to
with respect to certain public problems. Eventually everyone
forgets the particular purpose for which it was initiated; indeed,
it becomes like other established institutions in that persons,
asked what its purposes are, will give a variety of general and
rationalized answers in terms of accepted sentiments. In the end,
loyalty and implicit claims may arise with respect to what was in
the beginning conceived as a means to an immediate end.

Many recognized institutions of our society began in this
way. Ours is a society of many new occupations and types of
secular interest. It is also one in which there is freedom of as-

sembly and association. These are conditions favorable to this type of collective action.

When people undertake to establish a new organization to carry on some already accepted social function, there is a large element of lively collective behavior and of conscious enterprise in what they do. American colleges give us examples. Many American colleges were established as protest against prevailing systems of higher education. Methodists, Baptists, Catholics, Seventh Day Adventists established institutions in which their own young people would be educated without contamination by the "world." Normal schools were founded to train school teachers; agricultural colleges to train farmers and engineers. They were all special purpose enterprises. Most of them eventually broadened their purposes and programs and entered into open competition with other institutions of higher education, while at the same time trying to retain monopoly or at least a special advantage in their original field. In this they are like industrial enterprises which may start out, as did Henry Ford, producing one product for one part of the market and gradually come to produce a variety of products and for all parts of the market. Examples of this can be found in trade unions, social agencies, and perhaps even churches.

Arrested Development. Organizations which begin in social movements or which are initiated as enterprises do not necessarily run their course in this fashion. They may fail. They may be nipped in the bud. They may continue at a low level of success. The most that we can say is that if movements and enterprises are strongly successful and continue to be so institutional features will develop; the particular organization will find its place in the action structure of society. It is well to remember that every institution we see in operation had a beginning. It probably will not last forever, although it will develop some myth of its longevity, either by tracing its ancestry to a pre-historic hero, or by saying it was in the beginning, is now, and ever shall be.

We have presented some typical ways in which institutions begin. There are, however, certain kinds of collective enterprise which exist for long periods of time without getting full sanction of law and moral sentiment. Prostitution is such a case. There is a demand for it in all cities, in all countries, and in all ages. It takes on established forms, has its rules, and even established relations with police and courts. Professional stealing, as in the high-jacking of trucks carrying alcoholic liquor here and in England, depends, of course, on eventual sale of the stolen goods to respectable people who want to buy at cut-rates.

These established systems of enterprises are often subject to control by "rackets." A racket is a system of control, protection, and taxation in competition with the law, or perhaps in connivance with the established functionaries. The racket is more in conflict with the law than with the mores. So long as open legal sanction is not accorded businesses for which there is constant and ample demand, there will develop what one might call bastard institutions. The fields of activity in which they develop will depend upon the relation of law and law enforcement agencies to custom and consumer demand in a particular society.

Rackets also are related to insurance. In any society there are certain risks attendant upon living and working. Plate-glass windows may be broken. A doctor may be sued for malpractice. A crop or a stock of goods may be destroyed. These risks change with new invention and with social changes. Modern insurance schemes have developed around these risks. The government has entered the field with social security. And the rackets are in the wings waiting for someone who opens himself to the risk of blackmail. The student of institutions should have an eye out for the less legitimate enterprises which grow on the margin of any new system of institutions.

CHAPTER FIFTEEN

INSTITUTIONS AND THE COMMUNITY

Human aggregations may be viewed either as societies or as ecological communities. A society is described in terms of collective behavior, social relations, social usages and law, sanctions, status, and sentiments. The term community is used in two ways. Community of spirit, or religious community refers to a deep sense of common, that is shared, feeling. It is also used to refer to territorial groupings of people and institutions: a village, a town or a city is a community in this sense. The two meanings are found in most Western European languages, probably because the small territorial grouping and the sense of common identity and interests went together in rural society. We shall use the term community in the territorial sense of units which may be described in terms of spatial distribution of social institutions, competition, symbiosis and the division of labor by which a population produces and exchanges services and goods.

THE ENVIRONMENT

A community always exists in a physical environment. In modern communities, raw nature is buried beneath man's multiplied and stupendous artifacts; more than that, soil, water, and air are being modified in such a way as to threaten the very operation of the cities men have built. When the prevailing unit of human settlement was a village community living off its immediate environment life turned with the seasons; if the soil was exhausted or soured by cultivation it could be left fallow for a time, or burned over. In some cases a civilization deforested a large region, or so handled water that the rivers silted full and dried up; this may have taken centuries. Each civilization and the institutions within them have their effect on the environment.

Our technology of burning gasses, decomposing atoms, and putting all our wastes into water is rapidly changing our physical environment. Our free enterprises resist giving up the freedom to continue this pollution; our public bodies lack money and a clear mandate to stop it. At the same time we crowd people very close together at work, during transport from place to place, and in their eating, play and sleeping. It seems likely that this organization of life may have effects not only on the human individual organism during his lifetime, but also on the genetic future of the human race. This points to the need for investigations which require the collaboration of many scientists without regard to conventional divisions.

In technologically simple societies, communities are generally an obvious aspect of the landscape, easy to locate. In our world, while centers of cities are easy to discover, the actual limits of communities are difficult to find. To find some communities requires refined statistical work on the journey to and from work, retail trading areas, movements of perishable and of more durable goods, on listening to radio and watching television, newspaper circulation, and on financial affairs. London and New York are the organizing points of social and economic life for millions of people distributed at night over great areas, and assembled and redistributed by day, on week-ends and holidays in other ways according to age, sex, and occupation. In the United States the concept Standard Metropolitan Area has been developed by the Bureau of the Census to give a better notion of what is happening to populations and the institutions that mobilize them. Social institutions are distributed in relation to the movements of people.

THE LOCATION OF INSTITUTIONS

The most easily seen features of many institutions are the buildings which serve as headquarters and centers of their activities. But a building's location can be significantly described only with references to the movements of people and their activities. One way of describing institutions themselves is in terms of the mobilizing people.

A newspaper, for instance, has people at work at all times gathering news. They are deployed to the places where things are happening or expected to happen. Other people are gathered in a particular place, usually in the inner city, to rewrite, organize and make up the paper itself. The printing is usually done nearby if it is a daily paper. Then the papers are got out by trucks and planes to the streets, to houses and offices in a large area. The customers need not turn up at the newspaper office. Since the coming of television thousands of dollars worth of cameras are sent to places where news is expected to happen; sometimes there is suspicion that the news is rigged a little to make a good spectacle.

The mobilization for modern medicine is quite different. The capital goods of medicine are more and more concentrated in great clinics and hospitals. The nurses, technicians, book-keepers, dieticians, therapists and other auxiliary personnel are assembled there; the physicians "attend" at certain hours, although younger ones still in training act as "house officers" and stay on duty all hours. If and when he requires medical care the patient comes to the equipment, the beds and the staff. This is the reverse of what often happened in the past when the doctor or midwife went with a few tools to the patient. More and more the medical personnel remains fixed in one place day after day.

Education was always carried out to some extent at home, but nearly all children are now mobilized into school buildings daily and from an early age. Schools were placed at one time at what was thought easy walking distance from the most remote family. In the country, there was one teacher per school, with children of all ages. The centralizing of rural schools with the hauling of children to school in motor-buses lengthened the day away from home for the child, and made it possible to have all children taught in classes of one age. School districts were enlarged correspondingly, and local control of school declined.

In the cities, the same principle of having children walk to school prevailed. Since the population in cities clusters by income, religion, national origins and race, children were likely to attend schools with their own kind. While the school systems in the cities were administered by city-wide authorities, the individual schools often had a neighborhood flavor. Sometimes, the school authorities connived with influential parents and groups to set the school boundaries in such a way as to keep schools of certain neighborhoods free of Negro children of any class and of slum children of any ethnic group. At this point, sense of community enters. Formerly, the leaders of minorities insisted that time and safety alone should determine the boundaries of urban school districts. However, as the movement for racial equality has been accelerated, some of its leaders ask that the neighborhood principle be abandoned and that a principle of parity, that is, of proportionate mixing by children, by race and class be adopted. At the same time, some parents and neighborhood leaders demand that the people of the neighborhood be given control over the hiring of teachers. Thus comes a new case of the old struggle between local control and more centralized and bureaucratic administration. The upper-middle classes solve this for themselves by moving to suburbs where a smaller group may control schools and other institutions.

In large cities a great variety of institutions carry on their activities, with large bureaucratic staffs and having at some point contact with lay people of various classes who seek their services or come under their control. Each of them has its problem of locating its various activities in relation to other institutions and in relation to basic movements of population. Robert E. Park once said that "a community is a constellation of institutions." This seems especially true of modern cities.

R. D. McKenzie, who with Robert E. Park, brought the ecological viewpoint in to American sociology, distinguished *basic* from *service* institutions. Basic institutions furnish the economic base of the community; service institutions provide cultural services and distribute goods for consumption. The distinction refers to the function of a given institution in a region or community. A church generally "serves" the people of a locality; it is thus a service institution. The shrine at Lourdes performs a service for believers from all over the world who come there; but since it is the main source of income, it is the basic institution of the town of Lourdes.

The papacy, with its constellation of auxiliary institutions, including those who serve pilgrims, is the basic institution that give life and character to the Vatican and even to the city of Rome. A university is the basic institution of many a seat of learning, and a large state hospital is the same for many a small town, as surely as is the factory in a company town.

It seems increasingly true that the decision to maintain, close out, or move basic institutions is more and more taken by people who do not live nearby. If there is change in the basic institutions, it will be reflected in the local population, their number, character, level of living, and tastes. The service institutions have to adjust their activities to such changes.

McKenzie referred to the typical set of service institutions in a community of a given type as being its institutional *complement*, after the term used to indicate the number and kinds of men required to man a certain kind of ship. The complement will change in response to many factors. As the great shopping centers in suburbs and even the open country develop, the complement of service institutions in the center of cities and even in outlying villages may change. As families of a given class and religion move out of a city to suburbs the churches, clubs, and professional offices which serve them must either alter their programs to meet the needs of the incoming population, move out with the old population, or go out of business. Some institutions adjust themselves to new kinds of people more easily than do others. Protestant churches, generally bound as they are to ethnic groups and social classes, often do not survive a change of population. Catholic parishes, also generally ethnic in origin, may survive a change of ethnic group, but not without conflict. As the older Catholic groups move from the inner city to the suburbs, their older parishes decline in much the same way as did Protestant churches half a century ago.

Even when a given service is relatively free of class and ethnic peculiarities, people may prefer to be served by their own kind and in company of their own kind. This is very marked in religion, education, and medicine; less so in sports and entertainment; even less in purchasing clothing and groceries. Yet advertising often speaks of the class of fellow customers one will find in a shop. Ours is a service and consumption culture. Running counter to the grouping of consumers on community lines is the great development of insurance schemes and of public institutions which distribute services on an increasingly equalitarian, or at least impersonal, basis.

Perhaps the most persistent of all institutional nuclei is the family household itself. Any given one is likely to last less than half a human life-time, but they survive movement from coast to coast, from city to suburb. In a sense, such units are service institutions for each other. Suburbs are clusters of such households who expect support in their style of life from each other. This support may be more important than the support from kin, especially when the household seeks to maintain a style of life different from that of their kin on one side or both. Kin give another kind of support perhaps, but not always support in a style of life. Every kind of neighborhood tends to support some style of life, and creates certain risks for the family household.

It is not probable that any institution could be completely understood without study of the ecological conditions of survival of its operating units. Some institutions are largely supported and controlled by regional or other central bodies. A local community may thus have a better school than it could pay for alone. One of the functions of government is to iron out inequalities of financial and of moral and sentimental support of local institutions. Certain institutions are so dominated by sentiment that they seem impervious to ecological changes. But the units of every institution are in some fashion and in some measure subject to the survival of the human communities in which they exist, of the economy of wants of the population and of the technical resources available in the given culture and physical environment. In study of this matter the two meanings of community both come into play.

CHAPTER SIXTEEN

INSTITUTIONS AND THE PERSON

Institutions furnish the individual with a routine of life, patterns of expected behavior by which he will be judged, roles and offices to which he may aspire and toward which he may strive. Conversely, institutions exist in the co-ordinated and standardized conduct of individuals. The more subtle effects of institutions upon the personality of the individual are studied by psychologists; the pathologies of adjustment of individuals to institutions are treated by psychiatrists.

Status. In every society there are accepted social usages, but they are not the same for all persons. Boys and girls are distinguished from birth by costume and names. They are treated differently and expected to behave differently; constant emphasis is laid upon the different roles and careers which lie before them. They do not have identical rights and duties before the law. This is a difference of *status*. Persons of each status have their own special rights and duties, sanctioned by society.

Some societies recognize many statuses and assign individuals to them according to their race, sex, family, occupation, inherited wealth, religion, or various combinations of them. Indian society has an elaborate system of statuses, called castes. Japan has several. Our society has fewer fixed statuses; we proclaim an ideology of equality, and practice it in some measure, but we have an iron-clad special status for people of any known African descent.

In a society of few fixed categories of status and where movement is free, the person finds his place in the social structure. He has many choices to make, subject to his own capacities and opportunities, to such limitations of ascribed status as do exist, and to the nature of the social structure itself. We have a great variety of institutions and an extreme division of labor; the opportunities are many, but the individual may have limited knowledge of them and how to exploit them. The most important aspect of social classes in our society is unequal access to the means of attaining ambitions through education and acquisition of social skills. Institutions play a great part in the process of social differentiation which the person cannot escape.

Individuals in Institutional Life. The individual meets various institutions at different periods of his life, and for longer or shorter terms. He is considered part of his family from birth, but his position in it changes as he grows older. The state and some religious institutions claim him from birth until death; in these also, rights and duties change. In infancy and childhood he has little direct connection with the state; at a certain age he passes from the status of a minor to that of majority. Child offenders are dealt with by special juvenile courts. Children of certain ages may be required to go to school; young men may be called to military service, and so on. Still other institutions are met by the person only at later ages, and his relation to them may be contingent upon his other activities and roles. If he enters a certain occupation, he may be drawn into direct participation in the activity of a whole group of institutions. This leads to the distinction between *voluntary* and *involuntary* institutions.

Voluntary and Involuntary Institutions. Voluntary institutions are those in which the person is free to participate or not, as he chooses. Others are involuntary; a person is expected or compelled to participate in them. A child is inescapably part of a family; he may later renounce or desert it, although at some emotional cost. The school is involuntary for a certain period. All persons owe the state allegiance and some duties. Some institutions are voluntary in a limited way. One is free not to participate in them, but exercise of this freedom may be socially and economically costly. An adult does not have to take the job, but if he is able-bodied and does not work, relief agencies may not support him. No one has to become a physician; but once he does he cannot escape obligations put upon him by the organized medical system. A businessman is free to ignore trade associations, clubs, churches, and civic organizations; but if he does ignore them he may jeopardize his standing and his business. When a person enters upon a career each of his achievements or choices tends to bring with it some pressure to participate in institutions and to play certain roles; he exercises his freedom to refrain at his peril.

Conversely, there are limits on the right to participate in institutions and in offices in them. Women can receive communion in Catholic churches and sit in the gallery in Orthodox synagogues; but they cannot give communion or lead the rites. Control over determining who shall participate and in what capacity may be traditional, a matter of law or doctrine, a matter of status in the society, or it may lie with the functionaries of the institutions or with the body of the participants. We are in a period of great change in this matter.

Cooley [1] has said that a person enters into an institution only with a trained and specialized part of himself. As examples he mentioned "the legal part of the lawyer, the ecclesiastical part of a church member, and the business part of a merchant."

Institutions vary both in the degree of specialization demanded of persons and in the completeness of control over their lives. The lawyer may perform his professional duties satisfactorily and yet have a great deal of private life. A nun is expected to have no private life at all; even her secret meditations are expected to be pious. The saying that a woman's work is never done expresses the complete devotion to the family formerly, if not now, expected of the wife and mother.

Within the same institution, various degrees of specialization and of devotion are expected of different categories of people. In certain communities everyone is counted part of the church, but specially trained and dedicated persons, the clergy, devote their whole time and thought to the church and are expected to dress and act in a distinct way at all times.

Specialization as here conceived has two dimensions. One is that of knowledge and technique; the other, that of duties and prerogatives. The lawyer has expert knowledge; so have the priest, the businessman, and even the mother. But each of them has also prerogatives and duties by which he is distinguished from other people. Identification of one's self with one or more established sets of rights and duties is part of the process by which an individual becomes a person with a social identity.

FUNCTIONARIES AND OFFICES

The more specialized activities of an institution are carried on by functionaries who fulfill offices. An institutional office con-

---

1 C. H. Cooley, *Social Organization*, p. 319.

sists of a defined set of rights and duties vested in a person, but capable of being transferred to another person in some accepted way. This does not mean that a father, for instance, can be replaced in his family easily or completely, for personal attachment becomes too great. But when one becomes a father there is a pattern of expected conduct lying in wait for him. In other institutions, the functionaries can be changed within the individual units; at the funeral of an aged monarch the tears are not bitter and the mourners look out of the corner of their eyes at the beloved prince who will soon be happily crowned.

Impersonal Character of an Office. An office is impersonal in two respects. First, it is usually older than the individual incumbent and is expected to outlive him. Second, each incumbent is expected to behave, within limits, as have his predecessors. Ritual offices are the most impersonal, for in them the incumbent speaks in set phrases which he is not free to alter. The person in an office is judged by the expectations of the office. So long as he meets them, he is free from personal criticism. The office sets the limits of his responsibilities.

Personal Aspects of an Office. An office is personal in that the fulfilling of it requires the conscious identification of one's personal role with the historic office. The office is part of his experience. Deep emotions may be associated with it. It is also personal in that the individual may change the character of the office by his manner of filling it.

Opportunity of Initiative. Offices vary as to the opportunity they offer for personal initiative, and in the amount of responsibility of the individual to get results. The king of England enjoys great prestige, but does not make or carry out policies. The prime minister has less prestige, but is expected to get results. Some offices combine ritualistic and symbolic features with responsibility and initiative. Priests in Christian churches manage their sees and parishes as well as administer the sacraments.

Achievement of Results. In business institutions, officers are judged very largely by the results they achieve. They make decisions and are expected to see them carried out. Even active offices gather a certain amount of ritual, as is seen in the familiar custom of lending weight to words by having them uttered by industrial and financial figures.

NATURAL HISTORY OF AN OFFICE

Every institutional office has a history. Sects furnish a clear example. Joseph Smith was the founder and prophet of the Mormon sect. Brigham Young succeeded him, but he was not called a prophet. The founder is regarded as unique; after he dies a formula is developed by which some of his attributes are passed on to a successor. Eventually an office evolves, with defined prerogatives and a manner of succession. A social fiction is developed whereby the successors share the prestige of the founder.

Enacted and Crescive Offices. There are other typical lines of development. The presidency of the United States was defined in a written document. It was, in Sumner's terms, enacted rather than crescive; but, as is generally the case, the original enactment has been modified by experience. The present office is a product of precedent as well as of written prescription. Probably no office can be fully laid down in advance.

Changing Character of Offices. As an institution becomes established the character of offices changes, and new ones grow up. Duties and the exercise of authority are distributed among them. The relations of offices to one another and to the various classes of people who participate in the institution are its "working constitution."

Identification. As an office becomes sacred the individual who is to fill it may be separated from other people by a long discipline and is finally invested with the office in a ceremonial manner. These devices intensify the person's sense of identification with the office. He may be "called," as are the clergy. In psychiatric terms, he feels compelled to dedicate himself to the office. But institutions do not rely on a person's sense of compulsion alone as evidence that he should be invested with an office; devices are set up to test the validity of his call and to discipline his unbounded enthusiasm and sense of exalted righteousness.

Development of Instability. In a stable society, persons of succeeding generations identify the meaning and purposes of their lives with the offices of existing institutions. But there are periods in which this is not so. Some persons get a sense of a special mission not provided for in the institutions. They chafe under the bonds of institutions, and become restless. Such a situation is critical both for institutions and for persons.

Changes in Function. In a changing secular society there are many institutions in process whose offices are not clearly defined. The persons who fill such offices can and do show a great deal of individual initiative; in so doing they create the offices they fill. The rights and duties of the managing boards of universities and charitable organizations, as well as of their executive officers, are still in course of rapid change. Even in well-hardened institutions some offices offer opportunities for enterprise and initiative which may bring about changes in the office itself.

Selection of Functionaries. The persons who are to fill offices are selected in various ways. In business institutions the officers are supposed to be chosen because of their achievements and abilities, not because of family, race, or religion. In more sacred institutions it is but natural that more attention should be paid such characteristics. Yet many features and characteristics enter directly or indirectly into the choice of functionaries and leaders in most institutions. The engineer must have technical knowledge, but he must have certain human qualities if he is to become a manager, as many engineers do. He might have a hard time if he were a communist, no matter how hard he might work. The selection of functionaries is related to the general class structure of society. This is true both of those who are professionally active in institutions, and of those who are voluntary lay leaders. Every institution has its place in the class structure, as shown by the social selection of the people who play various roles and fulfill the various offices within it.

PARTICIPANTS IN INSTITUTIONS

Several categories of persons participate in an institution or at least have some occasional relations with it. The significant categories can be determined by study alone. A few examples were given in the discussion of classification of institutions. Two additional examples, characteristic of our society, follow.

The Social Agency. The people most actively and continuously concerned with social agencies are trained professional social workers, who may move from one agency to another. Formerly there were many volunteer workers. Managing boards and committees govern the agencies and assist in raising the necessary money; these people are chosen on the basis of their interest and their status in the community. They are generally large donors to the agency. The solvent members of the general population are contributors in a small way, but know little of the inner workings of the agency. Then there are the people, euphemistically called clients, who are looked after by the agency. There is little movement from one of these categories to another. The donors rarely become professional workers or clients; the clients almost never become donors, professional workers, or members of boards. In this case, the categories of people in the institution and the part played by each is clearly related to the general structure of society. A somewhat similar pattern is found in all institutions supported by philanthropic giving.

The University. The university shows similar categories, with certain significant differences. The governing boards are constituted in somewhat the same way. A professional group, the professors and administrators, devote their time to the university and have their careers within it. But the students occupy a quite different position, and seldom come from the poorest classes. The students continue, as alumni, to have a sentimental interest in the university and may even have a part in forming its policies.

The Spread of Participation. In both these cases the managing boards are persons of wealth and social position. The institution, although undoubtedly important to them, is incidental to their careers. The taking of such responsibility is expected of and urged upon them; they, too, consider it their right to act so. They are the patrons. The professional groups, social workers and faculty members, have their careers and living in it. They interpret the meaning of their lives in terms of the value of the institution to the community. They carry its main body of tradition and technique, and regard it as their right that the community should support them. In both cases a third group of persons directly receives services. Ordinarily they are in contact with the professionals, but not with the patrons. The "clients" of the social agency may have little or no sense of loyalty to the institution; it is simply a help in time of trouble. The social agency seldom has alumni. Students of universities have often remained sentimental about the universities which they attended and become loyal alumni upon whom the institutions depend for support. The college years were a prolonged social rite of passage as well as a time to learn how to make a better living. As a larger proportion of each age cohort attends university and as various social conditions change, the attitudes of students to the universities they attend has also changed. Many question the authority of the university to guide their studies and to control their behavior.

A fundamental change in the numbers and social characteristics of the people in one or more of the categories of participants may lead to unrest, to conflict and to change in the working constitution of an institution. All institutions depend upon the continued presence and availability of persons who may be involved in its ongoing activities. A change in the scale of operations of the institution may bring a crisis in the supply of people for its various roles. There are many rich people in our society, and the income tax is so arranged as to encourage them to give great sums of money to education. Yet the number of students and the cost of equipment have outstripped the supply of donated money. The government pays an ever larger portion of the cost of education. This may change the attitude of donors and may change the selection of trustees of universities.

Along with these changes may come related shifts in the meaning of the offices and roles to the people who play them.

Turnover. In an institution, the participants of different categories turn over at different rates. In universities students come and go most rapidly, or so it is expected. Younger staff in lower ranks move about more than those in higher ranks, although this may change in time of great demand for teachers and research people. In some inner city churches members turn over faster than do the clergy, whereas in stable communities the reverse is true. In prisons some prisoners and guards outlast a number of wardens. In any institution there may be some element whose members turn over more slowly than others. Those who move most slowly may informally gain greater power than they are supposed to have. They are the locals, or homeguards, as against the itinerants or cosmopolitans. Those who move more frequently may identify themselves more closely with some larger body, such as their profession; while those who move least may consider themselves most loyal to the local institution, and may work together against the more itinerant elements.

INSTITUTIONS AND THE LIFE OF THE PERSON

Institutions, it has been suggested, give order to the life of the individual. In early infancy and childhood his identity in the community is entirely determined by the family of which he is a member. Later he is identified with other institutions—the school, church, etc. Eventually he finds a job if he can, becomes a full-fledged adult citizen, and participates in some fashion in many institutions. Some of them influence his life without his becoming aware of it.

Self-Appraisal. From a fairly early age he develops a sense of his own identity, of the role he plays in the eyes of others and in his own eyes. He is also likely to conceive of himself in terms of his future, although it may not turn out to be what he expects. As he moves on through life he passes through a sequence of relations to other people and institutions; at each point—if he is at all introspective—he tries to square his past with the present, and to interpret the meaning of his present for his future. He sees life in a moving perspective.

Dominant Interests. Some of the institutions in which he has a part will mean much to him; others will mean little. To some persons, family life remains the sole dominating interest. The priest must leave his family and have his being in the church, although his family may gain prestige by his action. In the secular pursuits of business and industry many people find the leading interest of their lives, and all their hopes are set upon achievements in this field. Still others plug along at some job, but find the crucial prizes of life in their families, religious institutions, fraternal orders, local politics, charities, or what not. Thus each institution is an arena in which some people seek what they most want, while for others it is merely a casual or an incidental thing. While not all personal enthusiasms and aims are directed toward institutions, many of them are. So much is this true that the life-history of most individuals would be, in considerable part, an account of their relation to institutions. Subjectively, such a history would record how persons viewed these institutions and how they perceived themselves in relation to them; objectively, it would be an account of the assigned or achieved places in them.

THE CAREER

In some societies, each individual is assigned to a position in a set of statuses; thus is his career determined—his marriage mate, his occupation, his civic offices and the rights and duties which devolve upon him at each stage of his life and at each contingency in the life of his community. In our society a person is much freer than in most to make his own career. Yet people of certain backgrounds are more favored and free in their choices than are others. Women and persons of certain ethnic or racial identities are restricted in their careers by custom, prejudice, or institutional rule, if not by law. Even after formal restrictions have been removed, a hang-over of poverty, diffidence, fear, and of lack of education and social sophistication may still limit, in fact, effective free choice.

Schooling. One set of limits on the development of the person lies in failure to meet the demands which schools make. A child is expected to learn things in a fixed order and at certain ages. If he falls behind or drops out of school, he is considered a deviant. In some European countries the child, or his parents, must choose between divergent lines of schooling before he has reached the level of our high school. Some provisions are made in America for those who wish education at a later age, but there is still and will probably continue to be a certain fatality in the interruption of one's formal schooling.

Maturity. Meanwhile the person has attained the status of an adult, whether he wishes it or not. He must work for a living, unless he is of the favored few. Pride may prevent him from doing and learning the things conventionally appropriate to an earlier age. Thus when the person has reached the end of adolescence a great many things have happened to fix not only his habits, interests, and knowledge, but his social role and his probable career. The expected line of development of the individual tends to make decisions and actions irrevocable.

Bureaucratic Careers. Careers which tend to proceed by fixed steps are called bureaucratic. In the civil service, the army, and wherever the principles of seniority and selective examination prevail, careers tend to be of this type. In such careers, Karl Mannheim has said, one receives at each step a neat package of prestige and power whose contents are known in advance. Security is at a maximum and enterprise at a minimum. Many people believe that our society is becoming increasingly bureaucratic.

A measure of the bureaucratic tendency appears in many institutions. In school systems, in railroads and other large corporations, even in universities and social agencies there are signs of it. Wherever the knowledge and function of a kind of work become standardized it is likely to appear.

Exceptions to Bureaucratic Tendencies. In many fields of activity, career lines are not fixed. In institutions where they are fixed, some offices are filled from outside the line of expected bureaucratic advancement. When a new subject is introduced into the curricula of universities, the people who study and teach it will for a time come from irregular sources; such has been the case with sociology until recently. University presidents have likewise escaped the bureaucratic tendency. Judges of juvenile courts have not in the past been ground out of the regular legal and political mill. School superintendents and executive heads of social agencies often are not picked from those who have "faithfully served" in the lower ranks of their institutions. Although this matter has not been thoroughly studied, it appears probable that offices which require initiative and executive ability are difficult to standardize.

It may be that the careers of individuals can not be forced completely into institutional molds even in the most rigid of societies. Native abilities, extraordinary ambitions and efforts, and the contingencies of social change make for open places in the frozen structure of society. For most individuals, however, both the meaning and the course of life are closely bound to the institutional structure.

CHAPTER SEVENTEEN

SOCIAL CONTROL

In primary group life, the individual is sensitive to the actions and gestures of his intimate associates. In crowds there prevails a collective mood in which individuals lose the self-restraint of quieter moments. In both cases an informal collective control is exercised over the individual: in both appears that mutual responsiveness of human beings which is perhaps the ultimate basis of all social control.

INFORMAL CONTROL

A new element is introduced when conventional ways of behaving develop, as they inevitably do when people live together. Sumner designates as *folkways* the common modes of behavior accepted as natural and right in any group or society. Through them present behavior is controlled by that of the past. It is still a matter of individuals controlling one another, for the folkways are communicated from living persons to living persons. Each person becomes an agent of the folkways in so far as he himself adheres to them and gives his frown or his approving nod to other people, depending on whether they likewise depart from or conform to the folkways.

Sumner further divides folkways into *usages* and *mores*. Usages are merely practiced, whereas mores are considered necessary to group welfare and are sacred. In the terms used by Radcliffe-Brown, the mores are *sanctioned usages*.

All social usages have behind them the authority of the society, but among them some are sanctioned and others are not. A sanction is a reaction on the part of a society or of a considerable number of its members to a mode of behavior which is thereby approved (positive sanctions) or disapproved (negative sanctions). Sanctions may further be distinguished according to whether they are diffuse or organized; the former are spontaneous expressions of approval or disapproval by members of the community acting as individuals, while the latter are social actions carried out according to some traditional and recognized procedure.[1]

The *mores* are folkways subject to *diffuse sanctions.* Institutional control is distinguished by *organized sanctions;* it involves recognized rules, formal procedures for their application, and a structure consisting of persons acting in office. Anyone may lift his brow at a departure from accepted usage, or join with his neighbors in ostracizing someone who has violated the mores. Only the proper officers or functionaries may undertake the sanctioned procedures of an institution. None but very fanatical persons or those whole feelings have been extremely outraged interfere with a parent's way of looking after his children. Any one may suggest that the stock exchange is a den of thieves, but constituted authority alone may eject a broker from his seat.

The question is sometimes raised whether these concepts are applicable in a complicated society such as ours, where people constantly meet strangers and associate in changing situations. From study of industry and other situations where people associate in small groups it is clear that almost all such groups constantly develop rules with reference to the recurrent situations which they meet. If the group exists inside some larger institutional setting, it probably will set up rules which do not coincide with those of formal authorities. Medical students, who are usually assigned more work than they can do, arrive at implicit agreements about how much of it to do. College students, workers in industry, children at home all do this, and protect from punishment those of their fellows who conform to their rules; they have ways of making life miserable for those who transgress by living strictly up to the formal rules. As in most social control, the making and enforcing of informal rules generally involves some sort of unspoken bargain.

FORMAL CONTROL

The ultimate instance of institutional control is the law, as formally interpreted by courts and executed by police power.

1 A. R. Radcliffe-Brown, "Social Sanction," *Encyclopaedia of the Social Sciences* (1934), 13:531–534. Used by permission of the publishers, Macmillan Co., New York.

Some students have applied the term law to all social rules, whether systematically formulated or not, and whether or not subject to organized rather than merely diffuse sanctions. Roscoe Pound, however, limits law to "social control through the systematic application of the force of politically organized society." So defined, law is but one form of social control among others.

Law derives from many sources, among them custom, legislation, administrative orders and decrees. But none of these constitutes law in the strict sense until courts have passed upon them. Many usages and even mores are never embodied in law. Others may be. Justice Cardozo considered that a rule or convention was a part of law when it became so established that one could predict with reasonable certainty that a court would uphold it. According to this view much of the process of lawmaking occurs without legislation and before the matter reaches court.

A sociology of law would study the evolution of social rules, the nature and development of courts and their fields of jurisdiction, and the evolution of systems of thought used by lawyers and judges in arriving at decisions.

Courts have their history and functions which are not understood without reference to other institutions. According to the anthropologist Malinowski, the binding force of the law derives from the structure of institutions in the given society. Courts adjudicate, but do not form the relationships within families, in business, or between physician and client. Even in an orderly society, only a small part of all violations of rule which might be tried in court ever are so tried. While certain types of laws are enforced at the instance of the functionaries of the state itself, with respect to others the initiative is taken by persons representing the interests of other institutions or by proponents of some reform in the mores themselves.

Any institution is subject in some measure to the common stock of mores. In addition, it will be the vehicle of conscious and formal control over some limited phase of life and, usually, over some special group of persons. Against the background of the moral consensus of society, special groups of persons work out and apply formal rules and procedures to specific activities and interests.

Some institutions, such as the church and state, tend to exert authority over a wide range of activities and over all members of society. Their functionaries often attempt to bring to explicit formulation matters that have been subject to the mores, and to apply to them the formal procedures of the institution. Insofar as functionaries successfully set themselves up as the proper persons to define and enforce the mores, the latter take on the qualities of law.

Other institutions regulate only some very narrow aspect of life, such as the practice of a profession. In this case, the professional group consciously formulates and attempts to enforce rules. Although it may exert some control over the occasionally affected general public, the institution is, in turn, subject to the mores and popular usage. Professional medicine, for instance, cannot escape the general mores and popular beliefs with respect to healing. There are certain human activities which are not easily subjected to control by functionaries. Language, which has been called an institution, is one. Languages become highly elaborated without any formal teaching, and without any one having authority to impose standard usage. In literate societies, with universal schooling, teachers can punish pupils for their manner of speech or writing. Indeed, laws may be made for or against the use of a language. Academies may be set up to define proper use—as in France and Israel. But language, on the whole, goes on its way without great control by formal authority. F. S. Chapin spoke of language as being a diffused-symbolic institution, rather than a nucleated one. It appears likely that some human activities can be brought under formal control more easily than others.

Classification. Every institution involves some classification of the poeple of the society, according to the degree and manner in which they fall into the orbit of the institution. The relations between persons within each category, and between those of different categories, are defined. Institutional rules refer typically to the obligations of persons according to status and office.

Thus, however intimate its life may be, the family remains a system of sanctioned relationships between husband and wife, children, and other kin. The obligations of each to the others are defined in usage, in the mores, and in law. A citizen is a person who enjoys certain privileges in, and owes certain obligations to a state. Employers, managers, foremen, and workers in a factory; board members, donors, social workers, and "cases" in a social agency; trustees, presidents, deans, professors, students, and alumni of colleges; judge, jury, lawyers, witnesses, defendants, and plaintiffs in a court; physician, nurse, and patient—these are a few examples of institutional classifications of persons. When we say that the law is no respecter of persons, we mean that it treats them in terms of such instituted categories as are pertinent to the case in question, to the exclusion of matters irrelevant to it. The process of developing and changing such categories, with a reference to the complex current activities and interests within a society, is the very heart of the institutional process.

INSTITUTIONAL CONTROL IN THE PROFESSIONS

The processes of institutional control are well illustrated by the professions. The members of a full-fledged profession possess a technique and a body of knowledge pertaining to it. These they apply in performing some service for other members of society. So long as their competence is recognized by society at large, the members have a common status, and interests are shared by all of the members and may be injured by any one of them.

The persons who are served by the profession are interested only occasionally in its technique and knowledge. A body of unsystematic beliefs and practices may be adhered to by the general populace and communicated informally from generation to generation. In contrast with the general populace, however, the members of the profession are constantly and consciously interested in the matter involved, such as law, medicine, or accounting. Within the limited circle of the profession, technique and knowledge are systematized and passed on by formal means and in esoteric language. The professionals claim the sole right to judge knowledge and practice in their field of activity.

The Validation of Competence. A constant problem of professional control is that of determining who are members, and, therefore, colleagues. This problem is resolved in to two questions. First, who is competent to practice the profession? Second, who has a right to practice it?

The physician, the pharmacist, the surgeon, the midwife, the nurse, and the dentist all perform services relating to health. They at one time practiced rather independently of each other. Within the last century the lines between them have been revised and they have been drawn into a single institutional complex in which the place of each is defined. But at the same time some activities have passed from one of the occupations to another within the complex. Physicians have taken over obstetrics as part of their practice; the midwife has been put out of business in most parts of this country. The nurse is required to have much longer education than before. She now works only on patients who are under physician's care, but does many things which no one but a physician was formerly permitted to do. Many new techniques have to be assigned here and there in the system. Each of these occupations tries to set its own course of training and to get laws allowing them to choose who is to have a license to practice it. A part of the process of control is the drawing of the ever-changing lines between what is the domain of each and all of these related occupations. Those in a given branch are colleagues expected to stay within the bounds of the agreed upon definition of their area of competence.

The clear definition of the group of colleagues does not completely and forever settle the problem of keeping practice in their hands alone. It sometimes happens that scientists who are not physicians make discoveries which affect medical practice. If the discovered knowledge is not at once accepted by the professionals the scientist may accuse them of conservatism. Furthermore the populace persists in many beliefs and practices not approved by the profession, or may wish kinds of service which it does not give. Other persons continue to give these services. Baldness, about which the medical profession does not claim to know much, is a persistent source of profit to barbers and patent-medicine venders who claim they do know something about it. Anxiety and many diseases difficult to diagnose and cure are treated by various kinds of unlicensed practitioners, by religious cults, and at shrines. Certain medical and surgical services, notably abortion, are forbidden by law; since regular physicians will not give them, people resort to other sources. An organized profession, whether from high motives or low, has to deal with such vagaries of popular belief and usage if it is to dominate its particular field of interest. It has to reckon with popular tastes and beliefs.

One of the problems is that many laymen do not accept the profession's definition of the nature of health and disease. A profession always develops a philosophy about the nature of the problems it deals with and seeks a mandate to have its philosophy generally accepted. The medical professions in our time believe that all disease is due to natural causes, and inclines to biochemical explanations. Some people do not accept this conception.

They thus question the mandate of medical people to define what is proper diagnosis and treatment.

The number of professions has greatly increased in the last several decades. Each one has to determine the field over which it can claim monopoly on the ground that the professionals alone are competent in it and that it would be dangerous to allow others to practice; it has also to determine what definition of the nature of the problem should prevail and what authority (mandate) the profession should have to control thought and action.

Relations to Colleagues and to Clients. The relations of colleagues to one another and to their clients must be defined. The colleagues compete with one another for clients. The services offered are such that the client is not supposed to be able to judge their value with accuracy. If one buys a suit, he judges its quality by its wear. But a surgical operation or the advice given by a lawyer is not subject to lay judgment in the same degree. The patient may suffer and die under the best of treatment; a case may be lost by an expert lawyer. Each physician must, therefore, protect himself against criticism by saying that he has done all that medical science can do. His failures must be attributed to the state of technique and knowledge of the profession as a whole, not to his own shortcomings. He must allow the same defense to his colleagues, for if the impression gets abroad that some of the properly trained and licensed professionals are incompetent, the public may come to believe that none is to be trusted. The layman may then take the next step of daring to form a judgment as to matters of professional practice. Every professional must, therefore, curb the natural desire to praise his own work and to criticize that of his competitors.

From this situation proceeds the rule against advertising one's special qualifications. In some states, a physician is allowed to put on his window only his name and title. In other places, he may note his specialty. Such invidious distinctions as might be suggested by prominent naming of the school at which he studied and the hospital in which he interned are frowned upon.

The conditions under which one professional may accept a client who has formerly received the services of another, and the relations between the general physician to whom a patient comes and the specialist to whom it becomes necessary to refer his case are also problems of competition.

Another set of problems has to do with the duties of the professional toward his client, toward certain other individuals and toward the general public. Shall the physician report to a man's wife that her husband suffers from communicable venereal disease? Shall the priest report to police the confession of a crime? Shall a lawyer defend a person he knows to be a criminal?

Matters such as these cannot be settled by doctrine alone. As the technique of the professions changes, new problems of control arise. Changes apparently unrelated to the profession may make existing rules unworkable. Specialization may break up the coherence of the profession both as to knowledge and interests. The corporation lawyer and the criminal lawyer, for instance, may have little in common and may actually disagree about many problems. The specialist attached to a hospital and the general physician working in a poor neighborhood may likewise have little understanding of, or sympathy for one another.

Professional Etiquette, Code, and Creed. The rules governing these matters amount to a code and an etiquette of the profession. Both are produced by the professional group rather than by other parts of the society. The *etiquette* is a body of ritual which grows up informally to preserve, before the clients, the common front of the profession.

The *code* consists of rules elaborated to meet recurrent problems in the relations of the professionals to one another, to their clients, and to society at large.

Besides having an etiquette and a code, a profession is likely to have a *creed* which states its ideals in general terms. Thus, the medical profession exists to alleviate suffering, the legal profession to further justice, and so on. The creed, while seriously believed in, cannot be enforced by sanctions; the code can be so enforced if the profession has enough moral consensus. The ultimate penalty is expulsion from the group of colleagues. In reality, consensus is more easily maintained with reference to a creed than on the specific points of a code. There is also a tendency for the rules of a code to become matters of creed, more stoutly defended in words than by sanctions. At bottom all professional control—etiquette, creed, and code—rests upon the sense of community of status and of interest, among the members; that is, upon an implicit consensus.

Communication. The underlying consensus of a profession, as of any group, is maintained by intimate communication of its members. In a professional school much more than science and techniques is transmitted to the students. Traditional attitudes are communicated in asides by teachers who are themselves members of the profession. The students learn a lingo which expresses the fact that they are in possession of peculiar knowledge not given to laymen. Professional training is an initiation into a fraternity. One learns to guard its secrets, to cherish its ideals, and to have a feeling of being one of a group apart. The personality becomes identified with the historic professional group as symbolized in medicine for example by the figure of Hippocrates.

Sense of Honor. It is upon such close personal identification with a historic group having a special status, that a sense of honor ultimately rests. Honor combines features of formal rule with the scruples of conscience. Every person has some scruples of his own. They are not a matter of honor, for in following them he is responsible to himself alone. Every person is also subject to certain formal rules toward which his conscience is not especially acute; he obeys them, if he does, to avoid application of formal sanctions. Honor consists of a sense of conscientious scruple with reference to rules defined by a group and applicable to all its members. The person thus becomes compelled by his own conscience to live up to rules not of his own making. The most extreme manifestation of honor is formal suicide following an unavoidable breach of the rules of one's group.

Honor operates as a means of control only when the rules are specific, when there is consensus with respect to them, and when the person accepts them into his stock of moral compulsions. Within a professional group there is likely to be an inner circle who possess sufficient consensus to be governed by honor. In general, however, changes in technique and in the conditions of practicing a profession are inimical to rule by honor. For it is not sufficient that the members be conscientious; the rules must be clearly defined. In a democratic, mobile society, with a minimum of clear status, honor is difficult to maintain in its more extreme and rigid forms.

Conflicting Trends in Professional Control. Professional control seems to be currently subject to two conflicting trends. One is an increase in the number of specialized techniques with their relevant bodies of theoretical knowledge. The resulting elaboration of the division of labor has been accompanied by an increase in the number of occupations which are professional in character. At the same time there has been a change in the circumstances under which professional services are performed. The traditional professional man had many clients, any one of whom he might lose without great danger to his standing or living. Many professionals now have employers, in fact, if not in name. A lawyer, for instance, may live almost entirely from the patronage of one large corporation: in his office will be a number of other lawyers who, in effect, work for him on salary. A physician may be attached to a hospital or clinic, and have little outside practice. Engineers, accountants, nurses, and many other people of professional type are employed outright. Under these conditions the professional may be so dependent upon the good will of someone outside the profession that he is not entirely free to act with his professional group. Also the profession cannot easily discipline an individual who has a job of this type. Thus, autonomous professional control becomes difficult to maintain.

POLICY AND PUBLIC OPINION

Every institution has some relations with the larger public. It has interests to defend against the world at large; the final interest being its right to exist and to perform the functions which it does perform. The institution is ultimately sanctioned in some fashion by society at large.

Social Sanctions and the Family. In the case of the family, the sanction rests in the mores. The family furnishes the undoubtedly right way for people to live together and bring up their children. No one who wishes to establish a family has to justify this way of behaving. He may have to argue his own right to do it. People may think he is too young or too old, too poor, or that the mate he has in mind is not of the proper age, social class, race, or religion. His mother may think he should devote himself to her alone. The particular circumstances may be in question; marriage and family life as such are not.

Every family has also to keep up a "front" and to gain acceptance within some group of families. It becomes identified with a social class, or with a "social set" in which it plays a role. This role requires effort and conscious thought on the part of some members of the family. The family income will be budgeted among various kinds of expenditure according to the conception the family has of itself and according to the role it wishes to play and the group in which it seeks a place. Although the family as a type of institution is sanctioned by the mores, each separate family has to maintain, by a conscious effort, its place among other families. It has, indeed, a policy, although it is seldom admitted or put into words.

Shifts in Authority. At the same time, as society changes, the functions of the family change. In recent decades many institutions have arisen to take over control of various phases of the lives of children who are still under the guardianship of their parents. A parent is, in most places, no longer free to keep his children from school. Public authority may compel him to have his child inoculated against various diseases. Although general social doctrine still says that the parent is responsible for his children, a specific and conscious public opinion has developed with respect to education and health. Functionaries of other institutions may and do claim authority over the child, even against the will of the parent. This illustrates the manner in which an institution supported by the mores loses part of its authority to other institutions because of a change in public opinion.

Institutional Policy and Precedent. Other institutions, much more than the family, are impelled to define consciously their place in society and to justify their own existence. The functionaries develop a *policy* of action toward other institutions and toward individual members of society. This policy they state in terms of the values accepted by society at large; that is, in terms of the mores, and of the current social philosophy.

The policy will relate to those matters which the functionaries believe, from their experience, to concern in critical fashion the continued functioning of the institution. They will learn to scent remote dangers, and may consequently make a great to-do about some apparently small matter which might be taken as an unfavorable precedent. Policy, in short, involves seeing the present in the perspective of past and future.

The Catholic church, for instance, thinks of itself as eternal. Its essential problem is to save erring humanity. It must, however, meet the facts of life in a given age. It watches closely the slightest changes of law with respect to education, and interprets each with reference to its belief that education should be controlled by the church and by its knowledge that education under the church produces better Catholics. From time to time, the

Pope issues official statements on the relation of the church to the state, on marriage, birth control, and economic problems. In all these, a fine line is drawn between the particular occasion and the general principle or doctrine.

Other institutions, although they see their problems in a shorter perspective, develop an equally sharp eye for precedent. A real-estate board may interfere with the methods used in selling a given lot, because they might endanger the whole real-estate business and the place of agents within it. One such realty board spent a great deal of money opposing a law requiring property owners to clean the snow off sidewalks. This small item was seen as a step toward increased burdens upon real estate. Every such burden presumably decreases the desirability of real estate as an investment.

Interdependence of Institutions. In any policy lies some set of assumptions about the structure of the society in which the institution concerned has its vested place. The medical profession has an obvious interest in foundations, hospitals, medical schools, clinics, insurance, and all devices proposed for supplying medical services to the public. Even institutions which are often in conflict may depend upon one another's existence. The trade-union, which disputes some of the actions and prerogatives of employing corporations, must negotiate contracts with them. The functionaries of universities sometimes have to defend their policies against wealthy people, yet the American university has depended for support upon large gifts from just such people.

Internal Coherence. The maintenance of a policy depends upon the inner coherence of the units of the institution. If the functionaries do not have sufficient control to be accepted as official spokesmen, there can be no policy. Even a family cannot maintain its place unless its members can be counted upon to keep up a solid front; a skeleton cannot be kept in the cupboard without discipline.

Dominant Points of View. In the case of large institutions, the policy eventuates from a political process by which a dominant and accepted line of action and point of view emerge. In business institutions control is so completely in the hands of the entrepreneurs and managers that they may make the policies without much question from lesser employees. The managers are, however, held in check by the customer public. In professional groups, there develops a dominant point of view as to the interests of the profession and the proper way of pursuing them. If a considerable element of the profession refuses to accept this point of view, the policy cannot be carried out.

Influence of Current Events. Every institution is sensitive to some order of events with which its functionaries must keep abreast. This is particularly evident in secular institutions, such as the market. The price of a commodity, such as cotton, may be set by thousands of presumably rational judgments by buyers and sellers. Their judgments are based on news which bears on the probable supply of and demand for cotton for the season. Drought, pestilence, floods, and wars may affect supply and demand. Whatever agreements dealers make will be effective only if the agreements accord with the pertinent facts. Lloyd's, an association of insurance brokers in London, long ago developed a weather reporting service for practically the whole world, because this news was pertinent to their business of insuring ships and cargoes. These are examples of news which have no relation to the mores and the public mood, i.e., it is not political news. Other institutions are sensitive primarily to news of the political and moral state of the world. Messengers come to Rome to inform the Pope of social and political events that occur in the most obscure parts of the world. Large institutions develop research bureaus to ferret out facts pertinent to their affairs and to make predictions as to the probable effects on the institution. Whatever their doctrines, the functionaries of institutions must pay heed to the unpleasant facts of life.

The Newspaper. In this lies some of the significance of the modern newspaper. As R. E. Park [1] points out, the reporter who gathers and reports events, rather than the editor who comments upon them, has become the important figure in the modern commercial newspaper. The newspaper gathers and publishes news on the basis of which people can act with reference to specialized interests. By what is there reported, people judge which stocks to buy, the price to pay for cotton, or whether the home team is worth betting on. Generally speaking, the actions based on published news are taken in connection with institutions.

Incidentally, the newspaper also records, in its human-interest stories, the protests of individuals against the institutional order of society. Human-interest stories give some expression to the

---

1 R. E. Park and E. W. Burgess, *The City* (1925), Chapter 4, "The Natural History of the Newspaper."

moral pulse of society; they reveal society to itself. This is perhaps the reason why they are suppressed so severely in countries in which it is not considered proper that the general public should have a hand in the making of public policy.

Propaganda and Policy. The carrying out of a policy requires some control over public opinion. Insofar as an institution is subject to public opinion, it will carry on propaganda. If an institution has a solid place in the traditions of society, and if its functionaries are accepted as having authority, they can speak dogmatically to those who believe in that authority. In our society, many institutions lack traditional authority, and even those which have it are required to meet the counterpropaganda of conflicting forces. Propaganda is, in its essence, an attempt to get people to think and act as the propagandist would like them to.

Propaganda by secular institutions is not, as a rule, designed to change the popular conceptions of social welfare. It attempts rather to establish an association between the institution and existing values. Thus in our society, propaganda will generally make use of the terms *liberty* and *democracy* and, recently, of the term *social security*.

Propaganda must, however, go much further than mere association with accepted ideas. The functionaries have policies to carry out, and they must win support for them. So they must and do attempt to define the interests of the public. For instance, when chain stores are taxed with being inimical to the interests of small business, they respond by telling the public that in addition to their low prices they benefit society by employing many people. Even the churches, whose association with the mores is solid enough, engage in propaganda to show the value of specific programs of action and to convey to a somewhat indifferent world the conviction that the church promotes public welfare as currently conceived.

In a world so free and changing as ours, the ultimate problem of most institutions is that of maintaining the active good will of the public. Sumner went so far as to state that the aim of most modern institutions is to please the common man. In their efforts to do so, the functionaries of certain types of institutions, not too well grounded in the mores, have become expert in gauging and exploiting the mood of the public. Especially must those institutions which live by annual public appeals for funds, continually court good will. Thus, a social agency can by no means rely on a general sentiment in favor of charity; it has annually to prove to the public that the agency is the proper instrument to perform charity, that it knows how it ought to be done, and that the general obligation of persons to help the needy is specifically an obligation to give money at once to this agency. The constant and conscious effort of a great many organized forces to keep the active good will of people gives our society an air of always changing its opinions. This fact means not that we lack mores, but only that the institutions which carry on the organized life of our society are in a state of flux.

Part Four

—

Race and Culture

By

EDWARD B. REUTER
Late of Fisk University

CHAPTER EIGHTEEN

THE RELATIONS BETWEEN RACE AND CULTURE

Race and culture are in separate orders of reality: one is biological, the other is social. Genuine understanding of race and culture, therefore, depends upon clear comprehension of the distinction between biological and social processes, and of the interrelations among these processes in concrete reality.

ORGANIC AND CULTURAL VARIABILITY

Uniformity and Stability. In the racial character and cultural organization of human beings there is a high degree of uniformity and stability. All individuals are alike in original nature in that each embodies the same complex of physical, mental, and temperamental traits; the individuals of each generation are like those of each preceding one. In its fundamental aspects, the culture of every group is like that of every other group. Human nature, a product of primary group relations, is a common characteristic of mankind.

Along with uniformity and stability in racial character and cultural organization, there are also wide and important differences, as well as variation and change, in original characters and social traits. On the side of original nature, the three major independent variations are sex, race, and individual differences; in the social realm, variations may be classed as personal and cultural.

Organic Variability. In the organic realm, individual variability is continuous within the limitations of the species. Individuals of the same species vary from one another in height, weight, stature, and all other physical characters, but the fluctuations are always within a narrow range and cluster about a median point. Such differences are variations of the kind that may be produced by combinations of traits that vary quantitatively. In mental ability the range of variation is somewhat wide between the dullards and the men of talent, but intelligence is of the same quality in all; the differences are matters of degree. The range in temperament is probably as wide as in physique and mentality.

Cultural Variability. The range of variability is greater in the cultural than in the organic realm. The only limits in the former are those set by the physical structure of the organism, which makes impossible various types of life and behavior, and the nature of the material with which man must work. There are wide differences among peoples in their arts, techniques, and material culture; the differences are still greater in language, systems of thought, law, government, social organization, sentiments and attitudes, standards, and other elements of an immaterial nature.

INDEPENDENCE OF CONCEPTS

The Racial and Cultural Processes. It is essential to clarity of thought that the racial and cultural phenomena and processes be conceived as lying on different planes of reality. They are of independent origin, involve unlike mechanisms of transmission, and function to separate ends.

Race a Physical Concept. Races are products of the biological processes. The term *race* refers to a variety of mankind composed of individuals of common descent, a group with heritable traits sufficiently pronounced to set it apart from other human subdivisions. Races are indefinitely interfertile and intergrade with others of the same species.

A race arises as a single abrupt step or a series of sudden steps. Its origin is in a mutation, a biological accident, that produces an individual with transmissible physical structures new to the species. These characters are transmitted through the germ plasm and reappear unchanged in successive generations. The race thus begun may undergo change only by selective substitution in the process of biological adaptation. The whole genetic process culminates in the production of a biological individual: the origin is in mutation; the method of change is selection; the medium of transmission is the germ plasm; the mechanism is the chromosomes; the content is integrated structures; and the end result is a biological organism.

Culture a Social Concept. Culture is an outcome of social experience. It refers to the sum and organization of human invention and discovery, to the accumulated results of human effort. It includes the great variety of tools and other artifacts evolved during man's continued efforts to satisfy his needs; the subsidiary complex of sentiments and attitudes; the institutional structures and other control techniques operating to perpetuate the social order and make general the approved types of behavior; and the bodies of philosophical explanations of the world which help to make life intelligible and existence, in a measure, tolerable.

The culture process is thus separate from and contrasted at every point with the racial process. From small beginnings, culture grows through additions; it develops and changes through the incorporation of new items and the modification of the old practices, during use and transmission. Culture is transmitted through social contact and communication. Its origin is in human discovery and invention, its manner of growth is accumulation, its medium is communication, its mechanism is imitation and inculcation, its content is patterns of behavior, and its end results are types of personality and bodies of interrelated belief and practice.

INTERDEPENDENCE OF CONCRETE REALITY

Relationship between Racial and Social Processes. The racial and social processes are distinct and relatively independent and it is necessary to analyze each process apart from the concrete reality by means of which it gets expression. But at certain points they come together and interact, or operate simultaneously, to the same or different ends. It is necessary, therefore, to consider the relationships of the processes conceptually abstracted.

On a common-sense level, racial and cultural phenomena are coexistent, intimately interrelated, and mutually conditioned. Race facts are culturally defined and racial changes are brought about by social factors; on the other hand, culture facts are always observed as the possession of concrete racial groups.

There is, however, more than this superficial order of interdependency. The processes are not separated in concrete reality.

The human being has a dual inheritance: a complement of appetites and capacities characteristic of the organism transmitted biologically, and a body of habits resulting from present and past associated life.

Race as Conditioned by Culture. The individual is a biological unit whose nature is determined by the organic hereditary processes. But he comes at birth into a social environment, lives an associative life, and acquires a heritage and a personality as a result of interaction with other human beings. The subsequent working of the biological process is conditioned and controlled by the culture into which he is born and by the fact of associative life. The manner in which biological facts emerge from and are controlled by cultural facts may be shown by a simple example.

Domestication is a biological process. It is an alteration, by selective survival, of the native endowment of a race. The process presupposes heritable differences among individuals and a selective birth- or mortality-rate. The change resulting from individual differences and varying rates of birth or mortality is strictly biological. But the selection of survivors may be consciously controlled, be deliberate and purposeful, as in the case of political measures designed to reduce the number of feebleminded persons in a population. Here, a purely social fact controls the biological process, and domestication becomes as much a historical as a biological matter.

Similar control and direction of biological phenomena by social and cultural facts exist generally. The social and cultural facts fix the conditions of survival and so determine the direction and result of organic processes. Births and deaths are organic facts but their incidence is determined by cultural conditions. War is a social phenomenon that leads to racial transformation and decline. Slavery is a form of social organization determined by economic conditions but it leads directly to racial consequences. Marriage customs have direct and obvious racial consequences. Commerce and international trade are cultural phenomena, but they have racial consequences in the biological amalgamation of diverse stocks.

A low order of mentality is a biological fact. The social exclusion and the consequent association of the mentally deficient, and the appearance among them of characteristic folkways and divergent behavior patterns are purely cultural phenomena. But these cultural phenomena determine their marriage contacts which in turn determine racial phenomena.

Culture as Conditioned by Race. Certain biological facts bear a constant relation to cultural phenomena. The capacity of individuals determines the level of the human nature and culture that may be acquired and transmitted from one generation to the next; by controlling the level of individual achievement, the original equipment of human beings at birth controls the culture and social organization.

Sex, for example, is a biological fact probably without direct cultural connotation. But sex is an obvious basis for social organization and for the restriction and exclusion of individuals. In this way, sex gives rise to a wide range of subsidiary cultural phenomena.

Blindness is a physical or biological fact. But this fact limits the number and determines the kind of social contacts and, consequently, sets limits to personal development and group organization. Deafness, physical defect, mental deficiency, disease, and other biological facts and conditions limit contacts, and the consequent isolation may result in distorted personalities and retarded culture.

Race phenomena and processes are biological; cultural phenomena and processes are social. They are distinct types of reality and must be understood separately if they are to be understood at all. But in concrete reality the biological and social processes exist together and each influences the other. Hence the interrelations and mutual conditioning of the processes must also be understood in order to understand behavior phenomena.

CHAPTER NINETEEN

RACES AND CULTURE GROUPS

In the human realm, race has not been a particularly fruitful category. In common usage the concept is undefined and is used loosely to designate culture groups, language groups, or even political or class divisions as well as large groups which possess distinctive appearance because of common descent.

THE CONCEPT OF RACE

The Biological Concept. The biological conception of race is that of a permanent variety of mankind composed of individuals descended from a common ancestor who diverged, by mutation, from the previously existing racial type. A race is a division inferior to a species, yet possessed of constant transmissible traits sufficiently pronounced to characterize it as a distinct type. The distinguishing marks are of less constant character and of less biological significance than the traits which divide animals into species.

Few human groups meet these biological specifications necessary to form a distinct race. Human contacts throughout the human era have been such that racial groups when formed have not been long continued. In the modern world there are no clear-cut divisions, no human groups that meet the requirements of reasonably rigid biological definition. Local groups of remote districts are readily distinguishable but they are everywhere surrounded by scarcely distinguishable variants, and the remote local groups are united by various intermediate forms.

Hypothetical Races. Because of the biological impurity of the various existing racial stocks, the problem of classification is sometimes conceived as one of determining the original races from which the existing groups were produced by intermixture.

This is a problem of determining the ancestors from the heritable traits present in the mixed stock of the present day. The term *race* then refers not to existing concrete groups but to hypothetical constructs sharply divorced from tangible reality. The problems thus presented are important but they are purely speculative and aside from the present discussion.

Concrete Racial Groups. It is immediately obvious that no valid classification in biological terms of modern racial groups is possible. There are no sharp and stable lines of demarcation. Within any major group there are wide variations in stature, head form, pigmentation, facial angle, body proportions, and other physical characters. Individuals may be classified with any one of these as a criterion but, since there is no constant relation among the various physical traits, classification made with one as a criterion will not correspond to classification made on the basis of any other.

Biological traits are marks of individual organisms; biological facts are individual phenomena. A concrete race is a grouping of individuals having the same combination of heritable traits. But each individual in the modern world represents a mixture of traits, hence is not classifiable in any rigidly defined set of racial categories.

Race as a Statistical Concept. Because each individual differs from every other, there is no limit to the number of subtypes that may be set up in any large group. They may be classified according to any physical trait or any combination of physical traits. Since there is an indefinite overlapping of traits, there are as many races as one may desire to set up. Classifications are based on varying characters and there is no generally accepted system.

In this sense race is merely a statistical concept, and not a reality; there is no individual that conforms to type. Race is a statistical abstraction, an idealized set of characters, derived from the concrete, complex reality.

Races as Culturally Defined Groups. In sociological usage a race is a physical subtype of cultural formation. The biological origins and affiliations are relatively unimportant. It is a group with more or less permanent distinguishing characters to which the persons concerned, the members themselves or the members of outside groups, attach certain interpretations. The physical marks are meaningful only as a basis of identification that permits a type of cohesion.

RACE DIFFERENCES

Shared and Heritable Traits. However defined, the term *race* directs attention to the physical and biological aspects of man that are heritable in character and common to the members of a group.

Physical Characters. The individual variations among human beings in stature, body weight, skin color, and other biologically determined traits are within a very narrow range. Such differences, in all cases, are quantitative; they are differences in degree, not in kind.

Between concrete racial groups, however defined, the physical differences are less than the individual differences within a single racial group. The racial characters are averages of individuals comprising the group. The differences among such averages from one group to another are relatively slight. There is much overlapping. In pigmentation, for example, certain individuals of a dark race are of lighter complexion than many individuals of the lighter race.

The differences in physical characters seem in all cases to be biologically unimportant. It is not possible to show, for example, that the kinky hair, everted lips, long forearm, highly pigmented skin, and other physical traits of the Negro peoples, or the contrasted traits of the North European groups, are either good or bad.

The common idea that certain races or peoples are superior to others in some important traits is undemonstrated and appears to be without foundation. Such differences as exist are individual differences. Persons of keen senses and persons with defective senses are common in all groups. It may very well be that at a given time the percentages vary from one racial group to another. But the differences between groups as such, if and when shown to exist, are matters of statistical distribution; they are not racial traits.

Mental Characters. The members of each racial group have the same equipment of psychological characters. Perception, memory, the ability to form abstract conceptions, the capacity to inhibit impulses, and the other main mental characters of human beings appear to be the same in all racial groups. No qualitative differences, in the sense that some have mental capacities that others lack, have ever been shown to exist.

Such differences as may be observed are individual differences. Differences between and among groups are merely statistical averages; there are individuals of various degrees of mental ability in every group. If one racial group is mentally superior to another it is only in the sense of chance distribution. At a particular time one group may contain more superior individuals or fewer mentally incompetent individuals than another. That one group is able to produce a surplus of superior men each generation is conceivable, but neither historical nor biological evidence supports this theory.

The tendency to speak of superior and inferior races appears to do violence to the fact that these are concepts about individuals; applied to races or groups, such terms are either meaningless or carry a different, a merely statistical, connotation. It seems to be only in a statistical sense that one racial group may be said to be superior to another in mental capacity; there is apparently no racial group with any mental deficiency that would prevent cultural advance comparable with that of any other group.

Psychological Tests and Racial Differences. The crude findings of the early psychological tests showed marked differences among racial groups. Superficial interpretation, premature publication, and journalistic exploitation of such findings popularized the idea, in line with common prejudices and class biases, that gross racial differences exist in mentality.

But the results of the psychological tests, when adequately interpreted and competently understood, do not reflect group differences attributable to a racial factor. The tests in vogue are standardized on the basis of Anglo-Saxon and urban experience and education, hence they show differences in groups to the extent of differences in social experience and tradition. Differences in showings made on the tests are to be attributed to variations in the social heritage. That race is merely a chance element is shown by the fact that in the Army Tests the Negroes of certain Nothern states ranked above the whites of certain Southern states.

The measures of individual intelligence ratings, if granted to be valid, do not give the rating of a race. It is not possible to arrive at the qualities of a race by the addition of individual qualities or by taking an average of individual qualities. Differences between race groups exist as the tests show, but the tests do not show the differences to be attributable to race, if by race is meant the biological make-up apart from social experience.

THE SOCIOLOGICAL SIGNIFICANCE OF RACE

The Independence of Cultural Capacity. The physical differences among racial groups are slight and biologically unimportant. It has not been shown that the traits used by anthropologists in their classifications bears any constant relation to cultural capacity; mental differences among the racial groups have not been demonstrated.

The Isolating Effects of Race. The physical and visible marks of race are of great social and cultural significance. They differentiate between groups of people, and they condition contact and interaction by operating as barriers to communication across the group lines.

Visible marks of race are convenient criteria for classifications; they automatically assign individuals to categories. To the extent that these categories are social and cultural as well as physical, such classification defines personal experience, and conditions and limits participation in social life.

The cultural phenomena, caused by the fact that racial marks are treated as social values, are in no sense biological. They are not the result of race differences directly; they are the result of social attitudes directed toward the physical facts. The taboos and sanctions, not the biological facts, prevent full participation and achievement.

Race Marks as Social Values. Social attitudes may arise toward physical and biological traits. Each isolated racial group, and provincial men of all racial groups, look upon their own type as the only fully human form and tend to fear or despise men of other races. There is a vague, undefined fear of the strange, a spontaneous negative reaction from the unusual. This antipathy, an organic reaction largely below the conscious level, is a basis for negative attitudes towards individuals and groups of individuals who possess an outward appearance, food habits, moral customs, social beliefs, or behavior that differs from those familiar to the group.

In practically all places in the modern world the conspicuous marks of race, particularly skin color, are made the object of favorable or unfavorable estimation. They are the basis for differential treatment and for social and cultural exclusion.

Isolation and Retardation. The immediate effect of isolation, regardless of the conditions that induce it, is to prevent personal development and to retard the cultural advance of the excluded people. It narrows the range of contact and communication and makes difficult the meeting and association of men on the plane of equality and self-respect.

The relative slowness of change in primitive groups is due to the paucity of stimulating contacts, the lack of access to ideas current elsewhere, brought about by the fact of physical separation. The relative retardation of excluded individuals and groups —the Negroes, the working-class groups, and others within larger culture areas—is due to a similar narrowing of contacts brought about by social restrictions.

Group Solidarity. Individuals and groups excluded because of race and divergent appearance, whether it be by means of unformulated common understanding or by a legislative fiat of the ruling class, fraternize and develop a distinctive type of mind. The special environment inculcates a similarity of habits, manners, interests, beliefs, and traditions that facilitates contact and communication within the group and retards communication with other groups. The excluded individuals develop a distinctive folklore, and distinctive social and cultural traits.

This distinctive culture complex helps to augment the isolation of the group and to increase its internal cohesion. The traits peculiar to the group become the objects of ridicule and other types of persecution. Unable to discard them and gain membership in the dominant group, individuals strive for self-respect by exalting the qualities in which they differ. These marks thus become things of importance, emotionally charged symbols of group unity, that are defended with sectarian zeal. The new peculiarities lead to further exclusion and so to greater unity.

THE MIXTURE OF RACIAL GROUPS

The Process of Intermixture. The mixture of ethnic stocks is one of the uniform consequences of contacts among peoples. In all places where divergent peoples have come into contact for a period of time they have produced a hybrid offspring. The intermixture may be by way of formal intermarriage, sometimes by way of more casual, informal, and unsanctioned unions. If the association of the groups be long continued, the lines of demarcation disappear; one or the other or both of the originally divergent peoples are lost in the resulting mixed population.

The mixture of races has been in process throughout most of the human era. Its early incidence is indicated by the fact that many of the fossil remains of prehistoric man show that the individuals were descended from ancestors of different racial stocks, and the mixing of blood has continued in every area of contact to the present time.

Attitudes toward Racial Intermixture. The attitudes toward racial mixture vary from approval, through indifference or even apparent unawareness that race mixture is in process, to violent opposition that expresses itself in prohibitory legislation and mob violence. In the former situation the intermixture normally goes on by means of marriage forms that are conventional in the particular area. In the latter case intermarriage is rare, and contact and intermixture are for the most part outside of the marriage institution. The attitudes of approval and disapproval change the social aspects of the phenomenon; they apparently have no appreciable effect on miscegenation itself.

Every area of race contact is a particular historic situation characterized by unique economic and political conditions, and the racial attitudes in any area must be understood in terms of the historic development of the economic and political order.

Approval and Encouragement of Intermixture. When the social stocks are somewhat closely related and not strongly contrasted in physical type or culture, as are the various immigrant peoples of the American population, intermarriage commonly attracts little attention and arouses little opposition. It is often looked upon with positive approval, as an indication that the newcomers are being fully incorporated into the national group.

In certain areas and at certain times, marriage of European colonists or settlers into the native populations has been encouraged as a means of incorporating the natives into the existing culture, and of maintaining friendly relations with the native people.

The French in Canada manifested little antagonism toward the American Indians. They mingled freely with the Algonquin tribes, both on the coast and in the interior. Intermarriage was encouraged by the officials and by the Catholic missionaries.

Mixed marriages were numerous and a relatively large French-Indian population established a bond between the races.

In the Spanish colonies, for the most part, friendly relations were never established between the races; the conquerors were interested primarily in exploiting the area and the people. But there was a paucity of white women, and racial intermixture continued throughout the era without official or moral opposition. Intermixture was so extensive that it became the outstanding phenomenon of race contacts in Spanish America.

Popular Opposition. In other areas of contact, the mixture of races arouses more or less violent opposition. This is frequently the case where the physical and cultural differences between the races in contact are wide and obvious. But the explanation lies in the social relations rather than in the physical contrasts.

In colonial and settlement areas, opposition to miscegenation typically arises only after the introduction of white women.

The desire of the white women to keep a monopoly on the sex activities of the white men is frequently reinforced by the activities of the missionaries. The conditions of miscegenation violate the formal standards of the missionaries—which standards they are concerned to propagate—and arouse their violent and active condemnation.

Intermixture tends to break down the caste relations between groups. It thus generates opposition from two sources: the disturbance of the caste pattern of accommodation (the division into independent castes) arouses emotional resentment, and the control of the economically and politically dominant group is put into jeopardy by the weakening of the pattern.

For these or other reasons, opposition to racial intermixture may arise in areas in which the early attitudes were tolerant or positively favorable. Efforts to prevent miscegenation vary, according to the political exigencies of the situation, from the formally unacknowledged inculcation of caste prejudice, as in present-day Hawaii, to formal and legal as well as mob procedures, as in the Southern states of America.

Cultural Effects of Race Mixture. In popular and propagandist literature, great cultural importance is frequently attributed to race mixture.

The intermixture of races has often been associated with cultural phenomena of great human moment. The amalgamation of divergent racial strains seems everywhere to have preceded, accompanied, or followed profound changes in culture and social organization. The historic facts have been variously interpreted: in one view, it has been cited as a cause of cultural progress; in another, it has been cited in explanation of cultural decadence.

Either position involves a misconception of the relation between biological and cultural phenomena; the two do not stand in a causal relation to each other. The actual relation between race mixture and cultural phenomena is discussed in a later paragraph.

Biological Effects of Race Mixture. So far as the biological evidence goes, neither in-marriage nor out-marriage has any beneficial or injurious effects. The traits of individuals are determined by the genetic factors received from the immediate ancestry. The transmissible traits reappear in the offspring without regard to whether the parents are of the same or different racial strains. The marriage of closely related persons makes more likely the appearance in offspring of recessive traits; cross-mating decreases the likelihood that such traits will reappear. This, however, is a matter that has to do with the heritable traits of the parents; it is not a question of whether they belong to the same or different racial strains. Neither endogamous nor exogamous mating is able to produce any traits in the offspring that are not expressed or latent in the individual ancestry. Racial intermarriage, on the basis of the biological evidence from animal breeding as well as on the evidence from human marriage, is a matter of biological indifference.

Social Effects of Race Mixture. The immediate social effects of race mixture are to bring the races closer together in sympathy and understanding and to facilitate the process of assimilation.

The effect of biracial ancestry on individual status and personality depends upon the attitude people take toward racial intermixture. The fact of biracial origin makes the individual conspicuous and, where intermarriage is forbidden, self-conscious. The role and status of mixed bloods are stated in a later chapter.

RACIAL DETERMINISM

The Doctrine of Racial Determinism. The doctrine of racial determinism holds that the culture differences among population groups are expressions of innate factors. The racial, that is, biological, differences determine the possibilities of cultural advance;

because of the biological differences, an advanced culture is possible for some groups but is not possible for others.

Culture as a Function of Race. The doctrine of racial determinism errs in making culture a function of race. The culture differences that have existed for many centuries between the Negroids, Mongoloids, and Caucasoids are advanced as proof of the existence in racial groups of a determining factor other than diversity of historic experience.

In some cases the physical differences are posited as the foundation of the culture differences; the culturally backward peoples are believed to be more closely akin to the anthropoid apes than are the European stocks. But a greater similarity of the culturally backward peoples to the apes cannot be demonstrated and, if it could, it would justify no inference in regard to social qualities and mental abilities. The fact of physical resemblance demonstrates only the fact of physical resemblance. There is no known correlation between specific physical and mental qualities in the individual and so none in the race, which, in this respect, is simply a totality of individuals.

In some cases there is a direct assumption of mental inferiority. But the various attempts to discover racial differences in innate mental constitution have been uniformly unsuccessful.

It is the social background and the culture heritage that determine a race's status. Races have not lived in the same world and have not had the same experiences and opportunities. Hence their accomplishments cannot be attributed solely to innate characters, and cannot be attributed to race at all until the differences in opportunities and experiences have been equated. Culture is only casually associated with race, and such association as exists must be understood in historical terms.

Race Change and Culture Continuity. A culture has a high degree of continuity, a tendency to resist change and to change but slowly unless it be profoundly disorganized. This stability remains in the presence of heterogeneous biological changes of type. Heterogeneous types may be carriers of homogeneous cultures: all of western, central, and eastern Europe represents a general homogeneity of culture but a heterogeneity of racial type. In a smaller area, such as France or the United States, the same fact is yet more obvious.

The same is true of the various elements of culture that migrate separately. The English language, for example, persists in spite of the fact that it is used and transmitted by a large percentage of the people of the world and by the most diverse racial types.

Culture Change and Racial Stability. The converse is likewise true: homogeneity of biological type may go with heterogeneity of culture. This fact may be illustrated from almost any area of the modern world. The aborigines of the new world are fairly homogeneous as to racial type. But the culture differences as one goes from the Aztec to the Eskimo are as great as those between the African and the Eskimo or the African and the ancient Greek.

The specific racial type appears to be only a chance carrier of specific cultures. The language, technology, and other culture facts carried by a group are matters of historic accident. The change in culture of the American and the African branches of the Negro racial group is historical. Biologically the groups are the same; culturally they are different. The innate characters of the North European peoples are not essentially different today from those of 2,000 years ago, but the cultures are radically different.

RACIAL DOCTRINES

The Nature of Racial Doctrines. Racial doctrines are very numerous and very diverse, and they are held with the greatest of emotional certitude. These doctrines are to be understood as in part rationalizations of folk beliefs and in part as constructions of utilitarian origin.

Primitive Ethnocentrism. Most uncivilized peoples apply to themselves terms meaning men; for others they have less exalted terms. These are usually not rationalized; they are merely direct observation and report of differences between themselves and others unlike them. Sometimes the differences are accounted for by myths indicating the special favor of some deity.

In much of the current literature the same ethnocentric feeling appears and the same order of rationalization, with the exception that the rationalization is likely to run in terms of science rather than of deities. The superiority of the white man is accepted; the discussion revolves about the relative superiority of the branches of the white race, about the degree of inferiority of the other groups, or about the cause and explanation of the white man's superiority.

Political Constructs. In many cases the racial doctrines have been invented and propagated in the interests of some group or party. Count Arthur Gobineau, for example, produced his work to support the class and theological biases. In the preface to his work on racial inequality he points out that his theory was fabricated in support of certain clerical and social views, deliberately constructed as a tool to combat the "theorists of subversion" and the "eccentric liberalism" of his day and thereby uphold biblical revelation and the status and rights of the aristocratic caste. In spite of this frank and more or less naïve admission, the doctrine had a wide vogue; it was in line with the prejudices of the audience to which he spoke.

A great part of the more modern racial doctrines has been built up, consciously or naïvely, in the modern struggle against democracy. The whole eugenic doctrine, for example, unknown to most of its expounders and converts, is an aspect of race biology and a powerful antidemocratic tool. The mental tests, and this result was not anticipated by most of the practitioners, are valuable political tools for race control. The correlation of race with intelligence quotient was an inference elicited from the assumption of race superiority and inferiority, not the reverse.

CHAPTER TWENTY

CULTURE

No human group lives in a state of nature. Each group has a more or less elaborate and integrated social heritage, received from the ancestors and transmitted to the descendants. This heritage maintains the spatial and temporal solidarity of the group. Each new generation lives in and by the cultural remains of the earlier generations. The social heritage accounts for human nature and for its relatively unchanging character. Culture, which is coextensive with human life, is both a cause and an effect of the qualities that make life human.

THE CONCEPT OF CULTURE

Meaning of the Term. The term *culture* is used to signify the sum total of human creations, the organized result of group experience up to the present time. Culture includes all that man has made in the form of tools, weapons, shelter, and other material goods and processes, all that he has elaborated in the way of attitudes and beliefs, ideas and judgments, codes and institutions, arts and sciences, philosophy and social organization. Culture also includes the interrelations among these and other aspects of human as distinct from animal life. Everything, material and immaterial, created by man, in the process of living, comes within the concept of culture.

The Social Nature of Culture. No part of culture is inborn. It is a deposit from the activities of men as they endeavor to control reality for the satisfaction of their wishes. The members of each generation receive the cultural heritage from preceding generations and adapt themselves to it just as they do to climate and the other aspects of the physical environment. They use their inherited culture, add to it, and pass it on to their descendants. In an ultimate sense it exists only in men—in the habits, interests, and ideas of the members of the group. But it has a history of its own apart from any particular individual or group that receives, possesses, and transmits it. Culture may be treated as a reality independent of its present possessors. Language, for example, has objective reality as do religious dogmas, scientific theories, and law. Any given generation is a recipient and carrier. But the possession of the culture is a prerequisite to its transmission. It is not passed on in a merely physical sense; it becomes part of the life organization of each person who becomes a member of the group.

The Diversity of Culture Forms. Culture is characterized by its diversity; it takes a myriad of forms. The material devices and the idea systems vary from group to group; each people has its body of thought and custom, its characteristic way of life. Each culture goes its own way, persists in its own peculiar mode of life. The recorded differences between racial groups are often little more, sometimes nothing more, than culture differences. Each group is absorbed in its own culture; its thought and behavior are determined by the traditional materials. By the culture of a group, as distinct from culture in general, is meant the mode of life of the people. These culture differences among groups are in no way due to psychological and biological differences among peoples; they are caused entirely by external forces. They are the cause rather than the effect of racial differences.

Culture Diversity and Understanding. Culture is both an integrating and a segregating factor in human life and association. It makes for easy understanding and mutual appreciation among those who share the same heritage; it makes understanding difficult and appreciation rare among peoples of diverse heritages. A common language is necessary to communication. But even with a common language, the degree of understanding is limited except when there is a common background of belief, interest, and sentiment, a background that comes from participation in a common life.

The savage does not understand the white man; in the nature of the case he cannot do so. To understand the white man he must understand the white man's culture, or some considerable part of it. The converse is equally true: the white man does not understand the savage; he does not, in general, understand anything outside his own culture complex.

The same thing is true, in somewhat lesser degree, of men with closely related cultures as, for example, the people of two European states. A considerable lack of fundamental understanding exists between individuals and classes, such as an aristocracy and a peasantry, who possess different parts of a common culture. No individual possesses the whole of a complex culture. The particular part he possesses depends upon his social status and contacts. Thus, two individuals of the same culture may have in common only a few general elements, such as the supernatural beliefs, moral sentiments, and ethical ideas.

THE ORIGIN OF CULTURE

Culture as a Factor of Associative Life. The beginning of new culture facts at any given time or place is the result either of invention or of contact with and learning from other peoples; the culture facts are either created within the group or learned from outsiders. No part of the culture is inborn; no part is acquired or transmitted by way of the germinal inheritance. Culture originates from associative life and is elaborated in response to human need.

Invention. All culture facts begin as inventions. This is true regardless of the kind of achievement; ideas, types of behavior, and forms of social organization are as truly inventions as are the material devices. The new facts, produced in reaction to the previously existing situation, serve some definite immediate need, are added to the already existing body of culture, increasing its complexity, and are handed down to the following generations. The automobile, for example, in part replaces the horse; in part, it exists alongside. The living culture is therefore constantly changing and increasing in volume and complexity through the addition of new items.

The similarity of needs and the similarity of minds lead to the similarity of inventions in diverse areas. The bow and arrow, the invention of fire, the domestication of animals, and the fabrication of flood stories are illustrations of inventions independently created in different times and places.

In many cases inventions are in the nature of accidents—chance combinations of factors producing something new. In other cases failure or imperfection in transmission may produce a deviation that is in reality a new fact; the development of dialects through errors in speaking and the transmission of the errors are cases in point. Again, invention may come as an undesigned result of other activity; the domestication of animals, for example, which is one of the great inventions of the world, was probably an unforeseen outgrowth of the keeping of animal pets.

Where invention is something more than chance or accident, it is a personal achievement, usually of a superior mind; it involves the imaginative picturing of a group of relations before the relations have objective existence. An invention is a product of reflection leading to a new synthesis of elements. In the modern world invention is closely interwoven with science, and most of the modern contrivances are evolved; the steam engine, for example, is a combination of various minor, independently invented elements.

Borrowing. Once invented, culture facts spread: it is easier to copy and use things than to invent them. Within a particular group, so far as that group is concerned, culture comes chiefly from outside sources; wherever there is communication inventions spread. The spread may be in one direction; for example, the primitive group may have little to give but much to learn from the civilized group.

But there is always selection: only those things are accepted from the outside culture for which there is obvious need and which can be adjusted to the culture and the social patterns. The simple people readily accept the metal implements of the civilized group because of their obvious superiority to stone and bone tools, but in the realm of social organization and idea systems innovations are resisted and change is slow.

The Individual and the Group. In the last analysis all invention comes from individuals. Whether it be a word, an idea, an institutional detail, or a mechanical device, it originates as an individual expression. The group, as a group, never invents anything. Even in the case of such things as folk songs, which are frequently assumed to be of group origin, the inventor is a person; the illusion that they are group creations is due to the short interval of time between the invention and the group use.

The group performs two important functions in the culture invention. It provides the conditions conducive to the functioning of creative minds. In the case of a folk song, for example, the group gives the situation and the mental condition necessary to such creation. The act of invention is always related to the culture base: the innovating individual utilizes the existing culture facts and reshapes certain details into new combinations. It is in no case possible to go much beyond the culture base. The group furnishes the existing culture and gives the talented individual an opportunity to make a new contribution.

In addition to providing the cultural conditions in which the inventor works, the group performs a second essential function in the process of culture growth: it utilizes the inventions made, and preserves and transmits them to succeeding generations.

The Persistence of Culture Forms. A prime characteristic of culture is that it persists: most of the culture elements are passed on from generation to generation. Material objects outlive their creators and users. The habits determined by these objects or formed in response to the situation likewise persist and tend to reproduce the physical molds.

THE CONTENT OF CULTURE

Human Attitudes and Values. From the point of view of content, culture may be variously broken down into more or less complex subdivisions. Ultimate analysis of culture brings us to the examination of human attitudes and values, since it is these, in their various combinations and permutations, that constitute culture.

A common superficial distinction is often made between the material and the nonmaterial aspects of culture. The classification is not particularly helpful since it represents a somewhat arbitrary separation; external forms and material objects are in large measure meaningless when separated from the appropriate body of ideas and subjective reality.

A Classification of Culture Facts. According to one analysis, all the culture facts of any people are comprehended in nine fundamental divisions.[1]

  a. Speech
    Languages, writing systems, etc.
  b. Material Traits
    (1) Food habits
    (2) Shelter

---

1 Clark Wissler, *Man and Culture* (New York: T. Y. Crowell Co., 1923), p. 74.

   (3) Transportation and travel
   (4) Dress
   (5) Utensils, tools, etc.
   (6) Weapons
   (7) Occupations and industries
 c. Art
    Carving, painting, drawing, music, etc.
 d. Mythology and Scientific Knowledge
 e. Religious Practices
   (1) Ritualistic forms
   (2) Treatment of the sick
   (3) Treatment of the dead
 f. Family and Social Systems
   (1) The forms of marriage
   (2) Methods of reckoning relationship
   (3) Inheritance
   (4) Social control
   (5) Sports and games
 g. Property
   (1) Real and personal
   (2) Standards of value and exchange
   (3) Trade
 h. Government
   (1) Political forms
   (2) Judicial and legal procedures
 i. War

An Alternative Classification. Another classification divides culture into three categories: the *inductive*, the *aesthetic*, and the *control*.

INDUCTIVE. In the first category are included all bodies of knowledge that are inductively derived and all devices that are tested by practice or experience. Specifically, it includes such material objects as tools, machines, and various utilitarian objects; and such nonmaterial things as crafts, skills, techniques, logic, and scientific knowledge and method.

AESTHETIC. The second category consists of such material objects as works of art and the symbols and vestments of ritual; and such nonmaterial things as forms of recreation, the conventions of social intercourse, and aesthetic aspects of the fine arts.

CONTROL. The third category contains all those things that exercise a control influence on the group members. This category includes such material things as patriotic emblems, the insignia of authority, and other coercive objects or symbols; and such nonmaterial things as usages, moral standards, religious sanctions, and laws.[1]

The Types of Culture Content. The most obvious aspects of culture are the material parts, such as the tools, buildings, and utensils, used in the control of the external environment. Such aspects are form and space relations unlike those of nature; they are human rearrangements of matter. It is largely through the preservation of these external products of human activity that something of the nature of past cultures may be known.

A second distinguishable aspect of culture is the body of behavior patterns—habits, activities, and skills—of the people who produce and use the material objects. This habit system is to be understood as a product of the total culture complex and at the same time as a powerful factor in its perpetuation and elaboration.

Mental patterns are as real and as definitely a part of culture as are the material artifacts and the behavior patterns. The body of sentiments and attitudes, the type of mind, is determined by the culture and in turn reflects it. The human values—cleanliness, music, children, poetry, diamonds, nudity, and so on, and the attitudes toward them, derive from the culture rather than from original nature.

The social organization and institutional structures constitute a fourth aspect of culture. The relations to authority, laws of property, and family relationships are typical of this part of culture.

The symbolic elements of culture include all the nonmaterial tools that give control over the world of reality. Here are included language, graphic representation, mathematics, and other means of representing the outside world.

The organization of thought constitutes a final aspect of culture. This includes the whole body of science and philosophy as well as the beliefs of religion and magic.

---

1 James W. Woodard, "A New Classification of Culture," *American Sociological Review* (1936), 1:89–102, and "The Role of Fictions in Cultural Organization," *Transactions of the New York Academy of Sciences* (1944), Series II, 6:311–344.

THE CONDITIONING EFFECTS OF CULTURE

Stability and Persistence. The culture of a group, its mode of life, is perhaps more stable and persistent than its physical and racial character. The biological traits, as a result of selective birth- and death-rates or migration and intermixture, may undergo profound change in a relatively few generations. But the body of culture fact, in the absence of catastrophic phenomena, persists through successive generations with little alteration in fundamental character.

The Inflexibility of Culture Forms. The enduring nature of culture comes in part from the material persistence of the objective elements. Buildings, roads, books, machines, and like facts of relatively permanent character resist change and operate as facts of the geographic environment by setting a mold to which conformity is obligatory. The codes and institutions have a similar, if less obvious, inflexibility and enduring character.

The Formation and Persistence of Habit Patterns. To each individual culture comes from without. The existing pattern is a mold in which the plastic child is formed; inevitably the child acquires the mode of life of the group into which he is born. In all essential human traits the person is a product of the group and its mode of life. So early and complete is the conditioning of the child that many of the reactions to the restraints of culture are frequently ascribed to organic nature.

The habit patterns learned in the life of the group make difficult the formation of new habits. Early conditioning has a modifying effect on the organic structure, gives a set that is permanent. The acquisition of one mode of speech, for example, results in a development of the physiological speech mechanism that makes impossible the formation of certain other sounds. The same is true in regard to further acquisition of ideas; the learning of one thing may make impossible the subsequent learning of others.

The Culture Set and Personal Assimilation. The persistence of habits formed and the inhibiting effect they have on the formation of other habit complexes is readily seen in the case of individuals transplanted to a new culture situation. In a new environment the old habits, sentiments, and beliefs of the immigrant persist, and complete assimilation to the new culture is generally impossible. But the child of the immigrant acquires the new culture with the same ease as the native child; in general, it is extremely difficult to prevent his acquiring it.

THE DIFFUSION OF CULTURE

The Process of Diffusion. Culture facts are not only transmitted from generation to generation but they also spread from the place of origin and become incorporated in varying degrees in the culture of near and distant peoples.

The Culture Area. As a result, the culture forms current among a people generally bear considerable resemblance to those of neighboring peoples and a less close resemblance to those of more distant peoples. Within continental or other large areas there are broad resemblances; among the major geographic divisions there are sharp contrasts. In general, the cultural similarity is greatest where communication is easiest; the differences are pronounced where communication is limited.

The Culture Center. The first appearance of a culture fact is, of course, at some definite place, within some specific human group. From the place of origin, it spreads outward in the same way as the concentric circles on a pool spread from the point of disturbance. Ideally, the invention will reach its most highly developed form at the place of origin, this being at once the place where specific need led to its emergence and where it has the longest period of development. The invention will appear in increasingly diluted and modified form as distance increases from the point of origin.

But the area of diffusion is determined by contacts which, in turn, are determined in large measure by routes of travel. In consequence, the culture area tends to coincide with the geographic area. Certain traits of Eskimo culture, for example, with the center of dispersion about Hudson Bay, extend over a relatively narrow area east to Greenland and west through Alaska to Siberia, illustrating extreme distortion of the ideal pattern.

The Rate of Diffusion. Certain culture traits either do not spread spontaneously beyond the particular tribal group, or else they spread slowly ánd with difficulty. The language spoken by a group tends to remain its exclusive possession. Each group has its own language; one language may spread only by displacing another. Since the speech of each group is adequate to its needs, there is little tendency for one to displace another. The same thing is true of the forms of political and social organization and various other culture elements and complexes.

Some facts of culture diffuse widely and rapidly. This is particularly the case of elements that have an obvious superiority over items in current use, and of elements that supplement rather than displace items at present in use. The use of tobacco is a familiar illustration of quick and general diffusion. In the modern world, scientific discoveries spread so rapidly that the place of origin is a matter of indifference.

CULTURE CHANGE

The Pace of Culture Change. So long as a culture remains a living thing, it is in a state of growth and change. The pace of change is sometimes slow, as in a small and isolated primitive group, and sometimes rapid, as in the modern machine civilization. It is only the dead culture, as that of ancient Egypt or classical Greece, that remains as it was.

The Source of Change. Changes are due to the incorporation of new facts and relations. The new may come from without, by borrowing, as the phrase goes, from other peoples with whom the group is in contact. It may come as a consequence of indigenous invention or discovery. A good deal of change is in the nature of accident rather than of invention proper; as previously mentioned, many undesigned changes come about, as in language modification, partly in consequence of imperfections in the machinery for the inculcation of traditional forms.

The Order of Change. Change is usually most marked and rapid in the material and objective aspects of culture. It proceeds less rapidly and with increasing resistance through language, social customs, institutional forms, and thought systems, to modifications of the social organization and the moral order.

The unequal pace of social change is readily understood in simple terms. The deliberate adoption of a new element depends upon its simplicity, the degree to which its superiority to elements in current use is obvious, and the sentimental or other resistance its adoption encounters.

A new and simple material fact, as a new tool, weapon, word, or other utilitarian object adapted to the needs of the folk, is readily accepted and incorporated into the existing complex. It can be accepted as a single item supplementing or displacing other similar objects in current use. It involves, therefore, a minimum of habit resistance. The comparative efficiency of the new fact is obvious or readily demonstrable. Ordinarily, there is no sentiment surrounding utilitarian objects, hence no emotional resistance to change.

Apart from material elements, the superiority of the new to the old is seldom immediately obvious. In this case the new makes its way slowly even though its superiority may be easily demonstrated. Modern medicine, based on the germ theory of disease, displaces folk practices, based on alternative theories, very slowly as compared with the prompt folk acceptance and use of the automobile. This comparison shows how new inventions having an obvious use are accepted at a speedier rate than vitally important contributions not so easily recognized as superior. Where a degree of logical thought is necessary to understand or demonstrate the superiority of one value over another, as in economic and social discovery, there is generally no displacement of the old by the new.

In many cases the new invention or discovery meets emotional resistance because its adoption would disturb the old relations or institutions about which there exists more or less of sentiment. The opposition to rational changes in family arrangements, supernatural practices, economic organization, and governmental procedures arises in part from the fact that these institutions are grounded in sentiment and tradition. It arises, also, in part, from the fact that the existing order and its parts function to the welfare of the functionaries; the self-interest of the classes supports the conservatism of sentiment.

Finally, change is slow in all those aspects of culture that may not be atomized and adopted piecemeal.

The Direction of Social Change. The direction of change is determined, in the absence of catastrophe or major invention, by the inertia of the existing complex. There is ready acceptance of new items that supplement the present arrangements and further development along established lines; there is indifference to or active rejection of inventions that involve disturbance of habitual modes of thought and action or in any way run counter to the traditions and sentiments of the moral order.

The Undesigned Nature of Culture Change. A culture is an integrated system of objects and practices expressing the sentiments, attitudes, and philosophies of man. As a consequence, the invention or introduction of any new item effects, sooner or later, some modification and reorganization throughout the system. Such changes are generally neither designed nor anticipated.

On the level of mechanical invention the results are often direct and obvious. In a simple group the invention of the bow and arrow, or the adoption of firearms introduced from without, may result in an immediate economic prosperity and an increase in military power that change not only the mode of life of the group but also that of the surrounding peoples. The invention, or more properly the development, of the automobile brought changes not only in the transportation system but also in all aspects of the culture, including the mental and moral habits of the people.

Changes consequent upon material inventions are so easily seen as to give rise to a common idea that all culture change is initiated by mechanical discoveries. But discoveries in other realms of reality may be equally significant for culture and social change; not all the major inventions are in the mechanical realm. The germ theory of disease, with the resulting revolution in the whole dependent structure of medicine, and the theory of evolution have wrought changes in the whole mode of life of the people.

CHAPTER TWENTY-ONE

RACE AND CULTURE CONTACTS

The contact and intermingling of divergent stocks result in two distinct but related types of phenomena: the biological inter-mixture of the previously separated strains, and the fusion of their culture heritages. The former breaks down whatever there may have been of racial integrity; the latter disturbs more or less profoundly the cultural equilibrium established in the preceding period of isolation. Race problems arise in the transition from one period of racial and cultural equilibrium to another.

HISTORICAL CONTACTS

Primitive Peoples. Among the simpler peoples, wanderings and migratory movements seem always to have been the rule. The search for food or adventure, flights to escape attacks by enemies, spreading to escape the impoverishing results of their own multiplication, and other facts led to extensive wanderings. So general were these movements that the traditions of nearly every people are based on the story of a migration.

The wanderings resulted in contacts with neighboring peoples whose territory was invaded. In the resulting conflicts, old groups were broken up and new ones formed from the fragments. Powerful and aggressive groups overran the territory of smaller and weaker groups, imposed themselves as ruling classes, absorbed or were absorbed by the conquered peoples.

In the course of these conflicts resulting in the destruction of old stocks and the formation of new mixtures and blends, there was a more or less constant exchange of culture facts, the stimulation of invention, and the adaptation of old facts to new environments.

The Ancient World. So far as it is possible to follow the early history of peoples, they were constantly moving about. The peoples of eastern Asia migrated into Europe; those of central and western Asia moved into southern Asia; the North European peoples overran the Mediterranean area: the Central Africans overran southern Africa; the Alaskans migrated as far at least as Mexico, and the peoples of Mexico as far as Alaska. These and other similar movements and mixtures give a picture of prehistoric movements and contacts.

The civilization of the ancient world rose from the mixing of earlier groups and cultures. Babylon had its origin in the mixture of two different national and racial elements. Greece, Rome, and practically every other historic state were, in the beginning, mixtures of more or less heterogeneous ethnic elements, and their civilizations arose out of the culture fusion.

The ancient world continued and extended the mixing of blood and the fusion of heritages that characterized the earlier peoples.

The Period of the Discoveries. The period of the discoveries increased the race contacts that had been going on for countless ages. It was a period of contacts among groups previously separated, and of contacts on a larger scale than had anywhere existed previously.

The Modern Era. In the modern world the contact and intermingling of diverse ethnic and culture groups are incomparably greater than in any previous period; the mass contacts of diverse groups and divergent cultures are an essentially modern phenomenon.

Physical science and mechanical invention laid the basis for the modern world order. On the one hand, they brought power machinery and factory production which standardized and enormously increased the production of material goods; on the other, they perfected the means of rapid communication and developed cheap, easy, and rapid means of transportation. These made inevitable the present reduction of the world to a commercial and economic unit. The parallel development of popular education undermined the traditional controls. Science thus operated directly and indirectly for the economic and intellectual liberation and mobility of the individual man. The new freedom, physical and intellectual, in the presence of marked differentials in economic opportunity in different regions, got expression in an unprecedented migration, in the association of peoples previously widely separated, and in the exclusion or absorption of weaker peoples and the repopulation of whole continents by diverse and amalgamated stocks.

There were thus wholesale and indiscriminate contacts among ethnic strains wholly dissimilar, between peoples of varied degrees of development that had lived under widely different life-conditions. The highly civilized nations of Europe suddenly came into close relations with native races of contrasted culture and in contrasted climatic zones.

CONTACTS AND RACE RELATIONS

Universal Phenomena. However much the contacts of peoples may differ with time and place, there are certain phenomena of universal incidence. Below the multiplicity of detail in the concrete reality are the same stable factors. The disintegration of the native social order, the intermixture of racial strains, the fusion of cultures, and the disorganization of individual personality organization seem to recur in all areas of race and culture contact.

In the modern world, in the absence of insuperable political barriers to geographic mobility, population flows to those areas that offer or are thought to offer more tolerable conditions of life or superior opportunities for personal success. There is always appreciable inertia; the differential between areas must be sufficient to overbalance the ties of sentiment binding the individual to his homeland, and to offset the provincial fear of the new and strange.

The racial and cultural consequences of immigration are fairly uniform and the final outcome easily predictable.

Immigration movements are commonly between countries of somewhat similar cultures and on friendly relations. The initial contacts between the immigrants and members of the established population of the area are often marked by fear and suspicion, but they are seldom overtly hostile; the early negative reactions commonly disappear as association leads to understanding and appreciation.

Almost from the beginning there are transfer and blending of the cultures. In making their accommodations to the new situation, the immigrants rapidly lose their peculiar folkways and superficially identifying cultural characteristics, and acquire the social heritage of the area through their participation in the common life.

Intermarriage generally begins early and increases with growth in cultural similarity. This process results in time in the biological absorption of the numerically subordinate group or in the formation of a mixed population. No immigrant group maintains its physical identity indefinitely and seldom does so for even a few generations.

The period of transition from the old to the new culture heritage is marked by more or less widespread personal disorganization. This accompaniment of transition declines as the conflicting heritages become harmonized in a single system of social rules.

The Contact between Divergent Groups. Different types of phenomena appear where the territory of a militaristically impotent or culturally retarded people is occupied by representatives of a colonizing nation. The initial relations are largely or wholly a function of economic and political expediency.

The objective of the intruders may be frankly and openly predatory, the intention being to occupy the territory and exploit its resources. In these circumstances there is a minimum of consideration for the claims or welfare of the native people. They are more or less ruthlessly excluded from the area, reduced to slavery if the resources to be exploited call for an acclimatized labor force, or, in the event of armed resistance, they may be destroyed. In any event, the working relations presently established assign to the weaker people a servile status and subordinate role in the area formerly theirs.

In other circumstances a crude display and use of major force, by arousing hostility and resistance, would hinder or defeat the purposes of the occupation. The immediate objective may be trade with the native population, as in the British-Indian fur trade of the American Northwest. Where the occupation is ostensibly to protect the interest of an exploited group, the tangible benefits are more likely to accrue if the relations are friendly. In such cases the attitudes of the invaders are conciliatory, at least until their position is consolidated or until the natives appreciate the underlying motives of the foreign protectors.

The ultimate outcome is clear; whether the relations are friendly or antagonistic, the native population is presently reduced to a subordinate status. This may come immediately by the exercise of superior force and the enslavement of the native people, or it may develop as the economic forces imperceptibly undermine the position of the native group.

The Class Order and Personal Accommodation. The particular type of class order that comes to prevail depends upon the temper of the exploiting group and the exigencies of the situation; the work relations imposed define the patterns of behavior possible in the situation.

Individuals of necessity accept the conditions they cannot control; they conform to the rules imposed and consciously adjust their lives on the new basis. In time, as they are conditioned through the habit mechanism to the restrictions the order imposes, the new life becomes less burdensome; there is an internal adjustment to the external conditions. Around the status, as an established fact, there gradually develops an appropriate body of interests, sentiments, and attitudes; presently it comes to be accepted by master and servant alike as in conformity with the natural order.

This process is rendered easier by the fact that the class order tends to perpetuate and exaggerate the differences on which it was originally founded. The type of life, work, and responsibility determines the external traits of dress and manner as well as the beliefs and attitudes appropriate to the station in life. Moreover, the order is rationalized, explained in such a way as to justify and perpetuate it; a mythological history is built up about it; and the established religion provides it with supernatural sanctions.

To the extent that accommodation is achieved there is a state of harmony between the classes and races; often there is a high degree of social and personal sympathy and understanding.

Once firmly established, the class order tends to perpetuate itself; both the subordinate and the superior status are taken for granted. The duties, obligations, and roles are recognized and respected. The slave not only accepts his status, but may actually take pride in it and resent any effort of his fellows to escape the status.

THE INTERMIXTURE OF THE RACES

The Effect of Continued Association. Wherever divergent groups are in contact and association for a period of time, they produce a more or less numerous hybrid progeny. There seems to be no historic exception. If the association be long continued, the lines of separation tend to disappear as one or the other of the originally divergent peoples is lost in the resulting mixed-blood population.

Similar Peoples. Where the stocks are somewhat closely related and not sharply contrasted in culture and physical type, intermarriage goes on rapidly and commonly attracts little attention or opposition. The American experience is fairly typical of what happens when a common residence brings friendly peoples of similar culture into close association. In the relatively short period of American life, the older immigrant groups have merged into a common group and the rate of intermarriage of individuals of more recent entrance is such that their complete biological absorption into the general population is a question of only a few generations.

Divergent Peoples. Where the races in contact are sharply differentiated in skin color or other physical characters, or in culture and social status, the amount of intermarriage is commonly small. But physical and social differences between races are not insuperable barriers to intermarriage. The white pioneers of America in many regions took Indian wives, and similar marriages are frequent in various areas characterized by a paucity of white women. In a slave regime, once a friendly accommodation has been reached, racial intermixture may go on easily and rapidly.

In areas of contact where the exploitation of native peoples or resources goes on without formal master-slave relations, intermarriage and intermixture are commonly retarded. The class differences tend to harden into cast divisions marked by chronic friction and traditionally antagonistic attitudes. But intermixture is never wholly absent; half-castes appear and increase in number in every colonial area as in every area of settlement.

THE FUSION OF CULTURES

The Results of Contacts. Contacts with strange peoples result, also, in the disorganization of the simpler culture, the gradual assimilation of the weaker people, the transfer and fusion of heritages, and the final achievements of a new cultural equilibrium.

Culture Change and Conflict. The simpler peoples adopt and use various material elements of the more advanced culture. This process enriches the simpler culture but at the same time disorganizes the native economy and mode of life and makes the simpler group dependent upon further contacts. To secure the desired articles there must be an exchange of native goods. To secure the native goods in quantity for exchange involves a shift of occupation, a disturbance of work habits, and a reduction of work interest.

The change in economic organization is followed in time by changes in the more basic elements of the culture. The religio-superstitious system is disorganized and corrupted, partly as a consequence of economic change, and partly (particularly if there are missionaries present to attack the native and moral order) through the borrowing of practices and beliefs. Ultimately, through the decay or destruction of old institutions and traditional life-patterns, there is a more or less complete change in the fundamental social organization.

The transition is marked by competition between the alternative culture elements, particularly in those realms, such as religion and superstition, wherein there is no immediate objective measure of the relative efficiency of the competing units. In the course of culture fusion there is chronic conflict, overt or potential, between the sponsors of the competing systems. The defeated group strives to preserve or restore the lost or decaying standards, seeks to preserve its language and other signs of former unity, and builds an elaborate body of myth rationalizing the existing status.

Cultural Assimilation. The spread of culture resulting from the contact of unequally advanced peoples is largely a one-way movement; the subordinate or minority group in general has more to learn than the dominant group and the incentives to learning are greater and more obvious. The superiority of certain culture elements is patent and they are taken over immediately and without emotional resistance. Some familiarity with the technology and work techniques of the ruling group may be imposed as the work relations are established. An ability to use the language of the ruling group has obvious advantages.

Racial intermixture facilitates the process of personal assimilation and the culture fusion. The social heritages are in general most easily acquired in primary contacts and sympathetic association and are most readily and naturally transmitted to the young. The children of biracial ancestry are likely to be bilingual and to possess other elements of both cultures. In knowledge, habits, and sentiments they belong in some measure to each parent group.

Personal Disorganization. The foregoing in some part accounts for the fact that the period of cultural transition is one of wide personal disorganization. The change in work techniques and group practices disturbs the established habit systems and frees the individual, in a measure, from the traditional controls; it introduces new elements of insecurity into the life experience. The children of biracial ancestry in particular are exposed to two contrasting and conflicting sets of moral standards. With freedom and choice go personal disorganization and personal failure.

The breakdown of the control system favors the miscegenation of the races. The latter process is in itself, in most cases, a form of disorganization, being a violation of the customary practices and taboos. Irregularity in this respect, by weakening the control system, is conducive to the violation of other standards, and thus to further experimentation, failure, and possible personal demoralization.

A New Equilibrium. The assimilation of the native group is a protracted process always accompanied by disorder. It goes on at very unequal rates. Some individuals, because of fortunate chance circumstances, are brought into more or less close and personal relations with members of the ruling group and acquire an understanding and appreciation of its culture. This is particularly likely to be the case of children of biracial ancestry, and of all children in regions where native schools are established and missionaries active. Other individuals have little direct contact with the new culture, retain their traditional ways, and resist change long after the more mobile individuals have lost the old culture patterns.

The social disorder and cultural duality, incident to cultural fusion and assimilation, ultimately give way to a single set of enforced behavior patterns. The trend in every culture is toward equilibrium, toward order and status and uniformity. There may be a re-establishment of an old order through the assimilation of all individuals to it or there may be a new order resulting from fusion, but in any case one set of standards will in time replace the dual system. As this result ensues, personal disorganization and maladjustment decline and, when the equilibrium is complete, disappear.

MARGINAL GROUPS

Factors Leading to Marginal Groups. The effect of contact, operating through differential opportunity and through blood intermixture, is to produce cultural diversity; a larger or smaller number of individuals come to occupy, in status and heritage, a position between the contrasted cultures.

If the channels of cultural transition be unobstructed, the individuals who acquire the language and other cultural baggage of the dominant group pass into its ranks and participate in its life. This outcome is usual and typical of immigrant experience in America and elsewhere. Where caste or other barriers interfere with mobility, the cultural expatriates tend to form or to be formed into a special intermediate caste which may eventually assume the characteristics of a nationality.

When the physical marks of race are sufficiently pronounced so that the hybrid offspring are superficially distinguishable from the members of either parent group, the tendency to separation is stronger and more general. Unless the racial hybrids promptly disappear by intermarriage into one or the other parent group, they presently come to constitute a new racial strain in the population.

The Status of Mixed Bloods. These mixed-blood individuals are intermediate in physical type between the parents. As they increase in number the intermarriage and intermixture of the races are stimulated; the mixed bloods intermarry and intermix with both racial groups and a multiplicity of intermediate types bridges the gap between the parent races.

Socially and culturally, as well as biologically, the mixed-blood individuals commonly occupy positions intermediate between the two culture groups, thereby serving as cultural intermediaries between them. The mulattoes in the United States, the mestizos of Latin America, the Eurasians of Hawaii and elsewhere, and the part-native individuals in various colonial areas have an intermediate cultural position, and hybrid individuals everywhere achieve personal success higher than the more isolated and less mobile members of the subordinate group.

The two facts of (1) biracial ancestry and (2) distinctive status and achievement are often mistakenly assumed to stand in a cause and effect relationship. The intermediate social status, however, is not a direct result of the blood intermixture although the two facts are related.

The intermediate social status and the superior achievement are the results of social contacts. The hybrid individuals are more in contact with the dominant culture group, have greater mobility and freedom, and are more easily and quickly assimilated into the dominant culture than are the more isolated and less mobile members of the native population.

The Role of Mixed-Blood Groups. The social role of biracial marginal groups turns upon the administrative policy that obtains in the particular historical situation.

a) In the presence of two integrated and contrasted cultures, such as the Oriental and the European, there is no natural place and function for a marginal group. Unless the hybrids are absorbed into one or the other culture, they tend to become outcasts from both. If they are formed into a special caste it tends to be an inferior caste within one of the parent groups rather than a class intermediate between the two. The individuals who depart from the one civilization do not thereby approach the other; they simply lose status within the particular civilization. The hybrid individuals must content themselves with such status as is assigned them by the group with which they elect to be identified. In general they have no respected place and no special role in the biracial situation in the Oriental world.

b) In other areas, the presence of a mixed population is utilized to lessen the friction between the pure-blood groups. The independent organization of a hybrid middle-class may be encouraged and its growth fostered by catering to the aspirations of marginal persons without in full reality granting their wishes. The superior cultural worth of marginal persons may be recognized by preferential economic opportunities and by minor offices and inferior governmental positions, as in the British West Indies and in various Anglo-Indian areas. The result of this policy is to effect a fairly complete separation of the Europeanized and partly Europeanized individuals from the native population and to identify them with the ruling class by making them economically and morally dependent upon it. The native population is thus deprived of its natural leaders, and a middle-class cushion placed between the white aristocracy and the unassimilated native labor supply.

c) The ruling-class policy may be one of exclusion without special provision for the intermediate racial and cultural individuals. For the most part this is the method of dealing with the Negro population of the United States; it is essentially the policy of the self-governing colonies of South Africa; and it was the German native policy. No effort is made to establish relations that will secure harmony between the races; an impassable color line is drawn and no recognition given to the fact of cultural differences. The refusal to recognize superiority and to grant status and opportunity generates resentment and chronic discontent. The role of the marginal individuals tends to be that of leadership in the subordinate group.

RACE PROBLEMS

Nature of the Race Problem. Racial problems are expressions of disharmony between traditional status and current aspiration. They arise in areas wherein the attitudinal sets and the institutional patterns fail to comprehend the changing cultural and social phenomena. The nature of the race problem is an index of the stage that has been reached in the transition from the initial contacts and mixtures of groups to the final achievement of a new racial and cultural unity.

Race and Native Problems. Race problems, as distinct from the so-called native problem, seem to have their origin at the stage in the racial cycle at which biracial marginal groups become important and no adequate provision is made for satisfying their wishes. So long as the cultural lines between the races are distinct and clearly drawn, there may be a problem or a series of problems of an administrative order—problems of control, sanitation, labor, education, and the like—but there is no race problem. So long as the individuals are free to enter the dominant group and participate in its culture to the extent of their mastery of its elements, there is no race problem. Race problems proper arise at the point where the dominant culture group denies to individuals and groups who have mastered the culture an unobstructed opportunity to identify themselves with the dominant group and participate in its heritage.

Race Consciousness. When racial and cultural hybrids are excluded from full participation in the culture, resentment reinforces the sentimental bonds of unity. A sense of common interest arises; the conviction develops that their fortunes are involved in a common destiny. Like any natural group set apart in a population, they build up a characteristic body of sentiment, develop a provincial unity, and elaborate a mythology in the struggle for self-respect. Every minority that is excluded and persecuted tends to become militantly self-conscious.

Racial Separation. Where the lines of demarcation are entirely cultural they may be escaped by any individual who cares to conform to the majority standards. But where the differentiating characteristics are racial rather than cultural the individuals, regardless of personal traits and cultural achievements, cannot escape classification and the limitations of opportunity that go with it. The criteria of separation remain to the end of the racial cycle, that is, until such time as further intermixture erases the distinguishing marks of race.

Cultural Retardation. The discriminations by the dominant group lead to a disposition on the part of the excluded individuals to avoid cross-race contacts and the resulting humiliating experiences. There is established and maintained a more or less complete and voluntary segregation; isolating themselves, the hybrid and marginal individuals may undertake to work out a semi-independent social order.

Some degree of cultural retardation is an accompaniment and inevitable result of such separation. The pace of racial intermixture declines and the acceptance of cultural invention is impeded.

The excluded group elaborates a body of doctrine and fabricates a racial history to explain and justify its position in the inclusive social order. Its lack of power and prestige results in numerous compensatory phenomena that tend to intensify the isolation. The body of social opinion, for example, tends to be negative, to deny the values of the ruling group and to react adversely to all suggestions originating in it. In its extreme development, as in certain modern nationalistic minorities, the race-conscious minority becomes impervious to all facts conflicting with its emotional complex. Potential racial conflict is chronic and traditional.

Part Five

Human Ecology

By

AUGUST B. HOLLINGSHEAD
Yale University

Chapter Twenty-Two

THE ECOSYSTEM AND ECOLOGY

Men have long known that they, as individuals and groups, are dependent for their survival upon one another, upon other living things, and upon conditions existent in their environment. In the process of coping with conditions essential to the maintenance of life, all living things, from microorganisms to man, have come to inhabit communities composed of the same and different species. Each organism lives some place on the planet Earth. Each species of organism is distributed in time and place. There are observable interrelations and interdependencies between populations of organisms and their habitat. The complex of specific interrelations and interdependencies studied by ecologists between aggregations of organisms and the conditions imposed upon them by their habitat comprise an *ecosystem*.[1] Ecosystems range in size from all the forms of life on earth taken together to a small community of closely interrelated organisms living on the underside of a boulder in a woodland. Interdependence between living things and their habitat is the subject matter of *ecology*.

ECOLOGY

The basic concepts of ecology involve the linkages which connect organisms—plant and animal—to one another and to their habitat. These linkages enable species to survive from generation to generation in the same or different habitats.

Assumptions of Ecology. A primary assumption of ecology is that the ways of life of organisms are responses to the conditions of life which encompass them. These ways of life have evolved through time some place on the planet Earth. They are

---

1 L. R. Dice, *Man's Nature and Nature's Man: The Ecology of Human Communities* (Ann Arbor: University of Michigan Press, 1955), pp. 2–3.

subject to change as the conditions of life change, and organisms either adjust to the emergent conditions associated with their habitat or in time they disappear from the earth.

Origin of the Term Ecology. The term *ecology* was introduced into scientific literature in 1869 by the biologist Ernst Haeckel. It was derived from the Greek word οἶκος which symbolized house, abode, dwelling. In the Greek usage, the term included not only the dwelling place but also the inhabitants of the house and the everyday maintenance activities they carried on in it. In this sense, ecology is the study of living things, not as individuals but as members of a complex network of interconnected organisms (that range from the filterable virus to man) as they function in multiform environments which include the realm of physical nature, other plant and animal species, and other organisms of the same species.

THE ECOLOGICAL ORDER

Today we know that order exists among all living things, including man—an order that is the result of the competitive struggle for existence. This order has developed within and between species in place and time. The effect of this struggle is to bring about a distribution of the species and the individual, so that each lives, finally, in the place where he can survive and where he can best meet the competition with other organisms and species.

The Web of Life. All living organisms are bound together in a system of multiform, intricate, and ever-changing interdependencies. This has been called "the web of life." Darwin's famous instance of the cats and the clover is the classic illustration of this interdependence.[1] Darwin demonstrated that the network of life connects bumblebees, the fertilization of heartsease and similar plants, field mice, cats, villagers, and old maids one to another. Later studies have extended this fundamental principle to all types of organisms.

Competition. The competitive struggle for existence acts as a regulator of the number of individuals in all species and between species. This principle applies in time and place. It controls the distribution of living things and develops more or

---

1 Charles Darwin, *On the Origin of Species: A Facsimile of the First Edition* (Cambridge, Mass.: Harvard University Press, 1964).

less of a balanced relationship between numbers and available resources.

Stability and Change. Competitive factors produce relative stability between numbers of the population and the resources of their sustenance base for longer or shorter periods of time. Changes may be brought about by a shift in climate, an invasion of the habitat by some alien species, a famine, or an epidemic of disease. Invasion may lead to a rapid increase of the invading population and a sudden decline in numbers of the original population, if not the total destruction of the latter. Under ordinary circumstances any minor fluctuations that occur in the balance between species and their habitat are mediated without profoundly disturbing the existing routine of life. When a sudden and catastrophic change occurs, it upsets the conditions of life and releases energies that have previously been held in check.

The Biotic Community. Plants and animals living together in a shared habitat constitute a *biotic community*. The functional and structural organization that results from the interrelation and interdependence of different species within their common habitat enables each species to survive. A biotic community is comprised of a population of different plant and animal species, territorially organized and more or less adjusted to the conditions imposed by the space it occupies, and within which each species lives in a relationship of interdependence with other species that is essentially symbiotic. *Symbiosis* is, briefly, the mutual interdependence which exists between unlike species. For example, bees are dependent upon flowers for nectar to make honey, while many species of flowers are dependent upon bees, or other insects, to spread pollen so that fertilization and eventually reproduction of the plant will take place.

DIVISIONS OF ECOLOGY

In the discussion to this point, we have not attempted to differentiate between the three essential types of communities of interest to ecologists—plant, animal, and human. We will now turn to the consideration of the essential differences between them, discussing only briefly the relationship of plants, animals, and man to one another because the interest of the sociologist is focused primarily upon the human community.

The Ecological View of the Human Community. Reduced to its elements, ecologically the human community may be considered to be the product of seven interacting factors: (1) a population, (2) the area in which it lives, (3) the artifacts it possesses (technological culture), (4) its non-material culture (customs and beliefs), (5) availability of appropriate resources, (6) the uses to which these natural resources are put, and (7) the functions performed in the division of labor.

In the human community these seven interacting factors operate to produce its spatial distribution, social organization, position in a constellation of communities, and changes within the community.

Plant and Animal Ecology Differentiated from Human Ecology. Plants and animals live in communities which have been studied extensively by ecologists, but there is apparently no form of social relationship among plants that can be described as familial. The relationships between the different species are purely symbiotic, and competition tends to be unrestrained. In contrast, such relationships as exist among lower animals, particularly among the social insects, seem to be of the familial type.[1] In the case of the social insects, relationships are not based on tradition and maintained by consensus but are fixed in the structure of the organism and transmitted by instincts. One further point, among others, is the fact that animals communicate with each other and are able, under certain circumstances, to act collectively and in concert.[2]

Among human beings, some social relations, at least those between the sexes, are predetermined in a very general way by structure and supported by glandular potentialities. Certain other activities, especially those that have to do with acquiring sustenance, are determined by the association of competitive individuals. In the instance of man, as distinguished from plants and animals, social relationships are invariably conditioned by understandings, customs, and law rather than by structure or instinct. Besides this, man—at least civilized man—keeps records and is a time-building animal so that he lives in the past and future as well as in the present. The social order in man, which is transmitted not as a genetic but as a cultural heritage, performs somewhat the same function in human society as that performed

---

1 W. C. Allee, *The Social Life of Animals* (revised edition, Boston: Beacon Press, 1958).
2 J. P. Scott, *Animal Behavior* (Chicago: University of Chicago Press, 1958).

by instinct in animal society. In human society, therefore, social organization is embodied in customs and laws rather than in the physiological structure of its members.

There is every reason to believe that man, like other animal species, came into existence in a single area from which, in the course of human history, he has spread to every other part of the world. What racial differences now exist are to be attributed, however, less to the direct effects of physical environment than to the effects of isolation and of the inbreeding which this isolation imposed. Now that this isolation has so completely broken down under the influence of modern means of transportation, one of the historical conditions under which the races of mankind came into existence has effectively disappeared. The result is that there is not now, if ever there was among human beings, any such thing as a pure race.

History of Ecology. The preceding paragraphs indicate that ecology is divided into three broad fields: plant, animal, and human. Plant and animal ecology are confined, in very large part, to the life sciences of botany and zoology. Plant and animal ecology began to develop as separate disciplines in the 1870s,[1] but little systematic work was done on human ecology until about 1920 when Robert E. Park, Professor of Sociology of the University of Chicago, became interested in the implications of plant and animal ecology in the study of human communities, more particularly the city.[2] Park drew heavily upon the concepts of the plant and animal ecologists in his formulations regarding human ecology. During the 1920s, Park and his students in sociology developed what came to be known as "The Chicago School of Human Ecology."[3] In the 1930s, "The Chicago School" came under attack from non-Chicago sociologists.[4] In 1944, Hawley published a paper which pointed the way to bridging the gap that had developed between the Chicago and the non-Chicago human ecologists.[5] Since the end of World War II, a new generation of human ecologists has matured, and renewed interest has been kindled in the subject. However, a point at issue is the

1 T. A. Gouge, *The Ascent of Life* (Toronto: University of Toronto Press, 1961).

2 R. E. Park, *Human Communities: The City and Human Ecology* (Glencoe, Ill.: The Free Press, 1952).

3 George A. Theodorson [ed.], *Studies in Human Ecology* (Evanston, Ill.: Row, 1961).

4 Maurice R. Davie, "The Pattern of Urban Growth," in R. J. Kennedy [ed.], *The Papers of Maurice R. Davie* (New Haven: Yale University Press, 1961), pp. 121–145; Milla Aissa Alihan, *Social Ecology* (New York: Columbia University Press, 1938).

5 Amos H. Hawley, "Ecology and Human Ecology," *Social Forces*, 22 (1944), pp. 398–405.

question of whether human ecology should be a scientific discipline in its own right, such as economics, or should continue to develop as a substantive field within existing fields, such as sociology or medicine.[1]

SUMMARY

Viewed broadly, today, human ecology is conceived to be the study of man in his relation to environmental conditions—climate, water, soil, natural resources, atmosphere—and to other plant and animal species, as well as his interactions with definable societies and cultures on the planet Earth. In future years, however, as a result of man's efforts to overcome the limitations imposed on him by the earth's position in interstellar space, these factors, conditions, and limits may be expanded to man's ecological relationship to other planets. Confining our interests to this planet, it is now clear that the lives of all men are intertwined with the destinies of plants and animals and with the conditions imposed upon them by nature. Human beings are connected in vital ways to the conditions organisms impose on man, and man, in turn, places limiting conditions on other organisms by his exploitation of raw materials, energy, and other forms of life.

Stated simply, human ecology deals with society in its cultural and symbiotic aspects, that is with those aspects brought about by competition and by the struggle of individuals, in any social order, to survive and to perpetuate themselves. The social order includes that in which individual freedom is limited by the rules of a political society or by the customs and conventions of a personal and moral order such as exists in the family. Human ecology is, therefore, concerned with (1) *population* in all its vital aspects; (2) *social organization;* (3) the position and function of *power;* (4) *migration;* and (5) *changes in the spatial distribution of populations* through time. These points are taken up in succeeding chapters.

Ecology is the study of the vital and spatial relations existing between organisms of the same, similar, and divergent species and their environment. In the broad Greek sense, ecology ana-

---

1 Lowell Reid, *The Sociology of Nature* (revised edition, Baltimore: Penguin, 1962); Otis Dudley Duncan, "Social Organization and the Ecosystem," in R. E. L. Faris [ed.], *Handbook of Modern Sociology* (Chicago: Rand McNally, 1964), pp. 38–82.

lyzes not only how these organisms exist and the influences this process has on their mode of life but also the effects the organism has on the environment and the environment on the organism.

Ecological studies are classified within the three realms of plants, animals, and the unique mammal—man. Human ecology began to develop when men looked about them and discovered that human activities trace definite spatial patterns and form well-defined sustenance linkages that are, in part, a response to biological process and, in part, a reaction to culture. These discoveries led to the view that plant, animal, and human ecology are interrelated within the framework of life but that human activities, because of the influence of culture, must be viewed separately from those of plants and animals. This is not to say that human ecology is completely different from the other branches but rather that all three branches are correlatives in a biotic whole called life.

CHAPTER TWENTY-THREE

POPULATION

Since the surface of the planet Earth is divided into two principal parts—land and water—the basic fact that man is a terrestrial animal poses ecological problems. Man as a species evolved on land, and it is on land that he has built his societies. He has mastered the lands of the earth, but he has never colonized the sea. In the million or more years that man has been evolving into his present species, he has populated all the continents of the earth except Antarctica. As societies evolved, men learned how to exploit the natural resources of the earth in many ways—to hunt and fish, domesticate plants and animals, refine metals, and develop new procedures to utilize the resources of nature. But, although they have learned how to modify nature, they have not mastered it.

THE STRUGGLE FOR SURVIVAL

In the millions of years that elapsed before man developed culture, his survival as a species was dependent upon his ability to compete for his existence with other plant and animal species. The dilemma posed by evolutionary processes in the struggle for survival was stated clearly by the English economist, Thomas Malthus, in 1798 when he pointed out that man has the capacity to reproduce himself geometrically each generation—10, 100, 1,000, 10,000, 100,000—whereas his food supply increases arithmetically—10, 20, 30, 40, 50. In the long struggle for survival, man inherited along with other living species the capacity to reproduce himself faster than his food supply was able to sustain him. Thus, each organism is impelled by conflicting ecological urges: one urge leads it to struggle toward preserving its own existence to the utmost limits of its life span; the other urge leads the organism to continue, by procreation, the existence of the species and, in the case of man, the race to which he belongs.

The Dilemma of Numbers. If a species produces a large number of surplus individuals in each generation, a shortage develops in its food supply, thereby creating famine conditions and causing great numbers to die through starvation and disease; if it does not produce more individuals than are necessary for survival, it will be in danger of depletion from inroads of its natural enemies. Limitations on the food supply, which continually face all organisms, are normally solved through positive checks—famine, disease, and carnivorous and parasitoid enemies.

The Balance Between Numbers and Sustenance. The operation of the principal of overreproduction and the counterprinciple of positive checks tends, in simpler societies, to create and maintain in human communities a balance between (1) population size, (2) the available sustenance, and (3) the standards of living as defined by the group's culture. In each community, population tends to oscillate around a mean figure. Furthermore, this mean figure tends to remain relatively constant so long as the available sustenance is not appreciably increased or decreased. However, if the sustenance is increased substantially, an increase occurs in numbers or in the standards of living; if the sustenance is decreased for a prolonged period, numbers dwindle and the standards of living fall until a new balance is struck between numbers and food supply. Modern man, however, has learned to limit the ravages of famine and drought, to open up new areas for food production, and to control many communicable diseases.

Imbalance Between Numbers and Resources. Modern man has created many imbalances between the resources of an area and its population. When viewed from the perspective of the distribution of resources in a society and on the planet Earth, some communities are underpopulated whereas others are overpopulated. Speaking generally, a marked increase or decrease in the utilizable resources available to a population results in an increase or a decrease in numbers.[1] This principle is illustrated, on the increase side of the equation, by the remarkable growth of population in Europe, Asia, and the Americas during the last three centuries. The human population of the world in 1650 is

---

1 Gunnar Myrdal, *Asian Drama: An Inquiry into the Poverty of Nations* (New York: The Twentieth·Century Fund, 1968).

estimated to have been 545 million. In 1968, the Population Reference Bureau estimated the world's population at three billion. Man's numbers have increased over six times in the last three hundred years. What is of current concern is that the increase has accelerated during the last quarter of a century so that in 1968 there was a net gain in the world's population of some 70 million individuals. This was a daily increase of approximately 192,000 individuals. Most of this increase was concentrated in countries that were already overpopulated, where the standard of living was low and where a considerable portion of the inhabitants were, at best, undernourished and, at worst, faced daily by hunger and periodically by famine. The constantly increasing population, particularly in east and south Asia, Africa, South America, and the islands in the Pacific Ocean, presents man with his most critical problem from an ecological point of view.

This remarkable growth of population has been conditioned by cultural changes. New plants and animals have been introduced into different parts of the world; for example, potatoes were brought from the Americas to Europe and wheat from Europe to the Americas. The food yield of plants and animals has been increased tremendously by the application of genetics to agriculture, for example the development of hybrid corn. In the last three centuries men have tapped new sources of energy such as coal, oil, and natural gas and, in recent years, the atom. New techniques have been introduced into manufacturing such as the principle of interchangeable parts and the movable production line. The invention of the telegraph, the telephone, the radio and, more recently, television has enabled man to communicate with his fellow men over long distances. The resources available to a community's population multiplied, in the nineteenth century, after the development of steam-powered water and rail transportation and, in the twentieth century, with the development of automotive and air transportation. As far as man as a species is concerned, the planet Earth today is a single biosphere.

DEMOGRAPHY

The study of the vital processes of population aggregates is known as *demography*. There are two basic dimensions to demography: first, the static, which describes the number and composition of a defined population at a given time for a stated area; second, the dynamic, which analyzes the movement, growth or decline, and changes in the composition of the aggregate over a period of time for a stated unit of enumeration. From another point of view, demography might be defined as biosocial bookkeeping. Thus, its function is to record and analyze vital and social changes, over a temporal span, in the number and composition of the human units in communities and nations.

Bases of Demography. Reliable demographic knowledge depends upon accurate, detailed inventories of population (census enumeration) and careful, complete, and continuous registration of births, marriages, divorces, and deaths. Rarely, if ever, do demographic data collected within arbitrary territorial or time units coincide with an ecological unit. Ecologists are, therefore, definitely limited in their use of data compiled by the census and by bureaus of vital statistics. Nevertheless, compilations of demographic data from censuses and vital statistics are the best sources available to students of population, and the ecologist must resort to their adaptation for his purpose.

Ecology and the Distribution of Population. Every ecological area is characterized by a typical distribution of the population composing it, along age, sex, nativity, and occupational lines. Stated in other terms, ecological areas may, in part, be defined in terms of the spatial, biological, and social distribution of the population inhabiting them. The ecologist assumes that the characteristics of the population in a given area are the result of the competitive factors operating in the area. Therefore, a given population distribution is a reflection of the ecological factors operative in the area. Thus, a given distribution of biosocial characteristics enumerated for the population can be taken as suggestive of cultural organization.

The Population Pyramid. The population pyramid is a technique used to represent in a concise, graphic manner the complex variations of age, sex, racial, social, and economic conditions in a given population aggregate. Ordinarily, two or three variables are depicted in a single population pyramid, for instance age, sex, and nativity, or age, sex, and color. From this point of view, analysis of age, sex, race, nativity, and occupation is indispensable to a knowledge of the social, economic, and political processes which operate to form the structure of human communities. In metropolitan communities during the daytime, for example, the age-sex distribution correlates with different functional areas: the "downtown district" of the central city tends to have a higher ratio of males to females than the residential or suburban areas; the range of age varies from almost all adults in the center of the city to few adults and many children in the suburban periphery.

SOCIAL STRATIFICATION

The division of labor organizes the sustenance and maintenance activities of human communities. Occupation serves as the link that holds individuals to the social order. It connects each individual to many other individuals in three ways: *technologically*—through the specific manual and mental operations each participant in the organizational network carries out in the execution of work; *economically*—through the income yield of an occupation which provides a livelihood; and *socially*—through the prestige attached to the occupation in accordance with the mores of the community. The income yield and the prestige attached to an occupation create stratifications in the social order.[1]

Differential social evaluation characterizes practically all populations. Viewed from the perspective of the status structure, differential evaluations of occupational pursuits are related to: an individual's function in the economic system; his proportion of the group's sustenance (wealth); and his social status, plane of living, and ecological position in the community.[2] Technologic, economic, and social differences which obtain among members of occupational groups bind them into an interdependent stratificational structure that is pyramidal in form. Numerically, as one ascends the stratificational structure, a smaller and smaller number of individuals occupy each stratum. Socially, the strata are characterized by a developing *esprit de corps* as one moves from the inarticulate, unskilled lowest stratum to the closely organized corporate existence found in the higher strata.

---

1 Walter L. Slocum, *Occupational Careers* (Chicago: Aldine Publishing Co., 1966), pp. 76–87.

2 Peter M. Blau and Otis Dudley Duncan, *The American Occupational Structure* (New York: Wiley, 1967).

SPATIAL DISTRIBUTION OF POPULATION

The distribution of human population over the earth's surface is a product of the active interrelationships between cultural groups seeking sustenance and their geographic base. Population is, therefore, spatially as well as functionally distributed into patterns that correspond to the competitive factors operative in an area organized by a market. Economists, geographers, and sociologists, by pooling their knowledge, have found that the size, shape, and density of a given population distribution are products, in the main, of social organization; and, in turn, they have found that the social organization of a given people is a function of their culture. This functional interrelationship between population, culture, and ecology is the subject of systematic study.[1]

Four patterns can be identified objectively in the spatial distribution of the human species: (1) the world, (2) nations and states, (3) the region, and (4) the functional community.

The World Pattern. A map of world population shows seven areas of high density—the Japanese Archipelago, Indonesia, eastern China, northeastern India, Italy, northwestern Europe, and the east coast of the United States from Richmond to Boston. Six of these seven areas are on islands and the mainland of Eurasia. Stretching inland from western Europe toward the eastern part of European Russia there is a gradual drop in density. Central, northern, and southwestern Asia, Australia, most of Africa, South America, and North America, except eastern United States, are areas of low density. Areas of high and medium density follow coastal regions, and areas of low density are inland portions of the continents.

The National Pattern. If the nation is taken as a unit of analysis we find many variations in the density of its population. In the United States, population is variously distributed in the different census divisions. In 1965, 65.5 percent of the total population lived east of the Mississippi River and 34.4 percent west of the Mississippi; 52.6 percent of the population was in the North, 30.9 percent in the South, and 16.5 percent in the West. The density per square mile ranged from 340.1 in the Middle Atlantic states to 8.0 in the Mountain States. The population

1 Walter Goldschmidt, *Man's Way: A Preface to the Understanding of Human Society* (New York: Holt, Rinehart & Winston, 1959).

pattern in the United States is taking the form of definite metropolitan concentrations on the margins of navigable waters or adjacent to rich mineral and oil deposits. The ease with which industries using atomically generated electrical energy can be located near existing metropolitan areas will probably give rise to additional population growth near the present centers of concentration.

The Region. Population distribution within a region tends to follow relatively homogeneous geographic conditions of soil, climate, topography, and natural resources. Exclusive of metropolitan agglomerations, the density of population closely corresponds to food-producing areas. In the United States, areas of high density of the agricultural population are found east of a line drawn from Brownsville (Texas) through Wichita (Kansas) and Lincoln (Nebraska) to Winnipeg (Canada). West of this line, except in irrigated river valleys, large-scale grazing is the rule until the Pacific Slope is reached. This vast region is sparsely populated. In the valleys of the Pacific Coast states an intensive agriculture is accompanied by a high density of population. This is particularly true of the irrigated portions of the Sacramento-San Joaquin Valley in California.

The Functional Community. Functional communities are located around nucleated centers where lines of communication and transportation converge. Spreading out from the great metropolises are smaller centers located along lines of rail and highway transportation. Thus, population clusters into spatial patterns ranging in size from the many-millioned metropolis, such as New York City or Chicago, with a density of thousands of individuals per square mile, down to isolated ranches in the western mountains and on the high plains that stretch from west Texas to Canada.

SUMMARY

Population, in the *first* place, is not a mere statistical grouping but the distribution of the inhabitants of a discrete area into a vital structure which involves their age, sex, and race as well as other characteristics. *Second,* the number of inhabitants in the area is determined by their quest for sustenance within the competitive network of an organized market. *Third,* the population structure of an area may be conveniently analyzed by the use of the population pyramid as well as by other graphic and statistical techniques. *Finally,* the vital and social characteristics of the population in an ecological area reflect the operations of factors which repel, attract, segregate, and limit numbers in terms of the available resources.

Chapter Twenty-Four

ECOLOGICAL ORGANIZATION

Ecological organization is the product, in very large part, of the knowledge members of a society possess regarding the utilization of inorganic and organic resources available to them. Knowledge of the use of resources is learned, shared, and transmitted by the members of the society. Briefly, culture has enabled man to organize and, for the most part, control the resources necessary for his sustenance at a given point in time and place.

In general, man's widespread distribution on the earth is due to his ability to adapt his culture to meet his needs under a wide range of physical environments. The amount of technical knowledge available among a given people affects their capacity to utilize their environment for the satisfaction of their physical and social needs. Consequently, changes in culture generate changes in the forms of competition between communities, and these factors, in turn, result in modifications in the spatial and sustenance relations of human beings. Man's ability to utilize his environment for his own ends is reflected in the broad changes in his economy from primitive collectional to modern industrial societies.

DEVELOPMENT OF ECOLOGICAL ORGANIZATION

There is ample evidence that, as man's technical knowledge has increased, his dependence upon the natural resources of his habitat has been mediated by his increasing dependence upon other men. Evidence of this dependence is the existence of a steadily expanding market area and the increasingly effective and increasingly extensive division of labor among the many peoples of the earth.

The student of ecological organization may approach his task from the standpoint of anthropology and history or solely from the standpoint of large-scale twentieth-century societies as most American sociologists have done. The remainder of this chapter is concerned with outlining the main concepts involved in each approach.

ECOLOGICAL ORGANIZATION
VIEWED HISTORICALLY

Ecological organization was probably first centered on a familial and tribal basis; later, it was integrated on a political and territorial basis. There was apparently no definite period in history when society made the fundamental change by which it assumed the character of a territorial and eventually a political organization. The transition appears to have taken place at different times and under different circumstances among different people. The transition is still in process in isolated areas of the earth.

Viewed through time, man's ecological organization may be divided into four major types: *collectional and nomadic, horticultural and pastoral, settled village and town,* and *metropolitan.* Each ecological type is characterized by a distinct pattern of interdependencies between the population and the geographic environment, the organization of sustenance resources, the size of the communal area, the resources utilized by the inhabitants of the area, the spatial distribution of communities over the terrain, and, finally, the distribution of the population within and between communities. The general trend has been an evolutionary sequence in which the resources of this planet have passed from the simpler to the more complicated types of ecological organization. Concomitants of this trend are an increase in population density, an increase in the size of the area organized for sustenance purposes, and differentiation of function within and between communities and societies.

Collectional Societies. The simplest form of economic life known to man is represented by nomadic collectors who wandered over a wide territory gathering their food and other supplies from the environment. These men supplied their needs by appropriating what nature had to offer. The population must have been sparse because men lacked the knowledge necessary for a more intensive use of their environment. As time passed, emergent specialization occurred along sexual and occupational lines: men fished and made weapons; women dug roots, collected insects, seeds, and fruits, made clothing, cared for the young, and bore the burdens of the hearth. Occupational specialization existed within tribes. One man made arrows, another spears, a third medicine and charms, still another hunted rather consistently, and each man exchanged his product with another for the item he needed. There was tribal specialization also with one tribe gathering seeds, berries, and insects, another making salt, still others chipping flint and fishing. Intertribal exchange took place through barter, usually on the boundary between tribal lands, on a definite day, with the day and place protected by custom and reinforced by religious sanction.

Horticultural and Pastoral Societies. Horticultural and pastoral societies emerged from the collectional type when men learned to domesticate animals and cultivate plants. In horticultural and pastoral societies the collection of seeds, fruits, and game continued, but the people planted and tended their garden plots systematically and herded livestock, relying more on domesticated plants and animals for the things they needed than upon the bounty of nature. Men cared for the animals, hunted, fished, made weapons, and compounded medicine; women were the gardeners, food gatherers, and bearers of the household burdens noted in the preceding section. Economic specialization was more fully advanced with more trading at a regular market than in collectional economies.

A well-marked differentiation between herders and tillers developed in many parts of the world. Some people settled down on the land, whereas others followed their flocks and herds and thus became nomadic husbandmen drawing their sustenance mainly from domesticated animals. Nomadic pastoralists wandered over wide areas, coming into contact with several different tribes; when necessary these nomads traded animal products for the food and manufactures produced by tillers. Among nomads and tillers the market was periodic, usually held on the boundaries of territory claimed by both the pastoralists and the horticulturists. (Today, the Negritos of the Malay Peninsula and the Eskimos of North America have remained in one or the other of these phases of primitive economy.)

Settled Societies. Historically, fixed settlement on the land is traced back to the time, possibly 20,000 years ago, when kinship groups located in favorable environments combined horticulture and husbandry as their principal source of livelihood. In due course, the center of communal life became the compact, nucleated village built for protection and association. Outside the village, extended the open fields used for tillage, pasture, and gathering and crossed with paths radiating from one village to other villages. In these village communities territory was organized into nucleated settlement and rural hinterland.

The economic base of the village community was plant and animal cultivation for the satisfaction of sustenance needs. Each village aimed to be self-sufficient, but probably none was. Within each village, cloth, leather, shoes, pottery, metal, and tools might be manufactured by artisans who had become more advanced specialists than were the workers under nomadic economy. Some foods were processed and stored. Most villages probably remained agricultural, although some showed definite signs of becoming centers of local manufacture and trade. The village market held perhaps daily or weekly was the center of exchange between those who had specialized goods to sell or trade.

Town Societies. Town-centered societies developed historically from village societies when a trader class came into existence in a market village. The trader did business in his combined home-and-shop, both buying and selling there when possible. Often, however, he was forced to attend the market to purchase his wares and to wander from village to village peddling them while his wife remained at home managing the shop. The trader, located in the town, organized consumers and producers into a functional community which worked out its interdependence within itself and in relation to the outside world through the mechanism of a market where goods were bartered or bought and sold for money.

The organized market area of the average town extended over a radius of fifteen or twenty miles from the integrating center; within this hinterland many villages were located which served as the source of supply and the area over which goods were distributed.

Two types of towns gradually emerged: *first,* the local town described above; *second,* the prominent town with an extended trade. A favorable position, with respect to trade routes, waterways, hinterland, and natural resources, determined whether a town grew large or remained small. The large town became a commercial center, dominated by specialized traders and manufacturers who formed guilds or associations to protect their interests and to facilitate the organization of their market for exploitative purposes. Trade associations developed in some large commercial towns for the purpose of efficient organization of the market.

Metropolitan Organization. Gradually, some commercial towns grew into metropolises. A metropolis is the center which organizes, over a wide region, commerce, manufactures, finance, and business enterprise. The metropolis integrates and controls as many activities as possible over as wide a territory as communication and transportation permit within a competitive system. Economic dominance over a tributary hinterland characterizes the metropolis.

Metropolitan economy is the organization of producers and consumers mutually dependent for goods and services, wherein their wants are supplied by a system of exchange concentrated in a large city which is the focus of local trade and the center through which normal economic relations with the outside are established and maintained.[1]

Subordinate to the metropolis are cities, towns, villages, and the open country. These dependent units perform different functions in the elaborately organized network of ecological interdependence between metropolitan center and hinterland. Minute specialization in trade functions is found from wholesale through buyers, sellers, exchanges, common carriers, corporate organization, and finance. Each type of community is connected spatially and functionally to many other communities by a network of economic relationships.

CONTEMPORARY ECOLOGICAL ORGANIZATION

In modern societies economic functions are integrated around a market. Because not every location or individual has equal competitive ability, we find human activities and human beings segregated into different territorial and population distributions. Spatially distributed as consumers and producers, individuals living within the territory organized by the market constitute the trade area. Moreover, competitive interactions operative between individuals and their habitat give rise to specialization of function through which every territorial unit organized by a

---

1 N. S. B. Gras, *An Introduction to Economic History* (New York: Harper, 1922), p. 186. [Used by permission of the publishers.]

market is related to many other units. Functional specialization of industries integrated with lines of transportation and communication are the bonds which tie communities into an interdependent network. This web of functional specialization, communication, and transportation connects every individual with many other individuals who contribute to the satisfaction of his wants. In general, two forms of specialization of function may be differentiated: territorial and individual. These forms of specialization will be discussed in the following sections.

Criteria for Determining Ecological Units. Three fundamental categories are recognized in the analysis of what constitutes an ecologic unit: (1) man's utilization of the natural resources—land, water, minerals, and fuels; (2) organization of institutional agencies with respect to the consumption of their products; and (3) spatial distribution of institutional activities and population over the landscape. In our discussion of ecological areas or units, we shall begin with the largest—the region—and move successively to the smallest—the farmstead.

Ecological Areas. The *region* is a functionally organized unit made up of many interdependent communities integrated by a metropolis. The region is composed of the central metropolis surrounded by its suburbs and satellite cities; then further away are the smaller semi-independent cities, towns, villages, and open countryside. Size and shape of a region are determined by several factors, the most important being physiographic configurations, position of other metropolises, and lines and modes of communication. Modern modes of communication and transportation have organized the integral units in a functional complex so that each one is territorially differentiated and often specialized, yet all are inextricably connected by a commercial, industrial, financial, and cultural network into a structural-functional pattern that revolves around the regional metropolis.

The *metropolitan area* is the most easily recognized spatial distribution of institutions and populations in a region. It includes a central city, its suburbs, and independent satellites within a radius of approximately thirty miles from the downtown area. Localities within the metropolitan area comprise the built-up areas of urban agglomerations. Practically all of the gainfully employed members of the labor force commute on working days from their homes to their places of employment in the morning and back again in the evening.

Metropolis is the term applied to a city which economically and culturally dominates a region. The first requisite of a metropolis is its ability to draw into itself the products of one or more regions for processing, storage, trade, and transport. The second requisite is that its financial institutions dominate economic activities in the hinterland. Manufactures are usually situated in or near the city, but this is not a necessity, for manufacturing centers may be independent cities located at a distance from a metropolis, as for example Pontiac, Michigan or Bridgeport, Connecticut.

The *regional city* integrates the economic life of a metropolitan region. On the basis of function, regional cities may be grouped into three types: (1) *extractive-industrial*—Birmingham and Pittsburgh; (2) *commercial*—Atlanta and Dallas; (3) *commercial-food processing*—Omaha and Kansas City.

Two sets of factors entered into the development of regional cities in the United States: *first,* the development of the railways brought remote areas into competition with one another. Economic specialization ensued and cities arose at focal points where deposits of natural resources made manufacture on a large scale profitable or where rail lines converged or bulk was broken, giving these locations favorable positions in the competitive network. Today, rail lines and superhighways extend out from the regional city into the hinterland, connecting small cities, towns, and villages into an interdependent regional unity. Heavy-duty truck transport has accommodated itself to the earlier pattern established by the rail lines. Motor transport (automobile and truck) combined with the telephone, as a means of communication, and electricity, as a flexible source of energy available at any location in a region, have intensified the relationship between the city and its hinterland.

The *second* factor in the regional city's rise to power is the growth of national businesses administered through district headquarters located in a large key city. Facilities for handling the activities of the regional office are located in the regional city. Today, there is a strong tendency for many national concerns to select the same city as their regional headquarters. Instantaneous communication, via the telephone, and rapid transport of goods by air, motor, or rail bind the constituent territory closely to the regional metropolis.

Satellite cities are grouped around a central city but within the metropolitan area. The central city with her suburbs and satellites composes a city group. Satellite cities grow up adjacent to the central city as land values in the city rise, congestion occurs, and tax rates become prohibitive for industry. Ordinarily, a satellite city is created by the establishment of an industry or a group of industries on unimproved land outside the corporate city limits. The *centrifugal* factors of cheap land, low taxes, and space for operation and expansion push industry into these locations. Rapid transportation, easy communication, and electrical power facilitate this process. The result has been the movement of factories out of central cities and into suburban areas since the end of World War II. On the other hand, a series of *centripetal* factors, which include a large labor supply, nearness to a market, belt-lines, super-highways, and financial and administrative aid, draw industries close to the city. Thus, clustered around every metropolis are its satellite cities. Satellite cities are usually politically independent but subordinate units in the interdependent economic and cultural life of the metropolis. Strictly speaking, a region is united by the metropolitan area with central city and satellites, rather than by the metropolis alone.

The *provincial city* is local in its influence and organization. Its position with respect to larger centers enables it to develop and dominate a district which includes its own immediate area plus a number of towns and their trade areas. Provincial cities function in the integration of economic and cultural life between the regional city and the more remote rural territory. They are minor links in the metropolitan network. Motor transport, by filling in the gaps created during the railway era, increased the number, size, and power of small provincial cities.

The *rurban town* of from approximately 5,000 to 10,000 inhabitants with its outlying trade area forms an ecological structure which stands midway between the provincial city and the open country. Functionally, it unites the farm producer with the city consumer and the country consumer with the city producer.

Rurban towns support a minimum of one or more service agencies along each of the following lines: merchandising, marketing and finance, communication and transportation, processing of local products, education (including a high school), and professional, religious, and leisure organizations. Smaller towns are little specialized, bordering on the rural village which performs several functions in a single establishment. The larger towns are partially specialized. Most of their trade, however, continues to come from rural dwellers. Ordinarily, the rurban center is a county-seat town or at least the second town in the county.

Rural territory in the United States is composed of three kinds of ecological units: (1) the small town, (2) the neighborhood hamlet, and (3) the farmstead.

The *small town* or *village* is more rural or agricultural in its structure and function than the rurban center. Yet it functions as a link connecting farmers with larger urban centers. In size it ranges from about 500 to 4,000 inhabitants. Farmers living close to small towns patronize them for immediate needs such as groceries, overalls, work shoes, gasoline, and light repairs which cannot be done on the farm. Their children usually attend elementary school there, and most social activities center in the town.

The *neighborhood hamlet* is a simple service center, usually located at the juncture of two highways. In size it ranges from 25 to around 500 inhabitants. A general store or two, an elementary school, church, garage, service station, small lumberyard, repair shop, and a warehouse ordinarily complete the list of its service agencies.

The *farmstead* is the final consumption unit and the elemental production unit in American agriculture. From it go raw materials and foodstuffs to be fabricated and processed in world commerce, manufacture, and consumption. To it come finished commodities from the cities which it helps support; the cities, in turn, make possible the farm life of today.

These ecological units are not isolated or self-sufficient. Each is an interdependent unit in the complex metropolitan organization. Their size and structure are products of their functions in the competitive order of an organized series of markets.

URBAN PROCESSES AND STRUCTURE

Cities come into existence as a product of competitive interactions between people, market facilities, transportation and communication agencies, type of functions performed, and the resources provided by the site where they are located. Furthermore, the processes operative in the growth of cities are the same from the small provincial city to the large metropolis. Its organization varies with its size, economic functions, cultural peculiarities, and its position in the ecological network. Its physical structure tends to follow a characteristic pattern, with minor modifications due to topography and other unique factors. Processes operative in the organization of urban areas create the distributional pattern of institutions and people so typical of different cities. We shall now define and illustrate seven ecological processes underlying this phenomenon.

Concentration is the massing of human beings and human institutions in areas where nature or man has made conditions favorable to the satisfaction of sustenance needs. The principal factors responsible for concentration are the control of energy (animal, water, fuels—coal, oil, gas, and atomic), the development of machinery and industrial techniques and their application to the manufacture of goods, their transportation in the area organized by the market, and facilities for the rapid communication of information from one part of the market area to another.

Centralization is the integration of human beings and facilities around pivotal points at which social, economic, and cultural interactions occur most frequently. These focal centers are located where lines of transportation and communication converge. The center of community activities is associated with these focal points inasmuch as the essential community institutions locate as near to the center as possible.

Specialization is the sifting of similar social and population types or industrial and commercial facilities into specific districts. Competitive selection operative in the city forms hundreds of small apparently isolated clusters which, in reality, make up the substructure of the city. Banks, department stores, shopping centers, automobile rows, second-hand stores, wholesale districts, slums, and wealthy residential areas are all placed like the gaudy sections of a jigsaw puzzle in their proper places in the city's structure. Underlying specialization in an area is the competitive struggle for place and position in the community.

Invasion is the penetration of a specialized area by an institutional function or population group different from the one already there. It is a universal process in city growth. Its operation is a result of changes in competitive relationship among institutional agencies and population types within the city's framework.

Succession is a product of an invasion by a new function or population type into a specialized area or region. (This process will be discussed at some length in Chapter Twenty-Seven.)

Decentralization characterizes the tendency for selected segments of the population and particular types of institutions to move away from the center of the city and locate on the outskirts of the metropolitan area where space is available. Rapid motor transportation and electric power have accelerated the process. Thus, in the last quarter of a century we have observed the rise of vast shopping centers outside the central city and the rapid growth of the suburbs where middle- and upper-income groups have bought individual residences.

Routinization is the repetitious daily movement from place of residence to place of work or the shift into and out of the retail business, amusement, and wholesale districts by the city's population and those who use its services. The term refers also to the shunting about of goods within the city from storage warehouses to manufacturing plants or retail outlets.

CITY STRUCTURE

The structure of a city is contingent upon the operation of the seven ecological processes outlined above, for they create its pattern of distribution in space and time. The spatial pattern is integrated around the point of centralization where the largest number of individuals interact for the satisfaction of needs. Today, the city's spatial structure tends to follow definite patterns modified by local geographic and cultural conditions.

City growth occurs both from the center outward—*central growth*—and along local lines of communication and transportation—*radial growth*. Within the city the basic distribution pattern is a series of specialized areas extending from the center outward. In the expansion process each area encroaches on the contiguous one creating the dual invasion-succession process.

Geographical Zones. *The headquarters area or central business district* is the center of city life. Here are located the executive and administrative offices for finance, wholesaling, and manufacture. Found in the central area are the offices and agencies which integrate the city's life and function—department stores, hotels, theaters, municipal buildings, newspapers, and specialty shops, but few grocery stores. The highest land values are found in this area along with the lowest population density.

An *"interstitial area"* usually lies immediately outside the central area. It is characterized by high land values, but the buildings are deteriorated relics of the days before the center's functions began to invade the area. Along with light manufactures, here are the headquarters of vice, crime, and the men and women detached from their families who frequent cities. Poverty, personal disorganization, and delinquency exist here, as well as disciplinary and reorganizing agencies such as police stations, missions, settlement houses, and relief agencies. Interstitial areas are transitional areas. Many governmental projects have been aimed at converting them into either areas of workingmen's homes or into high-rent apartment areas.

The area of workingmen's homes is an area of flats in which shop and factory workers live. From about 1900 to 1940 this area was the second place of residence for European immigrants. Since the early 1940s, the typical area of workingmen's homes has increasingly been occupied by migrants from the rural south, white or black, and along the Eastern seaboard by large numbers of Spanish-speaking people from Puerto Rico or Cuba. In this area the family is the characteristic social unit. Grocery stores, bakeries, drugstores, shoe-repair shops, notion stores, and taverns are the principal businesses.

The high-class apartment and residential zone lies between the workingmen's and the commuters' homes. Along either side of the central arteries the apartment houses are strung out like high fences. Behind them, on the quieter streets, are homes still occupied by single families. Chain groceries, drugstores, specialty shops, and local theaters are the principal forms of business in these areas.

Suburban areas are composed of many specialized districts. Frequently on one side of a central city are found manufacturing satellite cities; on another, railroad yards; on a third, specialized residential suburbs; and completing the circle there may be intensified truck farms. There is a strong tendency for wealthy families to live in exclusive residential suburbs, while industrial workers tend to live in the less affluent suburbs. The suburban area normally ranges from thirty to sixty minutes of commutation time from the center of the city.

Differentiation within Territorial Areas. Within each specialized area are found many subdistricts (areas) characterized by: (1) *a few specific functions,* as in the financial and hotel districts; (2) *physical diversity,* e.g. skyscrapers or dilapidated frame-and-brick buildings in the ghetto; (3) *social distinctive-*

ness, as in the elegance and wealth of exclusive suburbs compared to the squalor and poverty of slums; (4) *a selection of population elements,* e.g. single adults in the rooming houses; and (5) *institutional adjustments,* as in the vice district where delinquent conduct is "normal." These are only a few of the many contrasts in the city's cultural districts. Each district is a product of competitive factors which draw into it appropriate functions and population elements and repel from it those who do not fit into its scheme of specialization or culture.

Studies of ecological organization have revealed that every type of human activity has a distinct pattern of distribution within and between the many specialized areas discussed in the preceding section. The explanation of this orderly distribution of cultural and social types is not wholly clear but may, perhaps, be regarded as an illustration of the general ecological principle that different types of human beings tend, with more or less inevitability, to drift into the particular niches in the territorial and cultural order in which they can most easily survive and then build up a variant culture within the framework of their interests.[1]

As society becomes more complex, an individual's function within it becomes more specialized, and differentiations into specific areas occur. Functional specialization creates the internal organization of a community. In this way competition more or less determines both the social niche (stratum) and the spatial niche (area of residence) an individual will occupy. In any event, the occupation by which an individual makes his living defines more or less adequately his place in the social and ecological orders.

In our civilization, the separation of place of work from place of residence has brought about most of the specialized residential areas found in all communities. A man functions within the economic sphere where he is needed because of the nature of his occupation; but within the noneconomic or familial sphere he lives where his tastes and interests dictate.[2]

SUMMARY

Ecological organization throughout the course of man's evolution on the planet Earth has been determined to an increasing

1 Albert J. Reiss, Jr. [ed.], *Louis Wirth on Cities and Social Life* (Chicago: University of Chicago Press, 1964).
2 Hans Blumenfeld, "The Modern Metropolis," *Scientific American,* 213 (1965), pp. 64–75.

degree by the knowledge man has gained in how to utilize the resources of his habitat. This knowledge is summarized in the word *culture*. While man has never been able to break the ties which bind him to nature, his culture has enabled him to modify these ties greatly. Viewed typologically, man's adaptations to nature have produced four basic forms of ecological organization —collectional and nomadic, horticultural and pastoral, settled village and town, and metropolitan. Each type of organization has been characterized by distinctive techniques to utilize the resources of nature in a given habitat. Moreover, each type has been dominant in a given phase of human history. In utilizing the resources of nature to meet his needs, man has developed specialized relationships to his habitat and to other human beings. He has also produced social structures, located in space and time, which enable individual human beings to live and work in communities. These communities range from the metropolis with millions of inhabitants to the small village and isolated family farm. Under modern conditions, the inhabitants of these varied communities are connected with one another by a network of market relations as well as by instantaneous communication and rapid rail, highway, and air transport.

Differentiation of function in the network of market relationships is accompanied by a series of ecological processes essential to the existence of the most complicated form of modern ecological organization—the city. These processes are: concentration, centralization, specialization, invasion, succession, decentralization, and routinization. The spatial and institutional structure of the city is controlled by the operation of ecological processes, as men compete for their livelihoods and other socially valued ends within the limits imposed by nature, intertwined with cultural factors in a vast multiform network of competitive relationships which tie them to one another and to their habitat on this planet.

CHAPTER TWENTY-FIVE

DOMINANCE

Throughout the course of human history man has organized his work and specialized his functions to meet his sustenance and social needs. In a particular society, individual men and groups of men have followed occupational pursuits which enabled them to produce the goods and services required for the maintenance of the community as a whole. A second principle, pertinent to the organization of human effort, is that specialization of function is accompanied by differential power relations between differentiated producing, transporting, and consuming units. Differential power relations between functional units—individuals, groups, organizations—imply inequality in decision-making among the interdependent units.[1] For specialized units to function meaningfully in the realization of social goals, there must be coordination between the participating units. This means that there is direction in the process. The activities of the participants in the productive, servicing, and distributive processes of communal life have to be controlled in some way by some unit or series of units. Ecologically, the controlling unit occupies a position of dominance.[2] A network of power relations links the dominant unit with all other producing and consuming units in the area it organizes. By so doing, it satisfies the population's ecological and social needs.

DOMINANCE DEFINED AND ILLUSTRATED

Dominance stated briefly, is the integration of diverse activities into a coordinated unity through the control of producing, distributing, servicing, and transporting processes in a society.

1 Gerhard Lenski, *Power and Privilege: A Theory of Social Stratification* (New York: McGraw-Hill, 1966), pp. 43–93.
2 Amos H. Hawley, *Human Ecology: A Theory of Community Structure* (New York: Ronald Press, 1950), pp. 220–222.

Dominance in human society depends upon the ability of some persons and groups to act, on the basis of funded experience and the news of changing events, to control the activities of other persons, groups, and institutions. Dominance may be exercised by competitive market processes where buyers and sellers meet or by deliberate planning on the part of government institutions.

Illustrations of dominance in this broad sense are: control by the United States of the money market through the medium of loans throughout the world, and control by Mecca of religious ideas in the Mohammedan world. Economic dominance arises from the control of transportation, communication, and market functions, whereas ideological dominance results from the ability to focus motivations on a particular item or idea in a certain place at a given time. Our general recognition that Paris and New York are the sources of feminine fashions illustrates this latter idea.

Center of Dominance. Ecologists have been more concerned with the influence of dominance on the competitive relations between communal units than in the process of dominance as an integral dimension of social organization. Thus, the location of dominance in the ecological network has been their central interest. In civilized societies, the center of dominance is generally the city. More specifically, the center of dominance in a city is the business section where financial institutions, executive authority, legal talent, and central offices of national concerns are located.

Gradients of Intensity of Dominance. It is characteristic of dominance, as it manifests itself in the processes of the marketplace, that control resides at the point of greatest activity (the city's business section), but its effects decline toward the periphery. The effects of ecological dominance extend just as far as social, cultural, economic, and political agencies centered in the city radiate in their control of activities located in the areas subordinate to the central authority. This principle is evident in both the growth of the city and in the expansion of the area influenced by it. Field investigations have shown that the intensity of control decreases as one moves outward from the center toward the margin of the area of dominance. This principle is known in general as the *dominance gradient,* and it holds good for many items, the best known of which (because they have been most thoroughly investigated) are newspaper circulation, trade, and traffic. Since the same forces which produce interdependence between center and margin for these three items have operated to create and maintain the existing territorial distribution of social and economic functions, newspaper circulation, volume of trade, and traffic flow may be taken as indices of the degree of dominance which an urban center exerts over the area it organizes.

One of the effects of television, radio, and the daily newspaper has been the extension of the area of urban dominance over an increasingly wider territory through the control of the news and advertising. This development was made possible by the perfection of instantaneous electronic communication and high-speed transportation. Although the dominance of the city in broadcasting and newspaper publication is important in the organization of modern life, it is the dominance of central banking, manufacture, and marketing which exerts the most pervasive influences upon the growth of cities and the areas subordinate to them.

DOMINANCE AND ECOLOGICAL POSITION

The competitive position of a given location in an area of interaction is determined by natural resources, that is, by physical conditions, and by the technological culture of a people. Usually both factors actively enter into the situation in such a way that it is impossible to separate the physical from the cultural; likewise, it is rather naïve to attribute determinism to one or the other. In its pristine state a site may possess every conceivable advantage, but it will not ordinarily attract human activities and institutions necessary for its development unless it comes into the competitive arena dominated by some distant center. For instance, New York City did not develop until its site became a frontier outpost in the colonial economy centered in London. The potentialities of Chicago as a site developed only after the railroad from New York made it the connecting point between the central continental hinterland and the world market.

CENTRALIZATION OF CONTROL;
DECENTRALIZATION OF OPERATION

The development of modern instantaneous long-distance communication, such as radio, television, telephone, and teletype, has brought about a reorganization of industrial and commercial activities. It has given rise to centralization of control and decentralization of operation in nationally and internationally organized businesses and industries. Executive control is concentrated where foci of communication converge; here the management of distant enterprises plans and directs operations in accordance with market demands. Industrial plants and commercial enterprises are so situated that they can most effectively meet competition throughout the area organized by the market.

Two trends are developing through the centralization of control and the decentralization of operations: *First,* centers of dominance serve to integrate activities over wider and wider areas. Stock and produce exchanges, executive offices, financial agencies, transportation headquarters, and the central communicative offices integrating the far-flung network of modern intelligence are the effective, dynamic integrators which dominate activities throughout a market area. *Second,* spatial separation of intelligence center from work center is developing direct communication and transportation between place of production and area of distribution. This trend has been accelerated in recent years by the development of large-scale air transportation of people and goods. In sum, such centers of dominance as New York, Chicago, and Los Angeles are becoming more powerful in controlling the ecological organization in the areas subordinate to them than they were a quarter of a century ago.

CHARACTERISTICS OF AN IMPORTANT CENTER OF DOMINANCE

In the dynamic center, every kind of function becomes highly specialized. While the physical parts of a spatially distributed ecological area integrated by the center of dominance may be physically far from the center, they are connected with it in three ways: through means of transportation and communication built and controlled by financial institutions in the city; through the organization of the market located in the specialized dominant center; and through specialization in interdependent economic, political, or cultural functions. Specialization reaches its highest form in the center of dominance but its influence extends to the margin of activity. The primary function of the center is to create an integrative relationship between the specialized parts which are dependent upon one another.

Another product of the intensive interrelationship existing

between the functional parts of our integrated ecological order has been the rise of specialized urban centers which are themselves dominant in a particular way. This is illustrated in the manufacturing phases of the automotive industry: for instance, Duluth ships ore; Toledo makes tools and gears; Niagara, aluminum; Akron, tires; southern mill towns, upholstery; and so on for hundreds of automotive parts in many other cities. In the Detroit area the interchangeable parts are assembled into the final product. With the assistance of the advertising and financial ends of the industry, located in New York City, the machines assembled in the Detroit area are finally purchased by consumers in all parts of the United States and the world market. In summary, thousands of productive, distributive, and servicing processes are located in hundreds of specialized centers spatially separated but functionally integrated through a few key centers which control all phases of the industry.

One of the most important trends in present metropolitan economy is the development of specialized cities and the subordinate areas they dominate. The industrial city, in turn, is essentially subordinate to a metropolis which integrates the multiform activities performed in its satellite cities and their tributary areas.

THE DYNAMIC CENTER

The place (in an area of competitive interaction) which can be most easily, quickly, and cheaply reached from the many locations in its suburban areas by information, goods, services, and human beings becomes the heart of the center of dominance. Thus, in New York City the core of the metropolis is Manhattan south of Fifty-ninth Street; in Chicago it is the Loop. Briefly, each city has its dynamic center usually typified as "the business district."

The concept of dominance implies that, within a territorially distributed culture complex, cultural achievements are concentrated in one or, at most, a few centers. The conditions which make achievement possible are located in the centers of dominance. Here the highest levels of culture are consolidated and then diffused to lesser centers and to the open country. The highest achievements have almost always been identified with cities. The city supplies a much larger percentage of distinguished men than its population ratio warrants, for most of a nation's leadership is developed in the city. The city influences politics more than its population justifies; it leads the society in fashions, morals, manners, attire, and language. In the city are located the institutions which supply creative leadership in all branches of art, science, business, politics, and religion. Sanitation, health, and welfare institutions were developed in the city. Today, the great universities, research foundations, art centers, libraries, museums, and hospitals are almost all located in metropolitan centers. These institutions are all dependent upon an economic surplus for their support. Great wealth, thus, represents a vital resource which can be, and is, used for the further creation of capital as well as for the advancement of culture in modern urban-centered societies.

DOMINANCE AND STABILITY

Theoretically considered, if the factors which produce a center of dominance remain constant in a competitive network of interdependent relations, then a condition of stability will result. The center should remain dominant so long as the factors which produced it continue to operate. In actuality, this condition is never realized, for the conditioning factors which produce a center are subject to intermittent fluctuations. Consequently, centers of dominance and the areas they dominate are subject to change. Viewed historically, old centers decline as new ones arise in response to emergent factors that change the pre-existing balance.

Each center, in its rise to dominance, passes through a series of changes which tend to integrate its activities and at the same time to disintegrate them. In this developmental series there occurs a period of rapid change, succeeded by a period in which the number of changes declines; then there emerges a phase of relative stability characterized by few changes. This latter period may last for a considerable time but tends inevitably to give way to another series of changes. As a city grows, its role as dominant integrator in its subordinate areas increases, but if a new competing center challenges an old center successfully then the old center gradually declines and the attributes of dominance associated with the old are transferred to the new center.

Competition plays a variable role in this process. During the interim phases of change in the life of a city, area, or region, competition increases in importance but, as adjustments are made to the new situation, custom and tradition actively enter the scene to influence the situation. As institutions become rigid and fixed, the role of tradition becomes more important and competition tends to decline. When such a condition develops, the activities of persons are routinized in response to custom and consensus. Thus, there emerges a relatively stable social order. This, in turn, will be broken down by the intrusion of new factors of a competitive nature which upset the cultural balance.

Briefly and abstractly we have presented an interpretation of the differences between competition as an ecological process and customary usages as a social process. Actually, competition and custom are correlatives—both are ordering processes. Competition, in ecological relations, gives rise to an integrative exchange of information and/or goods and services between competing units in a situation, whereas custom, as a social process, tries to fix by consensus between the interacting units the relationship attained by competition. *Competition* as a process is constantly trying to order ecological relationships within an unstable situation, whereas *custom* assumes that once a relatively stable condition has been attained it can be controlled more or less permanently by rationalizing activity in routine ways. Empirically, however, the equilibrium model assumed by custom and consensus is never attained. Thus, change is occurring, in fact, even though a center of dominance appears to be stable at a given point in time.

Historically considered, centers of dominance have maintained their position as long as the society they integrated has retained economic and/or political power over the satellite territories which they control. The historical record indicates that the world's centers of dominance have shifted northward and westward as one culture declined and a new one arose to integrate human activities. In this process, metropolitan centers have moved from river valleys, mountain fastnesses, and broad plains to the rims of the continents. Concomitantly, water-borne commerce has supplanted overland trade between one market center and another. Likewise, the market areas which dominant cities control have gradually increased until today we have only a few world metropolises. But such giants as New York and London are being successfully challenged by the rise of continental and oriental centers. The older cities try to rationalize their positions by appealing to treaties, past policies, and so on, when actually there is regrouping in world affairs in response to new conditions.

SUMMARY

Human beings organize their social activities by specialization of function. To have organization and specialization, social actions need to be coordinated and integrated by some individual, group, or institution able to exercise control. To exercise control, the more powerful individual or institution must have dominance over the less powerful. Thus, in the interaction that takes place between the units in the system there are *superordination* and *subordination*. Viewed ecologically, the superordinated unit, whether an individual or an institution, is dominant over the subordinated unit. Historically, dominance has been exercised in civilized societies by cities. Power, wealth, and planning functions have been centered in one or more cities which have dominated the subordinate hinterland. The exchange of information, goods, and services between center and hinterland has enabled the population to satisfy its organic and social needs for a longer or shorter period of time. While centers of dominance tend to persist through several generations, possibly even centuries or a few millennia, they are subject to change and challenge by new centers of dominance as competitive conditions change by the discovery of new processes, new resources, new modes of communication, and transportation.

Ecological dominance discussed in this chapter is only one kind of dominance existent in human societies. Other, and of course more familiar, forms are moral and political in nature. These forms are generally spoken of as "social controls" because they arise from social relations which we like to think of as rational. However, these more sublimated and sophisticated forms of control—if one may use the term "sophisticated" in this context —are related in the final analysis to the more elementary form of dominance described in the preceding pages, namely human control of the processes and conditions essential to the existence of the species from generation to generation under the circumstances imposed by nature and society.

CHAPTER TWENTY-SIX

MIGRATION AND MOBILITY

Migration is the movement of people, individuals or groups, from one locality to another. This process entails the transmission of cultural artifacts, traits, ideas, and techniques from individual to individual, group to group, and society to society. From the viewpoint of ecological theory, man adjusts to the conditions imposed upon him by the physical environment, to other men, and to the culture in which he lives. When conditions are stable the population of a community remains in relative balance with the sustenance available to it. Stated otherwise, there is an equilibrium between numbers and resources. The adjustment between numbers and resources is maintained by approximately equal birth and death rates over a shorter or longer time span. When some event or change in the conditions of life upsets this biotic balance, the spatial and sustenance relations of the population are altered. New adjustments have to be made to meet the changed conditions. Change in the relations of the population to its sustenance base may be brought about by drought, famine, floods, earthquakes, new technological knowledge, war, or an invasion of a society's territory by an alien people. Whatever the upsetting event or condition, the balance between the population and its sustenance base gives rise to new adjustments. Historically, one of the most common types of human reactions to changes in conditions of living is movement to another place.

Commentators upon human affairs who are disposed to take a broad and philosophic view of the human scene have been impressed by the profound historical significance and pervasive influence upon culture and society of man's wanderings from habitat to habitat. The fact that migrations involve new contacts and conflicts of peoples and culture has led social scientists to emphasize the importance of migrations, and the wars that are so frequently associated with them, as fundamental factors in the advancement of civilization. It is now generally thought that relative permanence and fixity, where they exist in society and culture, are largely a consequence of the isolation or absence of contacts between people with divergent cultures—a condition which a stable population tends to produce. Man appears to be emancipated by migration from the fixity of social institutions and the tyranny of tradition and custom which characterizes an isolated people. When a people migrates, it carries its old culture with it to its new home. Migrations usually bring two peoples with different cultures into close relationships.

THE MIGRATION PROCESS

Writers of the eighteenth and early nineteenth centuries attributed importance to migration and cultural conflict as the agencies by which a rational order progressively supersedes a customary and nonrational order. There has, however, been little effort expended by sociologists to analyze and distinguish the manner in which the different forms of migration actually take place or, for that matter, to define precisely what is included under the term migration. Ordinarily, migrations fall into three general classes: (1) *nomadic shifting* of people over wide areas for sustenance purposes; (2) *occupation of an area* for military, political, or economic purposes but, because most of the invaders are males, without normal reproduction within the conquering migrant group; and (3) *true migration* which involves both change of habitat and settlement, and possibly the amalgamation of the invaders with the indigenous population. When the newcomers and the previous settlers intermarry and their cultures become intertwined, the migrants are said to be assimilated. The second and third types involve the contacts of peoples with variant cultures and, especially, miscegenation between the invaders and the indigenous population.

Primitive Migrations. Migrations among primitive peoples were essentially mass shiftings of whole tribes from one area to another. More often than not, they were motivated by a search for food or plunder. Usually the migrations were warlike, resulting in the clash of divergent peoples. Out of these struggles came new adjustments. In short, early migrations were mass movements like the westward expansion in the United States and the great trek of the Boers in South Africa, a kind of swarming of the peoples seeking in the wide open spaces a new freedom where family and tribe might have opportunity to live, each according to its own conception of the good life.[1]

Wandering of People. The great classical migrations of antiquity were one wave of population following upon another. They were movements out into a strange land, movements which involved whole tribes who were pushed out of their customary habitats by war, famine, disease, or marked changes in climate. This wandering of people—*volkwanderung*—whose racial characteristics and tribal cultures were probably formed in isolation, finally settled them down together on the land. It was out of this conjunction of tribes, races, and cultures that civilization, as distinguished from the local and tribal cultures which contributed to it, has arisen.

Medieval Migration. The migrations of the Middle Ages were of a different kind. They were not movements of whole peoples but of individuals who performed specialized functions in the society. These migrants were merchants and middlemen, journeymen, handworkers, wandering knights, jugglers, and minstrels. This type of migration represented for the most part the movements of men in search of adventure and profit, not pioneers destined to extend the area of permanent settlement.

In the course of time the merchants settled about marketplaces and these centers became towns. Commerce, which began with the exchange of luxuries, was followed by a wider exchange of necessities. Thus, the expansion of trade extended the area of specialization and furthered the division of labor. So far as trade was free, it increased the area of economic interdependence and undermined the economic independence of the different regions.

Modern Migrations. Migrations during the last three centuries have, in the main, assumed the form of *individual and family movements* from one home to another. The effect of this form of migration has been to disperse peoples and to undermine traditional ancestral cultures. In the present century, the individual migrant is normally an industrial or agricultural worker who from necessity has to seek his fortune among strangers. Two notable exceptions to this generalization were the highly trained refugees who emigrated from Europe immediately before and after World

1 E. T. Mason, "Migration and the Food Quest. A Study in the Peopling of America," *Annual Report of the Smithsonian Institution,* July 1894.

War II and, more recently, emigrants from Cuba who have been largely well-trained business and professional people. Viewed generally, however, migrations in the twentieth century have been characterized by the movement of individuals with few skills from one country to another in search of a better life. Some of these migrations were motivated by political conditions in the home country, but several million unskilled workers have migrated from south and southeastern European countries to northern European countries since 1945 and have been employed in industrial plants in urban areas. This movement of rural and peasant workers to industrial areas has been a worldwide phenomenon in the post-World War II era.

In scope, modern migrations are: (1) *intercontinental,* involving the movement of peoples not only across national borders and cultural areas but also across oceans, or (2) *intracontinental* which may be of two kinds—(a) *international* such as the penetration of Italians into Switzerland, Germans into Poland, and Mexicans into the United States, or (b) *intranational* as the shifting of population from rural to urban districts, from east to west, north to south, and vice versa as in large continental countries such as Brazil, the Soviet Union, the Union of South Africa, and the United States. Two streams of migration have moved from one part of the United States to another during the last quarter of a century: rural peoples have moved out of the southern states to northern cities and Puerto Ricans have migrated from the island to the eastern cities on the mainland. Some of the current severe problems faced by our large cities are symptoms of the adjustment processes entailed in migration.

Conditions of Migration. The general compulsives discernible in migrations, both primitive and modern, continue to obtain although they vary in intensity and form depending upon the specific conditions under which they operate at a given time. Usually conditions underlying migrations are grouped into two broad categories: *changes in the physical environment* such as major climatic shifts, and *changes in the sociocultural environment.* Changes in either environment may act as expulsive or attractive factors in the migrations of peoples. Under primitive conditions most migrations were probably caused by a combination of both. Most modern migrations, however, have been conditioned by changes in the sociocultural environment. The motivation of an individual's decision to migrate may be traced to general economic, political, and social conditions both in the country of emigration and in the country of immigration as well as to personal desires for gain or for adventure.

The general conditioners of migrations since the Columbian Era of discoveries have been mainly economic (sustenance) in origin and development. The expansion of peoples in the past four centuries has been worldwide in scope and significance. The form of expansion from roughly 1500 to 1900 involved the establishment of a frontier settlement by a European or Asiatic country on the rim of an undeveloped continent. These settlements were usually political or economic outposts, oftentimes both. Since 1900, most immigrants have settled in urban areas and become employed in large-scale industrial processes or found employment in service activities or retail trade.

In the period from 1500 to 1900, capital from the homeland was sent to exploit the open resources in the new lands. Along with capital went overseers, engineers, and workers; later came settlers in areas where Europeans could settle successfully. Where they could not, Africans or Asiatics were imported. Migration tended to follow the path of capital in the exploitation of the new continents. Once the settlement structure developed, any modification in the techniques of organizing the economic life in these areas resulted in migration of workers and settlers to places where new exploitation of resources was occurring. Old areas of exploitation lost or gained population when a new cycle of development began. Thus, capital development, economic specialization, division of labor between interdependent areas, and general economic and political conditions motivated modern population movements, both intercontinental and intracontinental, internationally and intranationally.

Effects of Migration. Migration is a conditioning factor in the inception and development of new cultural forms. Customary and traditional ways of life give way to new forms as the migrant individual is freed from the repressive regime of custom characteristic of settled stable societies. The migrant individual's energies are released for creative as well as destructive thinking and acting. The migrant individual freed from customary restraints is able to roam in search of adventure.

Migrations disturb well-balanced adjustments of numbers to each other and to the sustenance base. New adjustments take place. Meanwhile, competition operates in one of three ways to determine the number and distribution of population units in any given area: (1) It tends to limit the number of inhabitants in the area to what the population was before the migration began unless new knowledge and techniques are developed for the utilization of the sustenance base. (2) If the conditions created by the intrusion are adverse, excess numbers will be expelled. (3) The new population may increase under the new forms of adjustment to the new habitat.

In its most elementary manifestation, man's competition with other men takes the form of the natural increase of births over deaths, in the course of which a people by the mere force of increasing numbers will occupy successively an ever-larger territory within the common habitat or within a territory over which another people has established some claim. Thus, a concomitant of natural increase may be territorial control as well as numerical predominance.

In this way there was a rapid expansion of European people overseas from the period of the great discoveries and explorations beginning in the latter part of the fifteenth century until the close of World War II. During this epoch peoples of European origin increased about twice as rapidly as the peoples in other parts of the world. Since the end of World War II, the non-European peoples of the world have increased more rapidly than the peoples of Europe and of European origin. The increase of non-European peoples in Asia, Africa, South America, and the islands of the Pacific in the post-World War II years is traceable to a more favorable ratio of births to deaths. This has resulted in a rapid natural increase of the populations in these areas of the world.

The excess of births over deaths has its origin in the ability of a people to increase and flourish under conditions imposed by the soil, climate, disease, and the existing social order, rather than in its ability to enforce its claims to the soil by military prowess. This struggle of competing peoples to expand within the limits of the human habitat ordinarily terminates in the most elementary form of control which the struggle of living organisms everywhere produces—the dominance of mere numbers—but population size is only one of many ecological factors which help determine the military potential of a people. With a balance in their favor, the economic and political dominance of one people over others can be achieved and long maintained in spite of numerical inferiority.

Migration and Settlement. To survive, any species has to come to terms with its habitat. In the case of man, this means that migrants must settle down some place. They become acclimated, and gradually they find the niche in the community in which they can live. Man's reactions to his environment are so multiform that he has covered the earth with his reconstructions and modifications of nature. He not only has altered the face of the earth but also recreated plants and animals and modified the natural conditions and order in which the different species came into existence. In addition to the process of naturalization in the biotic community, the migrant and new settler has to find a place in the social order which is imposed upon him as a stranger and newcomer by those already adjusted to the conditions of life in the community.

Socialization and Assimilation. The process by which the individual is incorporated in the customary and institutional order of a society is best described as *socialization*. The process by which a migrant group becomes fully adjusted to its new environment is known as *assimilation*.

The assimilation cycle involves successively, under ordinary conditions, competition, conflict, accommodation, assimilation, and eventually biological amalgamation into the society. Socialization and assimilation are complementary processes. Socialization takes place with the incorporation of every new generation into a society to which its members are indigenous. Assimilation is an intergenerational process. It involves the incorporation of a migrant group into an indigenous population. While socialization takes place in every generation, assimilation may take several generations before the descendants of a once-migrant group are fully incorporated into a society.

MOBILITY AS A CONCOMITANT OF MIGRATION

Population movements may be classified into two broad categories: migration, and mobility. In a strict sense migration entails mobility, that is, a specific kind of movement in space and time within a social framework, but mobility does not necessarily have to involve migration. In fact, in the modern world, movements of people, goods, and ideas within a social system have in many respects become substitutes for migration.

In general, one may say that with the development of instantaneous communication and high-speed transportation there is relatively less migration of persons and more mobility of persons, ideas, and commodities within an ecological system. We must distinguish, however, between those movements which are customary, such as the travel of executives from industrial plant to industrial plant by jet airplane, and those which involve some break in the routine of the individual's habits and the customs of a society. For instance, one cannot call a migration the daily cycle of movement of workers from their homes, perhaps in the suburbs, to their shops and offices in or near the center of the city. On the contrary, this is a simple, routine, habitual process. Such routine movements tend to crystallize and fix the structure of society. (This process was discussed above, on page 258.) On the other hand, movements which interrupt routine and create the necessity for some intelligent and creative action tend to undermine tradition and change institutions. They also usually involve migration from one place of settlement to another.

Modern man who, through the media of instantaneous communication, international finance, and integrated industry, has made the world tributary to him is not searching for a place in the wilderness which no hunter has disturbed or for some remote stretch of steppe or pasture where a shepherd can tend his sheep without fear of disturbance. The civilized man goes to the city to seek his fortune, to sell an idea, or to get a job. The place he looks for is somewhere in the ranks of an established social and economic order—not in the wilderness. This is why a considerable proportion of modern movement represents mobility within and between societies, as we have defined it, in contrast to migration as it existed among earlier peoples.

Social Mobility. All historical and contemporary societies are characterized by a greater or a lesser amount of social inequality. Social inequality arises from the differential evaluation of specialized pursuits men follow as they compete with one another for a place in the community. Some occupational pursuits are evaluated highly, such as financial managers and surgeons in American society. Other occupations carry a different and a lower position in the value structure, for example clerk in a supermarket. A few occupations are given a very low social position in the hierarchy of values—laboring in the fields or shining shoes.[1] A pecuniary value is placed upon practically all occupational pur-

1 Robert W. Hodge, Paul M. Siegel, and Peter H. Rossi, "Occupational Prestige in the United States, 1925–63," *The American Journal of Sociology*, 70 (1964), 286–402.

suits. The surgeon is paid highly for his services; the field laborer
is paid a meager wage. For the vast majority of men the income
they receive from their occupational pursuits is transformed into
goods and services. The income available to the individual and his
family determines his level of living. Where the individual lives
in the community and how he lives are controlled, in very large
part, by his ability to compete with his fellow men through the
mechanism of his occupational pursuits.

The quest for success in a network of competitive relations
in an ecological system may give rise to an individual's movement
in social space. If the questing individual is able to gain access to
a larger share of the community's wealth, increase his level of
living, move to a better home, and acquire new friends considered
to be in a higher social stratum than the one into which he was
born, we say he is *upward mobile*. If the questing individual is
unsuccessful in his efforts to maintain himself in the social stratum
into which he was born and slips downward in social status, we
say he is *downward mobile*. An individual who carries out the
occupational pursuit expected of him in a competent manner but
remains in the same stratum as his parental generation is viewed
as *socially stable*. In a general way, competition for a niche in the
community's ecological system is accompanied by movement in
social space for a larger or smaller number of individuals, while
the remainder of the population remains in the stratum characteristic of the parental generation.

SUMMARY

The migration of peoples brings cultures into collision.
Changes result from the shock. Previously established institutions
are destroyed or greatly modified. The ecological and social relations no longer tie the individual into the old, established cultural
orders. He becomes mobile and is forced to make new adjustments to the changed conditions. For the individual to survive he
must reorient his activities to the demands of his new environment—physical, social, and cultural. Out of the flux emerges a
new synthesis, a new order, which molds personalities and culture
elements into a functioning complex of correlated and integrated
culture traits. The phases of change which occur when a disruption takes place are known as *succession*. We discuss this concept
in Chapter Twenty-Seven.

CHAPTER TWENTY-SEVEN

SUCCESSION

The term *succession* is used to designate a sequence of changes associated with the organization of an ecological area during two or more time periods. The area subject to succession may range from a region to a segment of a community. Changes involved in a successional series are related to each other. The form and rapidity of successive changes are, in the main, consequent upon the component cultural factors active in the developmental organization of the resources of the area by its inhabitants. In most successions at least three types of changes occur which transform ecological relations in the affected areas: *First,* alterations take place in the spatial distribution of population units and institutional services; these alterations are accompanied by changed sustenance relations. *Second,* a new sociocultural order is formed, with fundamental changes occurring in many aspects of the pre-existent order. *Third,* a new population type with a characteristic composition normally accompanies a succession.

Succession involves the movements of population into and out of an area as well as changes in the uses of land in the area. Both aspects of the succession process (changes in population and land use) take place in time and involve changes in relationships of a vital, functional, and spatial nature. Succession (of a population type or land use) may be confined to a specific area within a city, or it may encompass an entire community or region. As such, succession may be regarded as a universal process applicable to every human group that ever existed on the earth's surface during a given era.

Succession encompasses all forms of orderly change which affect interactions of individuals in a community. Succession, also, entails changes in the physical structure of a community and gives rise to changes in the structure of the society. Three significant ideas are included in the term succession: (1) A human community at any given moment is composed of symbiotic and social relationships. (2) Viewed over a longer or shorter temporal span, changes in these relationships take place as competitive conditions change. (3) The changes that occur over the years compose a series leading to either the growth or the disintegration of the community.

TYPES OF SUCCESSION

Succession as a process may be classified into five types: (1) cultural, (2) territorial, (3) demographic, (4) occupational, and (5) land utilization. These types overlap, and they interact with one another.

Cultural Succession. In this category fall those phenomena known to the prehistorian as the "stages of culture" and to the historians as the "succession of empire." Prehistorians are concerned with the sequential development of cultures from the Eolithic Era to the dawn of civilization. To the historian, succession includes the rise of one civilization and the decline of another. For instance, the vicissitudes that mark the Christian Era are usually designated by historians as the Decline of the Roman Empire and the Medieval, the Early Modern, and the Modern periods.

Territorial Succession. Any habitable area on the planet Earth is subject to change of occupants. The long procession of known peoples who have invaded and settled South Africa is illustrative of this fact. First came the Bushmen, hunters who left interesting rock pictures in caves in the mountains as a record of their presence. Then came the Hottentots, hunters but herdsmen also; they had a great deal of trouble with the Bushmen who killed their cattle with poisoned arrows. In due course, the Hottentots drove the Bushmen into the Kalahari Desert. Following these came the Bantu, hunters and herdsmen, but also cultivators of the soil.

With the expansion of European peoples to the southern tip of Africa after 1500, the Dutch established themselves in Capetown and spread gradually inland. In the seventeenth and eighteenth centuries the European settlers expanded their numbers by an increase of births over deaths. By the early years of the nineteenth century, the descendants of the original European settlers had invaded the lands to the north and east of Capetown. The mixed European population, mainly of Dutch descent, were known as Boers. A large segment of this population began an aggressive invasion of the interior portions of South Africa about 1830 and became known as the Voortrekkers. With their families, livestock, wagons, implements, and firearms, they took over the lands. Settling the Transvaal and the Orange Free State, they conquered and enslaved the natives, raised large families, and lived on their extensive lands in patriarchal style. They became, as a result of their isolation, a separate society with their own language (Africaans), customs, and culture.

The Voortrekkers' way of life was changed by the discovery of diamonds (Orange Free State in 1872) and gold (Transvaal in 1884). The succession in South Africa which followed these discoveries was conditioned, in large part, by the influx of thousands of English. The British had established themselves militarily at Capetown at the beginning of the nineteenth century, and in the beginning their efforts were confined largely to coastal areas of the region. Within a few years after the discovery of gold and diamonds, however, they moved into the interior of South Africa in force. There they built Johannesburg, a cosmopolitan city—in fact, a modern world city like Hongkong, Tokyo, or São Paulo. In this way, they drew South Africa into the current of international trade and into the new world civilization. South Africa became a modern industrial nation, but the cultural influence of the Boers has not been lost, as exemplified in the Afrikaans language and possibly in the policy of apartheid.

South Africa is particularly relevant as an illustration of succession for three reasons: *First,* the settlement process outlined above exemplifies the general principle that, other things being equal, the simpler the technology of a people the larger the territory needed in proportion to its numbers to support its population. *Second,* within the competitive conditions prevailing in a market, the land eventually goes to the people who can extract the most valuable resources from it. *Third,* South Africa represents the five forms of succession we are discussing.

Demographic Succession. Demographic and territorial succession are intricately interwoven one with the other. The former cannot be separated from the latter, for with a change of territorial occupancy comes a change in population type and composition. The successive waves of population by which the American frontier advanced from the Atlantic Seaboard westward across

the plains to the Pacific Coast, each advance marked by a different population type, is an illustration of demographic succession on a national scale.

Territorial and demographic succession are involved also in
the intramural movements and shiftings of population incident to
the growth of cities. In the United States immigrant peoples ordinarily settled first in the so-called "areas of transition" near the
centers of cities. From there they moved by stages—one might
better say by leaps and bounds—from areas of first to areas of
second and third settlement. This movement was generally in the
direction of the periphery of the city and eventually into suburban areas.

In recent years the central thrust of demographic succession
in the United States has been the movement of millions of economically impoverished rural dwellers into the older portion of
our cities. These new migrants have become the successors of the
earlier immigrants from south and east Europe who settled in
these same areas roughly from 1890 to 1915. The latest migrants
have invaded these areas in large part since 1945. Today, it is
fashionable to refer to these areas as "ghettos," "innercities," and
"slums." Viewed ecologically, the newest migrants, whether they
are from Puerto Rico, Mexico, the rural south, or the mountains
of Appalachia, are an integral part of an invasion-succession sequence.

Occupational Succession. In an industrial society the occupational structure is formed on the basis of the different functions
individuals perform in the economy. The occupational structure
may remain relatively stable over long periods, but the individual
units in each occupation change over a relatively short term of
years. The base of the occupational structure is composed of
unskilled laborers, usually representatives of an unassimilated
ethnic or racial group who are new arrivals in the industrial
process, whereas the apex of the structure is composed of representatives of an assimilated segment of the population who are
the owners or managers of industry, finance, and large businesses.

The occupational structure of a given industry tends to be
made up of different ethnic or racial groups who have been
engaged in the industry for various lengths of time. As one migrant group becomes adjusted to the demands of the competitive
process, a new one generally enters the occupational pyramid at
the bottom. As individual members of each ethnic or racial group

rise in the social scale, individuals from other ethnic or racial groups are introduced at the base of the pyramid to carry on the activities of unskilled labor. In American society the new "hands" are ordinarily new migrants into the labor market of the area. When this occurs, a new invasion takes place, followed by succession, from the bottom of the pyramid toward the top, of those individuals and groups who are able to accommodate their activities to the demands of the market. As the upward mobility process continues, new ethnic and racial concentrations are found in specific occupations. Concomitantly, spatial redistributions of these population groups occur in different parts of the community, as the successful members rise in social status and move into different and usually better residential areas.

Land Utilization. Land is utilized differently under different conditions of settlement and market organization. Land utilization may be viewed as an index of the phase of development of the metropolitan economy in a region. Within the confines of the city the use and value of land indicate the point of dominance. Land values are highest at the center of financial and corporate activity and, other things being equal, they decline with increasing distance from the central area. Furthermore, land values reveal a definite succession as land utilization shifts from one type to another, for example from grain farming to truck farming to residential or commercial uses to factories and possibly office buildings.

CONDITIONS UNDERLYING SUCCESSION

The definitions and illustrations cited indicate in a general way the process ecologists refer to as succession. To understand how the process works we need to take into consideration the conditions precipitating the changes which give rise to succession and the forms the changes exhibit as they pass from one phase to another.

Etiology of Succession. Etiological elements in succession include the following: (1) Conditions obtaining in the biotic and physical environments may change, such as a modification in climate or the exhaustion of a natural resource. (2) The existent structure of ecological relations may be upset by a change in technology or other aspect of the culture, such as the development of automotive transport. A change in one aspect of a culture may and often does initiate change in many other aspects. (3) New interactions are created between people and institutions in response to cultural changes. (4) A new demographic complex may emerge as spatial and economic relationships are changed through adjustment of numbers to the sustenance base in response to new competitive conditions. New conditions may be viewed as intrusive factors in any existent situation. As these factors operate over time, they bring into existence a new succession.

Change of some kind is always occurring, although the rate and pace of particular changes may and do vary, sometimes greatly. Minor changes may be mediated without profoundly disturbing the existing routine of communal life. When, on the other hand, a sudden and catastrophic change occurs—war, famine, pestilence, or any change that upsets the biotic balance and alters the routine of customary behavior—it releases energies which up to that time had been held in check. A series of rapid changes may ensue which may profoundly affect the existing organization of communal life and give a new direction to the future course of events.

Human ecology assumes that if one could trace the origin of change to its source it would be found in the territorial and occupational distributions of peoples that are brought about by their struggles for existence. So far as this conception is valid, it assumes that most, if not all, cultural changes will be correlated with changes in the territorial organization and that changes in the territorial and occupational distribution will effect changes in the existing social organization of a people. The history of a society is, therefore, in one of its aspects, the evolution of a territorial organization. The human ecologist assumes that social change has its origin in some crisis, some break or interruption in established routines. Each crisis has a history that makes a comparative study of crises possible and, for the purpose of social theory, interesting. In fact, succession may be regarded as resulting from a series of recurrent crises.

Morphology of Succession. The beginning of a succession may be traced to a *crisis* in the lives of a people in the affected area. The crisis is a point in time and in the area from which events take a turn in a new direction: an invasion of an area by an alien people; a discovery of a new natural resource; a war or revolution; disease, drought, or famine; the development of a new technology. Whatever the stimulus for the crisis it almost invariably has a place in a definite configuration of events. Each succession, thus, has unique qualities which characterize its development. Successional changes ordinarily do not follow a rhythmic pattern. There is a tendency, however, in the development or decline of communities for a period of relative stability to be followed by a period of rapid change which, in turn, is succeeded by another period of relative stability.

Crises in human affairs have been systematically studied by different types of scholars. The dramatic aspects of business booms first attracted the attention of economists. Likewise, the catastrophic consequences of cholera in Europe attracted the attention of medical doctors. Both booms and epidemics were once regarded as chance events due to "acts of God," wars, or droughts. Later, it was discovered that business booms and depressions as well as epidemics of disease occur not by chance but as a phase of a clearly defined configuration of events.

SUMMARY

Succession as a temporal process involves changes in a territorial area along one or more dimensions: the age and sex structure of the population; its ethnic or racial composition; the distribution of the gainfully employed in different occupational groups; the users of land in the affected area. The efforts of individuals and groups of individuals to meet the conditions of life as they compete with nature, other plant and animal species, and with one another for a place in the community are the underlying conditions which produce successions in a communal area or a region.

Part Six

Social Problems

By

ALFRED McCLUNG LEE

Brooklyn College

of

The City University of New York

TOPICS (*cont.*)

CHAPTER TWENTY-EIGHT

TYPES OF SOCIAL PROBLEMS

A social problem is a question or issue about a development, a tendency, or a situation in human affairs that concerns one or more groups. It deals with a social difficulty said to require attention. Such attention takes the form of discussion and possibly also of agitation, investigation, and decision. It may lead to corrective, compensating, or adaptive action. Frequently social viewpoints differ and even conflict on the nature of a social problem or perhaps on whether or not it is a problem at all. A given formulation of a social problem is a part of the opinions typically expressed on the issue by members of one or more of the groups making up a public. Some social problems, such as those associated with depression or war, may concern a whole society and still be variously conceived and stated.

EXAMPLES OF SOCIAL PROBLEMS

Social problems are as varied as are the groups constituting society and the ills besetting mankind. Let us look at examples as they find expression in the behavior of individuals, of groups, and of society more extensively and as they are discussed in the mass media.

Individuals. An unmarried girl faces the tortures of an unwanted pregnancy and wonders how she could have been "so dumb." A young car thief from an "exclusive" subdivision gets "another chance" when the owner, his parents, and the police all agree to "cover up" for him after his promise "not to do it again." For the same offense, a slum youth may go to a reformatory or have his sentence suspended through the intervention of a politician.

Groups. Some teen-age hippies "turn themselves on" with marijuana. A group of white and Negro farm workers watch a mechanical cotton-picker bring economic, social, and psychic chaos into their lives. Human products of overcrowded slums and of disintegrating rural areas threaten the health and safety of all neighborhoods.

Society. The pollution of air and water threatens our cities and farmlands. Still another country joins the "nuclear club" with an atomic "hell bomb" explosion. The "population clock" of the world ticks on and adds each year the equivalent of another United Kingdom or Italy or more to the human total.

Mass Media. In discussing some of these items as social problems, a journal of opinion points to cynicism in high places. It alleges a "credibility gap" between facts and official utterances. It sets forth examples of arranged news and of other propaganda manipulations through the media of mass communication. On the other hand, other media assert that we must have faith in our over-burdened and dedicated leadership.

All such evidences of social problems are variously perceived and stated. For involved individuals and groups, they can be pressing, bitter, or even disastrous in their implications.

WHAT DO SOCIAL PROBLEMS HAVE IN COMMON?

What brings together for sociological consideration a Kansas dust storm and drug addiction? What do a slum uprising and an upturn in the incidence of syphilis have in common? All are problems of human beings living in groups and in society. All are perceived as social questions or issues requiring concerned attention and action. The integrating thread is that these are all questions confronting man in society. They are all aspects of the human lot. A knowledge of man, his groups, and his society can help us to understand social issues and how we might be able to cope with them. As a response to social problems, sociologists devote themselves to increasing our knowledge about man as a social entity and his life in his groups and his society. We can thus learn more about the social contexts of a dense fog laden with poisonous industrial fumes which sicken and kill those beneath it. We can see more of the social implications of a flood ripping through homes, factories, and eroded farm lands and thus discover more how society might work toward a social atmosphere in which preventive measures would become possible and even adequate.

HOW DO SOCIAL PROBLEMS DIFFER?

Social problems involve human beings, their groups, and their society and thus have significant human aspects in common. At the same time, they differ in important respects. One way of classifying these differences is in terms of the following seven features:

OVER-ALL CHARACTER. This is illustrated by illegal traffic in narcotics, by a breakdown in community ties or controls, by frictions among ethnic or racial groups, and by international conflict. This topic is discussed in the next section.

AGENT RESPONSIBLE. This is exemplified by an individual violation of law, interracial aggression, a general situation of economic depression or over-abundance, a natural catastrophe. Whether an economic depression results from the operation of natural forces beyond the control of individuals or from specific acts of leaders of government or business has been the subject of considerable debate. Viewed otherwise, available human agencies and economic measures have been useful in abating the severity of depressions. As these points suggest, dealing with agency is a complex problem. Who is responsible for a race-segregated ghetto —the migrants crowding into our cities? the tenement owners who continue to subdivide their holdings, raise rents, and refuse to spend money for needed maintenance and service? other owners who refuse to accept the migrants as tenants? or government officials who fail to plan and to act? A social problem usually arises out of multiple causes, better perceived as a complex social process, in which a tangle of agencies may be operative and in which the agents have quite narrow conceptions of their participation. The agency to be used for corrective measures is a separate problem, to be considered in terms of availability and effectiveness and not in terms of blame.

SOCIAL VISIBILITY. This is illustrated by contrasting covert abuses in government or business with the consequences of their revelation in a powerful news medium. What had been embedded in usage and hidden from public inspection by social ignorance becomes a matter of public outrage and the center of a public power struggle.

GROUPS CONCERNED. These may range from a neighborhood to a vocational group, a city, or the country, from a numerous but powerless racial group to a powerful but small elite.

MANNER PERCEIVED, DEFINED, OR STATED. This may be suggested crudely with such terms as "the white problem" and "the black problem," "100 percent Americanism" and "conscientious objection," "loyalty" or "conformism" and "dissent."

URGENCY. This may mean an endured annoyance, an organized effort to achieve gradual change through educational procedures, a demand for immediate government action by powerful groups, or a precipitation of spontaneous conflict as in a ghetto riot.

THE CORRECTIVE PROCEDURES VISUALIZED. This may stress education, agitation, picketing, recourse to the courts, lobbying in legislatures, petitions to administrators, boycotts, research, rioting, employment of specialists, construction of needed facilities, war, or the negotiation of peace.

These seven variables enter into all the following chapters of this part. Only the first one will be outlined in more detail here.

THE OVER-ALL CHARACTER OF SOCIAL PROBLEMS

A further classification of the over-all character of social problems must be rough at best. These six headings are helpful: (*a*) man-land relations, (*b*) periods in individual and family life, (*c*) atypical and deviant behavior, (*d*) aspects of major social institutions, (*e*) social divisions, and (*f*) social crises.[1] Reflecting the tangled web of human affairs, these categories all overlap. A decline in water resources, listed in (*a*), may disrupt the individual and family life of farmers (*b*), help develop interpersonal tensions to which atypical persons cannot adjust (*c*), focus attention on inflexibilities in educational facilities for their children (*d*), stimulate interracial and interclass agitation (*e*), and, if sufficiently persistent and acute, become a major social crisis (*f*). Here are additional illustrations of these six types of social problems:

Man-Land Relations. Problems having to do with man-land or ecological relations are those arising out of the conditions—including spatial relations—deriving from the physical environment.

---

1 Adapted from Elizabeth Briant Lee and A. McC. Lee, *Social Problems in America*, rev. ed. (New York: Holt, Rinehart and Winston, 1955).

They include questions of overpopulation, overcrowding, under-population, dislocations through international and intranational migrations, transiency, deficiencies and inflexibilities in urban design, the flights from rural areas to urban ghettos and from cities to suburbs, the camps of homeless refugees in many parts of the world, sudden changes in productivity, in distributive arrangements, and in other aspects of technology, and changes in the availability of land and other resources. Those concerned with national, regional, and town and city planning try to cope with such problems through suggesting patterns with which to adapt transportation, housing, and other facilities to changed conditions, but man-land problems also necessarily involve policy-makers for a great many other types of organization.

Periods in Individual and Family Life. Under this heading may be placed those problems which characteristically arise during certain periods of the life-cycle of an individual or family. These are such times as babyhood, childhood, adolescence, wage-earning years, premarital adulthood, child-rearing and post-child-rearing family life, retirement, and bereavement. Typical questions associated with such periods are: What are the social implications of birth control and family planning? How adequately are child adoptions handled? What about "black market" adoptions? What about children of broken homes, adolescent maladjustments, parent-youth conflicts? What is being done and can be done about sex education, lack of opportunities for the unmarried to meet, unwed mothers, divorce and desertion, disrupting illnesses and accidents, aging, retirement, bereavement? Sociologists and psychologists provide data and theoretical orientations to these problems, and educators, social workers, clinical psychologists, psychiatrists, and social policy-makers try to work out practical solutions.

Atypical and Deviant Behavior. Social problems may arise from the deviant behavior of those who are malformed in body, who are aberrant in mind, or who have had abnormal socialization experiences. Physicians, psychiatrists, psychologists, and social workers as well as special teachers can be helpful to such people individually and in groups. Sociologists are concerned with them as parts of our social environment and with how social programs and instrumentalities may effectively aid them. In our society, the atypical and the deviant include drug addicts, alcoholics, sex perverts, suicides, delinquents, criminals, the brutal, the excessively exploitative, accident victims, those responsible for accidents, those prone to be victims of delinquents and criminals, and those otherwise diseased physically and mentally. At the same time, they also include the famous and the especially talented. The atypical and the deviant are taken to be persons who do not conform to social norms sufficiently to keep from being regarded as different, queer, superior, inferior, unusually virtuous, or unusually evil. (See Chap. Five above.)

Aspects of Major Institutions. Under this heading can be placed examples of social control and manipulation, of community organization and disorganization. These aspects contribute to personal disorientation and disorganization as well as to personal stability and security. The major social institutions include the family, the educational, the economic, the governmental, the religious, and the recreational. All of these are shaken today with controversies and occasionally with scandals. What are the social uses of academic freedom for students and for faculty members? How far should young minds be opened and strengthened? To what extent should they be shaped? What is the nature of conflicts between management and workers? Why are nonwhite workers so disadvantaged in business and industry? Is bureaucratization a blessing or a threat to society? Perhaps it is both? How can consumers protect themselves against fraud in the marketplace? What is automation of so many organizational operations doing to people? Whose propaganda should one believe? How can we understand and cope with social power, with unwarranted and even antisocial controls, with harmful social manipulation?

Social Divisions. Under this title, we include principally *ethnic* and ethnic-like or *ethnoid segments, social strata,* and *occupational groups.* These cross-hatchings of our society result in the development of *social status groups,* each of which tends to be located in one social stratum and in one ethnoid segment and to be related to one general type of occupation.

The ethnic groups of the United States presently consist of the more or less absorbed immigrant groups from abroad and of various aboriginal American Indian tribes. These are slowly merging into new ethnoid segments (the "Colored" and the "white," i.e., the "Jewish," "Roman Catholic," and "Protestant." Quotation marks have been employed here to emphasize that these labels are indicative of *social identity* and background rather than of scientific biological classification or active religious practice.)

Our social strata reflect our custom of ranking ourselves and our fellows into "layers" according to presumed social prestige, power, and status. These strata are usually taken to be (*i*) the powerful and/or famous at the top—the "elites" of our society; (*ii*) the "big" people of localities or local elites, also called the "upper middle-class," (*iii*) the "better" people or "strainers," often designated the "middle and lower middle-class," (*iv*) the "common men," those below the "strainers" who have achieved "respectibility" through relatively stable patterns of striving or employment, and (*v*) the "ne'er-do-wells" at the bottom, also said to be the "lower lower-class," the stratum of the unstably and irregularly employed, the unemployed, and the unemployable— the poverty stratum.

The principal occupational groups into which we further divide these strata are those associated with the *occupational status ladders* of (*i*) the enterprisers, individuals and their families absorbed in some "game" of experimentation or exploitation in business, government, educational, recreation, or religion, (*ii*) the bureaucrats, those involved in maintaining themselves and in getting ahead in "the organization," whatever that organization might be, (*iii*) the vocationals and professionals, whose merchandise and major preoccupation consist of techniques of a trade or profession available for hire, and (*iv*) the artisans, artists, inventors, and scientists who are devoted to novelty, uniqueness, self-expression.[1]

From the crisscrossing of these divisions, as we noted above, our society develops social status groups at their junctures. Each social status group has a somewhat distinct group-culture and often its own special jargon, at times even its own dialect or language. Our many social status groups provide their members with orientations to society which differ and which sometimes come into competition and even conflict with one another. Misunderstandings among them are a continuing problem in our society. How can we benefit from our social diversity and minimize our intergroup tensions and conflicts?

---

1 These divisions of United States society and their nurturing of social status groups are discussed at length in A. McC. Lee, *Multivalent Man* (New York: George Braziller, 1966), esp. chaps. 14–17.

CHAPTER TWENTY-NINE

PERSPECTIVES ON SOCIAL PROBLEMS

The basic definition of a "social problem" differs only slightly among sociologists, but the contexts of theory and value into which the definition's terms may be fitted diverge widely. Our definition in the previous chapter is typical in that it stresses the setting of a social problem in public opinion. It thus relates the problem to the patterns of attention, perception, need, and expectation embedded for the members of a group or a society in a group-culture or culture.

A social problem is especially significant as a focal point of the concerned attention of a group's members. Without such concerned attention, no social problem exists. Many deprived group-members, for example, view with amazement the reactions of the more privileged to their life conditions.

SOCIAL PROBLEMS DEFINED

For the purposes of the discussion in this chapter and the next, our definition of a social problem can be given more of the character of a formula, each term of which permits some latitude in specification and even greater latitude in interpretation. The definition, divided into nine terms or aspects, is as follows: A *social problem* is (*a*) a *question or issue* (*b*) about *something*—a development, condition, tendency, situation, person, or group— (*c*) *perceived* (*d*) as a *social difficulty* (*e*) by *one or more groups* (*f*) which are giving it *concerned attention* (*g*) through *processes* of discussion, investigation, and decision-making, and possibly also of agitation, (*h*) with or without an *anticipation* (*i*) of achieving corrective, compensating, or adaptive *action*.

In the following, some references are made to one or more terms in this definition for the purposes of comparison. As will be seen, various perspectives bring social problems into relationship with considerations other than their setting in public opinion. In moving from the level of opinion in any investigation and discourse to a more probing and analytical one, we need to be aware that we are changing the character and the social context of our discussion.

MAJOR DIFFERENCES IN PERSPECTIVE

When sociologists go beyond a basic definition of a social problem, divergences in perspective become marked. These variations reflect contrasting uses of terms, contrasting values, contrasting conceptions of the nature and services of sociology and of sociologists in our society and in the world.

We cannot divide all the available perspectives up into neat categories, but we think it instructive to examine briefly some of the principal ones. We shall do this through offering definitions for twenty principal terms that are useful keys to such overlapping frames of references: (*1*) social deviation, (*2*) social pathology, (*3*) social disequilibrium, (*4*) impediment to progress, (*5*) maladjustment, (*6*) cultural lag, (*7*) conflict of interest or value, (*8*) anomy, (*9*) disorganization, (*10*) dysfunction, (*11*) social change, (*12*) social reconstruction, (*13*) social reform, (*14*) social engineering, (*15*) social policy, (*16*) social strategy, (*17*) action research, (*18*) social experimentation, (*19*) applied sociology, and (*20*) clinical sociology.

Sociologists usually fit two or more of these terms into their orientation. It also needs to be recognized that there are sharp differences in viewpoint concerning some of the definitions, especially when those definitions involve values or ethical positions. The following discussions are offered as a way of highlighting many of the variations of emphasis in the field and of suggesting ways to judge the differences.

1) *Social Deviation* is a departure from the socially anticipated that is sufficiently great and sufficiently obvious to attract attention. The deviation may be in the character or in the behavior of an individual, a group, a social structure, or even a society. A society is only adjudged deviant in terms of the norms of another society, not of its own current norms.

Whether or not a person or a behavior instance is deviant is not an absolute or a universally accepted decision. Like a social problem, it depends upon the norms of those who are its current judges. Such norms vary among groups, among societies, and through time. At a given time, each group or society differs from others in the degree to which it tolerates deviation, in the sanctions or homogenizing pressures it brings to bear upon deviants; in other words, on the extent to which various deviations are perceived socially as social problems. Social deviation includes intellectual, religious, artistic, economic, and political nonconformism as well as delinquency, crime, addiction, and mental illness.

What is typically specified as normal societally is reflected in legislation, administrative and judicial acts, and in orthodox ideology and criteria for what is legitimate. An official judgment as to what is deviant reflects popular consensus only as it is weighted or distorted by the deciding representative of an existing power structure. There are significant contrasts many times between what a deviant person thinks he has done and what an official perceives that deviant's action to have been.

All deviant behavior is not evidence of pathology or disorganization, of social disequilibrium or anomy, but some of it may be so interpreted. Deviant behavior also includes the constructively experimental, the creative, the usefully innovative.

2) *Social Pathology* refers to the "diseased" condition of some aspect or of all of society. It is a departure by a person or a group or a society from its norm of social health. The term is borrowed from the healing arts by simple analogy and with little adaptation.

This orientation pictures relevant social problems as symptoms of a social illness. This view, in extreme form, holds that our culture is sick, that we are all more or less disordered mentally, and that our society must become the "patient" of social specialists. Deviations from a social norm are no longer, in consequence, so clearly taken to be abnormal in public opinion. In this view, the specification of "normal" becomes increasingly difficult.

Some social pathologists stress the impact of social disorder on the individual. They see "distinct problems such as suicide, narcotism, and racial and ethnic tensions . . . as *symptomatic* of fundamental dislocations of the social structure," especially of "crisis-generating aspects of our basic institutions." The "several problems falling within each area of social disorder" can be analyzed, in one conception, in terms of (*i*) symptomatology, (*ii*) statistical evidence, (*iii*) social latencies, (*iv*) social and cultural dynamics, (*v*) case study insights, (*vi*) personal latencies, (*vii*) situational dynamics, and (*viii*) social types.[1]

To paraphrase our definition of a social problem, the concern of a social pathologist can be seen as an effort to achieve analysis on a more fundamental level than that of public opinion. In place of popular perceptions, the social pathologist attempts to substitute those of trained, experienced, and motivated specialists who presumably can diagnose the situation and guide the use of available remedies in hope of a cure.

The use of the organic analogy here and elsewhere in sociology distorts the character of society, its constituents, and its problems. It assumes a higher degree of integration and of articulation than one can actually observe in society. It glosses over distinctive differences between biological and social processes and structures. It suggests the attempt to borrow the mantle of authority of the medical practitioner even though the social practitioner has no choice eventually but to be judged on his own merits.

3) *Social Disequilibrium* and its positive counterpart, social equilibrium, have long enticed those who seek in the imageries of the physical and biological sciences a way to conceptualize the changing interdependent relationships in society. "In a broad sense *equilibrium* denotes some kind of balance among a plurality of interrelated social phenomena. This balance may be manifest or merely latent; it may be posited as objectively real or as purely analytical; it may be either static or dynamic."[2] Rather than on such a physiological or medical analogy as that used in social pathology, this conception usually rests on a physical one. The equilibrium may be one that modifies through time, but it is the "normal" state toward which the social "system" tends to return after the termination of events making for temporary imbalance of disequilibrium. Such an abstract conception may be suggestive to some, but it can easily distort social theory through oversimplification and through a bias often built into its formulation. Because criteria for social equilibria tend to be stated in terms of the maintenance of an existing power complex, advocates of equilibrium-disequilibrium theories frequently appear to oppose social experimentation or even social change.

---

1 H. A. Bloch and Melvin Prince, *Social Crisis and Deviance: Theoretical Foundations* (New York: Random House, 1967), p. 15.

2 Walter Firey, "Social Equilibrium," pp. 654–655 in Julius Gould and W. L. Kolb, eds., UNESCO *Dictionary of the Social Sciences* (New York: Free Press, 1964), p. 654.

4) *Impediments to Progress.* Progress is such a popular conception for social change in a desired direction that some sociologists have tried to give it scientific usage. In this light, a social problem is an impediment to social progress. Whether or not such an impediment will inevitably be swept aside by the impersonal social forces operating historically depends upon one's interpretation of social historical data. An alternative is to assign great influence in the stimulating of social change to the gifted leader or to the dedicated action group.

Conceptions of progress already accomplished or to be achieved depend upon ethical judgments, upon the popularly accepted goals and values of a people in a time and place. Such conceptions have now been replaced in general scientific usage by those associated with the ethically neutral term, *social change,* in an effort to transcend the culture of the analyst's time and place. Judgments about alleged social progress are data for sociological consideration rather than scientific conclusions. "The progress of humanity . . . cannot be proved either true or false. Belief in it is an act of faith." [1]

5) *Maladjustment* indicates that some aspect of society is failing to perform as socially anticipated or required. It implies departure from a condition of satisfactory behavior and suggests the possibility of adjustment or re-adjustment, of a return to something resembling a previous condition. Like the term, maladaptation, maladjustment often carries with it the sense of a *systemic* model drawn from physics or biology, but this need not be the case. It can be a term for a problem in personal or social organization or interaction on which concerned attention may possibly achieve corrective action.

6) *Cultural Lag* "occurs when one of two parts of culture which are correlated changes before or in greater degree than the other part does, thereby causing less adjustment between the two parts than existed previously." [2] It is thus a kind of maladjustment that may be overcome by cultural adaptation. It is illustrated by the lag which developed in this century between the rapidly increasing potentialities of the automobile on the one hand, and the design and construction of adequate highways in this country on the other.

1 J. B. Bury, *The Idea of Progress* (re-issue: New York: Dover, 1955), p. 4. *Cf.* Morris Ginsberg, *The Idea of Progress: A Revaluation* (London: Methuen, 1953).

2 W. F. Ogburn, *On Culture and Social Change,* ed. by O. D. Duncan (Chicago: University of Chicago Press, 1964), p. 86.

Cultural lag is thus a way of analyzing certain types of social problem. It represents a judgment of the relative adaptation to changed conditions by the culture traits in question. It may refer to an issue, development, tendency, or behavior pattern. As such, it raises these difficult analytical questions: Is resistance to change in an aspect of society necessarily undesirable? Cannot unevenness in cultural change also be seen in other lights than that of "lag," for example as stimulating creative tensions? Does not "cultural lag" resurrect in another guise many of the indeterminable implications of "social progress"? Is not belief in the benefits of better highways for speedier motor vehicles an act of faith based on transient considerations? Does not cultural lag lead to a kind of reductionism by overemphasizing the immediate effects of particular changes rather than their broader social-historical context?

7) *Conflict of Interest or Value* frequently enters into terms of our definition of a social problem. Both interest and value color the manner in which something is perceived by one or more groups as a social difficulty. Interest may be as varied as are the objects toward which individuals or groups are attracted and to which they accept or assign value. Confrontations between groups with contrasting interests can take the form of accommodation, competition, or conflict. Social problems include questions on which contrasting interests and values lead groups to struggle for contrasting conceptions and solutions as well as to engage in such more overt conflicts as interracial and interethnic outbreaks and even wars.

8) *Anomy* (also: *anomie*), from its Greek derivation, means lawlessness or normalessness. In sociology, it has come to be used in these two principal ways: (*a*) It refers to a *social* "state of deregulation" arising from a disequilibrium in which social forces are freed and "their respective values are unknown and so all regulation is lacking for a time." [1] This is usually interpreted as a situation in which there is a conflict of norms and a lack of social enforcement. (*b*) It refers to *personal* confusion, disorientation, desocialization, disorganization, and antisocial behavior. Such personal behavior may or may not be due to an anomic social situation.

Social anomy thus resembles social disorganization. Their differences are ones of emphasis. Personal anomy, on the other

---

1 Emile Durkheim, *Suicide: A Study in Sociology*, ed. by George Simpson (Glencoe, Ill.: Free Press, 1951), p. 253.

hand, differs from personal disorganization by including other types of normless and lawless behavior as well.

9) *Disorganization* is used sociologically in connection with both the social and the personal. Social disorganization is "a decrease of the influence of existing social rules of behavior upon individual members of the group." Individuals frequently break social rules, and there is thus continually some tendency toward social disorganization. Such disorganization when incipient is ordinarily offset by activities which reinforce existing rules. "The stability of group institutions is thus simply a dynamic equilibrium of processes of disorganization and reorganization." [1] As this suggests, there is a reciprocal relationship between personal and social disorganization.

The personally disorganized include those disorganized by social influences and also those disorganized by disease and by natural catastrophes. It is at the same time difficult to distinguish those who are disorganized from those who might better be called unorganized. The latter includes individuals so marginal genetically in their physical or mental equipment as to be unable to function normally in society. The disorganized and unorganized may both find themselves in deprived groups. Both may notably fail to adjust to dislocations due to technological change, depressions, and wars.

Social disorganization is thus what is taken at a given time and place, in a given social situation, to be a disturbing deviation from "normal" social organization. Personal disorganization is similarly what is taken at a given time and place, in a given social situation and in terms of the values of a given society or group, to be an undesirable deviation from "normal" personal organization as revealed by appearance or behavior. The use of these terms presents the sociologist with problems of developing criteria for what constitutes problematic deviation as well as of understanding for whom it is problematic.

10) *Dysfunction*, in a social sense, "refers to a *designated* set of consequences of a *designated* pattern of behavior, belief, or organization that interfere with a *designated* functional requirement of a *designated* social system." [2] This definition, as well as

1 W. I. Thomas, *Social Behavior and Personality*, ed. by E. H. Volkart (New York: Social Science Research Council, 1951), pp. 234–235.
2 R. K. Merton, "Social Problems and Social Theory," pp. 775–823 in Merton and R. A. Nisbet, *Contemporary Social Problems*, rev. ed. (New York: Harcourt, Brace & World, 1966), p. 818.

the term itself, suggests a straining for an impression of precision beyond what an adequate sampling of social data can sustain. The consequences of a pattern of behavior are dependent on changing situational factors. A designated functional requirement can scarcely be an absolute matter; it would be from the standpoint of some particular group interest and value orientation that should be recognized and specified. For one to speak of a "social system," which is necessarily a customary fiction or myth about the nature of social organization, one would have to select the fiction of one particular group together with the interests and values that that fiction would favor. Once one realizes the ramifications of these interest and value implications of a "social dysfunction" or "social function," the conception becomes no more precise, no more manageable, and no less relative than others we have been discussing.

11) *Social Change* refers to any limited or general alteration in social structure and process, in social issues, or in the social character or behavior of persons, groups, or society at large. It may be stimulated or precipitated by any type of incident or tendency or development. The term has displaced "progress" because of the latter's ethical or culture-bound, time-bound, group-centric, and ethnocentric implications. It is also favored over "evolution" because many writers persist in finding progressive and organic connotations in that term even though "social change" and "evolution" can well be defined as approximately synonymous.

Social change may or may not refer to adjustive or adaptive behavior. It includes both adjustive and maladjustive modifications as well as alterations or mutations which appear to be neither.

12) *Social Reconstruction* is "a production of new schemes of behavior and new institutions better adapted to the changed demands of the group." [1] It is a deliberate effort at social reorganization through planned change. Such planned change must needs be attempted in the midst of highly complex social processes, and therefore unanticipated consequences of such an effort may come as surprises or even as disasters to the planners. Our knowledge of social change still leaves much to be desired, but few would say that we should not attempt deliberate, planned change in

---

1 Thomas, *op. cit.*, p. 235.

order to try to cope more adequately with the many disturbing aspects of our social situation. The social reconstruction so stimulated may not please its initiators, but that may not be too relevant in judging the social benefits obtained.

13) *Social Reform* is a conception resembling social reconstruction. The sociologist of social change includes it in his subject matter, among the data he studies. The sociologist of social problems conceives of his job *as a sociologist* as being that of fact-gatherer and analyst. He studies and can give informed assessments of the workability of plans for stimulating or inhibiting social change. On the other hand, the development of plans for the reorganization or reconstruction—the reform—of a part or all of society is in the province of social engineers, politicians, agitators, and reformers. If such practitioners of arts and powers of change utilize the findings and counsel of social scientists, they may save time and social wear-and-tear thus gaining in effectiveness and efficiency.

14) *Social Engineering* includes efforts at social planning, manipulation, and change for predetermined purposes. The services of trained sociologists as social engineers are now sought by many types of firms and agencies for the improvement of their personnel relations, product design, advertising and other forms of publicity, sometimes called image-management, and of dealings with and controls over other firms and agencies. Problems related to the ethics of the social engineer are occupying more and more of the time of committees of the professional sociological societies.

When a sociologist becomes a social engineer or a social reformer, he is still called—with the inaccurate connotation that he still functions as a scientist—a sociologist. Unfortunately, such terms as "social engineer" and "social reformer" do not appear to carry sufficient professional prestige even though they are certainly more accurate and appropriate.

15) *Social Policy* is a somewhat consistent course of procedure or conduct in social affairs, especially in the behavior of those in control of an organization. It may or may not be publicly announced. It may or may not be consciously formulated. There is often a contrast, at least in detail, between an organization's ostensible policies and those apparent in its activities, its actual policies.

Sociologists concerned with social problems often speak of

themselves as being policy-oriented or action-oriented. By this, they mean that their investigations in connection with social problems are planned to provide bases for policy formation or modification, in other words to guide decision-makers in re-thinking the policies controlling the actions of organizations under their control.

16) *Social Strategy* is a term closely related to social policy. It refers to procedures to be used in implementing social policies and especially changes in social policies to the best advantage of the interests or program being forwarded. Through comparative studies of strategies and through the testing of strategies in limited situations, sociologists can aid those planning social programs.

17) *Action Research*, or action-related research, might also be called policy-related research. It is research carried out as scientifically as the involved sociologists can make it and planned to deal with policy and strategy aspects of a social problem. As sociologists are able to establish more adequately the value to subsidizers of thoroughly scientific research, this type of investigation and analysis becomes more possible.

18) *Social Experimentation* is a loose term which has often been criticized. The term, experiment, suggests the using of human beings in test situations without respect for their civil rights, but such an extreme sense is not the only tenable one. Those in positions of social decision-making responsibility are constantly confronted with the possibility of making more or less experimental decisions. An agency, bureau, union, or corporation which fails to find and accept fresh ways of dealing with its changing problems starts to rigidify and to decline in effectiveness. Experiments with changes in policy and strategy can often be tested in aspects of an organization's program before being accepted for use more generally.

19) *Applied Sociology* "is not government or politics, nor civic or social reform. It does not itself apply sociological principles; it seeks only to show how they may be applied. It is a science, not an art. The most that it claims to do is to lay down certain general principles as guides to social and political action."[1] Original contributions to sociological knowledge arise from the work of applied as well as of "pure" sociologists. The

---

1 L. F. Ward, *Applied Sociology*, chap. 1, reprinted in Israel Gerver, *Lester Frank Ward* (New York: Thomas Y. Crowell Co., 1963), pp. 58–59.

former are more directly concerned with the marshalling of facts and theories for the guidance of the social reformer or social engineer in the solution or mitigation of social problems. The latter try to limit themselves to what they take to be the more basic sociological problems. As we shall see in the next chapter, the applied sociologist first tries to find the sociological problems underlying the social problems with which he is concerned. The alleged purity of the "pure" sociologist has been at times merely a rationalization for concern with problems of relative social insignificance or for the avoidance of controversial data.

The distinction between applied and "pure" sociologists is thus more one of possible emphasis and of actual sponsorship than of precise definition. The Society for the Study of Social Problems, dating from 1950 and formally organized in 1951, has helped to give a greater impetus and a higher status to applied sociological work.

20) *Clinical Sociology* or the clinical study of society is an approach to applied sociology. It is a method of investigation that stresses the participant observation of spontaneous as well as of planned behavior in actual social situations. It is the concerned, objective, intimate, continuing, and thoughtful observation, critical evaluation, and absorption into evolving theory of the spontaneous social responses to corrective or manipulative efforts. It is thus the first-hand study and diagnosis of social problem situations.[1]

As in the foregoing discussions of related matters, that which might well be called the sphere of the social practitioner should not be confused with that of the clinical sociologist—the fact-gatherer, diagnostician, and theorist of dynamic social-problem situations. The social practitioner is concerned with carrying on efforts at social reform, social reconstruction, or social engineering. When he patterns his work after a clinical model, the social practitioner has his eye especially on considerations of practitioner-client relations, sometimes called "bedside manner." He attempts to use the wisdom in client relations and particularly to develop the autonomy from client prescriptions nurtured by other types of clinical practitioner. When the clinical social practitioner "recognizes that he has the problem of helping his client *learn*

---

1 A. McC. Lee, "The Clinical Study of Society," *American Sociological Review*, XX (1955), 648–653, and "The Challenge of the 'Clinic,'" chap. 22 in *Multivalent Man* (New York: George Braziller, 1966), esp. pp. 330–331.

CHAPTER THIRTY

PROBLEMS:
SOCIAL AND SOCIOLOGICAL

Science is one type of response to human problems. It owes its development to the concerned curiosity of talented men and women about such questions. The stimulating problems are especially the recurrent and persistent ones with which existing theories and techniques have somehow failed so far to cope. The tested observation that does not fit existing knowledge, the arrogance of vested authority, the threat of social disaster, the death of a mother from cancer, the alcoholism of a father, the slaughter of loved ones in a riot or a war, and millions of other personalized evidences of minor and major human problems affect the lives of millions. Such problems also so influence the lives of a few thousands directly or indirectly that they become creative scientists. They turn to systematic study, to searches for new "answers" to the problem that touched them. They are alert especially to the possible significance of *unanticipated* observations, the source of a great deal of new knowledge.

The intricately interrelated fabric of scientific knowledge—physical, biological, and social—is the weaving together of the experiences scientists have gained in millions of such searches for answers to general and specific, directed and derived problems. At any given time and in all the various specialities, the accumulated knowledge does not consist of absolutes. It is in effect a report on the best currently available estimates of reality and of how to cope with it. These estimates are always subject to further revision in the light of new and more dependable data.

The general attitudes and methods of scientists, regardless of field, stress observation and imagination. They call for the accumulation, verification, and understanding of sense experiences, and they recognize that imagination leads scientists on to new questions, new hypotheses, new sources of data, and new research techniques. As scientists have disciplined their thoughts and tested their imaginings with careful observations, they have gradually refined more and more useful and precise tools and techniques for observation, measurement, generalization, and at least limited prediction. With such tools and techniques, they have produced more and more dependable guides for meeting human needs and desires.

SOCIOLOGY AS A RESPONSE TO SOCIAL PROBLEMS

Sociology, like other social sciences, owes its appearance and development to those who dedicate themselves to a study of pressing and burdensome human problems. Physical and biological scientists concern themselves with certain aspects of strife, race, alcoholism, drug addiction, disease, prostitution, physical handicaps, and many other problems. Social scientists find in such problems significant aspects which are typically social and through the study of which they can contribute understanding and mitigation. Sociology has grown especially as a response to problems raised by migration and assimilation, by ethnic and racial differences, by industrial and urban unrest, by rural disorganization, by problems of morale in wartime and in depression, by persisting poverty, and by other social stimulants to personal disorganization.

Social problems, as popularly stated, can do little more than initiate a sociologist's concerned investigation. As the sociologist works with them, he has to probe more deeply than such a conception drawn from public opinion can take him. Thus, the superficial social problems are replaced, in effect, by more comprehensive and probing conceptions of them, i.e., by sociological problems.

SOCIOLOGICAL PROBLEMS

These are questions or issues so stated that they reflect a broader, comparative perspective on social problems and on their social settings. Such statements also often lead to more and more fruitful and accurate investigations. A sociological research may start with (*a*) a social problem as popularly discussed, (*b*) a more fundamental and probing reformulation of a social problem, or (*c*) a problem discovered through critical reconsiderations of sociological data, method, and theory in the light of accumulating research reports and changing events. Regardless of the definitions of problems and of the statements of hypotheses they might make at the outset of an investigation, sociologists constantly strive for more basic and precise ways of conceiving their research problems as they proceed.

To permit rigorous and productive investigation, each sociological research problem must be given precision in the wording of its plan and hypotheses, be subject to study through available methods, facilities, and personnel, and be brought into relationship with relevant social theory. This is not at all to say that social importance or scientific significance should be sacrificed in order to achieve greater precision or to depend only upon already-tested methods or theory. Determination to attack important social problems can sometimes score surprising gains in spite of weaknesses in method, facilities, and personnel.

On going from a social to a sociological statement of a problem, such questions as the following are raised concerning the nine aspects of the initiating social problem set forth in our definition at the outset of the preceding chapter.

a) How is the question or issue being stated by members of various groups?

b) To which development, condition, tendency, situation, person, or group do group-members point as basic to the problem? How accurate are such popular diagnoses? How significant are they?

c) How do popular perceptions of the problem differ? From what do the differences appear to arise?

d) For whom is the problem said to be a social difficulty? What kind of a social difficulty?

e) What group or groups define it as a social difficulty? In what terms? For whom?

f) How much and what kind of concerned attention are those involved giving to the difficulty?

g) What processes of discussion, investigation, decision-making, and agitation are being used in connection with the difficulty? How are they being employed?

h) What significance may be attached to the outcome anticipated from such concerned activity? In other words, what are the goals of those involved in the problem? How significant are differences in goals?

i) Does corrective, compensating, or adaptive action appear to be possible? If so, can research provide guidance for suitable policy changes and strategies for the relevant organizations? Is such guidance likely to be accepted and used? On what probable terms? What other alternatives exist or can be created?

From such probings can emerge a broadly sociological understanding of the social problem in its many ramifications. This understanding generally leads to new lines of investigation, new researchable sociological hypotheses, that take understanding and guidance further.

The distinction between a "social" and a "sociological" problem rests on the difference between a problem from the world of affairs, as crystallized in public opinion, and a problem as it is stated by sociologists in their striving for greater understanding and guidance. The popular formulation of a social problem may or may not be precise; it is *particularistic,* i.e., it is practical, focuses on immediate concerns, lacks account of the broader setting. A developed statement of a sociological problem is relevant to its broader setting in social history and social theory; it is as precise and concise as it can be made.

By this distinction, we do not mean to imply a rejection or belittlement of the study of social problems as such. Sociologists need to understand social problems and to concentrate upon sociological problems that underly the most important and pressing social problems confronting mankind. They also need to concentrate upon them in such ways that their findings will be useful socially.

FOUR PROBLEMS: ALTERNATIVE FORMULATIONS

Through brief illustrations from four deep-seated and persisting areas of social concern, let us suggest further the nature of the distinction between the social and the sociological statement of problems. The four areas have to do with the "generation gap," urban riots, drug addiction, and poverty.

The Generation Gap. Differences in outlook between generations are a recurring social problem. Especially when life-conditions are rapidly changing, as they are now, youth and their parents speak "different languages." Currently, the popular news periodicals, radio, and television run sensational items about "student revolts," "flower children," "hippies," and angry young men and women in a hurry to cope with life as they find it. To the bewilderment of their elders, youth figure prominently in urban riots, civil rights sit-ins, resistance to the military draft, drug addiction, automobile "drag races," and all the rest. To the frustration of young people, elders appear to close their minds against trying to understand changes that youth contend are long over-due.

Few of the participants in struggles, demonstrations, or rejections related to the generation gap are free enough from emotional involvement to hold a broader perspective on what is happening to and around them. Youth talk about the bigotry, vested interests, and rigidity of their elders. Elders demand harsh and arbitrary measures against student rebels, against juvenile delinquency and youthful shortsightedness.

The sociologist tries to look at the "generation gap" and its ramifications more broadly—both in time and comparatively. He attempts to find tenable and accurate answers to such questions as these: What are the demands of youth? What are the demands of elders? From what sources do these demands spring? What would be the likely outcome if such sets of demands were accepted and implemented? How can our institutions, with the aid of youth and the cooperation of elders, meet more adequately and constantly the challenges of changing life-conditions and the needs of all groups?

Urban Riots. Such conflicts may take on frightening dimensions. Those of the 1960's especially occasioned the fear that the United States was drifting into organized insurrection. Some talked of a "second civil war." During one week in July 1967, at least 164 Americans were slaughtered and 2,100 wounded in riots in cities of the United States.

Some police departments bought war equipment—armored cars, machine guns, gas guns, masks, and grenades. Vigilante organizations sprang up. Extremist societies took on new vigor and presumed justification. Both whites and nonwhites stockpiled guns and ammunition. Conflict myths and rumors were widespread.

The communications media blossomed with references to black power, soul brother, poverty, deprivation, civil rights, nonviolent resistence, integration, segregation, desegregation, white racism, and black separatism.

The assassination in 1968 of the Rev. Martin Luther King, Jr., the Nobel Prize winning apostle of nonviolence, precipitated civil disorders in more than 125 cities even though it also brought home forcefully to a great many the durable wisdom of his teachings of nonviolent resistance.

Popular discussions of riots—whether in bars, country clubs, or Congress—are usually the confused airings of prejudices. They seldom reflect the sympathetic and open-minded exercise of intellect. In order to provide a more dispassionate and accurate guide for policy decisions, especially in government and business, President L. B. Johnson established in 1967 a National Advisory Commission on Civil Disorders. He asked the Commission to find out "What happened? Why did it happen? What can be done to prevent it from happening again and again?" The resulting document, though tempered with political considerations, is a long step towards understanding urban unrest and disorder as a popular social problem. Examples of the Commission's findings are:

"Our Nation is moving toward two societies, one black, one white—separate but unequal. . . . This deepening racial division is not inevitable. . . . Segregation and poverty have created in the racial ghetto a destructive environment totally unknown to most white Americans.
"What white Americans have never fully understood—but what the Negro can never forget—is that white society is deeply implicated in the ghetto. White institutions created it, white institutions maintain it, and white society condones it. . . .
"The economy of the United States and particularly the sources of employment are preponderantlv white. In this circumstance, a policy of separate but equal employment could only relegate Negroes permanently to inferior incomes and economic status."

The Commission made a series of specific recommendations for the purpose of ending "the destruction and the violence, not only in the streets of the ghetto but in the lives of people." [1] It agreed that, at best, measures repressive of violence can only buy time in which to substitute integration for segregation.

Such a report is about as far as an official analysis of such a social problem can take us. It is created, and it remains in the world of public affairs. It is necessarily a political document.

---

[1] National Advisory Commission on Civil Disorders, *Report* (New York: Bantam Books, 1968), pp. 1–2, 404, 483.

Sociologists can and do use such reports as starting points and then push on to deal further with the questions raised and to ask and attempt to provide answers for other, more basic questions: How deep-set are racism and tribalism? What are their social and psychological ramifications? Can they be eliminated? Can we have a society in which tribalistic class and ethnoid groups do not persist in maintaining special privileges for themselves at the expense of other class and ethnoid groups? Can formal and informal socialization procedures in American culture be changed so as to develop generations of citizens dedicated to the solution of differences by means of discussion, negotiation, and perhaps forceful but nonviolent aggression rather than through recourse to violence?

Intellectual leaders need to learn how to view fully and accurately the implications of violence on many levels of human thought, emotion, and behavior. This can only be done in an atmosphere of free academic inquiry, in terms of daring sociological and other scientific hypotheses. Wishful thinking will not eliminate violence nor its social implications from either cities or international affairs. Only an intimate and careful examination of the nature of violence, its uses, and the conditions under which it occurs can equip us to indicate how to replace it with other and less damaging procedures.

Drug Addiction. This is not only a physical problem but also a mental and social one. A committee of the World Health Organization defines drug addiction as "a state of periodic or chronic intoxication detrimental to the individual and to society, produced by the repeated consumption of a drug (natural or synthetic)." In the United States, those addicted to opiates are estimated at some 60,000, and those to alcohol, a drug usually considered as a separate issue, at perhaps 6,000,000. With the proliferation of "dangerous drugs"—drugs legally available only on a physician's prescription—for "sprees" and for regular use among the American people, and especially with widespread experimentation with marihuana, the situation has become quite complex and threatening.

Not only are drug addicts a pressing social problem, but the inaccurate overplay of news reports on addiction makes sensible corrective measures difficult to obtain. Sensational news stories about addicts robbing and killing to get themselves drugs, and about drug use among suburban youth and ghetto delinquents continually overstate or distort the situation and panic government officials, parents, and the press itself.

Sociological studies of drug use and addiction avoid this panic-thinking so often surrounding the social problem. In addition to the contributions being made by physiologists, psychologists, and psychiatrists to the understanding and control of drug use and addiction, there are many useful lines along which sociologists are working: What are the social settings of drug use and addiction? What happens to the people involved when such settings are modified or eliminated? In a social sense, how do people become addicts? How do pushers or sellers of drugs operate? How are they organized and supplied? Why is addiction now so concentrated among young male urban delinquents, especially among young Negroes and Puerto Ricans of slum neighborhoods? What are the social consequences of existing governmental efforts to control the distribution and use of dangerous drugs? What are the social consequences of existing methods of treatment for addicts? Of what significance are the group-cultures developed by addicts? Of what significance are group organizations of drug-using addicts and of addicts who have quit using drugs?

Poverty. In our "affluent society," poverty is something that we usually either minimize or try to explain away. Only in times of economic crisis, in an urban rebellion, or during poor people's marches on city halls, state capitols, or Washington, D.C., do mass media bring poverty into popular discussion as a crucial social problem. Even then, some commentators find it easy to infer the necessity, however regrettable, of some minimum percentage of poverty and that the existing percentage is probably an "irreducible minimum." They may also dwell on the relative nature of poverty, that is, on how much better off a poor person is in America than in India or Africa. Be that as it may, the vast majority of Americans continue to have little or no direct or accurate knowledge of the effects of deprivation, hopelessness, how one falls into poverty, and how one might climb or be helped out of it.

Who are the poor? Even this aspect of the problem is controversial. Both politicians and serious academic students of the subject are accused of "playing the numbers game." It depends on how "poverty" is defined for any given time and place. Between 1947 and 1966, the percentage of families having a money income of less than $3,000 (in terms of constant 1966 dollars) dropped from 30 to 14. Among unrelated individuals not in families during the same years, the percentage with a comparable income of $1,500 declined from 52 to 37. Such flat categories ignore, however, differences in living conditions and purchasing power in various parts of the country as well as non-money income. On the basis of more inclusive and flexible criteria for "poor persons," the Bureau of the Census estimated that members of poverty families dropped from 20 to 14 percent of the total between 1959 and 1966. Unrelated individuals in poverty diminished from 47 to 39 percent in the same period.

Why are the poor poor? A breakdown of figures based upon many different definitions of poverty points to certain significant generalizations: In a predominantly white society that has not outgrown old prejudices, color is the prime handicap. Other disadvantages for wage-earners are lack of education, age (especially when 65 years or older), being female, illness, and a crippling or disabling condition of long duration. In a conservative estimate for 1966 made by the U. S. Census Bureau, more than 41 percent of nonwhites are "below poverty level"; comprehended in this figure are half of all nonwhite children under 18 years of age. Comparable estimates point to less than one-eighth (12 percent) of all whites as being below the poverty level; this fraction includes one-eighth of all white children under 18.

Why do the poor remain poor? Sociologists are discovering that the poor become poor and remain so because they are problem individuals, members of problem families, or victims of majority prejudice. Lack of income is a symptom of such a problem or complex of problems. A four-year study in St. Paul, Minnesota, in 1948–52 indicated that 6 percent of all the city's families "were suffering from such a compounding of serious problems that they were absorbing well over half of the combined services of the community's dependency, health, and adjustment agencies." Seven percent of all St. Paul families were then dependent, 11 percent maladjusted, and more than 15 percent plagued with ill health; a total of 41 percent were receiving social agency services.[1]

Thus, as sociological probing proceeds, such vague generalities as "poverty" tend to be displaced by a variety of much more specific terms and conceptions.

---

1 Bradley Buell and associates, *Community Planning for Human Services* (New York: Columbia University Press, 1952), p. 9.

CHAPTER THIRTY-ONE

PROBLEM FAMILIES I:
CHILD AND YOUTH

The solving of solvable personal and family problems is much of the business of living. The difficulties persons and families may encounter become social problems when they can be solved, if at all, only with outside aid, or when they are solved in a way so deviant as to arouse the concern of others, or when they are apparently unsolvable and have become social concerns. These myriad problems, each so unique in its manifestations to the person or family affected, can only be outlined here. The problems of deviation are discussed in Chapters 1–5 in connection with processes of socialization.

Focal points among personal and family problems to be treated in this chapter are (1) procreation, (2) problem homes, (3) juvenile delinquency, and (4) sex.

PROCREATION

Social problems clustering about human procreation include abortion, sex education, birth control, planned parenthood, illegitimacy, maternal and infant mortality rates, child defects, and unwise and inadequate adoption facilities.

Abortion. Unwanted pregnancy may lead to abortion or to unwanted and perhaps unwed parenthood, so-called illegitimacy. As yet, our society permits no legal escape from pregnancy resulting from rape, incest, or other extramarital sexual relations unless —as in a few states—it can be diagnosed as therapeutically necessary. Since most state laws allow abortion only to save a mother's life, 8,000–10,000 legal abortions are performed annually in contrast to a rough estimate of more than one million "criminal" abortions. Illegal abortions have now become the largest single cause of maternal deaths in this country. Following the lead of California, Colorado, Maryland, and North Carolina, many states are changing their laws to permit abortions when pregnancy threatens the physical or mental health of the mother, when it appears the child will probably have physical or mental defects, or when the pregnancy has resulted from rape. A hospital board must pass on such abortions. Unless such laws are liberalized as well as enacted in additional states, they will continue to provide relief in only a small percentage of the cases.

Education, Control, and Planning. More and more, sex education from an early age, birth control devices and medicines, and planned parenthood teachings are diminishing both unwanted pregnancies and the need for abortions. In recent years, in consequence of a dramatic shift of policy, the Federal government and most of the states have undertaken to sponsor and subsidize research, clinical aid, and education in birth control both in the United States and abroad. Because this development is recent, dating only from the early 1960's, great strides in it are still needed to cope with the existing—and still growing—problems.

Illegitimacy. In terms of recorded births per 1,000 unmarried women 15–44 years of age, illegitimacy mounted from 7.1 in 1940 to 23.6 in 1966. The increase is attributable to both the whites and the nonwhites, but the difference between the rates for the two sectors has lessened: The nonwhite rate has gone up by 2.7 times, but the white rate has risen by 3.2. In terms of the percentage illegitimate among all births, the greatest part of these increases came in 1955–65; from 1.9 to 4.0 for whites and 20.2 to 26.3 for nonwhites, from 4.5 to 7.7 for all. In 1966, the nonwhite illegitimacy rate was a little more than six times that for whites. Women 15–19 are mothers of two-fifths of the illegitimates whether white or nonwhite. Nevertheless, because there are so many unmarried women of this age category, the rate of illegitimate births for this category is relatively low. It did not rise as rapidly from 1940 to 1965 as did those for other age groups.

Mortality. The partial socialization of medicine has helped cut maternal and infant mortality rates. In the period between 1940 and 1966, maternal deaths per 1,000 live births dropped from 3.2 to 0.2 for whites and from 7.7 to 0.7 for nonwhites. Comparable rates for infants less than one month old declined from 27.2 deaths to 15.6 for whites and from 39.7 deaths to 24.8

for nonwhites. The improvement during the rest of the first year of life has been marked; white infant deaths dropped from 16.0 to 5.0, and nonwhite, from 34.1 to 14.0. Americans cannot take great pride, however, even in an over-all rate of 22.1 deaths during the first year of life recorded in 1967, the lowest to date. It was higher than recent estimates made for more than a half dozen countries of northern Europe, Australia, New Zealand, and Japan.

Handicapped Children. Hereditary and other child defects as well as accidents and disease take their tolls in crippled, retarded, and mentally ill children. Over 450,000 crippled children benefit each year from the medical services provided with Federal assistance. Special money-raising projects such as the "March of Dimes," social service agencies, research scientists, and innovative physicians and surgeons are making substantial contributions to the prevention and correction of such handicaps as well as to the aid of those who have to live with a handicap. The damaging effects to unborn children of certain diseases and of certain drugs misused during pregnancy have aroused wide concern and are being subjected to special study and efforts at control. Comprehensive statistics on child handicaps and on the success in coping with them are not available, but efforts to deal with them remain far from adequate.

Adoption. Unwanted children, if they are fortunate, either become wanted or are given for adoption. About 150,000 children are adopted each year, 70,000 by relatives and 80,000 by nonrelatives. A growing number, but still only about 60,000, are placed by social agencies. Even an adoption through the placement services of a well-organized, ethical, professional agency is a delicate arrangement; it has a good chance of reasonable success only with mature and patient adoptive parents. The children adopted through family channels and without professional guidance may face difficulties from which recourse is difficult and embarrassing. An exploitative and irresponsible "black market" in babies still operates by catering to couples who are not considered good risks by recognized social agencies.

PROBLEM HOMES

Problem individuals usually grow up in problem homes. If not, they help to create problem homes. Such homes are frequently below the poverty level, but they are found on all economic and social levels. Their members often lack education, but they may have any degree of education. One or more members may suffer from physical or mental defects or illnesses. One or both parents may be absent because of death, imprisonment, hospitalization, or desertion; the one parent present may be divorced or never have married.

All families living together are groups of people in some continuing pattern of interaction, and interaction includes conflict and tension as well as accommodation and love. Since children need both affection and discipline, and demand both, the mere presence of conflict or tension in a home does not make it a problem home. Excessive conflict and tension can, however, undermine the child's sense of identity and security. They can be the problem matrix for a problem personality.

Even the fact of deviance from some accepted pattern of family behavior is not necessarily a basis for regarding a family's home as fraught with problems of a type to be called "social." Deviant families include those which are constructively enterprising and innovative as well as those containing the antisocial, the delinquent, the criminal, and the mentally ill. Intergenerational misunderstandings and conflicts, reflecting both a rapidly changing society and deep and unresolved interpersonal conflicts, can further push children toward rebellious or destructive behavior.

Many substitutes for the problem home have come into existence. Their character depends to a large degree upon the family's social and economic resources and status. The wealthy turn their rejected children over to servants or governesses or send them to boarding schools in winters and special camps in summers. Voluntarily or with governmental assistance, others depend upon relatives, friends, or other private arrangement or have their children placed in an institution or a foster home. Some 330,000 children, with one or both parents living, are now cared for through public and private welfare agencies, one-third or less in the current equivalent of "orphan asylums" and industrial schools and the rest in foster homes. These estimates do not include private arrangements by parents themselves. Possibly half of those living with foster parents enjoy reasonable security as they presumably wait for an opportunity to return to their parental homes. The other 100,000 find themselves trapped in a damaging environment and have little hope of escape.

According to the Child Welfare League, almost half of the

children in foster care are there to escape parental neglect, abuse, and exploitation. The rest, also largely rejected, are taken from broken homes and homes handicapped by economic, mental, and physical problems. When foster homes are available and can be made to fit the needs of the child, foster parents can make almost magical contributions to a child's welfare, but the rising volume of children in need, the shortage of foster parents, the use of crowded temporary arrangements, and the lack of money and of professional services are all defeating the procedure in too many cases.

When such substitutes for problem homes are not available or workable, the physically and mentally beaten or distorted products of such homes afflict our schools, social and police agencies, and general social life. Statistics are lacking on how many children, said to be tens of thousands, are brutally battered or killed each year by their own parents. Writers and politicians more easily discuss juvenile addiction and delinquency than focus needed attention on problem families. Fanned especially since the 1940's by our wars and urban riots as well as by technological change, by contrasting affluence and deprivation, and by more vivid and immediate mass communications, the increase of problem homes has been evident and continuing.

To a degree, social legislation, subsidies, and affluence have lessened one characteristic of the problem home, exploitative child labor, with its toll of maleducation, crippling accidents, and impaired health. Both whites and blacks, aged six to fifteen years, now have at least a nominal school enrollment of 99 percent. The largest block of such child labor remains among farm families, especially families of migratory workers.

JUVENILE DELINQUENCY

Juvenile courts were started in this country in 1899 as a way of providing more humane and perhaps curative treatment for young offenders. In theory, a juvenile court judge takes a parental role. He tries to serve the interests of the delinquent child. He investigates the offense but also all other apparently relevant aspects of the case. This requires a relaxation of rules of evidence and of many courtroom procedures used in criminal cases for the protection of the accused. It also means rather extensive possible controls over child and family. When the theory is fully and adequately applied by a well informed and well motivated judge, he can offer a model of procedure and results which has beneficially influenced criminal court thinking and should influence it more, but the powers of the juvenile court have admittedly at times been abused.

Juvenile courts handle not only the range of adult-like offenses which children might commit but also such behaviors as incorrigibility, frequenting the streets at night, truancy from school, and running away from home. Most such courts also have jurisdiction—depending upon state laws—over dependent and neglected children and youth and sometimes also over custody, guardianship, adoption, and support cases.

Instances of juvenile delinquency that come to juvenile courts comprise only a small fraction of the offenses committed. For this reason and because the term, "delinquency," like the term, "crime," has a legal significance, instances not brought to police or court attention are sometimes called examples of proto-delinquency, *i.e.*, "primary" or "basic" delinquency. As nearly as one can learn from informal reports of police and social workers, probings of sociologists and psychiatrists, and imperfect official statistics and investigations, proto-delinquency occurs among the children and youth of all social status groups even though cases reaching the courts come disproportionately from the less advantaged class, ethnic, and racial groups. For boys, these offenses are most often stealing and acts of carelessness and mischief; for girls, sex acts, unruliness, and running away from home. In approximate order of frequency, the most common types of proto-delinquency among middle-class boys are: theft, vandalism, driving offenses, ungovernability, assault, alcohol, and sex; for middle-class girls, they are: alcohol, driving offenses, theft, vandalism, ungovernability, sex, and assault. Many of these offenses either do not come to the attention of the police at all or are handled by them quietly and privately in negotiation with the youths and their parents.

How can we come to an understanding of the widespread and apparently increasing juvenile delinquency of our society—with its parallels in so many other countries? Perhaps sociologists have learned most in response to this question by their probing analyses of the group-cultures of children and adolescents—whether non-delinquent, proto-delinquent, or delinquent. These group cultures differ in various status groups (groups defined compositely by class, ethnic, and vocational characteristics) in our society.

Obvious aspects of these group-cultures are seen in the behavior patterns of lower-class street gangs, of middle-class scout troops, informal clubs, cliques, college fraternities and sororities, and of upper-class sets, cliques, adjuncts to parental clubs (city and country), and boarding school groups.

The activities of all these groups reflect, sometimes positively, sometimes negatively, the common orientation of the related parental status group toward social institutions and symbols of authority. Whether male or female or both, these youth groups have about them the character of both an offensive and defensive compact to achieve their own objectives in a world largely controlled by parents and other adults. Such groups introduce their members to group-patterns (folkways and mores) of value and behavior which are passed on with some modification from the older to the younger members. Members contend that these group-patterns provide them with a more realistic orientation to the actual business of living than they can find in the formal teachings of the school and churches (societal conventions and morals). Such group-patterns deal with interpersonal competition and conflict, jostling for prestige and influence, which pay off both immediately among youths and then later in formal and informal adult groups, ranging from gangs, unions, clubs, sales forces, political organizations, and casual cliques to corporate management groups. Just how far these patterns are defined in society as legitimate or at least tolerable and at what point they become proto-delinquent or legally delinquent is too academic a question for the participants. Proto-delinquency is often a test of ability and willingness to conform to group ideals for male and female behavior. The point at which proto-delinquency becomes delinquency is often a matter of etiquette or just luck.

To a degree, the kind of formal and informal groups into which juveniles are caught up depends upon the neighborhood in which they live and, when it differs, the one in which they go to school. It also depends upon chance acquaintanceships. These points suggest the theory of differential association, the theory that companions are a primary source of delinquent and criminal values and behavior patterns. Granted juvenile group continuity, certain areas continue to rank high in delinquency through many immigrant waves.

The group-cultural and differential association approaches do not explain fully the lone delinquent. Such a person raises considerations of unique individual characteristics such as a psychologist or psychiatrist might diagnose, but the lone delinquent also reflects social influences which are of professional concern to the sociologist. The extent to which violence and the flouting of morality have been exploited by television and comic books is just one part of an atmosphere in which both individual and group-participating delinquents find themselves stimulated to commit offenses, and indeed, stimulated to regard offenses as socially acceptable challenges. The commercial exploitation of child and teen-age fads by toy manufacturers, clothing distributors, and musicians and the exaggeration and glamorization of violence, drugs, and sex by journalists are also significant parts of this situation.

In all this, children and youth are, in effect, caught up in the unrecognized but powerful cross-purposes of our society, our societal many-valuedness or multivalence. Americans want their children to achieve reasonable success in society, but our schools often function to increase pupil preoccupation with sports and fun, and to dramatize the academic as the concern of bores who do not know "the score." They want their children to get certain diplomas as tickets to desirable social statuses, and perhaps to become even somewhat "cultured." On the other hand, they recognize—in a largely subconscious but forceful manner—that initiation into the ways of dealing with people and of avoiding social restraints or "trouble" will carry their offspring most directly to whatever kinds of statuses they themselves regard as influential. Such parental aspirations help to catch youths up in popular activities and games that involve them in enticing dangers—hopefully without being hurt or caught: sex without pregnancy or perversion, drugs without lasting addiction, stealing and vandalism without a "record," and the rest.

SEX

Advertising, entertainment, and gossip stimulate young people to preoccupation with sexual exploration and experimentation. Often without adequate instruction or even accurate suggestions, youth are given vague caveats about not going "too far." During the same overcrowded and emotionally confusing years, they need to solve problems of personal autonomy and career in the approaching adult world as well as those of rating, dating, and mating. Even the allegedly fun-filled years of dating present more anxieties than journalists and fiction-writers will ordinarily admit. Little wonder that so many difficulties haunt this period of life and become recognized as social problems—especially when the real problems of youth are further compounded by the imaginings, projections, and jealousies of their elders.

The conception of what it means in any given group to "be a man" or "be a woman" drives youth to extreme exploits to "prove themselves." These ideas play significant parts in excesses in drinking, smoking, car-racing, and sex. Since these conceptions are rapidly changing, those who are not too securely adult and male or female often find such behavior most alarming and incomprehensible.

Sexual offenses in which young people or adults may be involved are: assault (mild, serious), rape (forcible, statutory), fornication (unlawful coitus by the unmarried), adultery (unlawful coitus by the married), incest (sexual relations between individuals closely akin), criminal abortion, noncoital sexual relations with a minor, indecent exposure, disseminating "obscene" materials, homosexual relations (with a minor, with an adult), bestiality, and prostitution.

In popular discussion, prostitution and sexual promiscuity are often confused. A prostitute sells sexual services; a sexually promiscuous person enters into sexual acts outside of wedlock either for hire or as an amateur. Prostitutes include streetwalkers, inmates of red-light houses, those available on call, and independents operating in their own apartments. Most prostitutes are female catering to a male clientele, but there are also male prostitutes catering to females, and prostitutes of both sexes serving homosexual clients. With the relaxing of taboos, this ancient "profession" has suffered more in recent years from the competition of promiscuous amateurs than from the police. With noncommercial sexual partners more available, and wisdom concerning personal hygiene often lacking, venereal diseases have again become a serious threat to public health since World War II in spite of the highly effective medical treatments freely available to counteract them.

Just how far the enforcement of laws can be used to counteract the prevalence of socially condemned sexual behavior is an old controversy. Laws prohibiting sexual intercourse between consenting adults outside of wedlock are difficult to apply. Those dealing with abnormal relations between a man and a woman or two members of the same sex, when both parties consent, lend themselves as much to blackmail as to the preservation of public morality. In consequence, efforts are being made in the United States to eliminate from the criminal category homosexual acts between consenting adults. To date, only Illinois has enacted such legislation. That many a case of rape, fornication, adultery, and incest is hidden by protective friends and relatives remains no secret to concerned social workers, physicians, nurses, and clergymen who try to repair some of those damaged in such incidents.

While efforts to "legislate morality" have thus promised much more than they have accomplished in the control of sex offenses, they appear to have been most useful in the area of aiding the young to grow up with greater freedom from molestation and seduction. The current emphasis upon sex education from an early age and upon more adequate parent education will probably do even more to reduce the need for so much concern with sexual social problems.

CHAPTER THIRTY-TWO

PROBLEM FAMILIES II: ADULTS

Science and technology rapidly change our occupations both in character and in educational level needed for regular employment. They lengthen our lives and contribute to tensions that shorten our lives. They modify the opportunities and techniques of the criminal. They make it possible for a great many more people to live to be old, to retire, to be dependent, and thus to require care and treatment. They delay death and, by curing certain disorders, change the frequency of types of terminal illness and accident.

Crucial aspects of occupation are job security, human resistance to change, alienation, and loyalty. Social problems associated with health involve sick families, the unequal distribution of medical care, the faulty communication of medical instructions by physicians and nurses to patients, quackery, and habituation to such potentially harmful substances as tobacco, alcohol, "mind-changing" chemicals, marihuana, narcotics, and sedatives. Crime and the criminal can be better understood and controlled through taking a broader, less prejudiced view than the common legalistic and narrow problem-solving ones so common in society. This generalization also applies to the institutions for punishment and/or rehabilitation and re-assimilation which too often actually provide training and contacts for criminals. Among the social problems of old age, the tendency of the aging to think of retirement in fanciful terms has led to many tragedies. Gerontology and geriatrics as well as Golden Age Clubs (by whatever name) are joining with public and private insurance and pension schemes to help cope with the rising tide of the aging and to aid them in finding worthwhile activities. Other than death itself, the social problems of human tragedy include bereavement, the exploitation of survivors by morticians and others, and the incidence and conditions of suicide.

Changes in science and technique have thus radically affected all the topics to be discussed in this chapter: (1) occupation, (2) health, (3) crime, (4) old age, and even (5) death. Other adult problems, such as poverty, unemployment, the unemployable, underprivileged minorities, divorce, desertion, and deviation, are discussed in other chapters.

OCCUPATION

Employment today is largely mass employment, the sequel to mass education and the concomitant of mass housing, mass communications, and mass selling. Our lives are arranged around assembly lines, feeders to them, and distributors from them. We are part of complexes controlled by automated and computerized systems of selection, recording, and manipulation of personnel, materials, operations, and money. Today control of managerial talent is the principal means of increasing the concentration and growth of industrial-political power in key American corporate networks.

What social problems do significant publics see in the kinds of occupations available in our evolving society? They have to do principally with job tenure, ingrown barriers to change, lack of involvement, and loyalty.

Job Security. For mass business, most wage-earners need to be skilled in only a few operations at any given time, and these operations can be learned in a relatively brief period. Some few workers still hold their jobs through being all-round journeymen in a given craft, but such skilled artisans are in short supply. In order to cope with the problem of their own interchangeability and replaceability and of fluctuations in the labor market, wage-earners are highly unionized in mass industry as against only about 30 percent so in nonagriculutral pursuits over-all. On the whole, unorganized wage-earners, including the vast majority of those in agriculture, have longer hours and less income than those in unions. While union work stoppages irritate affected publics, they only account for the loss of less than one-fifth of one percent of the total estimated working time of wage-earners each year.

An advertisement of the Advertising Council (organized advertising's "public service" instrument) suggests the extent to which our highly technical civilization is no longer dependent upon long-term apprenticeship. Here are excerpts from it:

"You say typists are in short supply? How long does it take to train somebody to become a good typist? About two months. In two months, the shortage of typists could disappear. . . .
"No welders around? Four months of crash training is all it would take to hatch a new, skilled batch.
"Draftsmen, machinists, welders, assemblers, molders—the story is the same. A few months' training could work wonders. . . .
"Many of America's top corporations are already spending millions to train people, including Negroes and other minorities, for skilled jobs."

The largely unorganized typists, with their low pay scales and chancy job security, could not assure the new recruits a living wage, but long experience has forced the other craftsmen mentioned to utilize collective union action to maintain pay scales both for themselves and for any newcomers.

Ingrown Barriers to Change. The above advertisement is headed, "The Skilled Labor Shortage Is a Myth." It does not mention the extent to which organized labor attempts to maintain such a shortage as a way of protecting its own bargaining position with management. Granted a basis for the cooperation of management and organized labor in such crash specific training, two other prerequisites not mentioned in the advertisement are *motivation* and an adequate level of *general education*. For the technologically displaced, there are the added possible problems of *inflexibility* and *location*.

Those of any ethnic or racial group who have adapted themselves throughout their early years to "making it" through public welfare allotments, part-time or temporary jobs, or illicit rackets have great difficulty changing their patterns of motivation and work to meet the demands of a five-day-a-week job. In a milieu that places little value on education, with uneducated parents and with personal exposure to a poorly staffed school, their educational level at the end of compulsory schooling may have been as much as three or more years below their age potential and, for that matter, below their own actual potential.

If candidates for training are older, their attachment to a way of life—even though it no longer provides gainful employment—may have made them highly resistant to change. With wife, children, friends, and family connections as well as a house and community ties in one locality, they may also fail to accept an opportunity through re-training in another area even though their current location holds no promise for the future. Customary human ties of family and neighborhood give those with narrow horizons much of their sense of security. To break them and to accept even a subsidized training program elsewhere would appear to them to be taking a high risk.

Is Alienation Something New? The traditional artisan allegedly had a proud identity with his product. The contemporary assembly-line worker is said to be lacking in any personal involvement in his. This oversimple contrast leads sentimentalists to speak of the "alienation" or estrangement of the assembly-line worker from his task as part of the "tragedy" or the "malaise" of our times.

There are still handicraft workers earning their living under conditions similar to those of the artisans of a century or two ago. They weave tweeds in Donegal and the Outer Hebrides; they carve wood in the Italian Alps and Kashmir; they embroider in Belgium, the Mediterranean islands, and Hong Kong; they paint complicated scenes on wooden screens in India. Unorganized and lacking adequate governmental protection from exploitation, they work long hours for modest incomes. They cope with the confinement, pressure for production, and low wages as best they can, but most of them can scarcely be said to have great pride in their products. It is the way of life that they know and to which they are inured. As in this country, an occasional artisan —a cabinet-maker, motor mechanic, stonemason—is a master of his trade and takes a real and creative delight in it. Our unalienated handicraft workers are often employed in making prototypes for others to copy. Many of them are hobbyists.

On the other hand, assembly-line workers often express to interviewers the relative freedom they feel in a routine job which they can leave behind after each day's relatively short "hitch." They sell a part of their time to do a not-too-demanding task, and then they live their lives elsewhere—at home, in hobbies, in games, in sociability, in self-improvement. They are neither enchanted nor disenchanted with their work, neither estranged from the productive process nor deeply involved in it. On the job, their rhythmic routine permits them to think about many other things.

Viewed thus, "alienation"—so far as the "alienated" are concerned—may be more of a benefit than a tragedy. Identification or involvement would make it easier for the corporation to claim a worker's loyalty; noninvolvement makes it easier for the union.

Loyalty. In each corporation or agency, there is usually a struggle in process between those who get their security from identifying themselves with the organization and its management —the *"organization men"*—and those who get their sense of security from a union, a personal reputation for technical ability, or a shrewd sense of how to play the game of climbing. Both business and political entrepreneurs place high value upon loyalty, especially upon the part of their salaried employees, and they try to develop arrangements that will give such employees more and more of a vested interest in being loyal to them personally and to their organization. As a part of nurturing such loyalty in white-collar employees, as well as of developing their competence, national corporations move them from one of their cities of operation to another. This stimulates a sense of rootlessness and interchangeability in all things except the corporate or agency connection. They work in interchangeable offices and live in interchangeable houses and suburbs, equipped with similar schools, churches, clubs, and people. Both men and women are caught up in the corporation or agency community which takes precedence over any temporary living or other arrangements.

The ethnic, racial, political, and economic homogeneity of such suburbs and corporate or agency communities raises fundamental questions about the increasing lack of adaptability by organization families to changing life conditions. Their social distance from urban and rural social problems insulates them from precise knowledge about the underprivileged and makes them bulwarks of anti-reform efforts.

HEALTH

In all its forms, disability keeps about two and one-quarter percent of our employed population away from work and about two percent of our children away from school on any given day. More than half of those absent have some respiratory disorder, and about one-sixth, an injury. Women are more subject to illness, but, when employed outside the home, they lose less workdays per year than do men. Persons over sixty-five are incapacitated about two and one-half times as many days as those under sixty-five.

These generalizations do not include the unemployed, the unemployable, the institutionalized, and those in the armed forces. The latter, because of such considerations as age limitations, more available medical services, and promptings from first sergeants, have about half the absentee rate of civilians. About 12 percent of the white and 15 percent of the nonwhite population have chronic illnesses and activity limitations.

Social problems in the health field to which sociologists are giving attention include: (*a*) sick families, (*b*) unequal distribution of medical care, (*c*) communication of medical instructions, (*d*) quackery, and (*e*) habituation to harmful substances.

Sick Families. General practitioners, psychiatrists, social workers, and others working with the ill and injured frequently conclude that their patient should be the family rather than the individual. Whole families become sick, disorganized, or confused, and their members find it difficult to help reverse the downward spiral—the joint reinforcement of unhealthy family relationships. The individual patient may be symptomatic of a family disorder.

In another day, physicians and clergymen collaborated with each other and with family friends to try to work out a kind of family therapy. To a degree, they still do, but, under contemporary conditions, a new type of practitioner has developed. The *family therapist* is a psychiatrist, psychologist, or social worker who specializes in attempting to work out the conflicts and other difficulties of troubled families. Psychiatric clinics, family service agencies, child guidance clinics, and hospital social workers are developing such therapy, but they need more and more research guidance and specially trained staff in order to make their efforts as effective as necessary on all social and economic levels. The family research of sociologists and interdisciplinary research on socialization are contributing heavily to the development of family therapy.

Unequal Distribution of Medical Care. A great deal of health care is geared to the treatment of critical conditions rather than to the maintenance of health, and even this has been largely out of the reach of the poor. The development of voluntary health schemes helped to broaden the clientele for health care and to provide a stronger preventive orientation. Since the legislation of

1965, the Federal Medicare program for persons sixty-five and over and the Federal-grant Medicaid program for the medically indigent have considerably extended the availability of health care and are stimulating its use for health maintenance.

Voluntary Plans. More than 80 percent of all Americans are covered by voluntary hospital insurance plans, and about 75 percent, by surgical insurance. The voluntary hospital insurance pays almost three-quarters of the hospital costs of those covered. Altogether, voluntary insurance plans pay about one-third of the costs of health and medical care of those covered. In general, these plans serve those regularly employed and their families. They can usually be continued into retirement.

Medicare is administered through the Social Security offices of the Federal government. Basic Medicare is financed by the Social Security tax payed by those employed. Supplementary Medicare insurance is voluntary and is financed half by the individual's monthly payments and half by general Federal revenue funds. Those enrolled in Medicare now amount to about one-tenth of the entire population. When fully used, Medicare takes care of a substantial share of hospital costs for the elderly and two- to three-fifths of medical expenses. Medicare also benefits groups other than the elderly; it relieves voluntary health agencies of the high expense of insuring older people and thus helps to keep their rates from rising as rapidly as they otherwise might.

Medicaid. Until recently, the indigent could turn only to such institutions as the clogged "charity" clinics and hospital wards for limited and grudging health care. Federal Medicaid grants to states now cover from one-half to four-fifths of the costs of a five-point program that offers: in-patient and out-patient hospital services, tests, X-rays, physicians' services wherever furnished, and skilled nursing homes for those over twenty-one. By 1969, more than four-fifths of the states and territories had set up such programs. As of 1970, only states participating in Medicaid can receive Federal aid for the health care costs of those on public assistance. Many states are broadening the Medicaid program to total health care, including dentistry, dentures, eyeglasses, physical therapy—whatever is needed. Who is eligible? It is usually few more than those on a public assistance level even though health costs can hit families above that level in a disastrous manner. A 1967 Social Security amendment places a top income limit at one and one-half times the state's allowance for aid to families with dependent children.

Remaining Health Care Distribution Problems. Crucial to the success of our whole broadening health care program is the development of more adequate numbers of physicians, nurses, laboratory technicians, and administrators. Of only slightly less importance is the speeding of research into means of utilizing health care facilities more efficiently as well as the provision of better designed and more extensive facilities.

Communication of Medical Instructions. Even more significant than poverty in the unequal distribution of medical care are (a) lack of knowledge on how to obtain available health services and (b) inaccurate communication between the physician or nurse and the patient. The first point should also include the emotional blocks nurtured by ethnic and class tradition in which a physician or nurse is a suspect stranger, not one of "our kind of people," and in which there is still great faith in folk medicine and even magic. Studies of the amount of malcommunication in medical practice have startled both physicians and sociological researchers. Efforts are now being made to provide standardized, simplified (where appropriate cartoon-like), printed instructions for the use of physicians with their patients. Such instructions increase many times the efficiency of therapeutic communication.

Quackery and unethical practices in the health field are not at all things of the past. While even their definition is still subject to controversy, current guesses place their costs to the people of the United States at some two billion dollars a year. Even more important than this vast sum is the human suffering and death due to the failure of pretended curatives.

Among licensed medical practitioners, carelessness and lack of up-to-date knowledge probably do more damage to patients than fakery and fee-splitting. The persistence of unethical practices represents the failure of government and of professional societies to police adequately the licensed practitioners of the curative arts. Such practices are quackery at its worst.

One of the difficulties with defining other types of health quackery arises from the large potentiality of faith in any curative process. A great many religious denominations teach faith healing, to be sought with or without medical aid depending upon how inclusive and exclusive faith healing is thought to be. The faith may be placed in a person, a relic, a supernatural influence, a doctrine, a type of treatment, or a medicine. While modern scientific medicine can make high claims to effectiveness, medical practitioners have recognized many times the contributions of faith healing to the curative process. They are also aware that dependable medicines and curative procedures have come to us from the folk medicines of many peoples. Hence the vagueness of defining the boundary between legitimacy and quackery in aspects of the health field is likely to persist. Pseudo-scientific and even quite unscientific health cults, the manipulation of fancy but unsound machines, the prescription of expensive but useless medicines, and dangerous experimentation with X-rays continue and require careful and critical scrutiny and policing. Perhaps the most susceptible to unscrupulous quacks are those pathetic people seeking a magical way to deal with an incurable disease or with old age. What is clearly damaging or exploitative quackery demands police action. That which may harmlessly give hope and faith requires understanding permissiveness.

Habituation to Harmful Substances. Physiologically harmful substances are found in use in all societies. Sanctioned tradition often prescribes the kinds of substance used, the methods of their employment, and the extent to which they may be taken. Social scientists have made cross-cultural studies of the social correlates in various societies to the types of addiction to harmful substances. They also examine the social situations in the United States and elsewhere in which people begin and then continue to use harmful substances, the consequences of such habituation in other aspects of their lives, and the social conditions under which anti-habituation therapy can be most effective.

The most widely used harmful substances to which Americans are habituated are tobacco (especially in the form of cigarettes) and alcohol. For every 100,000 *cigarette smokers,* 112 die each year at age 35 as a consequence of smoking; at 40, such deaths take 205 a year; at 50, 1,173. The warnings about lung cancer, emphysema, bronchial infections, and heart disease by the United States Public Health Service and the American Cancer Society have begun to cut into cigarette smoking. Because of their vivid clinical knowledge of the consequences of smoking, fewer physicians now smoke; this is especially the case with specialists in ailments attributable to smoking. Researchers have answered the contention that it may be too late for a habituated smoker to give up; they have shown substantial physical benefits to ex-smokers even though they may have smoked for many years.

Some 80 million Americans are said to drink alcoholic beverages at least occasionally, and more than 6 million have enough of a problem with alcohol to be called alcoholics. Alcoholism covers a range of illnesses of considerable complexity. The tendency of police and many others to punish the alcoholic as "just a drunk" does more to aggravate than to aid to cure such diseases. Members of the voluntary association Alcoholics Anonymous work with the police and the hospitals in order to change the treatment of alcoholics to a more therapeutic emphasis. They also try to help each other avoid the use of alcohol.

Other harmful substances to which people are habituated seem endless in number. They include especially the so-called "hard drugs" such as opium derivatives and cocaine, the psychedelic drugs such as LSD, the mescalin group, marihuana, and the psychotropic drugs, namely, the sedatives, tranquilizers, and stimulants. As we indicate in our discussion of drug addiction (pp. 315–316), relatively few Americans are caught in the disastrous grip of the hard drugs and the psychedelics. There are about one hundred times as many alcoholics as there are hard-drug addicts. While precise comparable figures are lacking, the costs of tobacco and alcohol in illness and death appear to outrank those of the other harmful substances. It is difficult to say how to rank the third most prevalently used group of partly harmful and partly helpful substances, the psychotropic drugs. The proportion of adult U.S. population using tranquilizers, whether prescribed or obtained otherwise, grew in 1957–67 from 7 to 27 percent. In 1967, about 13 percent took sedatives and 6 percent took stimulants other than alcohol. Groups with relatively high prevalence of psychotropic drugs display low rates of escape drinking; groups with low prevalence exhibit high escape drinking rates.

CRIME

Legally, a criminal is a person who has violated a criminal statute, has been caught, and has been adjudged guilty. This is a legal definition which sociologists accept as a social datum to be studied, but it leaves far too many significant questions unanswered for it to be accepted as more than what it is, a legal artifact. For example, to what extent do criminal statutes accurately specify what is socially damaging behavior? Of those who disobey legal injunctions, how many and who are likely to be convicted? What about those who illegally, but as a matter of conscience, refuse to obey what they regard as immoral laws? What about the so-called white-collar criminality—bribery, adulteration of products, crooked bookkeeping, fee-splitting, etc.— that is so underrepresented in crime statistics? These questions are of far more than academic significance. They reflect the changing power struggles and popular concerns of our society. Pro-labor politicians have looked into the iniquities of those whom Theodore Roosevelt called the "malefactors of great wealth," and pro-business politicians have sought out law violations of labor leaders.

The need for more fundamental conceptions of criminality and the criminal than mere legalisms and police practices or judicial norms requires us to free ourselves from narrow, problem-solving viewpoints. When we try to see the criminal as a person in his social settings—as he has experienced his environment and as his associates have experienced him throughout his life—we get closer to an understanding of the nature of criminal acts. The criminal becomes more than just a trouble-maker who has to be "fixed." Narrow problem-solving neglects the fact that very few life histories in our society are free from some delinquency. It also tends to sever the study of crime from "normal" and "decent" society even though our multivalent norms for the use of force and violence, for the "cutting of corners" in business, politics, and personal affairs, for the protection of "our own folks," and for the exchange of "favors" make distinctions between criminal and socially acceptable behavior blurred and arbitrary.

In studies of punishment, rehabilitation, and re-assimilation of the criminal into society, a broad approach is imperative in sociology. What is the nature of a prison community? What obstacles does the informal organization of prisoners raise against the re-assimilation of ex-prisoners into the outside community? In many ways, the crux of such matters probably lies in our philosophy of punishment as it is popularly held. This philosophy is largely one of "an eye for an eye," of vengeance for vengeance, which made rough sense under tribal conditions but which does not work; it neither prevents nor diminishes crime. After the popular theatricality of the courtroom in which attorneys play out a ritualistic game rather than help judge and jury to a sensible social solution of a given case, we impound the one convicted law-breaker in ten or twelve who has been caught and whose attorney fails to get him released or acquitted. Thus we think we cope with the threat of criminals to society. Then, in both prisons and mental hospitals, we entrust the defenseless and socially condemned to persons who, on the whole, are badly trained, poorly motivated, underpaid, and who not infrequently abuse their tremendous power. Ignored in most cases by all but politicians, an occasional writer of an exposé, and a few do-gooders, little wonder that such institutions chiefly serve purposes other than rehabilitation. All credit should certainly be given, however, to servants of such institutions who are competent and dedicated and do hold to their integrity despite conditions of employment and who find ways to help their charges to discover a "way back."

Emerging from sociological investigations is a view that we should be able eventually to develop a society with patterns of healthy maturation available to most people. These would be patterns that would force fewer minds into antisocial paths than do our present ones. We should also be able to develop ways to rehabilitate criminals rather than to harden them in their antisocial tendencies. Police may eventually become sufficiently professionalized, with increasing social work orientation, so that they can treat their cases more like patients than enemies. This change has already proceeded far in the police work done with women and children in some of our more enlightened city governments.

OLD AGE

The twentieth century has seen a phenomenal lengthening of life expectancy in the United States. For white males, it has gone from 48 to 68 years; for white females, from 51 to 75. For nonwhite males, it has risen from 33 to 61; for nonwhite females, from 35 to 67. An extended life of physical and mental health has long been a human dream. Today, with longer lives in store, the problems have developed of how to remain reasonably healthy and how best to utilize the extra years. A new scientific discipline, gerontology, has come into being to provide this knowledge; it consists of a systematic interdisciplinary investigation of aging. At the same time, special practitioners are evolving techniques with which to help cope with the nonmedical problems associated with aging; this coordinate discipline is called geriatrics.

With 31 percent of the American population now aged forty-five or over and 10 percent sixty-five or over, sociologists are focusing on problems of "full life planning." Of more immediate concern are problems of gainful employment for men and women over forty-five, of adaptability to less demanding careers after middle age, of the nature and practicality of "retirement" schemes, and of how to provide proper housing and diet for elderly couples and lone individuals. Work on these problems includes research into social techniques for relieving the feeling of being unneeded, unwanted—or even ostracized—which can lead to burdensome illnesses and mental breakdowns.

Participation in the labor force (which includes looking for a job) drops to about 83 percent in the 55–64-year-old age group, and then to 27 percent among those sixty-five and older. It is estimated that by 1980, only 22 percent of those over sixty-four will not be living in retirement. Especially in blue-collar pursuits, the last decade before sixty-five becomes one of increasing unemployment and job-changing. "Dead-end" jobs younger men would not take become attractive. Many older men and women find openings for themselves in governmental organizations where their political contacts can give them security for a while in a lower pressure job during their declining years.

Social Security benefits, including Medicare, ease somewhat the problem of financial security for retired people over sixty-four (in some cases beginning at sixty and sixty-two), but Social Security payments provide only a meager income on which to live. Private pension and insurance schemes and part-time employment now make many of the aged more comfortable, and such plans are now often included as a fringe-benefit of employment.

Many oldsters fantasy an easy and uncomplicated "life of Riley" as the ideal situation for retirement. They often sell their home, cut old ties, and move to a "retirement area." Then, they wonder what they should do next. Some drift back to their old haunts. Others get sick and die. Only a few thrive on retirement-area living in spite of its strangeness to their previous way of life. A more successful adjustment to retirement can be built around a new career in which the talent and wisdom of years can be helpful to those who need and request aid or in which a former hobby can become a center of continuing work-interest. Dependable later careers include gardening, repair-work, clerical tasks, and volunteer assignments. Women appear more often to be able to make such an adaptation than do men, especially when they like housekeeping or simple office tasks and have someone for whom to do it. Golden Age Clubs (under a variety of names) are helpful in bringing older people together for socializing, for the exchange of shop talk about retirement problems and opportunities, and for special events.

How to provide smaller, more efficient homes for the elderly in which individuals and couples can be near desirable community facilities—including if possible relatives and old friends—and be assured of an adequate diet is a pressing problem. Programs of taking hot meals to the elderly are becoming more available and are helping to solve a part of the problem. Part-time housekeepers who drop in at scheduled hours during each week also assure the maintenance of healthful standards and routines for the aged either at community expense or at a manageable charge.

With research physiologists predicting life expectancies of 100 and more years, sociologists have tremendous problems to help to solve in this area.

DEATH

The prolongation of life has had the effect of decreasing the percentage of our population living in a widowed state. From 1930 to 1967, the percentage of widowed men dropped from 6.3 to 3.2, and that of women, from 15.6 to 12.2. Those who do not remarry are mostly men and women fifty-five and over.

Three problems of striking concern related to death are (*a*) family adjustment to "life minus one," (*b*) the commercial exploitation of survivors, and (*c*) the incidence and conditions of suicide.

Clergymen, social workers, and psychologists concern themselves with the shock of death and with techniques for helping survivors "to go on" after bereavement. The knowledge that has been developed by sociologists of basic family interaction patterns, routines, and rituals has been helpful in raising the competence of such specialists to meet this problem. The ease with which morticians (funeral directors), monument and cemetery-lot salesmen, photographers, and others have been able to prey upon grief-stricken survivors has often been described and so has the confiscatory size of some of their bills. Many Jewish, Roman

Catholic, and Protestant leaders have now worked out ways to preplan with family members through the medium of a Memorial Society for their eventual deaths. Such societies enter into continuing contracts with whatever business firms appropriately should be utilized by survivors at the time of a family death. The result is dignified arrangements at a negotiated price.

In the United States, suicide is more common among older, white, single, divorced, or widowed men of high or low social status. Statistically, in a society murder and suicide appear to be inversely related, *i.e.*, the more of one, the less of the other. As one would expect from this, suicide declines in wartime. These figures have been held to demonstrate an innate aggressiveness or violence in men, but the frequency of both murder and suicide is too low, and the statistics are much too undependable for such a generalization. Many deaths listed as due to alcohol, drugs, overeating, or accident would possibly be seen as instances of suicide were one able to interview the deceased.

CHAPTER THIRTY-THREE

PROBLEMS OF MINORITIES: RACIAL, ETHNIC, CLASS

Social myths are treasured, but they are costly. Sometimes they become disastrous. Race, ethnic group, and class are such social myths. They are myths because their existence depends on imaginary and unverifiable theories. They are disastrous because these theories become justifications for group self-glorification and for the exploitation and even destruction of other groups.

ETHNOCENTRIC MYTHS ABOUT RACE

There is one human race. Physiological differences within it are too blurred to provide accurately inclusive racial subcategories. At most, we can identify racial types and then observe that mankind overwhelmingly falls between such types. These generalizations of scientific findings have not prevented many groups from nurturing social myths about allegedly superior "races" and nationalities. These myths have also downgraded other "races" and evenutally led, for example, to the Nazi racist extermination program directed against Jews, Poles, and other minorities.

Changing Ethnic Amalgams. There are groups identified as being of a common ethnic background. Some such groups speak or have a tradition of having spoken a common language. They have an oral and, many times, a written tradition, with literature, music, and customs. All such traditions are selective folk-constructions, amalgams of prestigious tales and theories, rituals and patterns of status and control. Even though the possessors of such social myths could not accurately claim for them to be other than aspects of the many-stranded human heritage, they have used them as bases for the exploitation of "lesser" peoples. Thus, down through history, one dominant ethnic amalgam after another has made disastrous use of such a myth.

Social Classes or Strata. There are more or less distinct social classes or strata in all complex societies. They represent a ranking of ourselves and other into "layers" according to presumed social prestige, power, and status. Social myths to justify upper-class status and control have included those of divine right, superior "breeding," and special education as well as theories derived from the social myths of racial and ethnic superiority. The excesses of European nobles and of American "robber barons" were justified by such social myths. At many times and places, members of lower social classes have paid bitter prices for this social myth, sometimes quite willingly, but usually just without choice.

A Country of Minorities. The United States is a country of minorities which are called racial, ethnic, and class. We are all members of minorities, and none of us, of a majority. That may appear offhand to some to be a noncontroversial statement, but it is a very difficult generalization for members of disadvantaged minorities to accept. They say: What about the "Wasp" (White Anglo-Saxon Protestant) majority? Isn't there a Wasp "establishment" because there is a Wasp majority in our society? It would be more accurate to say that those in power in our society—the so-called Wasp "establishment"—have a predominantly Wasp appearance because they conform to the customs and utilize the symbols specified in Wasp ethnic mythology.

New racial, ethnic, and class amalgams are emerging in the United States. They are amalgams made up through the intermixture not of pure types but of earlier amalgams. The Anglo-Americans, for example, are called Anglo-Saxons, but what of their Celtic, Danish, Italian, Norman French, Norse, Spanish, and many other ancestors, probably including Mongoloids, Moors, and African Negroes? The amalgam now called the "Wasp" has an even more complicated background. Many a so-called Wasp is descended principally from immigrants who were German, Scandinavian, French Huguenot, Scotch Irish, or other non-Anglo-Saxon. The racial and ethnic diversity of the Jews has been described many times, and Germans, French, Italians, Poles, Russians, Spanish, and all other ethnic groups and nationalities are similarly cosmopolitan in background. Each of the groups is not at all the same as the others, but it is another mixture in different racial and ethnic proportions drawn from the same range of strains and materials.

How did we become so mixed in background? Two parents do not appear to complicate our racial and ethnic heritage very much. They may give themselves the "brand names" of being Irish and Italian or German-Jewish and Swedish or English and African Negro. But that is just a start. Let us go back three centuries, 10 generations rather than just one. Then we each had 1,024 forebears in that generation (minus possible duplications). Go back six centuries, 20 generations, and we each had 1,048,576 ancestors in that generation (minus inevitable duplications). Where did all those people come from? Are you sure? What does this suggest about the ethnic or racial "purity" of our family trees? Even the carefully edited genealogies of large family connections suggest the extent of our ethnic diversity, and anthropologists can assure us from their studies of living people and of human remains—regardless of our immediate parentage—of our racial impurity.

What are the social problems? Parents worry about the possibility of a son or daughter marrying "the wrong [racial, ethnic, class] type." Householders in segregated neighborhoods worry about getting a neighbor of "the wrong type." Employers and employees in segregated situations have similar anxieties. How should we analyze these social problems? What would be a more sociological formulation of such problems?

Despite sensational press items, young men and women most often marry people rather similar to their parents in physical, ethnic, and class characteristics. On the other hand, granted reasonable compatibility, mixed marriages can provide kinds of stimulation both for the couple and their offspring that make for unusual achievement. Their deviance from the usual pattern may give both the couple and their children a special sense of challenge. Granted a willingness to accept a "different" neighbor and a refusal to be panicked into a hasty and unwise sale, such a change in a neighborhood is not at all likely to result in itself in financial loss or in an undesirable situation. Both employers and employees have usually wondered after a time why they had once opposed mixed employment. The social problems associated with intermarriage, mixed neighborhoods, and mixed employment are, therefore, basically those of *uninformed prejudice,* of *scape-*

goating, and of a *splintering society* in which greater and greater
social distances are separating groups which appear to differ in
terms of race, ethnic background, or class.

OUR SPLINTERING SOCIETY

The United States is becoming residentially a more segregated society than ever before. A few contrasting figures can
illustrate the point: In 1950–66, the central cities of our metropolitan areas went from 12 to 24 percent Negro; meanwhile the
percentage in the urban fringe dropped from 5 to 4, and in smaller
cities, towns, and rural, from 11 to 10. New York City's percentage
of Negro population rose from 10 to 18; Washington's, from 35 to
66; Atlanta, Memphis, Newark, and New Orleans all passed 40;
five others among the 30 largest went beyond 30 percent. During
that period, the percentage of the country's blacks living in
metropolitan cities rose from 43 to 56 and in smaller cities, towns,
and rural areas declined from 44 to 31. This growth reflects
natural increase plus a net migration from the South in 1940–68
of about four million underprivileged nonwhites. Even with
losing so many, the South's nonwhite population rose from 9.9 to
11.6 millions in that period.

Other nonwhite minorities are not so widely distributed as
are the Negroes. In order of size, they include the Mexicans,
Puerto Ricans, Indians, Japanese, Chinese, Filipinos, and a number of smaller groups. Except for the rapidly assimilating Japanese, they appear on the whole to be subjected to the same
segregated living arrangements as are the Negroes.

Segregative tendencies affecting our *white ethnic minorities*
are not so readily apparent. Neighborhoods in larger cities
and towns and whole suburbs assume the coloration of one or
another ethnic or religious group. In the case of self-segregated
towns, this tendency goes so far that public schools and other
public institutions such as churches, clubs, and business organizations take on a religious and ethnic orientation. In urban
neighborhoods, private schools and other ethnic, ethnoid, i.e.,
merged-ethnic or ethnic-like, and ethnoid-class institutions help
to maintain segregation and a separate group-culture.

School Desegregation. For all the talk of the desegregation
of our schools, stimulated particularly by the important Supreme
Court desegregation decision of 1954, the vast majority of Ameri-

can pupils still attend segregated classes. In the South by 1966, only 25.8 percent of all Negro pupils and 29.1 percent of Negro teachers were in at least *nominally* desegregated schools. Nationally in 1965, 79.9 percent of white first and twelfth graders were in segregated or only nominally desegregated (10 percent black or less) schools; 72.0 percent of the black first graders and 61.7 of the twelfth graders were in classes 80 to 100 percent Negro. All but 5 percent of the black pupils in metropolitan areas of the South and Southwest are in overwhelmingly black schools. This is what the first dozen years of "desegregation" accomplished in the schools.

How Many "Melting Pots"? These are hints of the situation, but just how much American society is splintering along ethnic and class as well as racial lines is difficult to determine. Our ethnic and racial groups are merging into four separate class-stratified "melting pots." These ethnoid or ethnic-like segments of our society are the three white ones, the "Protestant," "Roman Catholic," and "Jewish," and the "Colored." The religious terms are used here and by many people strictly for social designation; they do not imply any specific degree of orthodoxy or of adherence. What is emerging is a kind of four-fold cultural pluralism.

The Viability of "Cultural Pluralism." The virtues of religious identification and the glories of various ethnic heritages have often been recited. They can be enjoyed and utilized within the context of over-all American culture and with simultaneous participation in over-all American society. It can easily be demonstrated that our society has much yet to gain from each of the ethnic heritages represented in it. But let us look at the problem side of "cultural pluralism," of maintaining a society divided among discrete but *unequal* ethnoid groups. Just as the principle of "separate but equal" failed in our political life because such separate facilities as schools could be neither equal nor as good as desegregated ones, we cannot possibly implement an ideal— even if we held it—of assuring separate but equal status, prestige, and power to each of our ethnoid segments and to their cherished cultural heritages. Since we cannot do this, we merely continue the present situation of ethnoid inequality and of intolerable handicaps for the members of the less privileged ethnoid segments, especially groups that are merging into the nonwhite ethnoid segment. Those from any background who have "made it" in American society have helped to convey contributions from their cultural heritage as well as their own personal contributions to American society more generally, to the more general "melting pot" or stratified amalgam which is emerging.

Separatism as a Step Toward Assimilation. Few social paths lead directly from A to B—whatever or wherever A and B might be. Thus, when the various waves of immigrants came to the United States, they frequently created their own ethnic neighborhoods or towns and institutions as bulwarks against assimilation. Try as hard as they might in our dynamic society, such efforts at self-segregation and cultural perpetuation succeeded chiefly in slowing down a group's eventual engulfment in the larger society, not in preventing it. Irish, Germans, Jews, Italians, and many others found the various types of group solidarity—political, business, religious, social—useful in establishing themselves in the American environment. Group solidarity gave members a kind of quick power which certain of them at least could exploit. Sometimes such group efforts also provided easy targets for "backlash," that is, anti-minority excesses. Jewish and Catholic buildings and cemeteries, for example, were desecrated, and bizarre propaganda tales of "Popish" and Zionist "plots" were spread by hate groups. In spite of such conflict and excess, the phase of ethnic separatism started to pass for all such white groups when many of their members had achieved a reasonable degree of status and power and when individual members could feel more assured of being able to compete within the larger society with a reasonable chance of success.

NONWHITES AS A SPECIAL CASE

Almost all American groups have embedded in their traditions flight from oppression and persecution. Efforts are thus frequently made to apply the experiences of white groups to the current struggles of the nonwhites and especially of the Negroes. Certain parts of such analogies hold fairly well. The persistence and irrationality of anti-Jewish prejudices are often cited. Some European peasants lived under conditions little if at all different from those of American Negroes under slavery. In some ways, the peasants were worse off because those controlling them did not regard them as their property; when not needed, they could turn the peasants out onto the roads to starve—as on occasion they did. Among other analogies, there is that of the mother-centered family and the high alcoholism rates of both the Irish and the Negroes. But for all the similarities, one very high hurdle to assimilation and even to fair treatment remains: The Negroes, Indians, many Puerto Ricans and Mexicans, Japanese, Chinese, Filipinos, and a range of smaller groups are not white. In a British-American world, the French, Russians, Greeks, Spanish, and other "white" immigrants—after a suitable degree of "Americanization"—became relatively unnoticeable and acceptable. Those who were dark or who had the social label of being non-white remained noticeable. They thus have to be considered as a special case, and not just as another group about to rise in the usual manner on the American status ladder. It would appear that they are rising and inevitably will continue to rise, but in the forseeable future they will probably do so as nonwhites in an overwhelmingly white but mixing society.

Who are the nonwhites? The large bulk of them in the United States are called Negroes, blacks, or Afro-Americans. This is too easy a label. Like the white segments of our population, the American Negro is far from being "pure" anything and certainly not "pure African." He is a new amalgam: a substantial part derived from African ancestors but with sizeable genetic contributions from his American Indian and European forebears. A "pure Negro" is about as rare in the United States as a "pure Nordic" is anywhere. *Like ethnic-labeling, race-labeling in the United States is largely a matter of social usage rather than of physiological fact.* Negroes have often found it convenient and not difficult to pass as American or Asiatic Indians or, if they are light, as Latins. In current efforts to construct a black folk mythology similar to those for white groups, African folklore and other cultural materials are stressed to the exclusion of the Negro's Indian and white heritages. Perhaps in consequence of a stage characterized by "Black Power," "Black is beautiful," and other separatist slogans, the assimilation of the blacks into the general American "melting pot" will be facilitated. In this sense, a significant parallel to other ethnic groups is suggested.

The other large nonwhite groups, the Mexicans, Puerto Ricans, and Indians, the first two of which contain many members who are socially labeled white, are likely to continue in the future as they have in the past to merge gradually into the white and colored ethnoid segments. Their chief problems, like those of the blacks, are those associated with a poor educational background and prejudiced treatment.

MUST THE POOR BE WITH US ALWAYS?

Many of the social problems of race, ethnic group, and class are associated with disproportionate power or with disproportionate poverty. Depending upon the criteria used, somewhere between one-third and one-half of all nonwhites make up from one-fourth to one-third of those living below the poverty level. Of the remainder many are members of deprived white ethnic minorities or of handicapped and damaged "Wasp" families.

Our usual solution to the problems of poverty today, in our alleged "war on poverty," is to provide training and jobs for those trainable and employable and welfare payments for the rest. As a part of what is evolving as a "culture of poverty," welfare payments mean the creation of a conflict situation between the public assistance employees (who control inspections and recommend allotments) and their welfare clients. The arrangement is expensive both financially and in terms of the antagonistic relationship it nurtures. In consequence, a *guaranteed minimum income* for all families and separate individuals has been put forward as a less controversial and more constructive way of handling the poverty problem. This would be, in effect, "income tax payments in reverse" for those below a certain income level.

Those who assert that such a "dole" would sap the ambition of its recipients and cement poor individuals and families into a poverty status are shown, in reply, the extent to which an assured minimum income can give people the security and dignity with which to try to make a better solution for their problems. Except for the ill and crippled who might not be able to make such a struggle, those who are able would be likely to do better on such a guaranteed minimum income than on the "bitter charity" of the welfare payment obtained from the "prying" public assistance investigator.

Chapter Thirty-Four

PROBLEMS OF COMMUNITY
AND SOCIETY

Modern transportation and communication devices have expanded greatly the area in which we can have a sense of community with other people. At the same time, we are often surprised at the great social distances that separate physically nearby neighbors and associates. Professors in adjoining offices can belong to quite different local, regional, and world communities and scarcely know each other. A woman and her household "day help" can be from such different communities that they see one another only as caricatures and not as actual persons.

Locally, community refers to the people living or working in a given place who have developed some sense of common interest and of communicating with one another. Community is also used interchangeably with a public, the commonwealth, and even society at large. In each of its uses, common interests and intercommunication continue as key characteristics. Society is the largest social entity, short of humanity, with which we identify ourselves. Through its many parts, it functions as arbiter and carrier of the over-all cultural heritage in which we participate.

We shall outline social and sociological problems frequently in community and society which we have not already discussed. These we group under the following headings: (1) local community conditions, (2) mass manipulation, (3) natural catastrophes, (4) depressions, inflations, (5) pollution and waste, (6) overpopulation, and (7) wars, cold and hot.

LOCAL COMMUNITY CONDITIONS

Whether they are rural, suburban, or urban, local communities are subject to such problems as poor morale, underdevelopment or neglect, inadequate planning, over-exploitation, decay, and isolation. These can be exacerbated by the intergroup tensions and conflicts mentioned in the previous chapter. Such conditions also depend very much on the relations of a community to the over-all power structure of the region and society in which it is located.

Poor morale is a tell-tale symptom of a general problem in a local community. A community without the human resources or capital with which to meet its most pressing needs is likely to have a sense of being hopelessly underdeveloped or decaying and thus of poor morale. The automobile revolution has destroyed the excuse for a great many village centers, has made possible the emergence of integrated shopping centers and regional schools, and has brought about the construction of superhighways through many congested districts. Overexploitation and unwise planning, or none at all, have spread blight over large urban, suburban, and rural areas. Rather than stay and fight for a revitalization of a community by helping to discover and exploit new opportunities, the more vigorous citizens are likely to move to areas with more obvious assets. The discouraged, the members of underprivileged minorities, and the ill and damaged are likely to remain in the decaying area.

Isolation is a significant aspect of local community problems. The decaying urban, suburban, and rural communities are not visible to those who might aid in the solution of pressing problems. Prosperous communities with high morale, well developed or overdeveloped facilities, and a dynamic growth situation preoccupy their inhabitants and keep them from being aware of depressed conditions over the next hill, across the river, or even along the commuter train's right of way. The routine activities of the members of many privileged communities never bring them to see the blighted conditions they help to create through their business and political decisions.

Can a community be recreated? Conscientious social workers have long seen the redevelopment of community as the best way available to help rehumanize our depersonalized and demoralized urban, suburban, and rural areas. They have tried to make the nurturing of community participation and "grass-roots" leadership central to their proposals for a "war against poverty." In doing so, they immediately clash with the determined and entrenched opposition of the existing politico-economic manipulators of those who live in blighted areas. Such politico-economic entrepreneurs prefer to utilize "poverty funds" in ways that strengthen their own organizations while incidentally "doing what they can" for the poor.

Without the provision of adequate resources and social opportunities for the poor within the existing power structure of society, separatist types of community and social organization develop. Classical examples of this are the nationalist movements in Ireland, Wales, Brittany, and Sicily. In this country, Black Nationalist efforts to form separate social structures are of this nature.

MASS MANIPULATION

Basic services are provided for mass society by communications media, schools, and politico-economic instruments of production, distribution, finance, and control. To an extent, at any given time and place, such social instruments represent and serve popular interests and needs. To the extent to which they do not, they become more or less recognized social problems. Their lack of adaptation to popular desires demonstrates built-in institutional resistance to change and also reflects the manipulative efforts of power-seekers and of special-interest groups.

Except for the very few government and contributor-supported stations and channels, radio and television derive their income from advertisers. Newspapers depend on advertising revenues for almost three-quarters of their income, and it has been adequately shown by expensive failures that they cannot exist competitively in our society without advertising. In its early years the *Reader's Digest* obtained the largest circulation of any American magazine without advertising, but eventually it too tapped the vast resources available to it through paid advertisements. Periodicals generally (other than newspapers) receive three-fifths of their income from advertising. A large share of newspaper and magazine subscription income on the other hand has to be reinvested in the costly struggle to maintain high circulation figures among the groups advertisers wish to reach. This struggle typically takes the form of exploiting sports coverage, comic strips, continued fiction, women's features, and similar entertainment rather than of providing more accurate news coverage or better politico-economic guidance or representation. Broadly conceived, the interests of advertisers and of subscribers would perhaps tend to converge, but advertisers caught up in their daily struggles for business may be led to take quite narrow views of their interests and are able to communicate these concerns forcefully to the media with which they deal.

Even though many books are subsidized for propaganda purposes or written noncontroversially in order to attract larger audiences as in the textbook market, the book publishing industry is our freest medium of communication. It is controlled chiefly by estimates of editors, publishers, bookstore operators, and librarians as to popular needs and interests. Even though there still are a great many book publishing firms, large corporations are taking control of more and more of the industry. Whether this will eventually have a restrictive effect remains to be seen.

The steady beat on mass society of the advertising messages, slanted news, and sensationalized entertainment in our mass media tends to promote many times a callousness and occasionally a sense of hopeless panic among readers and listeners. Our schools, from nursery classes through graduate seminars, are mostly caught up in the same web of control and orthodoxy. They appear to be demanding and absorbing, but students often find them little more than a time-filling activity, an impersonal daily ritual. Fortunately, thousands of dedicated teachers try with some success to make our schools more directly to interest and to serve the needs of our young people. Their devoted efforts have done miracles in the awakening of interest and the developing of talent. In times of crisis, as exemplified by student strikes against educational irrelevance during the 1960's, some needed reorganizations of high schools and colleges are being made.

NATURAL CATASTROPHES

Forest fires in Oregon and New Jersey, earthquakes in Alaska and California, tornadoes and drought in the Middle West, hurricanes and floods from Texas to Maine, all are frequently in the news. They join with more local catastrophes such as hail and lightning damage to remind us constantly of forces far from controlled by modern technology and only partly compensated by insurance.

The spectacular nature of such catastrophes and their recurrence have stimulated efforts to cope with them and to insure against their consequences. Sociologists have been interested in how such efforts have made for the wiser planning of water control by states and on a multi-state basis. Such planning has also facilitated the planned control of other resources. As weather-control becomes increasingly possible, its planning necessities will have wide social implications. For the meeting of the consequences of catastrophes as they arise, sociologists are proving themselves to be increasingly helpful to the Red Cross, emergency, police corps, and national guard units both in preplanning and training and also in meeting the complexities of an actual emergency situation.

DEPRESSIONS, INFLATIONS

Economic crises involve society at large and have sweeping social consequences. At the end of the Great Depression of the 1930's, the modest New Deal welfare-state projects had met effective opposition not only from organized business but also from multitudes who were panicky and confused in the face of uncertainty. A booming war economy quickly replaced such efforts and gave us a sense of prosperity. With constant modifications, that war economy has continued ever since the end of World War II, through the Cold War with the Soviet Union and Red China, the Korean Intervention, the Undeclared War in Viet Nam, and minor involvements. After the 1930's, rather than depressions from time to time, the American economy has had "recessions" or "periods of consolidation and adjustment."

There is a popular view that both depression and inflation contain an arbitrary element and that they are convertible the one into the other. While this popular belief oversimplifies societal complexities, the economic climate is influenced by major politico-economic strategy decisions concerning international tension, war, credit restriction, capital investment, inflationary "guide lines," welfare funds, the relative value of currencies, and all the rest. Hence, there is a popular feeling of remoteness from crucial decision-making, and as a result a lack of involvement or representation in the determination of basic policy change. This provides the cognitive basis for popular mythologies in which scares about Communism and rightist "take-overs" substitute for judicious analysis. Panaceas offered by propagandists of the right, left, and center outweigh sensible considerations of what is possible and desirable socially.

Responsible economists now hold that wise politico-economic planning and control can keep our economy from either depression or inflation. As this view becomes more widely understood and held, social pressures to follow a more stable and appropriate course will perhaps gradually prove adequate. This type of social adjustment need not be confused with either doctrinaire capitalism or doctrinaire socialism. It is likely to be a blend of both. Sociologists are concerned with how such arrangements can help to "shock-proof" society and in what the consequences of greater stability may be upon continuing human welfare.

POLLUTION AND WASTE

The pollution of our environment with smog, automotive exhaust gas, pesticides, synthetic fertilizers, sewage, garbage, junk, and noise—not to mention atomic waste—only occasionally reaches the spectacular notice of death reports and the release of sensational scientific and government reports on health damage. On the island of Manhattan, the exposure of non-smokers to carcinogenic fumes has been estimated as equivalent to two inhaled packages of cigarettes a day. Wonders have been done in the construction of dependable water supply and sewage disposal systems, but both water and sewage problems continue to outstrip our solutions for them. The outpourings of sewage and industrial waste are a growing menace to human health and survival.

In *Silent Spring* Rachel Carson relates how pesticides indiscriminately slaughter a great many useful insects and birds and also shorten and complicate human lives. Dangerous agricultural and industrial chemicals sometimes penetrate eggs, butter, meat, and bread. They contaminate fruit, vegetables, and drinking water. Once people could flee from polluted air, water, and food of the city and find refreshment "on the farm." Now they have no such refuge to which to turn; farms themselves become centers of pollution. Social concern grows as to whether or not such chemical alterations in our natural environment can be more adequately controlled. After all, we are adapted to our natural environment and indebted to it for the maintenance of our lives.

OVERPOPULATION

Discussions of relative overpopulation and underpopulation have to take into consideration four complicated variables: (*1*) population, (*2*) environment in the sense of physical resources, (*3*) stage or general level of the arts of production and distribution—the arts we use in making our physical resources available to meet human needs and desires, and (*4*) the standard of living viewed in an average sense but with the implication that it varies from group to group within a society. As a society's population increases, it can be sustained by bringing more resources into production and distribution, by improving the arts, or by lowering the level of living. Population increases through lowering the death rate or raising the birth rate. A sudden increase in available resources (such as followed the opening of the Americas to colonization by peoples with advanced arts) or marked improvement in the arts (such as the modern technological revolution) can at least temporarily raise the mode of living until population again catches up and begins to depress it.

These relationships are usually referred to as the "man-land ratio." In *Societal Evolution*, A. G. Keller summarizes the ratio thus: "population tends to increase up to the limit of the supporting power of the environment (meaning above all, land), on a given stage of the arts, and for a given standard of living—that is, for a given stage of civilization."

Within a society, differences in standards and modes of living and in fertility among the various social-class groups further complicate the application of the ratio. Some groups limit births as they strain to maintain or improve their mode of living. Others take a more relaxed view of reproduction. The application of the man-land ratio within each group is more specific than, and varies from, the average of society as a whole.

At its present rate of increase, world population will again double in the next forty years. Many countries are doubling theirs now each twenty years. To put it quite briefly, public health measures have cut most of the world's death rates, but they have not yet offset such declines by cutting the birth rates. This leaves a net annual gain in world population of more than 60 million a year, a figure equal to the present population of Brazil or of the United Kingdom plus Belgium. Each decade this means a world population increment equal to more than all the people in the Western Hemisphere.

Many relatively underdeveloped countries are increasing at rates of between 3 and 4 percent a year. These are countries which share the condition of undernourishment existing among two-thirds of the world's population. Latin America's over-all annual population rise is 3.0 percent; that of Africa, 2.4; of non-Soviet-Russian Asia, 2.2; of the United States, 1.3; of the Soviet Union, 1.2; of Europe, only 0.9.

Cannot human ingenuity provide food for additional billions of humans? There are limits both to ingenuity and to the bounty of the earth. Not only that, but each year additional millions are being added to the more than two billion who are now undernourished, without adequate living facilities, and an increasing burden upon the more fortunate inhabitants of earth. Even in the United States, we have not solved the increasing problems of crowding, lack of economic opportunities, the spread of disease, and overbreeding.

Under the leadership of politicians of many religious faiths and with bipartisan backing, the United States government and those of most of our states have in recent years begun to take active parts in the development and dissemination of birth-control information, techniques, and materials. Both the Federal government and university research agencies are providing scientific and technical aid upon request to countries around the world for the development of birth control programs and also of improvement programs in the agricultural and industrial arts and sciences.

Effective campaigns to provide mass-education in birth control procedures and to raise the levels of technical competence are the two recourses now being pushed to try to bring the man-land ratio more into balance. The time for action is short. The world population "clock" ticks faster and faster, and the "have-nots" become a more and more pressing threat to the "haves."

WARS, COLD AND HOT

Wars and the rumors of wars are disastrous strands in human history. These include the "peacetime" international tensions, military aid, and even economic and military interventions that we call "cold war." Preparing for wars, conducting them, and suffering their consequences consume a large share of the energies and capital of mankind each year. Prior to the Spanish-American War, Americans were preoccupied with wars for autonomy, wars of expansion, including our genocidal efforts against the American Indian, and wars against secession. As a result of expanding military and business adventures signalled by the Spanish-American War, the United States now supports a military establishment on which the "sun never sets," a phrase once used of the British Empire. It is an establishment which involves extensive military "aid" and "intervention."

The involvements of individual Americans in such efforts currently amount to between ten and twenty percent of each person's income in the form of taxes, not to mention, for males, the possibility of military service and even death in action. Other costs are not so obvious. They are the consequences of subjecting millions of young men to brutalizing routines and philosophy, the maintenance of huge industrial vested interests in destruction, and the tendency for both propaganda and educational media to be "prussianized." Above all, important and even urgent reforms and programs are dissipated or destroyed by war. Woodrow Wilson's "New Freedom" was a war casualty in 1917. F. D. Roosevelt's "New Deal" rapidly lost momentum as the United States went towards war in 1939–41. The Kennedy-Johnson "New Frontier" languished through the distractions of the Viet Nam Undeclared War of the 1960's.

In such a brief discussion of cold and hot wars as social problems, we can only suggest a few salient aspects. The subject and its literature are vast. Basic questions are being asked now as to how inherent war and bellicosity are to man and to man's society. The weight of evidence indicates that patterns of personal and social conflict and of emotional involvement in conflict are learned; they are not innate or instinctive. Cross-cultural studies of war, even though primitive data are scarcely relevant to a consideration of industrial societies, do not prove that human societies are always warlike or even that they need to be in order to survive. As Willard Waller concludes, in *War in the Twentieth Century*, "Any valid theory of war . . . must consider the fact that it grows out of the totality of our civilization. . . . War settles nothing because defeated nations will not accept defeat.

CHAPTER THIRTY-FIVE

SOCIAL RESEARCH, PLANNING, AND ACTION

More and more, social research now is joined with planning and action in efforts to cope with social problems. This growing importance of social research is not, however, without its own problems.

If social research is to be useful, it must be scientific. That is to say that social research must be thorough-going, accurate, and as free as possible from distortion or omission through considerations of special interest.

On the other hand, social planning and action are matters of art, of practical strategy. They not only require close attention to special interests; they are most likely to be done by representatives of special interests. At best, social planning and action are done under direction sufficiently composite and representative to assure fairly proportioned attention to all interest groups most concerned.

The social scientist perennially faces this difficulty, often called the conflict between "theory" and "practice," between the conclusions of the scientists based upon evidence and the decisions of the man of action based upon evidence *and* special interest and wisdom concerning strategy. As the various sciences have matured and have made contributions to phase after phase of our social life, the impatience of the actionist with the theorist has necessarily been tempered. The invasion of the social scientist has proceeded, and the actionist has developed a respect for him.

The services of sociologists in researching some of the great social problems of our times have included especially their work on intergroup prejudice, tension, and exploitation, on minority groups, on marriage and the family, on socialization, on delinquency and crime, on congestion, population shifts, and community decay, on the social deviants, on social work, and on domestic and international violence. The evidence and conclusions of social scientists on these and other subjects are being presented and gaining substantial attention in administrative, legislative, and judicial units of all levels including the United States Supreme Court and international tribunals, in corporation board rooms and union halls, and popularly through the press, radio, and television.

SELECTED READINGS

The Quick Reference Table (inside front cover) provides a representative list of general textbooks in sociology, with cross-references to this College Outline. Here are listed (A) other over-views of the field, (B) standard reference works, (C) leading sociological periodicals, and (D) selected readings for each chapter of this Outline.

A. OVER-VIEWS OF SOCIOLOGY

Bates, Alan P. *The Sociological Enterprise.* Boston: Houghton Mifflin Co., 1967. Sociology as subject and profession.

Berger, Peter L. *Invitation to Sociology: A Humanistic Perspective.* Garden City, N.Y.: Doubleday Anchor Books, 1963. A lucid book "intended to be read, not studied," an invitation to an "exciting and significant" intellectual world.

Falding, Harold. *The Sociological Task.* Englewood Cliffs, N.J.: Prentice-Hall, 1968. What sociologists are trying to do.

Inkeles, Alex. *What Is Sociology? An Introduction to the Discipline and Profession.* Englewood Cliffs, N.J.: Prentice-Hall, 1964. Addressed to the person considering sociology as a career.

Horowitz, Irving Louis. Professing Sociology: Studies in the Life Cycle of Social Science. Chicago: Aldine 1968. Institutional setting of sociology, the locale where sociologists make their living and legitimize their careers.

Lundberg, George A. *Can Science Save Us?* 2nd ed. New York: Longmans, Green, 1961. Dwells on "the regrettable fact that good intentions are not a substitute for good techniques in achieving either physical or social goals." Brief statement of positivist position.

Lynd, Robert S. *Knowledge for What? The Place of Social Science in American Culture.* Princeton: Princeton University Press, 1939. An appraisal of "elements of strain and disjunction" in American life and a critique of social science.

Mills, C. Wright. *The Sociological Imagination.* New York: Oxford University Press, 1959. Plea for "addressing ourselves to issues and to troubles, and formulating them as problems of social science."

Simpson, George. *Man in Society: Preface to Sociology and the Social Sciences.* Garden City, N.Y.: Doubleday, 1954. Stimulating treatment of basic issues.

Stein, Maurice, and Arthur Vidich, eds. *Sociology on Trial.* Englewood Cliffs, N.J.: Prentice-Hall, 1963. Critical papers re-assessing the social roles of sociology and of sociologists.

B. STANDARD REFERENCE WORKS

Encyclopedia of the Social Sciences. 15 volumes. New York: Macmillan, 1930–1935.

International Encyclopedia of the Social Sciences. 17 volumes. New York: Macmillan and Free Press, 1968.

Sociological Abstracts. See under section (C) "Leading Sociological Periodicals."

Fairchild, H. P., ed. *Dictionary of Sociology.* New York: Philosophical Library, 1944.

Faris, Robert E. L., ed. *Handbook of Modern Sociology.* Chicago: Rand McNally, 1964.

Gould, Julius, and W. L. Kolb, eds. *A Dictionary of the Social Sciences.* New York: Free Press, 1964.

Merton, Robert K., Leonard Broom, and Leonard S. Cottrell, Jr., eds. *Sociology Today: Problems and Prospects.* New York: Basic Books, 1959.

Mitchell, G. Duncan, ed. *Dictionary of Sociology.* Chicago: Aldine, 1968.

Parsons, Talcott, Edward Shils, Kaspar D. Naegele, and Jesse R. Pitts, eds. *Theories of Society: Foundations of Modern Sociological Theory.* New York: Free Press, 1961.

C. LEADING SOCIOLOGICAL PERIODICALS

American Journal of Sociology. 1895– . Bi-monthly. University of Chicago Press. Reports of research, theory, method, critical analysis; book reviews.

American Sociological Review. 1936– . Bi-monthly. American Sociological Association. Reports of research, theory, method, critical analysis; book reviews.

American Sociologist. 1965– . Quarterly. American Sociological Association. Professional forum, employment bulletin, news notes, announcements, official reports and proceedings.

Annals of the American Academy of Political and Social Science. 1890– . Bi-monthly. Each number devoted to special topic. Comprehensive book review section.

The Family Coordinator. 1952– . Quarterly. National Council on Family Relations. Education, counseling, and services.

Journal of Health and Social Behavior. 1960– . Quarterly. American Sociological Association.

Journal of Marriage and the Family. 1938– . Quarterly. National Council on Family Relations. Theory, research interpretation, critical discussion.

Rural Sociology. 1936– . Quarterly. Rural Sociological Society. Scientific study of rural life.

Social Forces. 1922– . University of North Carolina. Scientific social study and interpretation.

Social Problems. 1953– . Quarterly. Society for the Study of Social Problems.

Sociological Abstracts. 1952– . Eight issues plus annual index. Brief summaries of thousands of articles and books published all over the world. Arranged under standard specialty headings. Index makes it easy to locate items on any subject.

Sociological Analysis. 1940– . Quarterly. American Catholic Sociological Society.

Sociological Quarterly. 1960– . Quarterly. Midwest Sociological Society.

Sociology and Social Research. 1916– . Quarterly. University of Southern California. Research reports, discussions.

Sociology of Education. 1927– . Quarterly. American Sociological Association. Interdisciplinary and international.

Sociometry. 1937– . Quarterly. American Sociological Association. Research reports in social psychology.

Southwest Social Science Quarterly. 1920– . Quarterly. Southwestern Social Science Association.

Trans-Action: Social Science & Modern Society. 1963– . Monthly. To further popular understanding and use of the social sciences.

D. SELECTED READINGS FOR EACH CHAPTER

Part One: Socialization of the Individual

Chapter 1: Individual and Environment

Bandura, Albert, and R.A. Walters. *Social Learning and Personality Development.* New York: Holt, Rinehart & Winston, 1963. Standard and deviant personality patterns and their modification.

Barnouw, Victor. *Culture and Personality.* Homewood, Ill.: Dorsey Press, 1963. Anthropological textbook.

Brim, O.G., Jr., and Stanton Wheeler. *Socialization After Childhood: Two Essays.* New York: Wiley, 1966.

Clausen, John, and others. *Socialization and Society.* Boston: Little, Brown, 1968. Symposium on socialization theory and research.

Cohen, Yehudi A., ed. *Social Structure and Personality: A Casebook.* New York: Holt, Rinehart & Winston, 1961. Interdisciplinary and cross-cultural integration.

Cooley, Charles Horton. *Social Organization: A Study of the Larger Mind.* 1909. *Social Process.* 1918. *Human Nature and the Social Order,* rev. ed. 1922. New York: Scribner's. Noted contributions to theory of socialization.

Elkin, Frederick. *The Child and Society: The Process of Socialization.* New York: Random House, 1960. Brief textbook.

Erikson, Erik H. *Childhood and Society,* 2nd ed. 1963. *Young Man Luther: A Study in Psychoanalysis and History.* 1962. *Identity: Youth and Crisis.* 1968. New York: W.W. Norton. Synthesis of neo-Freudian and anthropological data and theory.

Flavell, J.H. *The Developmental Psychology of Jean Piaget.* Princeton: Van Nostrand, 1963. Authorized summary and interpretation of Piaget's contributions to socialization.

Goodman, Mary Ellen. *The Individual and Culture.* Homewood, Ill.: Dorsey Press, 1967. To what extent can a man determine his own destiny? Interdisciplinary consideration.

Goslin, D.A., and D.C. Glass, eds. *Handbook of Socialization Theory and Research.* New York: Rand McNally, 1968.

Gottschalk, Louis, Clyde Kluckhohn, and R.C. Angell, eds. *The Use of Personal Documents in History, Anthropology, and Sociology.* New York: Social Science Research Council, Bulletin 53, 1945.

Haring, Douglas, ed. *Personal Character and Culture Milieu.* New York: Syracuse University Press, 1956. Anthropological readings.

Honigmann, John J. *Personality in Culture.* New York: Harper & Row, 1967. Anthropological viewpoint, data.

Hsu, Francis L.K., ed. *Psychological Anthropology: Approaches to Culture and Personality.* Homewood, Ill.: Dorsey Press, 1961.

Hunt, Robert, ed. *Personalities and Cultures: Readings in Psychological Anthropology.* New York: Natural History Press, 1967. 18 selections dealing with specific issues and/or cultures.

Kaplan, Bert, ed. *Studying Personality Cross-Culturally.* Evanston, Ill.: Row, Peterson, 1961. 24 papers on theory, methods, and findings.

Kluckhohn, Clyde, and H.A. Murray, with D.M. Schneider, eds. *Personality in Nature, Society, and Culture,* 2nd ed. New York: Alfred A. Knopf, 1953. Important symposium.

Lindesmith, Alfred R., and Anselm L. Strauss. *Social Psychology,* 3rd ed. New York: Holt, Rinehart & Winston, 1968. Esp. part 4, "Socialization and Interaction," and part 5, "Deviance."

Mead, George Herbert. *On Social Psychology: Selected Papers.* Ed. with an introduction by Anselm Strauss. Chicago: University of Chicago Press, 1964. Socialization theory.

Stoodley, Bartlett H., ed. *Society and Self: A Reader in Social Psychology.* New York: Free Press, 1962. Readings emphasize influence of social structure.

Whiting, John W.M. *Field Guide for a Study of Socialization.* New York: John Wiley & Sons, 1966. Detailed plan for study of child rearing in six different societies.

Whiting, John W.M., and Irvin L. Child. *Child Training and Personality: A Cross-Cultural Study.* New Haven: Yale University Press, 1953. Interdisciplinary consideration of data on 75 primitive societies.

Chapter 2: Roles

Entries for chapter 30 also treat with role in various aspects.

Bennis, Warren G., Edgar H. Schein, and David E. Berlew. *Interpersonal Dynamics: Essays and Readings on Human Interaction.* Homewood, Ill.: Dorsey Press, 1964.

Emmet, Dorothy. *Rules, Roles, and Relations.* New York: St. Martin's Press, 1966. A philosopher considers sociological findings concerning roles and culture.

Goffman, Erving. *The Presentation of Self in Everyday Life.* 1959. Man as actor in diverse social situations. *Interaction Ritual.* 1967. Study of face-to-face interaction in natural settings. Garden City: Doubleday Anchor.

Goffman, Erving. *Encounters: Two Studies in the Sociology of Interaction.* Indianapolis: Bobbs-Merrill, 1961. "Fun in Games" and "Role Distance."

Goffman, Erving. *Behavior in Public Places: Notes on the Social Organization of Gatherings.* New York: Free Press of Glencoe, 1963. Exploration of organization of face-to-face interaction.

Shibutani, Tamotsu. *Society and Personality: An Interactionist Approach to Social Psychology.* Englewood Cliffs, N.J.: Prentice-Hall, 1961. Includes extensive discussion of roles.

Strauss, Anselm L. *Mirrors and Masks: The Search for Identity.* Glencoe, Ill.: Free Press, 1959.

Chapter 3: Child and Family

Benson, Leonard. *Fatherhood: A Sociological Perspective.* New York: Random House, 1968. In family and in community life.

Bossard, James H.S., and Eleanor Stoker Boll. *The Sociology of Child Development,* 4th ed. New York: Harper & Row, 1966. Eclectic treatment plus original contributions.

Eisenstadt, S.N. *From Generation to Generation: Age Groups and Social Structure.* New York: Free Press of Glencoe, 1956. Analysis of how societies transmit culture from adults to young.

Fyvel, T.R. *Troublemakers: Rebellious Youth in an Affluent Society,* new ed. New York: Schocken Books, 1964. Mostly on English youth but with chapters on European, American, and Russian youth as well.

Handel, Gerald, ed. *The Psychosocial Interior of the Family: A Sourcebook for the Study of Whole Families.* Chicago: Aldine Publishing, 1967. In 23 writings, an attempt to show that diversity of work which constitutes the nucleus of a potentially coherent framework for family study.

Heiss, Jerold, ed. *Family Roles and Interaction: An Anthology.* Chicago: Rand McNally, 1968. 36 readings relevant to the concerns of role theory.

Hoffman, M.L., and Lois W. Hoffman, eds. *Review of Child Development Research.* New York: Russell Sage Foundation, vol. 1 (1964) and vol. 2 (1966).

Klein, Josephine. *Samples from English Cultures.* London: Routledge & Kegan Paul, 1965. 2 vols. Summary and analysis of studies of socialization patterns in diverse English status groups.

Miller, Daniel R., and Guy E. Swanson. *The Changing American Parent: A Study in the Detroit Area.* New York: John Wiley & Sons, 1958. Details on the rearing of a population sample of nearly 600 children.

Miller, Daniel R., and Guy E. Swanson. *Inner Conflict and Defense.* New York: Henry Holt, 1960. Social factors and child-rearing practices that predispose children to favor particular methods of resolving conflict.

Minturn, Leigh, and William W. Lambert. *Mothers of Six Cultures: Antecedents of Child Rearing.* New York: John Wiley & Sons, 1964. Representative of Kenya, India, Mexico, The Philippines, Okinawa, and U.S.A.

Sears, Robert R., Eleanor E. Maccoby, and Harry Levin. *Patterns of Child Rearing.* Evanston, Ill.: Row, Peterson, 1957. How 379 American mothers brought up their children from birth to kindergarten age.

van Gennep, Arnold. *The Rites of Passage* (Orig. published 1908). Transl. by M.B. Vizedom and G.L. Caffee. Introd. by S.T. Kimball. Chicago: University of Chicago Press, 1960. Ceremonies accompanying an individual's "life crises."

Znaniecki, Florian. *Social Relations and Social Roles: The Unfinished Systematic Sociology.* Chicago: Science Research Associates, 1965.

Chapter 4: Courtship, Marriage, Divorce

Adams, Bert N. *Kinship in an Urban Setting.* Chicago: Markham Publishing Co., 1968. Study of 800 young married adults in a middle-sized city.

Bell, Norman W., and Ezra F. Vogel, eds. *A Modern Introduction to the Family,* rev. ed. New York: Free Press, 1968. 52 selections include comparative, cross-cultural materials.

Bell, Robert R. *Marriage and Family Interaction,* rev. ed. Homewood, Ill.: Dorsey Press, 1967. Dating, courtship, marriage, parenthood, marriage breakdown and alteration.

Bowman, Henry A. *Marriage for Moderns,* 5th ed. New York: McGraw-Hill, 1965.

Burgess, E.W., Harvey J. Locke, and Mary Margaret Thomas. *The Family: From Institution to Companionship,* 3rd ed. New York: American Book, 1963.

Cavan, Ruth Shonle. *The American Family,* 3rd ed. 1963. *American Marriage: A Way of Life.* 1959. *Marriage and Family in the Modern World: A Book of Readings,* 2nd ed. 1965. New York: Thomas Y. Crowell.

Christensen, Harold T., ed. *Handbook of Marriage and the Family.* Chicago: Rand McNally, 1964. Useful symposium.

Clemens, Alphonse H. *Design for Successful Marriage* (formerly *Marriage and the Family: An Integrated Approach for Catholics*), 2nd ed. Englewood Cliffs, N.J.: Prentice-Hall, 1964.

Coser, Rose Laub, ed. *The Family: Its Structure and Functions.* New York: St. Martin's Press, 1964. The family as an institution, not as a source of specific social problems.

Eshleman, J. Ross. *Perspectives in Marriage and the Family.* Boston: Allyn & Bacon, 1968. Text with readings; structural-functional and symbolic interactional.

Farber, Bernard, ed. *Kinship and Family Organization.* New York: John Wiley & Sons, 1966.

Geiger, H. Kent, ed. *Comparative Perspectives on Marriage and the Family.* Boston: Little, Brown, 1968.

Goode, William J. *The Family.* 1964. Emphasizes complex relations between family systems and larger social structure. Ed. *Readings on the Family and Society.* 1964. To complement his text, *The Family.* Englewood Cliffs, N.J.: Prentice-Hall.

Goode, William J. *World, Family, and Revolution.* New York: Free Press, 1963. Comparative study of family as institution.

Komarovsky, Mirra, with Jane H. Philips. *Blue-Collar Marriage.* New York: Random House, 1964. Special study of lower-class families.

Landis, Judson T. *Building a Successful Marriage,* 5th ed. Englewood Cliffs, N.J.: Prentice-Hall, 1968.

Landis, Paul H. *Making the Most of Marriage,* 3rd ed. New York: Appleton-Century-Crofts, 1965.

McKinley, D.G. *Social Class and Family Life.* New York: Free Press, 1964. How social stratification influences family organization and values.

Nimkoff, M.F., ed. *Comparative Family Systems.* Boston: Houghton Mifflin, 1965. Cross-cultural comparisons illustrated by cases from twelve cultures.

Nye, F. Ivan, and Felix M. Berardo, eds. *Emerging Conceptual Frameworks in Family Analysis.* New York: Macmillan, 1966. Symposium.

Rodman, Hyman, ed. *Marriage, Family, and Society: A Reader.* New York: Random House, 1965.

Schneider, David M. *American Kinship: A Cultural Account.* Englewood Cliffs, N.J.: Prentice-Hall, 1968. An anthropological approach.

Shanas, Ethel, and Gordon F. Streib, eds. *Social Structure and the Family: Generational Relations.* Englewood Cliffs, N.J.: Prentice-Hall, 1965. Stress on intergenerational relations and kin network.

Simpson, George. *People in Families: Sociology, Psychoanalysis, and the American Family,* new ed. Cleveland: Meridian Books, 1966. Integration of Freudian and sociological viewpoints.

Stephens, William N., ed. *Reflections on Marriage.* New York: Thomas Y. Crowell, 1968. Focuses on mate choice and family roles and relationships.

Sussman, Marvin B., ed. *Sourcebook in Marriage and the Family,* 2nd ed. Boston: Houghton Mifflin, 1963. 75 readings, unified by life-cycle plan of organization.

Winch, Robert F., and Louis Wolf Goodman, eds. *Selected Studies in*

Marriage and the Family, 3rd ed. New York: Holt, Rinehart & Winston, 1968. Introduction and 62 articles on American and foreign data.

Chapter 5: Deviants

Angrist, Shirley S., Mark Lefton, Simon Dinitz, and Banjamin Pasamanick. *Women After Treatment: A Study of Former Mental Patients and Their Normal Neighbors.* New York: Appleton-Century-Crofts, 1968.

Baumeister, Alfred A., ed. *Mental Retardation: Appraisal, Education, and Rehabilitation.* Chicago: Aldine, 1967.

Becker, Howard S., ed. *The Other Side: Perspectives on Deviance.* New York: Free Press of Glencoe, 1964. Symposium developed under the auspices of the Society for the Study of Social Problems. Supplementary text.

Becker, Howard S. *Outsiders: Studies in the Sociology of Deviance.* New York: Free Press, 1963. Supplementary text.

Becker, Howard S., Blanche Geer, and Everett C. Hughes. *Making the Grade: The Academic Side of College Life.* New York: John Wiley & Sons, 1968. Includes discussion of problems associated with superior performance.

Bloch, Herbert A., and Melvin Prince. *Social Crisis and Deviance: Theoretical Foundations.* New York: Random House, 1967. Short text on social pathology; sick society requires treatment.

Clinard, Marshall B. *Sociology and Deviant Behavior,* 3rd ed. New York: Holt, Rinehart & Winston, 1968. Comprehensive and authoritative text on social deviation, deviant behavior, and social control.

Cohen, Albert K. *Deviance and Control.* Englewood Cliffs, N.J.: Prentice-Hall, 1966. Effort to develop a general theory of deviance.

Coser, Lewis A. *Men of Ideas.* New York: Free Press, 1965. Roles of the creative.

Edgerton, Robert B. *The Clock of Competence: Stigma in the Lives of the Mentally Retarded.* Berkeley: University of California Press, 1967.

Erikson, Kai T. *Wayward Puritans: A Study in the Sociology of Deviance.* New York: John Wiley & Sons, 1966. Discussion of theory of deviance in terms of societal reaction followed by application to Puritan New England.

Goffman, Erving. *Asylums: Essays on the Social Situations of Mental Patients and Other Inmates.* Garden City: Doubleday, 1961. *Stigma.* Englewood Cliffs, N.J.: Prentice-Hall, 1963. Participant observations.

Gowan, John Curtis, George D. Demos, and E. Paul Torrance. *Creativity: Its Educational Implications.* New York: John Wiley & Sons, 1967.

Jessor, Richard, Theodore D. Graves, Robert C. Hanson, and Shirley L. Jessor. *Society, Personality, and Deviant Behavior: A Study of a Tri-Ethnic Community.* New York: Holt, Rinehart & Winston, 1968. A research report.

Lefton, Mark, James K. Skipper, Jr., and Charles H. McGaghy. *Approaches to Deviance: Theories, Concepts, and Research Findings.* New York: Appleton-Century-Crofts, 1968. Eclectic research-oriented approach to study of deviance.

Lemert, Edwin M. *Human Deviance, Social Problems, and Social Control.* Englewood Cliffs, N.J.: Prentice-Hall, 1967. Collection of his papers.

MacAndrew, Craig, and R.B. Edgerton *Drunken Comportment.* Chicago: Aldine Publishing Co., 1969.

Pasamanick, Benjamin, Frank R. Scarpitti, and Simon Dinitz. *Schizo-*

phrenics in the Community: An Experimental Study in the Prevention of Hospitalization. New York: Appleton-Century-Crofts, 1967.

Rubington, Earl, and Martin S. Weinberg, eds. *Deviance: The Interactionist Perspective: Text and Readings in the Sociology of Deviance.* New York: Macmillan, 1968. Emphasis on mental illness, alcoholism, homosexuality, drug addiction, shoplifting, and traffic violation.

Rushing, William A., ed. *Deviant Behavior and Social Process.* Chicago: Rand McNally, 1968. 48 readings on 10 types of deviant behavior.

Scheff, Thomas J. *Being Mentally Ill: A Sociological Theory.* Chicago: Aldine, 1966. In terms of norms or residual rules and of role theory.

Scheff, Thomas J., ed. *Mental Illness and Social Process.* New York: Harper & Row, 1967. Reader.

Simmons, Ozzie G. *Work and Mental Illness: Eight Case Studies.* New York: John Wiley & Sons, 1965.

Susser, Mervyn. *Community Psychiatry: Epidemiologic and Social Themes.* New York: Random House, 1968. Causes and distribution of socially-based mental illness.

Weinberg, S. Kirson, ed. *The Sociology of Mental Disorders: Analyses and Readings in Psychiatric Sociology.* Chicago: Aldine Publishing, 1967.

Weiner, Leonard, Alvin Becker, and Tobias T. Friedman. *Home Treatment: Spearhead of Community Psychiatry.* Pittsburgh: University of Pittsburgh Press, 1968.

Wilkins, Leslie T. *Social Deviance: Social Policy, Action, and Research.* Englewood Cliffs, N.J.: Prentice-Hall, 1965. Effort to bring together in a text the needs of social action and the techniques of social research.

Chapter 6: The Person and Social Policy

Bury, J.B. *The Idea of Progress: An Inquiry into Its Origin and Growth.* London: MacMillan, 1920. Variously reprinted.

Freud, Sigmund. *Civilization and Its Discontents* (Orig. published 1930). Transl. and ed. by James Strachey. New York: W.W. Norton, 1961.

Gouldner, Alvin W., ed. *Studies in Leadership.* New York: Harper, 1950. Symposium.

Kosa, John, ed. *The Home of the Learned Man: A Symposium on the Immigrant Scholar in America.* New Haven: College & University Press, 1968.

Lynd, Robert S. *Knowledge for What? The Place of Social Science in American Culture.* Princeton: Princeton University Press, 1939.

Ogburn, William Fielding. *Social Change,* rev. ed. New York: Viking Press, 1950.

Sumner, William Graham. *Folkways.* Boston: Ginn, 1907. Variously reprinted. See chaps. 19, 20.

Part Two: Collective Behavior

Chapter 7: The Field of Collective Behavior

Cooley, Charles H. *Social Process.* New York: Chas. Scribner's Sons, 1918. A classic treatment of human society, emphasizing the tentative and exploratory character of the on-going process that takes place in human group life. Provides a good background for the more specific study of collective behavior.

Freud, Sigmund. *Group Psychology and the Analysis of the Ego* (1921). London: Hogarth Press, 1953. The well known effort of the founder of psychoanalysis to deal with the problem of group behavior from the standpoint of his scheme. Reflects an orthodox psychoanalytic treatment of a number of important problems in collective behavior.

Lang, Kurt and Gladys Lang. "Collective Behavior," *International Encyclopedia of the Social Sciences*, vol. 2, pp. 556–564. New York: Macmillan and Free Press, 1968. A recent authoritative statement of the nature of the field of collective behavior.

Lang, Kurt and Gladys Lang. *Collective Dynamics*. New York: T.Y. Crowell, 1962. A systematic sociological treatment of the field of collective behavior, with detailed discussion of its major sub-areas. Original theoretical analyses are advanced. A valuable basic textbook.

LaPiere, R.T. *Collective Behavior*. New York: McGraw-Hill, 1938. One of the early efforts to present a systematic organization and analysis of the field of collective behavior. While outdated, the discussion contains many challenging observations.

Mannheim, Karl. *Ideology and Utopia*, transl. by Louis Wirth and E.A. Shils. New York: Harcourt, Brace, 1936. A famous sociological treatise, of particular value to an understanding of the formation of a mass society, and the consequences of this for social thought and social organization.

Milgram, Stanley, and Hans Toch. "Collective Behavior: Crowds and Social Movements" in Gardner Lindzey and Elliot Aronson, eds., *The Handbook of Social Psychology*, 2nd ed., vol. 4, chap. 35. Reading, Mass.: Addison-Wesley, 1969. Outlines the nature of collective behavior from the standpoint of psychology. Has an extensive and helpful bibliography covering psychological work.

Park, Robert E. "Collective Behavior," *Encyclopedia of the Social Sciences*, vol. 3, pp. 631–633. New York: Macmillan, 1930. A valuable condensed exposition of the nature of collective behavior written by the scholar most responsible for establishing collective behavior as a field of study.

Smelser, Neil J. *Theory of Collective Behavior*. New York: Free Press, 1962. A valuable and systematic analysis, seeking to introduce a general theory that covers all segments of the field of collective behavior. Sees and treats collective behavior in terms of a structural-functional view of society.

Turner, Ralph H., and Lewis M. Killian. *Collective Behavior*. Englewood Cliffs: Prentice-Hall, 1957. The most widely used introductory textbook on collective behavior. Has a good organization of the major segments of the field and gives a simple and clear theoretical discussion. The value of the book is increased by the inclusion of numerous descriptive accounts of concrete instances of collective behavior.

Turner, Ralph H. "Collective Behavior" in R.E.L. Faris (ed.), *Handbook of Social Psychology*. New York: Rand-McNally, 1964. A recent condensed account of the field of collective behavior, presenting additions and new views to the treatment in the author's introductory textbook.

Young, Kimball. *Social Psychology*, 3rd ed. New York: Appleton-Century-Crofts, 1956. Chaps. 9, 12, 13. A readable elementary treatment of important problems in collective behavior.

Young, Kimball. *Source Book for Social Psychology*, part 6. New York:

F.S. Crofts, 1927. Contains a number of excellent first hand accounts of different instances of collective behavior.

Chapter 8: Elementary Collective Behavior

Backman, E. Louis. *Religious Dances in the Christian Church and in Popular Medicine*, transl. by E. Classen. London: Allen & Unwen, 1952. Shows the play of primitive forms of religious behavior under conditions of crowd-like experience. Significant in the study of religious movements.

Bresson, Bernard L. *Studies in Ecstasy*. New York: Vantage, 1967. Presents accounts showing the emergence of ecstatic behavior under conditions of social and personal disturbance. Relevant to the topic of the resolution of social unrest.

Cleveland, C.C. *The Great Revival in the West, 1797–1805*. Chicago: Univ. of Chicago Press, 1916. An excellent historical treatment of the Great American Revival, showing the emergence of various forms of primitive religious behavior under conditions of collective excitement and contagion.

Davenport, F.M. *Primitive Traits in Religious Revivals*. New York: Truth Seeker Co., 1905. A very fine discussion of primitive forms of expressive behavior under conditions of intense crowd excitment.

Durkheim, Emile. *The Elementary Forms of Religious Life,* transl. by J. W. Swain. New York: Macmillan, 1915. A famous theoretical treatment of the origin of religious sentiment in the collective excitement of tribal life. A pronouncedly sociological explanation in terms of the unitary character of the group.

Hecker, J.F.C. *Dancing Mania in the Middle Ages*. New York: Twentieth Century Publishing. The classic account of the dancing manias in Europe during stressful conditions in the middle ages. Excellent source material for an analysis of wide spread collective excitement.

Janis, Irving, and Carl Hovland. *Personality and Persuasion*. New Haven, Conn.: Yale Univ. Press, 1959. Covers psychological and experimental studies, seeking to identify and measure factors and conditions that shape decisions.

Lowenthal, Leo, and N. Guterman. *Prophets of Deceit: A Study of the Techniques of the American Agitator*. New York: Harper, 1949. An excellent analysis of agitation as carried on by the leaders of mass movements. A valuable counterpart to studies of agitation at the grass roots level.

Mackay, Charles. *Extraordinary Popular Delusions and the Madness of Crowds*. Boston: L. C. Page, 1932. A classic account of a variety of collective crazes, showing the play of crowd phenomena. A valuable source for material to be used in the analysis of extended crowd behavior.

Martin, Ira J. *Glossolalia in the Apostolic Church*. Berea, Key.: Berea College Press, 1960. An informative treatment of "speaking with tongues," one of the most interesting expressions of collective excitement in primitive religious settings.

Merloo, J. A. M. *Patterns of Panic*. New York: International Universities Press, 1950. One of the better known efforts to reduce panic behavior to different types. A good source of information on the peculiarities of panics.

Mooney, James. "The Ghost Dance Religion and the Sioux Outbreak of

1890." Edited by A.F.C. Wallace. Chicago: Univ. of Chicago Press. From the *Fourteenth Annual Report of the Bureau of Ethnology*, Part 2. Washington: Government Printing Office, 1896. This is a classic treatment of a religious cult among the American plains Indians which led to overt rebelion. A valuable source on social unrest that turns to a religious expression.

National Advisory Commission on Civil Disorders. *Report*. Washington: U. S. Government Printing Office, 1968. New York: Dutton, 1968. Presents the findings of the United States riot commission in an intensive study of the series of urban riots. Contains excellent materials for an understanding and analysis of riots. Offers little theoretical explanation.

Park, Robert E. and Ernest Burgess. *Introduction to the Science of Sociology*, 2nd ed. Chicago: Univ. of Chicago Press, 1924. Chaps. 12 & 13. The earliest systematic discussion of the topic of collective behavior. The scheme of treatment has provided the framework for most of the subsequent efforts to map out the field. Contains an excellent bibliography.

Silvert, K.H. ed. *Expectant Peoples: Nationalism and Development*. New York: Random House, 1963. Deals with the awakening of nationalist feelings in present day Latin-America, showing incipient efforts to move collectively under modern conditions of social transformation.

Chapter 9: Elementary Collective Groupings

Allport, G.W., and L. Postman. *The Psychology of Rumor*. New York: Henry Holt, 1947. Generally regarded as the best treatment of rumor from the standpoint of psychological factors. Should be compared with Shibutani, *Improvised News*.

Bauer, Wilhelm. "Public Opinion," *Encyclopaedia of the Social Sciences*, vol. 12, pp. 669–674. New York: Macmillan, 1934. An authoritative treatment, written primarily from the standpoint of the interests of traditional political theory. A lesser concern with social processes.

Berelson, Bernard, and M. Janowitz, eds. *Reader in Public Opinion and Communication*, 2nd ed. New York: Free Press, 1966. A good collection of articles dealing with different dimensions of mass communication and the process of forming public opinion.

Bernays, Edward L. *Propaganda*. New York: Liveright, 1938. An early well known discussion of propaganda by one of the foremost public relations experts of our era. The theoretical treatment is not profound but the practical observations are important.

Blumer, Herbert. "Public Opinion and Public Opinion Polling," *American Sociological Review*, vol. 13 (1948), pp. 542–544. A treatment of public opinion as a social process, reflecting the social organization present in a society. Polling is viewed critically from this standpoint.

Brown, Roger W. "Mass Phenomena" in Gardner Lindsey (ed.), *Handbook of Social Psychology*, vol. 2, pp. 833–876. Cambridge: Addison-Wesley, 1954. A comprehensive review of the literature dealing with crowds and related phenomena. Heavy emphasis is placed on psychological studies, such as laboratory and quasi-experimental work. A good reference source.

Canetti, Elias. *Crowds and Power*. New York: Viking Press, 1966. A significant recent effort by a German scholar to explain the nature of crowd behavior and the influence of the crowd in the shaping of civilization. While largely speculative, it is full of important insights.

Cantril, Hadley. *The Invasion from Mars*. Princeton: Princeton University Press, 1940. Classic account of crowd behavior taking place among thousands of listeners who construed a radio program as a *bona fide* report of an invasion of Martians in the New York area. A valuable source of information of the play of rumor and alarm under conditions of mass communication.

Chaplin, J. P. *Rumors, Fear and the Madness of Crowds*. New York, 1959. A recent effort to analyze the topic of collective alarm in terms of the mechanisms of crowd behavior.

Chapman, D. W. "Human Behavior in Disaster," *Journal of Social Issues*, vol. 10 (1954), no. 3 (entire issue). A series of articles by contemporary scholars dealing with the reaction of people to disaster situations, based predominantly on actual observational studies.

Chicago Commission on Race Relations. *The Negro in Chicago*. Chicago: Univ. of Chicago Press, 1922. In many ways still the best account and analysis of a single widespread racial riot. An intensive study, yielding much material worthy of further analysis.

Choukas, Michael. *Propaganda Comes of Age*. Washington, D. C.: Public Affairs, 1965. A thoughtful treatment showing and explaining refinements in the use of propaganda.

Cohen, Jerry, and William S. Murphy. *Burn, Baby, Burn*. New York: Dutton, 1966. An interesting and informative semi-popular treatment of recent riots in the Negro ghettoes in large American cities.

Davison, W. Phillips. "Public Opinion" in *International Encyclopedia of the Social Sciences*, vol. 13, pp. 188–196. New York: Macmillan and Free Press, 1968. A more recent treatment dealing with the political role of public opinion, its measurement and its relation to communication.

Dewey, John. *The Public and Its Problems*. New York: Henry Holt, 1927. A penetrating analysis of the "public" as a group, throwing much light on the nature and role of public opinion.

Elli, Frank. *The Riot*. New York: Coward-McCann, 1967. A recent treatment of the phenomena of riots, of value primarily in bringing together different views.

Ellul, Jacques. *Propaganda: The Formation of Men's Attitudes*. New York: Knopf, 1965. A recent attempt to analyze the nature of propaganda and show its operation in forming the views and attitudes of people.

Hardman, J. B. S. "Masses," *Encyclopaedia of the Social Sciences*, vol. 10, pp. 195–201. New York: Macmillan, 1933. An authoritative discussion of the nature of "masses," summarizing the literature up to 1932 and outlining a thoughtful view.

Harvey, Ian. *The Technique of Persuasion*. London: Falcon Press, 1951. Considers the devices used in trying to influence and direct the views and attitudes of people, especially through modern means of communication. Of value for an understanding of propaganda.

Institute for Propaganda Analysis. *Propaganda Analysis*, vols. 1–4 (1937–42). A valuable series discussing the nature and modes of operation of propaganda. Much can be gleaned through a careful readings of the materials.

Janis, Irving. *Air War and Emotional Stress*. New York: McGraw-Hill, 1951. One of the better discussions of the reaction of people in their personal and communal life to bombing from airplanes.

Key, V.O., Jr. *Public Opinion and American Democracy*. New York: Knopf, 1961. One of the more renowned analyses of public opinion in terms of its formation and role, especially in a democratic framework. Needs to be read by any student of public opinion.

Kornhauser, William. *The Politics of Mass Society.* Glencoe, Ill.: Free Press, 1959. An excellent discussion of the nature of a mass society in relation to the political process. Shows the significance of the presence or absence of organized groups in affecting the operation of a mass society, expecially in terms of political control.

Kracauer, Siegfried, and Paul L. Berkman. *Satellite Mentality.* New York: Praeger, 1956. Contains valuable observations with regard to the psychological processes in play in a mass society.

Larrabee, Eric, and Rolf Meyersohn. *Mass Leisure.* Glencoe, Ill.: Free Press, 1959. A good selection of articles dealing with different aspects of the problem of leisure as one of the central features of modern mass society. Throws much light on the position and role of mass members as consumers.

Le Bon, Gustav. *The Crowd: A Study of the Popular Mind* (1895). New York: Viking Press, 1960. This is the classic treatment of the crowd. It has influenced scholarly and lay thought throughout the world. Its central theses have by now been largely rejected or revised, but the work is full of valuable observations and insights.

Lederer, Emil. *The State of the Masses.* New York: W.W. Norton, 1950. A well known work by a German scholar, viewing modern society in terms of the play of "masses" of people, especially as it relates to the political role of the urban proletariat. The author is inclined to view the mass as a large crowd.

Lee, Alfred McClung. *How to Understand Propaganda.* New York: Rinehart, 1952. (Especially Chaps. 7–8). A penetrating treatment of the major factors in play in propaganda. An excellent introduction to the subject.

Lee, Alfred McClung. "Public Opinion in Relation to Culture," *Psychiatry* (1945) 8:49–61. A short but valuable statement on the nature of public opinion, showing its place in, and influence on, the shaping of collective life.

Lippmann, Walter. *The Phantom Public* (Orig. pub. 1925). New York: Free Press, 1965. An early but valuable analysis of the nature and role of public opinion by one of its most sensitive and thoughtful observers.

Lynes, Russell. *The Tastemakers.* New York: Harper, 1954. Discusses the sets of people who are placed in position that enable them to shape popular tastes. Helpful to an understanding of fashion and public opinion.

Martin, Everett D. *The Behavior of Crowds.* New York: Harper, 1920. A systematic effort to analyze and explain the nature of crowds, chiefly from the standpoint of psychoanalytic theory.

Merton, R. K. *Mass Persuasion.* New York: Harper, 1946. An interesting and thoughtful study of the efforts to induce the public purchase of Liberty Bonds during World War II. The analysis is made by a distinguished American sociologist.

Meusel, Alfred. "Proletariat," *Encyclopaedia of the Social Sciences,* vol. 12, pp. 510–518. New York: Macmillan, 1934. An early authoritative treatment of the nature and play of the large segment of our modern industrial society known as the proletariat. The analysis is of value for an understanding of both crowds and masses.

Neumann, Franz. *The Democratic and the Authoritarian State.* Glencoe, Ill.: Free Press, 1959. This work contains considerable discussion on the nature of mass society and its political operation under differently organized systems of modern society.

Ortega y Gasset, Jose. *Revolt of the Masses.* New York: W.W. Norton,

1932. The best known and most influential effort to identify the nature of mass society and to show its disintegrative effects on social order and discipline. This work by the renowned Spanish philosopher has set the mould for much of the political thinking on the role of the "masses."

Public Opinion Quarterly, special spring issue, vol. 27 (1963). Presents divergent views and treatments of the topic of public opinion. A valuable source.

Reisman, David et al. *The Lonely Crowd*. New Haven: Yale Univ. Press, 1950. By now, a famous analysis of the condition of the "modern man" in contemporary society. Seeks to identify basic type of orientation of people to the indigenous character of modern group life, placing stress on the psychological separateness of the individual. Has important observations on mass society.

Rosenberg, Barnard, and David White, eds. *Mass Culture*. Glencoe, Ill.: Free Press, 1957. A helpful collection of articles dealing with the more expressive side of the life of people in a mass society. Contains thoughtful discussion of the influence of mass communication.

Ross, E.A. *Social Psychology*. New York: Macmillan, 1908. An early treatment of crowds, social contagion and related phenomena, seeking to establish principles of explanation. Very readable. Contains interesting accounts of diverse forms of collective behavior.

Rudé, George. *The Crowd in History*. New York: Wiley, 1964. One of the better treatments of crowd behavior, having the merit of being empirically well grounded through careful historical study. Is concerned chiefly with crowds during periods of crises in Western Europe during the 18th and 19th centuries.

Selznick, Philip. *The Organizational Weapon*. New York: McGraw-Hill, 1952. An excellent analysis of the tactics of infiltration and manipulation in large scale organizations in modern society. Much light is thrown by this approach on the character of modern mass society as well as on mass political movements.

Shibutani, Tamotsu. *Improvised News, A Sociological Study of Rumor*. Indianapolis: Bubbs-Merrill, 1966. The most thorough analysis of the rumor process to be found in the literature. Views rumor in the context of group life, seeing it as a collective means of defining the world under conditions of uncertainty and anxiety.

Sidis, Boris. *Psychology of Suggestion*. New York: Appleton, 1898. Although written many decades ago this work is still a valuable treatment of the nature and play of suggestion in the shaping of thought and action. Much of the analysis has direct application to crowd behavior.

Sorel, Georges. *Reflections on Violence* (Orig. pub. 1908), transl. by T. E. Hulme and J. Roth. New York: Collier Book, 1960. A famous treatise, of greatest value in outlining the nature and the decisive role of collective myths in the formation and direction of large social movements.

Wallace, Anthony F. C. "Mass Phenomena," *International Encyclopedia of the Social Sciences*, vol. 10, pp. 54–58. New York: Macmillan and Free Press, 1968. A brief treatment of mass apathy, panics, mob behavior, collective crazes, and social movements. Reflects a different meaning of the term "mass."

Chapter 10: Social Movements

Adams, Brooks. *The Theory of Social Revolutions*. New York: Macmillan, 1913. One of the earlier efforts to outline a theory of social revolutions.

While considerably out of date, contains many insightful views that need to be taken into account.

Arendt, Hannah. *The Origins of Totalitarianism*. New York: Harcourt, Brace & World, 1966. Has valuable theoretical views on the background and formation of Nazism, Fascism, and Communism, of great relevance to the study of massive social movements in contemporary society.

Barbash, Jack. *The Labor Movement in the United States*. New York, 1958. An excellent discussion of the emergence and development of organized labor in the United States. The treatment is particularly relevant to an understanding of general social movements.

Brink, William and Louis Harris. *Black and White: A Study of U. S. Racial Attitudes Today*. New York: Simon and Schuster, 1967. One of the more thoughtful presentations of material on the current transformation in self-conception and political orientation of American Negroes.

Brinton, Crane. *The Anatomy of Revolution*, rev. ed. New York: Random House, 1957. This work by an eminent American historian is recognized as an outstanding theoretical analysis of revolutions. Based on a comparison of four major social revolutions in the Western world during the past three centuries.

Cantril, Hadley. *The Psychology of Social Movements*. New York: Wiley, 1941. One of the few attempts to develop a systematic theory of social movements. Deals with different kinds of social movements from the standpoint of a uniform psychological scheme.

Down, T. C. "The Rush to the Klondike," *Cornhill Magazine*, vol. 4 (1898), pp. 33–43. This short account has been recognized for a long time as a perceptive account of the Alaskan gold rush. Typifies the collective behavior usually found in the case of gold rushes, diamond rushes, and land rushes.

Edwards, L.P. *The Natural History of Revolutions*. Chicago: Univ. of Chicago Press, 1927. A suggestive analysis of social revolutions from a sociological point of view. Sees revolutions as a natural growth out of a given complex of social conditions.

Essien-Udom, E.U. *Black Nationalism*. Chicago: Univ. of Chicago Press, 1962. Based on a first-hand study of the "Nation of Islam" or as more popularly known, the Black Muslims, a religious cult emphasizing separatism and self-development on the part of American Negroes.

Fairweather, Eugene R. ed. *The Oxford Movement*. New York: Oxford Univ. Press, 1964. This collection of essays treats one of the interesting quasi-religious movements of modern time (known also as "Moral Rearmament") which has recruited its members internationally from the elite layers of modern society.

Fall, Bernard B. *Ho Chi Minh on Revolution*. New York: Praeger, 1967. A thoughtful and perceptive presentation of the objectives and strategy of the North Vietnamese revolutionary movement, throwing much light on movements seeking simultaneously liberation from colonial imperialism and the formation of an agricultural communistic society.

Finney, Charles G. *Lectures on Revivals of Religion*. ed. by W. G. McLoughlin. Cambridge: Harvard Univ. Press, 1960. An informative treatment of revival efforts in organized religious bodies, casting much light on the conditions that have to be faced in the resurrection of religious sentiment. Of relevance to the topic of expressive movements.

Füllop-Miller, Rene. *Leaders, Dreamers, and Rebels,* transl. by E. and C.

Paul. New York: Viking Press, 1935. While not systematic, this work presents a rich fund of insights on the formation of modern massive revolutionary movements, showing the role of leaders in the growth of popular discontent.

Gluckman, Max. *Order and Rebellion in Tribal Africa.* Glencoe, Ill.: Free Press, 1963. An illuminating treatment of nativistic movements in African tribal societies. One of the better discussions of this type of social movement.

Greer, Thomas H. *American Social Reform Movements since 1865.* New York: Prentice-Hall, 1949. Deals with a series of reform movements in the United States. Of value chiefly as a reference work, giving brief but satisfactory accounts of different movements.

Gusfield, Joseph R. *Status Crusade.* Urbana: Univ. of Illinois Press, 1963. An analysis of the Women's Christian Temperance Union movement from a sociological point of view, emphasizing the importance of social status as the driving force of the movement.

Gusfield, Joseph R. "The Study of Social Movements," *International Encyclopedia of the Social Sciences,* vol. 14, pp. 445–450. New York: Macmillan and Free Press, 1968. A brief characterization of "directed and undirected" movements, the career of social movements, bureaucratization of movements, and their relation to mass society.

Heberle, Rudolf. *Social Movements.* New York: Appleton-Century-Crofts, 1951. An important theoretical analysis of social movements, based largely on polictical movements in twentieth century Europe.

Heberle, Rudolf. "Social Movements—Types and Functions," *International Encyclopedia of the Social Sciences,* vol. 14, pp. 438–444. New York: Macmillan and Free Press, 1968. Deals with the social-psychological characteristics, organization, strategy and tactics, and the functions of social movements.

Hoffer, Eric. *The True Believer.* New York: Harper & Row, 1951. A reflective treatment of modern social movements, done through an analysis of the makeup and orientation of members who become irrevocably committed to the ideology of the movement.

Hofstadter, Richard. ed. *The Progressive Movement: 1900–1915.* Englewood Cliffs: Prentice-Hall, 1963. An interesting effort to treat a political movement in terms of the shifts in status of social classes. Represents a more recent type of social approach in history.

Huberman, Leo and Paul M. Sweezy. *Cuba: Anatomy of a Revolution.* New York: Monthly Review, 1961. A helpful account of the Castro revolution in Cuba. While the authors are sympathizers of the movement their discussion retains an objectivity that yields important theoretical principles for this type of revolution.

Jacobs, Paul and Saul Landau. eds. *The New Radicals: A Report With Documents.* New York: Random House, 1966. Discusses the new types of radicals and revolutionists that are emerging in contemporary times, especially among the new generation of youth. Of indirect value in suggesting the influence of the social setting in shaping the form and character of social movements.

Johnson, Alvin et al. "Agrarian Movement," *Encyclopaedia of the Social Sciences,* vol. 1, pp. 489–515. New York: Macmillan, 1930. An authoritative discussion of social and political movements among peasants and farmers. Contains excellent material on social discontent and its organization. Excellent bibliography.

King, C. Wendell. *Social Movements in the United States.* New York: Random House, 1956. An abbreviated but readable and useful analysis of social movements. The theoretical scheme is simple even though not profound. A good introduction for beginning students.

Kraditor, Aileen S. *The Ideas of the Woman Suffrage Movement, 1890–1920*. New York: Columbia Univ. Press, 1965. An informed discussion of the important suffragette movement around the beginning of the present century. Throws considerable light on the topics of ideology and tactics in the formation of social movements.

Kroeber, A. L. *Style and Civilization*. Ithaca, N. Y.: Cornell University Press, 1957. The work of an eminent anthropologist. Has important insights on the nature, the role and the career of fashion.

Kropotkin, P. *Memoirs of a Revolutionist*. Boston: Houghton Mifflin, 1899. This autobiography by a Russian prince who became a famous revolutionist illuminates many of the social factors operating in revolutionary movements, especially in the shaping of career lines.

Neumann, Franz. *Behemoth*. Oxford: Oxford University Press, 1942. An enlightened and insightful analysis of the Nazi movement in Germany, yielding valuable observations for an understanding of revolutionary movements.

Niven, Charles D. *The History of the Humane Movement*. London: Johnson Publishing, 1967. A valuable treatment of a general social movement which laid the basis for a variety of specific reform movements.

Nystrom, Paul. *The Economics of Fashion*. New York: Ronald Press, 1928. Contains interesting information on the difficulties in trying to control the trend of fashion.

O'Dea, Thomas F. *The Mormons*. Chicago: Univ. of Chicago Press, 1957. An authoritative account of an important religious sect, showing its formation and accommodation in American society. An important addition to the literature on religious movements.

Olgin, Moissaye J. *The Soul of the Russian Revolution*. New York: Henry Holt, 1917. In many ways the best study of the germination of revolutionary sentiments among the Russian people under the Tzarist regime. Supplies excellent material for an understanding of the early stages of revolutionary movements.

Rainwater, Clarence E. *The Play Movement in the United States*. Chicago: Univ. of Chicago Press, 1921. A monograph on a less spectacular type of movement. Of value in showing important features of the process of formation of general social movements.

Reed, John. *Ten Days that Shook the World*. New York: Modern Library, 1935. A first hand observation of the final stage of the revolutionary movement of the Bolsheviki in gaining political control in Russia in 1917. Throws theoretical light on revolutionary behavior.

Rotberg, Robert I. *The Rise of Nationalism in Central Africa*. Cambridge: Harvard University Press, 1965. A valuable treatment of nationalist movements in tribal Africa following World War II.

Schapiro, J. Salwyn. *Movements of Social Dissent in Modern Europe*. Princeton: Princeton Univ. Press, 1962. An insightful treatment of different forms of protest in recent European history. Contributes helpfully to an understanding of social discontent, its dissemination and its crystallization.

Shirer, William L. *The Rise and Fall of the Third Reich*. New York: Simon & Schuster, 1960. A comprehensive and discriminating account of the Nazi movement in Germany. Of particular value in considering the later stages of a massive social movement that succeeds in gaining political control and power.

Toch, Hans. *The Social Psychology of Social Movements.* Indianapolis: Bobbs-Merrill, 1965. A recent attempt to analyze social movements from the standpoint of the principles of social psychology. Provocative and illuminating.

Tracy, J. *The Great Awakening.* Boston: Tappan & Dennet, 1842. Although an old work it still has much value as a treatment of the widespread religious revival at the beginning of the nineteenth century.

Trotzky, Leon *The History of the Russian Revolution.* New York: Simon & Schuster, 1936. In many ways the best and most insightful of the histories of the communist revolution in Russia, chiefly because of the eminent role of the author in it. The treatment is replete with significant theoretical analyses of different aspects of revolutionary movements. This is a rich source of material for the construction of a theory of revolutionary movements.

Van Langehove, Fernard. *The Growth of a Legend.* New York: Putnam, 1916. The best account in the literature tracing the formation of a single legend. Shows the play of crowd processes.

Wagner, D. O. *Social Reformers.* New York: Macmillan, 1934. Is helpful in identifying the distinctive characteristics of reform movements as reflected in their type of leaders. Useful particularly since so little attention has been given to the analysis of reform movements as a type.

Wallas, Graham. *Human Nature in Politics,* 4th ed. New York: Macmillan, 1950. A well known work centering around the thesis of "balked dispositions" as the impelling factor lying behind reform and revolutionary movements.

Wittenmyer, A. *History of the Woman's Temperance Crusade.* J.H. Earle Co., 1878. The classic account of the early prohibition movement in the United States. Deals on an intimate and concrete basis with agitation in the early stages of the movement.

Zinn, Howard. *SNCC: The New Abolitionists.* Boston: Beacon Press, 1964. A perceptive account of the youthful agitators and organizers seeking to arouse southern Negroes to a posture of active protest. Much of the discussion is relevant to analysis of protest movements in their early stages.

Part Three: Institutions

Chapter 12: Institutions Introduced and Defined

Blau, Peter M., and W. Richard Scott. *Formal Organizations.* San Francisco: Chandler Publishing, 1962. General work reporting research on the inner workings of bureaucratic organizations.

Cooley, Charles H. *Social Organization.* New York: Charles Scribner's Sons, 1909. Glencoe: Free Press, 1956. The classic work which defines primary groups and shows their relations to institutions. Chapters 3, 28.

Eisenstadt, Shmuel N. "Social Institutions," *International Encyclopedia of the Social Sciences.* New York: Macmillan and The Free Press, 1968. 14:409–428.

Faris, Ellsworth. *The Nature of Human Nature.* New York: McGraw-Hill, 1937. Chapter III, "The Primary Group: Essence and Accident." A book of essays on social psychology.

Malinowski, Bronislaw. *Argonauts of the Western Pacific.* New York: Dutton, 1922, 1961. An early classic of modern social anthropology, showing functional interrelations of institutions.

————. "Culture," *Encyclopaedia of the Social Sciences*. New York: Macmillan, 1931. 4:621–646. Contains statement on the functions of institutions.

Mead, George H. *Mind, Self and Society*, edited by Charles W. Morris. Chicago: University of Chicago Press, 1934, 1962. The main body of work of a father of the social psychology of interaction among humans.

————. *The Social Psychology of George Herbert Mead*, edited by Anselm Strauss. Chicago: University of Chicago Press Phoenix Books, 1956. Selections from *Mind, Self and Society*.

Merton, Robert K. "The Role-set," *British Journal of Sociology* 8 (1957): 106–120. See also his *Social Theory and Social Structure*. New York: Macmillan, 1968, pp. 41–45, and 422–438. Collection of main articles of the author.

Parsons, Talcott. *The Social System*. Glencoe: Free Press, 1951. A general treatise on human society, with some sections on medical institutions.

Redfield, Robert. *The Folk Culture of Yucatan*. Chicago: University of Chicago Press, 1941, chapter 10. "From Holy Day to Holiday." Study of three communities: a folk village, a somewhat modern town, and a city.

Sumner, William Graham. *Folkways: A Study of the Sociological Importance of Usages, Manners, Customs, Mores, and Morals*. Boston: Ginn, 1907. New York: New American Library, 1960. For this chapter see especially paragraphs 40, 41, 45, 61, 63, and 67.

Webb, Beatrice and Sidney Webb. *English Local Government*. New York: Longmans, Green, 1927. A famous study of the parish in England, showing that it was no longer adequate as the institution to look after the poor.

Weber, Max. *Economy and Society*. New York: Bedminster Press, 1968. vol. III, chapter XIV, "Charisma and its Transformations." Translation of his main sociology work, of which the original was published in 1921 in German.

Chapter 13: Kinds of Institutions

Cooley, Charles H. *Social Organization*. New York: Charles Scribner's Sons, 1909. Glencoe: The Free Press, 1956.

Goffman, Erving. *Asylums*. Garden City, New York: Doubleday, 1961. Report, based on prolonged observation, of the "under life" of a "total institution."

Homans, George C. *The Human Group*. New York: Harcourt, Brace, 1950. A book on the nature of human groups, based on a comparison of many cases.

Jencks, Christopher and David Riesman. *The Academic Revolution*. New York: Doubleday, 1968. A wide-ranging study and criticism of the many kinds of institutions of higher education in this country.

Park, Robert E., and Ernest W. Burgess. *Introduction to the Science of Sociology*, 2nd edition. Chicago: University of Chicago Press, 1924. "Sects and Institutions," pp. 872–874. The first American textbook on sociology geared to research. Now out of print.

Radcliffe-Brown, A.R. "The Present Position of Anthropological Studies," *British Association for the Advancement of Science*. Centenary Meeting (London, 1931), section H, p. 13. A programmatic statement on the aims and methods of social anthropology and sociology.

Sanford, Nevitt, ed. *The American College*. New York: Wiley, 1962. A symposium on colleges and the American student.

Chapter 14: Institutions in Process

Ashby, Eric. *African Universities and Western Tradition*. Cambridge: Harvard University Press, 1964. A series of lectures comparing American, British and the new universities in Black Africa.

Clark, S. Delbert. *The Suburban Society*. Toronto: University of Toronto Press, 1966. General treatment of suburban life, with special study of certain suburbs of Toronto.

Gans, Herbert J. *The Levittowners: Ways of Life and Politics in a New Suburban Community*. New York: Pantheon Books, 1967. Based on participant observation.

Gusfield, Joseph. *Symbolic Crusade: Status, Politics and The American Temperance Movement*. Urbana: University of Illinois Press, 1963. Tells what happened to an organization that was temporarily successful.

Hughes, Everett C. *Students' Culture and Perspectives*. Lawrence: University of Kansas Press, 1961. Chapter IV, "Quality and Inequality: American Educational Enterprises." Lectures on the culture developed by medical students to meet their problems and one lecture on how American colleges develop.

Kerr, Clark. *Uses of the University*. Cambridge: Harvard University Press, 1963. Lectures on trends in the organization and curricula of American universities.

Park, Robert E. "The City: Suggestions for the Investigation of Human Behavior in the Urban Environment," *American Journal of Sociology*, XX (1915): 577–612. Reproduced in Park, R. E., and E. W. Burgess, *The City*.

Park, R. E., E. W. Burgess, R. D. McKenzie. *The City*. Chicago: University of Chicago Press, 1925. Classic statement proposing study of modern cities.

Powell, Sumner C. *Puritan Village. The Formation of a New England Town*. Boston: Anchor Books, 1965. How English immigrants invented new institutions to make life orderly in the wilderness.

Jenks, Christopher, and David Riesman. *The Academic Revolution*. New York: Doubleday, 1968.

Chapter 15: Institutions and the Community

Daedalus. vol. 96, no. 4 (Fall, 1967). A symposium on "America's Changing Environment."

Fichter, Joseph H. *Southern Parish: Dynamics of a City Church*. Chicago: University of Chicago Press, 1951. A detailed account of the activities of a Catholic parish.

Hall, Edward T. *The Hidden Dimension*. Garden City, New York: Doubleday, 1966. On the role of physical distance in human interaction.

Hawley, Amos H., ed. *Roderick D. McKenzie on Human Ecology*. Chicago: University of Chicago Press, 1968. Contains several basic papers on human ecology.

McKenzie, R. D. *The Metropolitan Community*. New York: McGraw-Hill, 1933; New York: Russell and Russell, 1967. The classic work on the ecology of cities.

Schuyler, Joseph B. *Northern Parish*. Chicago: Loyola University Press, 1960. A study of an ethnically mixed Catholic parish in New York City.

Chapter 16: Institutions and the Person

Cains, Leonard D. "Life Course and Social Structures," pp. 272–309, in Faris, Robert E.L., ed., *Handbook of Modern Sociology*. Chicago: Rand McNally, 1964. Shows how the biological and social life-cycle are related.

Cooley, Charles H. *Social Organization*. New York: Charles Scribner's Sons, 1909; Glencoe: Free Press, 1956. Chapters XXVIII, XXIX, "Institutions and the Individual," pp. 313–341.

DeVos, George, and Hirashi Wagatsuma. *Japan's Invisible Race: Caste in Culture and Personality*. Berkeley: University of California Press, 1967. An account of the place of the outcast Buraku people in modern Japan.

Frazier, E. Franklin. *The Negro in the United States*, rev. ed. New York: Macmillan, 1957. Comprehensive account of Negro institutions.

Glaser, Barney G., ed. *Organizational Careers*. Chicago: Aldine, 1968. Collection of articles on careers in various organizations.

Gouldner, Alvin W. "Cosmopolitans and Locals: Toward an Analysis of Latent Social Roles—I, II," *Administrative Science Quarterly*, 2 (1957–58), 281–306 and 444–480.

Jordan, Wilbur K. *Philanthropy in England, 1480–1660: A Study of the Changing Pattern of English Social Aspirations*. London: Allen & Unwin, 1959. On institutional changes at the time of the English Reformation.

Parsons, Talcott, and Kenneth B. Clark, eds. *The Negro American*. Boston: Houghton, Mifflin, 1966. Symposium on the present economic and social state of Negro Americans.

Ross, Aileen D. "Organized Philanthropy in an Urban Community," *Canadian Journal of Economics and Political Science*, 18:474–486, 1952.

Sumner, William G. *Folkways*. Boston: Ginn, 1906; New York: New American Library, 1960. Sections 61, 73.

Weber, Max. *Economy and Society*. New York: Bedminster Press, 1968. vol. III, chapter XI, "Bureaucracy." Contains classic statement on bureaucracy.

Chapter 17: Social Control

Becker, Howard S., Blanche Geer and Everett C. Hughes. *Making the Grade: The Academic Side of College Life*. New York: Wiley, Inc., 1968. The students' view of what counts in college.

Becker, Howard S., Blanche Geer, Everett C. Hughes, and Anselm L. Strauss. *Boys in White: Student culture in medical school*. Chicago: University of Chicago Press, 1961. A study of how students cope with the demands of medical school.

Blauner, Robert. *Alienation and Freedom: The Factory Worker and his Industry*. Chicago: University of Chicago Press, 1964. A comparison of the attitudes of workers in several different industries.

Carlin, Jerome E. *Lawyer's Ethics: A Survey of the New York Bar*. New York: Russell Sage Foundation, 1966. A survey of how law is practiced in a variety of firms.

Carr-Saunders, Alexander M., and P. A. Wilson. *The Professions*. London: Oxford University Press, 1933; London: Cass, 1964. A comprehensive study of the development of professions and professionalism in modern England.

Hagstrom, Warren O. *The Scientific Community*. New York: Basic Books, 1965. The social organization of scientific research.

Parsons, Talcott. *The Social System*. Glencoe: Free Press, 1951. Contains sections on professions.

Part Four: Race and Culture

Chapter 18: The Relations Between Race and Culture

Banton, Michael. *Race Relations*. New York: Basic Books, 1968. Textbook and reader. Comparison of typical patterns over the world.

Berry, Brewton. *Race and Ethnic Relations*, 3rd ed. Boston: Houghton Mifflin Co., 1965.

Boas, Franz. *Race, Language and Culture*. New York: Free Press Paperback, 1966 (originally publ. 1940). Compendium of famous anthropologist's original findings.

Brace, C. L., and M. F. Ashley Montagu. *Man's Evolution: An Introduction to Physical Anthropology*. New York: Macmillan Co., 1965.

Count, E. W., ed. *This Is Race*. New York: Henry Schuman, 1950. Useful selection of scientific papers on race.

Dunn, L. C., and Th. Dobzhansky. *Heredity, Race, and Society*. New York: Penguin Books, 1946. Popular statement by two leading zoologists.

Frazier, E. Franklin. *Race and Culture Contacts in the Modern World*. New York: Alfred A. Knopf, 1957. "Racial problems" considered as one aspect of the cultural situation created by the expansion of European civilization.

Mead, Margaret, Th. Dobzhansky, Ethel Tobach, and Robert E. Light, eds. *Science and the Concept of Race*. New York: Columbia University Press, 1968. Inventory of current knowledge and research on questions of race.

Park, Robert E. *Race and Culture: Essays in the Sociology of Contemporary Man*, ed. by E. C. Hughes and others. New York: Free Press Paperback, 1964 (originally publ. 1950). Basic contributions on race and culture by a famous sociologist.

Rose, Peter I. *The Subject Is Race: Traditional Ideologies and the Teaching of Race Relations*. New York: Oxford University Press, 1968.

Simpson, George E., and J. Milton Yinger. *Racial and Cultural Minorities: An Analysis of Prejudice and Discrimination*, 3rd. New York: Harper & Row, 1965. Comprehensive one-volume treatment of racial and cultural minorities. See esp. chaps. 2, 5.

van den Berghe, Pierre. *Race and Racism: A Contemporary Perspective*. New York: Wiley, 1967.

Chapter 19: Races and Culture Groups

Allport, G. W. *The Nature of Prejudice*. Cambridge: Addison-Wesley Publishing Co., 1954. Readable survey and analysis.

Barron, Milton L., ed. *Minorities in a Changing World*. New York: Alfred A. Knopf, 1966. Representative problems in United States and other countries.

Benedict, Ruth, and Gene Weltfish. "The Races of Mankind." *Public Affairs Pamphlet* no. 85. New York, 1943. One of the most widely circulated anthropological statement on race.

Berry, Brewton. *Almost White*. New York: Macmillan, 1963. Jackson

Whites, Lumbees, Croatans, Narragansetts, Nanticokes, and other mixed groups.

Bettleheim, Bruno, and Morris Janowitz. *Social Change and Prejudice.* New York: Free Press, 1964.

Blalock, H. M., Jr. *Toward a Theory of Minority-Group Relations.* New York: Wiley, 1967. Theoretical propositions based upon empirical data.

Gordon, Milton M. *Assimilation in American Life: The Role of Race, Religion, and National Origins.* New York: Oxford University Press, 1964. Comprehensive discussion of pluralism in its various forms.

Lee, Alfred McC. *Fraternities Without Brotherhood.* Boston: Beacon Press, 1955. Survey of racist practices in United States college social fraternities and of anti-racist tendencies.

Mack, Raymond W., ed. *Our Children's Burden: Studies of Desegregation in Ten American Cities.* New York: Random House, 1968.

Marx, Gary T. *Protest and Prejudice: A Study of Belief in the Black Community.* New York: Harper & Row, 1967. Sample survey based on about 1,100 Negroes.

Osofsky, Gilbert, ed. *The Burden of Race: A Documentary History of Negro-White Relations in America.* New York: Harper Torchbooks, 1968.

Reimers, David M. *White Protestantism and the Negro.* New York: Oxford University Press, 1965.

Rose, Arnold M., and Caroline B. Rose, eds. *Minority Problems: A Textbook of Readings in Intergroup Relations.* New York: Harper & Row, 1965.

Rose, Peter I. *They and We: Racial and Ethnic Relations in the United States.* New York: Random House, 1966. Brief introduction to sociology of intergroup relations.

Shibutani, Tamotsu, and Kian M. Kwan, with Robert H. Billigmeier. *Ethnic Stratification.* New York: Macmillan, 1965.

Vander Zanden, James W. *American Minority Relations: The Sociology of Race and Ethnic Groups,* 2nd ed. New York: Ronald Press, 1966.

Williams, Robin M., Jr. *Strangers Next Door.* Englewood Cliffs, N.J.: Prentice-Hall, 1964.

Znaniecki, Florian. *Modern Nationalities.* Urbana: University of Illinois Press, 1952.

Chapter 20: Culture

Beals, Alan R., and George and Louise Spindler. *Culture in Process.* New York: Holt, Rinehart & Winston, 1967.

Benedict, Ruth. *Patterns of Culture.* New York: Penguin Books, 1946. Synthesis of culture theory illustrated chiefly with Zuñi, Dobu, and Kwakiutl customs.

Chapin, F. Stuart. *Cultural Change.* New York: Century Co., 1928. Lucid and wide-ranging discussion, still relevant.

Ford, Clellan S., ed. *Cross-Cultural Approaches: Readings in Comparative Research.* New Haven: HRAF Press, 1967. Contrasting ways of analyzing information on human behavior, social life, and culture.

Herskovits, Melville J. *Cultural Dynamics.* New York: Knopf, 1964. Nature, structure, and modification of culture.

Hertzler, Joyce O. *A Sociology of Language.* New York: Random House, 1965.

Kroeber, A. L. *Anthropology,* rev. ed. New York: Harcourt, Brace & World, 1948. General text, extensive discussion of culture.

Kroeber, A. L., ed. *Anthropology Today: An Encyclopaedic Inventory.*

Chicago: University of Chicago Press, 1953. Important symposium; many aspects of culture discussed.

Lee, Alfred McC. *Multivalent Man*. New York: George Braziller, 1966. Man's multivalent socialization in multivalent culture.

Linton, Ralph, ed. *The Science of Man in the World Crisis*. New York: Columbia University Press, 1945. Viking Fund symposium; stress on applications of knowledge about culture.

Moore, Frank W., ed. *Readings in Cross-Cultural Methodology*. New Haven: HRAF Press, 1961. Companion to Ford Book above.

Potter, Jack M., May N. Diaz, and George M. Foster, eds. *Peasant Society: A Reader*. Boston: Little, Brown, 1967. Studies of peasant society and culture.

Redfield, Robert. *The Primitive World and Its Transformations*. Ithaca: Cornell University Press, 1953.

Chapter 21: Race and Culture Contacts

Barbour, Floyd B., ed. *The Black Power Revolt: A Collection of Essays*. Boston: Porter Sargent, 1968. Black Power in history, as concept, in action, and as personal expression.

Barron, Milton L., ed. *Minorities in a Changing World*. New York: Knopf, 1967. 33 articles and essays written in 1959–66: a comprehensive introduction.

Bettelheim, Bruno, and Morris Janowitz. *Social Change and Prejudice*. New York: Free Press, 1964.

Burma, John H. *Spanish-Speaking Groups in the United States*. Durham, N.C.: Duke University Press, 1954.

Cahnman, Werner J., ed. *Intermarriage and Jewish Life*. New York: Harzl Press, 1963.

Clark, Kenneth B. *Prejudice and Your Child*. Boston: Beacon Press, 1963.

Fichter, Joseph H. *Social Relations in an Urban Parish*. Chicago: University of Chicago Press, 1954.

Frazier, E. Franklin. *Black Bourgeoisie*. New York: Free Press Paperback, 1965. Frustrations and insecurities, behavior, values, and attitudes of middle-class American Negroes.

Gans, Herbert J. *The Urban Villagers: Group and Class in the Life of Italian-Americans*. New York: Free Press of Glencoe, 1962.

Glazer, Nathan, and Daniel Patrick Moynihan. *Beyond the Melting Pot*. Cambridge: M.I.T. Press and Harvard University Press, 1963. Examination of New York City's Negroes, Puerto Ricans, Jews, Italians, and Irish.

Goldstein, Sidney, and Calvin Goldscheider. *Jewish Americans: Three Generations in a Jewish Community*. Englewood Cliffs, N.J.: Prentice-Hall, 1968.

Gordon, Milton M. *Assimilation in American Life: The Role of Race, Religion, and National Origins*. New York: Oxford University Press, 1964. Problems of prejudice and discrimination.

Greeley, Andrew M., and Peter G. Rossi. *The Education of Catholic Americans*. Chicago: Aldine, 1966.

Heller, Celia Stopnicka. *Mexican American Youth: Forgotten Youth at the Crossroads*. New York: Random House, 1966.

Herberg, Will. *Protestant—Catholic—Jew: An Essay in American Religious Sociology*, rev. ed. Garden City: Doubleday Anchor Books, 1960. A sympathetic interpretation.

Hesslink, George K. *Black Neighbors: Negroes in a Northern Rural Community.* Indianapolis: Bobbs-Merrill Co., 1968.

Kramer, Judith R., and Seymour Leventman. *Children of the Gilded Ghetto.* New Haven: Yale University Press, 1961.

Kung, Shien Woo. *Chinese in American Life.* Seattle: University of Washington Press, 1962.

Lee, Calvin. *Chinatown, U.S.A.* New York: Doubleday, 1965.

Lenski, Gerhard. *The Religious Factor: A Sociological Study of Religion's Impact on Politics, Economics, and Family Life,* rev. ed. Garden City: Doubleday Anchor Books, 1963. Extensive study of religious ramifications in daily life based on 600 Detroit interviews.

Lewis, Oscar. *La Vida: A Puerto Rican Family in the Culture of Poverty— San Juan and New York.* New York: Vintage, 1968. Intimate data on lives in poverty in midst of an affluent society.

Liebow, Elliot. *Tally's Corner: A Study of Negro Streetcorner Men.* Boston: Little, Brown, 1967. A world of violence and ever-shifting relationships.

Mack, Raymond W., ed. *Race, Class, and Power.* New York: American Book, 1963. 33 articles emphasizing significance of power distribution.

Rand, Christopher. *The Puerto Ricans.* New York: Oxford University Press, 1958.

Segal, Bernard E., ed. *Racial and Ethnic Relations: Selected Readings.* New York: T.Y. Crowell Co., 1966. Problems and changing social processes.

Senior, Clarence. *The Puerto Ricans: Strangers—Then Neighbors.* Chicago: Quadrangle Books, 1965.

Sherman, C. Bezalel. *The Jew Within American Society.* Detroit: Wayne State University Press, 1961.

Sklare, Marshall, ed. *The Jews: Social Patterns of an American Group.* Glencoe, Ill.: Free Press, 1958. Studies of immigration, religiosity, community relations, and attitudes toward Israel.

Steiner, Stan. *The New Indians.* New York: Harper & Row, 1968. An effort to interpret the thoughts and acts of contemporary American Indians.

Tuck, Ruth D. *Not with the Fist.* New York: Harcourt, Brace, 1946. Mexican-Americans.

U.S. Bureau of Labor Statistics and Bureau of the Census. *Social and Economic Conditions of Negroes in the United States.* Washington: U.S. Government Printing Office, 1967.

Weinberg, Meyer, ed. *Integrated Education: A Sourcebook.* Beverly Hills, Calif.: Glencoe Press, 1968. American developments compared cross-culturally.

Whyte, William F. *Street Corner Society,* 2nd ed. Chicago: University of Chicago Press, 1955. Social structure of an Italian slum area during the depression as seen through the "corner boys."

Williams, Robin M., Jr. *Strangers Next Door: Ethnic Relations in American Communities.* Englewood Cliffs, N.J.: Prentice-Hall, 1964. Summary of field research in American communities.

Yinger, J. Milton. *Anti-Semitism: A Case Study in Prejudice and Discrimination.* New York: Anti-Defamation League of B'nai B'rith, 1964.

Part Five: Human Ecology

Chapter 22: The Ecosystem and Ecology

Duncan, Otis Dudley, "Human Ecology and Population Studies," in Philip M. Hauser and Otis Dudley Duncan (eds.), *The Study of Population.*

Chicago: University of Chicago Press, 1959. Discussion of the significance of human ecology to the demographer, emphasizing general
perspective, heuristic principles and concepts, and specific hypotheses.

Duncan, Otis Dudley and Leo F. Schnore, "Cultural, Behavioral, and Ecological Perspectives in the Study of Social Organization," *American
Journal of Sociology* (1959–1960), 65:132–153. A statement of the
advantages of the ecological approach over the cultural and behavioral
approaches in explaining variation and change in certain patterns of
social organization.

Firey, Walter. *Land Use in Central Boston.* Cambridge, Mass.: Harvard
University Press, 1947. A criticism of ecological theory and an analysis
of certain aspects of human ecology.

Hawley, Amos H. *Human Ecology: A Theory of Community Structure.* New
York: Ronald Press, 1950. An attempt to develop a full and coherent
theory of human ecology from the contributions of plant and animal
ecologists to an investigation of the nature and development of community structure.

Jones, Emrys. *Human Geography.* New York: Praeger, 1966. A comprehensive analysis of the relationships man bears to the earth and its many
configurations.

Landis, Paul H. *Population Problems.* New York: American Book, 1956.
An interpretation of population within a cultural and social framework
emphasizing these factors as forces in the biological behavior of man.

McKenzie, R. D. "The Ecological Approach to the Study of the Human
Community," in R. E. Park and others, *The City.* Chicago: University
of Chicago Press, 1925. The first formal definition of the field of human
ecology by a sociologist.

McKenzie, R. D. "The Scope of Human Ecology," in George A. Theodorson
(ed.), *Studies in Human Ecology.* Evanston, Ill.: Row, Peterson, 1961.
The first systematic statement of the scope of the field of human
ecology.

Mezerik, A. G. *The Pursuit of Plenty.* New York: Harper, 1950. A discussion
of man's power to destroy, create, and act constructively as a planetary
force.

Mukerjee, R. *Social Ecology.* New York: Longmann, Green, 1945. An attempt to organize and integrate the theory of human ecology.

Osborn, Fairfield. *The Limits of the Earth.* Boston: Little, Brown, 1953. A
realistic appraisal of the resources of the earth in relation to man's
future.

Park, R. E. "Human Ecology," in Ralph H. Turner (ed.), *Robert E. Park
On Social Control and Collective Behavior.* Chicago and London:
Phoenix, 1967. A discussion of human ecology as an attempt to investi-
gate the processes by which the biotic balance and social equilibrium
are maintained and how the transition is made from one relatively
stable order to another following disturbance.

Park, R. E. *Human Communities: The City and Human Ecology.* Glencoe,
Ill.: Free Press, 1952.

Quinn, James A. *Human Ecology.* New York: Prentice-Hall, 1950. Selected
materials covering areal structure, ecological processes, and spatial
distribution, which clarify and systematize the field and also point out
weaknesses, gaps and contradictions in the theory.

Schnore, Leo F. *The Urban Scene.* New York: Free Press, 1965.

Theodorson, G. A., ed. *Studies in Human Ecology.* Evanston, Ill.: Row,
1961.

Toynbee, Arnold J. *A Study of History.* Edited by D. C. Somervell. New York: Oxford University Press, 1957. *Reconsiderations.* London: Oxford University Press, 1961.

White, Leslie A. *The Evolution of Culture.* New York: McGraw-Hill, 1959.

Wirth, Louis. "Human Ecology." in *Louis Wirth on Cities and Social Life,* edited by Albert J. Reiss, Jr. Chicago: Phoenix, 1964. An essay on the development of human ecology as a scientific discipline and as a supplement to other methods of social investigation.

Chapter 23: Population

Brown, Harrison. *The Challenge of Man's Future.* New York: Viking Press, 1960. An examination of man's past and present and an attempt to picture the future based on the clues derived from the study of past and present.

Chandrasekhar, S. *Hungry People and Empty Lands.* London: Allen & Unwin, 1954. A discussion of demography emphasizing the unevenness of international population distribution and growth of different national populations, with recommendations for a comprehensive population policy.

Frazier, E. Franklin. *The Negro in the United States.* New York: Macmillan, 1956. A sympathetic examination of the role of Negroes in the social structure by a distinguished black sociologist.

Hatt, Paul K. (ed.). *World Population and Future Resources.* New York: American Book, 1952. A compilation of papers on the relationship of potential growth of the world population to resources for human sustenance and its mediation by man's mastery of science and technology.

Hauser, Philip M. *Population Perspectives.* New Brunswick, N.J.: Rutgers University Press, 1960. A detailed presentation of the growth of world population and the relations between theory and numbers.

Hauser, Philip M. "Urbanization: An Overview," in *The Study of Urbanization* edited by Philip M. Hauser and Leo F. Schnore. New York: Wiley, 1965. A comprehensive perspective of impression, hypothesis, and available literature on the processes and consequences of urbanization.

Loomis, C. P., and J. A. Beegle. *Rural Social Systems.* New York: Prentice-Hall, 1950. Part 2. An attempt to convert rural sociology research findings into a body of scientific knowledge by presenting a conceptual interpretation of phenomena which have social structure or are value oriented.

Lorimer, Frank (ed.). *Culture and Human Fertility.* New York: International Documents Service, Columbia University Press, 1955. A study of the relationship of cultural conditions to human fertility in nonindustrial and transitional societies.

McCleary, George F. *The Malthusian Population Theory.* London: Faber & Faber, 1953. A restatement of Malthusian theory of population and a consideration of the extent to which it fits the facts confronting the world in the mid-twentieth century.

Steward, Julian H. *Area Research: Theory and Practice.* New York: Social Science Research Council (Bulletin 63), 1950. A distinguished anthropologist examines and discusses cross-cultural research as it has developed in the twentieth century.

Vidal de La Blanche, P. M. J. "Distribution of Population," in his *Principles of Human Geography.* New York: Henry Holt, 1926. A discussion by a geographer of group life within an environmental setting.

Woytinski, W. S., and E. S. Woytinski. *World Population and Production.* New York: Twentieth Century Fund, 1953. An outline of world economic forces and trends during an era when mechanization overtook the economy of the civilized world.

Chapter 24: Ecological Organization

Breese, Gerald W. *Urbanization in Newly Developing Countries.* Englewood Cliffs, N.J.: Prentice-Hall, 1966. An exploratory discussion of urbanization and the modernization process based on an extended study of the literature and firsthand examination of the field.

Burgess, E. W. "The Growth of the City," in *Studies in Human Ecology,* edited by George A. Theodorson. Evanston, Ill.: Row, Peterson, 1961. A republication of his original hypothesis of concentric zones as the basic pattern of urban spatial structure.

Childe, V. Gordon. *Man Makes Himself.* New York: Mentor, 1951. Classic statement of the effect of man's technology and numbers upon his cultural development.

Freedman, Ronald. "Cityward Migration, Urban Ecology, and Social Theory," in *Contributions to Urban Sociology,* edited by E. W. Burgess and Donald Bogue. Chicago: University of Chicago Press, 1964. An examination of sociological theories focused upon evidence accumulated by the "ecological method" concerning the settlement patterns of recent migrants.

Gans, Herbert J. *The Urban Villagers.* New York: Free Press, 1965. A careful study of the impact of urban redevelopment on the social life of an area in the inner city of Boston, Massachusetts.

Gist, Noel P. and Sylvia Fleis Fava. *Urban Society,* 5th ed. New York: T. Y. Crowell, 1964. A broad-scope examination of urban sociology in the modern world.

Greer, Scott. *The Emerging City.* New York: Free Press, 1965. A penetrating study of the city of the future.

Hadden, J. K., and E. F. Borgatta. *American Cities: Their Social Characteristics.* Rand McNally, 1965. A description of the salient characteristics of cities within the framework of human ecology.

Hall, Peter. *The World Cities.* New York: McGraw-Hill, 1966. An ecological analysis of the location, growth, structure, and characteristics of the cities man has built through the rise of his civilizations.

Hatt, Paul K. "The Concept of Natural Area," in *Studies in Human Ecology,* edited by G. A. Theodorson. Evanston, Ill.: Row, Peterson, 1961. A critical, inductive study of the natural-area concept applied to an urban subarea.

Hauser, Philip M. "Urbanization: An Overview," in *The Study of Urbanization,* edited by Philip M. Hauser and Leo F. Schnore. New York: Wiley, 1965. A comprehensive perspective of impression, hypothesis, and available literature on the processes and consequences of urbanization.

Kroeber, A.L. *A Roster of Civilizations and Cultures.* Chicago: Aldine, 1962.

Leakey, L.S.B. *Adam's Ancestors: The Evolution of Man and his Culture.* 4th ed. New York: Harper, 1960.

Mitchell, Robert B. (ed.). "Building the Future City," *Annals of the American Academy of Political and Social Science,* November 1945. A volume of *The Annals* devoted to consideration of the future development of cities based upon the technologic, economic, and social environment of the future.

Shaw, Clifford R., and Henry D. McKay. *Juvenile Delinquency and Urban Areas.* Chicago: University of Chicago Press, 1942. An outstanding study of the spatial distribution of juvenile delinquency and its relationship to urban subareas.

Sjoberg, Gideon. *The Preindustrial City.* New York: Free Press, 1965. A survey of the preindustrial city, a community that arose without stimulus from the form of production associated with the European industrial revolution.

Thompson, Warren S., and David T. Lewis. *Population Problems,* 5th ed. New York: McGraw-Hill, 1965. A classic text dealing with population theories, controls, growth, decline, composition, and migration and the natural and social factors affecting them.

Zorbaugh, Harvey W. "The Natural Areas of the City," in *Studies in Human Ecology,* edited by George A. Theodorson. Evanston, Ill.: Row, Peterson, 1961. A discussion of the need to base statistics of human behavior in the urban environment on the natural areas of the city.

Chapter 25: Dominance

Mayer, Harold M. "A Survey of Urban Geography," in *The Study of Urbanization,* edited by Philip M. Hauser and Leo F. Schnore. New York: Wiley, 1965. A discussion of the major advances in urban geography and their value as predictive devices in many types of planning.

McKenzie, R. D. *The Metropolitan Community.* New York: McGraw-Hill, 1933. A discussion of the narrow metropolitan community and the various aspects of the broader metropolitan region—its economic and social unity and methods of delimitation.

Mighell, Ronald L. *American Agriculture: Its Structure and Place in the Economy.* New York: Wiley, 1955. A picture of the structure of agriculture, its separate parts, how the parts are assembled, and how the whole fits into the economy of the nation.

Russell, Sir Edward J. *World Population and World Food Supplies.* London: George Allen & Unwin, 1954. The age-old issue of the man-to-land ratio is given a careful look, and the perspective is not difficult to understand.

Thompson, Warren S., and David T. Lewis. *Population Problems.* 5th ed. New York: McGraw-Hill, 1965. A classic text dealing with population theories, controls, growth, decline, composition, and migration and natural and social factors affecting them.

Weigert, Hans W., and V. Stefansson (eds.). *Compass of the World.* New York: Macmillan, 1944. (Especially articles by Quincy Wright, F. W. Notestein, and Frank Lorimer.) An appraisal of the impact of geography on world politics with a discussion of regional and demographic factors in the shifting balance of manpower.

Woldenberg, M. J., and Brian J. L. Berry. "Rivers and Central Places: Analogous Systems?" *Journal of Regional Science* (1967), 7: 129–139. An exploration of the nature and extent of a systems analysis framework as the basis for future growth of geography in its relationship to other sciences.

Chapter 26: Migration and Mobility

Bernard, William S. and others. *American Immigration Policy: A Reappraisal.* New York: Harper, 1950. A reappraisal of United States policies on immigration covering background, effects of quota systems on population growth, processes of immigrant adjustment, and experiences of other nations with immigration.

Bogue, Donald. "Internal Migration," in Philip M. Hauser and Otis Dudley Duncan (eds.). *The Study of Population*, Chicago: Chicago University Press, 1959. A summary of some methodological lessons in migration research acquired from a long-range program of research in population distribution.

Carroll, J. Douglas, Jr. "The Relations of Homes to Work Places and the Spatial Pattern of Cities," *Social Forces* 30 (1952): 271–282. A series of hypotheses concerning the relationships between home and work which operate to create urban patterns and the implications for planning.

Davie, Maurice R. *World Immigration*. New York: Macmillan, 1936. The most comprehensive statement of the movements of world population from early modern times until the middle 1930s. The large movements of population since 1940 are not included in this pioneer study.

Drake, St. Clair, and H. R. Clayton. *Black Metropolis*. New York: Harcourt, Brace, 1945. A penetrating analysis and extensive study of social life in the major Negro area of a large city.

Ferenczi, Imre. "Proletarian Mass Migration, 19th and 20th Centuries," *International Migrations* 1 (1929): 81–88. A geographer and anthropologist discusses the interaction of culture and environment to explain the social life and areal patterns of adjustment of representatives of different types of economy.

Freedman, Ronald. "Cityward Migration, Urban Ecology, and Social Theory," in *Contributions to Urban Sociology*, edited by E. W. Burgess and Donald Bogue (eds.). Chicago: University of Chicago Press, 1964. An examination of sociological theories focused upon evidence accumulated by the "ecological method" concerning the settlement patterns of recent migrants.

Gaulle, Omar R. and Karl E. Taeuber. "Metropolitan Migration and Intervening Opportunities." *American Sociological Review* 31 (1966): 5–13. A report of a study using data from 1955 to 1960 that replicates Stouffer's study of migration and intervening opportunities.

Park, R. E. "Human Migration and the Marginal Man," in *Robert E. Park on Social Control and Collective Behavior*, edited by Ralph H. Turner. Chicago and London: Phoenix, 1967. A discussion of the effects of migration and the processes of acculturation, assimilation, and amalgamation of racial stocks.

Sorokin, P. A. *Society, Culture, and Personality*. New York: Harper, 1947. An imaginative statement of interdependencies between the three basic dimensions of sociological theory; recommended for its broad scope, but it is somewhat dated today.

Taeuber, Karl E., and Alma F. Taeuber. *Negroes in Cities*. Chicago: Aldine, 1965. A study of a significant social problem utilizing quantitative research methods to achieve better understanding, including detailed analysis of the contemporary situation and longitudinal data from over 100 years.

Chapter 27: Succession

Breese, Gerald. "The Daytime Population of the Central Business District," in *Contributions to Urban Sociology*, edited by E. W. Burgess and Donald J. Bogue. Chicago: Chicago University Press, 1964. A discussion of the need to study the central business district of metropolitan areas as the focus of urban life.

Breese, Gerald. *Urbanization in Newly Developing Countries.* Englewood Cliffs, N.J.: Prentice-Hall, 1966. An exploratory discussion of urbanization and the modernization process based on an extended study of the literature and firsthand examination of the field.

Brown, Harrison. *The Challenge of Man's Future.* New York: Viking Press, 1960. An examination of man's past and present and an attempt to picture the future based on the clues derived from the study of the past and present.

Davie, Maurice R. "The Pattern of Urban Growth," in *The Papers of Maurice R. Davie,* edited by R. J. Kennedy. New Haven: Yale University Press, 1961. An inductive study of one city showing spatial distributions of various data and a criticism of the concentric-zone hypothesis.

DeVos, George, and Hiroshi Wagatsuma (eds.). *Japan's Invisible Race.* Berkeley, Calif.: University of California Press, 1966. A cross-cultural examination of social stratification and caste organization with particular reference to Japan, but also excellent articles of Indian caste in this volume.

Duncan, O. D. and A. J. Reiss, Jr. *Social Characteristics of Urban and Rural Communities, 1950.* New York: Wiley, 1956. A careful analysis of the data available on rural and urban communities in the United States.

Hatt, Paul K. and A. J. Reiss, Jr. (eds.). *Cities and Society.* Glencoe, Ill.: The Free Press of Glencoe, 1957. A reader in urban sociology emphasizing the relevance of problems to the city as a mode of life.

Johnson, Charles S. *Patterns of Negro Segregation.* New York: Harper, 1943. A primarily social and only partly ecological description and theoretical discussion of the segregation of Negroes in the United States.

Lieberson, Stanley. *Ethnic Patterns in American Cities.* New York: Free Press of Glencoe, 1963. An analysis within a systematic framework of one urban social problem in ten cities.

Lind, Andrew W. *Island Community: Ecological Succession in Hawaii.* Chicago: University of Chicago Press, 1938. The succession of economies in Hawaii traced through its changing position with regard to world trade.

McKenzie, R. D. "The Ecological Succession in the Puget Sound Region." *Publications of the American Sociological Society* 23 (1929): 60–80. An analysis of the succession of economies in a region under the influence of developing modes of transportation.

Park, Robert E. "Succession, An Ecological Concept," in *Robert E. Park on Social Control and Collective Behavior,* edited by Ralph H. Turner. Chicago and London: Phoenix, 1967. A theoretical discussion involving succession in all recurrent irreversible sequences of social or areal change.

Pirenne, Henri. *Medieval Cities.* Garden City, N.Y.: Doubleday, 1956. A general discussion of the economic awakening and the birth of urban civilization in Western Europe during the Middle Ages.

Ratcliffe, Richard W. "Efficiency and the Location of Urban Activities," in Robert M. Fisher (ed.). *The Metropolis in Modern Life.* New York: Doubleday, 1955. A discussion of the locational distribution of urban activities dealing with the structure and arrangement of land use.

Wirth, Louis. "Localism, Regionalism, and Centralization," in Albert J.

Reiss, Jr. (ed.). *Louis Wirth on Cities and Social Life*. Chicago and London: Phoenix, 1964. A discussion of the capacity of members of a society to act collectively in the shifting trend to centralization.

Part Six: Social Problems

In lieu of specific references to chapters 28 and 29 the following list of textbooks and readers especially devoted to social problems is provided. Topics dealt with in each book are summarized after each entry.

Becker, Howard S., ed. *Social Problems: A Modern Approach*. New York: Wiley, 1966. Symposium. Problems of life cycle (adolescence, education, work, aged), of deviance (delinquency, crime, mental illness), of community and nation (race, organization, poverty, inequality, housing, urban renewal, popular culture), and of the world (population, new nations, war).

Bredemeier, Harry C., and Jackson Toby. *Social Problems in America: Costs and Casualties in an Acquisitive Society*. New York: Wiley, 1960. Those who fail to meet standards, materialism, self-reliance, competition, negotiated exchange, acceptance of defeat, refusal to accept defeat. Text with readings.

Cuber, John F., William F. Kenkel, and Robert A. Harper. *Problems of American Society: Values in Conflict*, 4th ed. New York: Holt, Rinehart & Winston, 1964. Major economic problems, the city, population, marriage, education, religion, leisure and recreation, race, physical and mental health, old age, crime and the criminal, juvenile delinquency, deviations, pressure groups.

Dentler, Robert A. *American Community Problems*. New York: McGraw-Hill, 1968. Brief text on social problems seen in a community context —urban and rural.

Dentler, Robert A. *Major American Social Problems*. Chicago: Rand McNally, 1967. Text with readings. War and national defense, poverty, ethnic relations, rural and urban problems, adult crime, juvenile delinquency, narcotics, mental disorders and illnesses, population.

Dynes, Russell R., Alfred C. Clarke, Simon Dinitz, and Iwao Ishino. *Social Problems: Dissensus and Deviation in an Industrial Society*. New York: Oxford University Press, 1964. Community, family, education, religion, science, medical care, mass communications, mass leisure, ethnic and racial groups, integration, mental illness, criminal deviation.

Eisenstadt, S. N., ed. *Comparative Social Problems*. New York: Free Press, 1964. Reader. Individual's retreat from role performance (suicide, alcoholism, illness, mental illness), crises in life cycle, sexual identity, and family (youth, old age, women, family stability), work and unemployment, community development, leisure. Cross-cultural comparisons emphasized.

Elliott, Mabel A., and Francis E. Merrill. *Social Disorganization*. New York: Harper, 1961. Juvenile delinquency, adult offender, sex offender, alcoholic, industrial problems, mentally disorganized and deranged, suicide, family disorganization and tensions, desertion, divorce, community disorganization, rural community, political corruption, crime, mobility, migration, unemployment, religious and racial minorities, revolution, totalitarianism, war.

Faunce, William A. *Problems of an Industrial Society*. New York: McGraw-Hill, 1968. Industry's social aspects, automation, technology and society.

Gold, Harry, and Frank R. Scarpitti, eds. *Combatting Social Problems*:

Techniques of Intervention. New York: Holt, Rinehart & Winston, 1967. Poverty, unemployment, education, race relations, urban change and development, mental illness, crime, juvenile delinquency, drug addiction, alcoholism. Reader.

Gouldner, Alvin W., and S. M. Miller, eds. *Applied Sociology: Opportunities and Problems.* New York: Free Press, 1965. Symposium sponsored by the Society for the Study of Social Problems. Criminal community, military, business, labor unions, health organization, race relations, criminology and delinquency, community, family, law, aged, mental illness.

Horton, Paul B., and Gerald R. Leslie. *The Sociology and Social Problems,* 3rd ed. New York: Appleton-Century-Crofts, 1965. Vested interests and pressure groups, crime and delinquency, problem families and family problems, religious problems and conflicts, social class (poverty and opportunity), race problem, urban and rural communities, mass communications, personal pathologies, health and medical care, civil liberties and subversion.

Kane, John J. *Social Problems: A Situational-Value Approach.* Englewood Cliffs, N.J.: Prentice-Hall, 1962. Population explosion, physical health and medical care, mental health, aging and aged, juvenile delinquency, crime and criminal, narcotic addiction, alcoholism, suicide, Negro, Jews, Roman Catholics, marriage and the family, religion, education.

Landis, Judson R., ed. *Current Perspectives on Social Problems.* Belmont, California: Wadsworth, 1966. Crime and deviant behavior, race and ethnic group problems, population explosion, family instability, urban problems and poverty, political dissent.

Lee, Elizabeth Briant, and Alfred McClung Lee. *Social Problems in America,* rev. ed. New York: Holt, Rinehart & Winston, 1955. Text with readings. Changing resources, population, city and country dwellers, planned parenthood, problem periods in family life, education, employment, political power, mass communications, recreation, physically ill and handicapped, mentally deficient and diseased, delinquent and criminal, leadership, class and status, race, ethnic difference, depressions and catastrophes, riots and wars, social work and social action.

Lindenfeld, Frank, ed. *Radical Perspectives on Social Problems: Readings in Critical Sociology.* New York: Macmillan, 1968. Education, sex and the family, the city, law and authority, crime, work and leisure, poverty, racial inequality, power, warfare state, mass society, the new left, radical ideology, utopian practice and perspectives.

McDonagh, Edward C., and Jon E. Simpson, eds. *Social Problems: Persistent Challenges.* New York: Holt, Rinehart & Winston, 1965. Reader. Urbanism, mass culture, alienation, economics, political problems, education, family, race relations, population, crime and delinquency, personality problems.

McGee, Reece. *Social Disorganization in America.* San Francisco: Chandler, 1962. Brief text illustrated with digests of studies on the disorganized individual, group, organization, and society.

Merton, Robert K., and Robert A. Nisbet, eds. *Contemporary Social Problems,* 2nd ed. New York: Harcourt, Brace and World, 1966. Symposium. Mental disorders, juvenile delinquency, crime, drug addiction, alcohol, suicide, sexual behavior, population, race and ethnic relations, family disorganization, work and automation, poverty, disrepute, community disorganization, war and disarmament.

Peterson, William, and David Matza, eds. *Social Controversy.* Belmont,

California: Wadsworth, 1963. Contraceptives, divorce, education, organized crime, homosexuality, ethnic minorities, school segregation, immigration, working-class democracy, Joe-McCarthyism, the suburb, mass culture. Statements pro and con on each issue.

Raab, Earl, and Gertrude Jaeger Selznick. *Major Social Problems*, 2nd ed. New York: Harper & Row, 1964. Text with adapted readings. Juvenile delinquency, crime, group prejudice, immigration, family, schools, dependency.

Rosenberg, Bernard, Israel Gerver, and F. William Howton, eds. *Mass Society in Crisis: Social Problems and Social Pathology*. New York: Macmillan, 1964. Crime, marriage, delinquency, mental problems, mass terror (concentration camps, police violence, thought control), genocide, war, segregation, automation, politics, slums, drug addiction.

Scanzoni, John H., ed. *Readings in Social Problems: Sociology and Social Issues*. Boston: Allyn & Bacon, 1967. Issues within institutions: political, religious, kinship, educational. Social class and social differentiation. Deviancy and its control.

Shostak, Arthur B., ed. *Sociology in Action: Case Studies in Social Problems and Directed Social Change*. Homewood, Ill.: Dorsey Press, 1966. Population, education, religion, physical and mental health, community development, race relations, casualties and crime, political action, poverty at home and abroad, peace, militarism.

Weinberg, S. Kirson. *Social Problems in Our Time: A Sociological Analysis*. Englewood Cliffs, N.J.: Prentice-Hall, 1960. Juvenile delinquency, adult crime, sex offenses and deviations, organized gambling, alcoholism, drug addiction, personality disorders, suicide, marital conflicts, family conflicts, adolescence, old age, ethnic prejudice and discrimination.

Winter, J. Alan, Jerome Rabow, and Mark Chesler. *Vital Problems for American Society: Meanings and Means*. New York: Random House, 1968. Population explosion, assimilation, Negro strategy, shared values, political controls, church-state problems, punishment, sex equality, criminal justice, police, violence, civil disobedience, military-industrial complex, cold war, student deferment, guaranteed income, poverty, bureaucracy, hang-loose ethic, pluralism, extremist politics, social planning.

Chapter 30: Problems: Social and Sociological

1. The "Generation Gap"

Blos, Peter. *On Adolescence: A Psychoanalytic Interpretation*. New York: Free Press Paperback, 1966.

Coleman, J. S. *The Adolescent Society: The Social Life of the Teenager and Its Impact on Education*. New York: Free Press, 1961.

Committee on Adolescence, Group for the Advancement of Psychiatry. *Normal Adolescence*. New York: Charles Scribner's Sons, 1968. From biological, cultural, and psychological viewpoints.

Douvan, Elizabeth, and Joseph Adelson. *The Adolescent Experience*. New York: Wiley, 1966.

Erikson, Erik H. *Identity: Youth and Crisis*. New York: W. W. Norton, 1968. From a psychoanalytic and comparative cultural viewpoint.

Feuer, Lewis S. *The Conflict of Generations*. New York: Basic Books, 1968. Study of student movements throughout the world.

Gottlieb, David, and Charles Ramsey. *The American Adolescent.* Home-
    wood, Ill.: Dorsey Press, 1964.
Josephson, Eric and Mary, eds. *Man Alone: Alienation in Modern Society.*
    New York: Dell, 1962. Selections from a variety of viewpoints, espe-
    cially on youth.
Kenniston, Kenneth. *The Uncommitted: Alienated Youth in American So-
    ciety.* New York: Harcourt, Brace & World, 1960.
Kenniston, Kenneth. *Young Radicals: Notes on Committed Youth.* New
    York: Harcourt, Brace & World, 1968. Study of American opposition
    to involvement in Vietnam.
Konopka, Gisela. *The Adolescent Girl in Conflict.* Englewood Cliffs, N.J.:
    Spectrum, Prentice-Hall, 1966. Suggestions for community and pro-
    fessional response to problems of adolescent girls.
Kovar, Lillian Cohen. *Faces of the Adolescent Girl.* Englewood Cliffs, N.J.:
    Spectrum, Prentice-Hall, 1968. Study of conformist and deviant per-
    sonalities through in-depth interviews.
Rosenberg, Morris. *Society and the Adolescent Self-Image.* Princeton:
    Princeton University Press, 1965.
Sebald, Hans. *Adolescence: A Sociological Analysis.* New York: Appleton-
    Century-Crofts, 1968. From a structural-functional perspective.
Smith, Ernest A. *American Youth Culture: Group Life in a Teen-Age So-
    ciety.* New York: Free Press, 1962.

2. Urban Riots

Barbour, Floyd B., ed. *The Black Power Revolt: A Collection of Essays.*
    Boston: Porter Sargent, 1968. By leading spokesmen for Black Power.
Bennett, Lerone, Jr. *Confrontation: Black and White.* New York: Pelican,
    1966. Social-historical background and interpretation of current situa-
    tion.
Brink, William, and Louis Harris. *Black and White: A Study of U.S. Racial
    Attitudes Today.* New York: Simon and Schuster, 1967. Based on
    Newsweek-Harris surveys and interview documents.
Carmichael, Stokely, and Charles V. Hamilton. *Black Power: The Politics of
    Liberation in America.* New York: Vintage, 1967. A political framework
    and ideology.
Cohen, Jerry, and William S. Murphy. *Burn, Baby, Burn: The Watts Riot:
    The Los Angeles Race Riot, August 1965.* New York: Avon, 1967.
    Synthesis of journalistic materials.
Conot, Robert. *Rivers of Blood, Years of Darkness.* New York: Bantam,
    1967. Dramatic summary of data on Los Angeles 1965 riot.
Hayden, Tom. *Rebellion in Newark: Official Violence and Ghetto Response.*
    New York: Vintage, 1967. Summary of observations and documents.
Killian, Lewis M. *The Impossible Revolution: Black Power and the American
    Dream.* New York: Random House, 1968. A sociological study.
Lee, Alfred McClung, and Norman D. Humphrey. *Race Riot,* new ed. New
    York: Octagon, 1968. Sociological study of 1943 riots in Detroit, Los
    Angeles, and Harlem.
National Advisory Commission on Civil Disorders. *Report.* New York: Ban-
    tam, 1968. What happened in the riot-torn summer of 1967? What
    should be done about it?
Wills, Gary. *The Second Civil War: Arming for Armageddon.* New York:
    New American Library, 1968. Summary of interviews and observations.
Wright, Nathan, Jr. *Black Power and Urban Unrest: Creative Possibilities.*

New York: Hawthorne, 1967. By a clergyman-sociologist leader in Black Power.

3. Drug Addiction

Barber, Bernard. *Drugs and Society.* New York: Russell Sage Foundation, 1967. A sociologist's analysis.

Blum, Richard, and associates. *Utopiates: The Use and Users of LSD-25.* New York: Atherton Press, 1964. The who and why of LSD.

Borgatta, Edgar F., and Robert R. Evans, eds., *Smoking, Health, and Behavior.* Chicago: Aldine, 1968. Symposium on tobacco.

Cavan, Sherri. *Liquor License: An Ethnography of Bar Behavior.* Chicago: Aldine, 1966. What people do in bars.

Kessel, Neil, and Henry Walton. *Alcoholism.* Baltimore: Penguin, 1965. Summary of findings by two British practicing psychiatrists.

Laurie, Peter. *Drugs: Medical, Psychological and Social Facts.* New York: Penguin, 1967.

Lindesmith, Alfred R. *The Addict and the Law.* Bloomington: Indiana University Press, 1965. Description and assessment of existing official controls over addiction in the U.S.

O'Donnell, John A., and John C. Ball, eds. *Narcotic Addiction.* New York: Harper & Row, 1966. Comprehensive symposium.

Pittman, David J., ed. *Alcoholism.* New York: Harper & Row, 1967. Symposium on cross-cultural, physical, psychosocial, and sociocultural aspects.

Trice, Harrison M. *Alcoholism in America.* New York: McGraw-Hill, 1966. Comprehensive analysis in relation to family and work life.

Yablonsky, Lewis. *Synanon: The Tunnel Back.* Baltimore: Penguin, 1967. A study of an antidrug-community program for the rehabilitation of addicts.

4. Poverty

Balogh, Thomas. *The Economics of Poverty.* New York: Macmillan, 1967. Consequences of poverty throughout the world.

Caplowitz, David. *The Poor Pay More: Consumer Practices of Low-Income Families,* new ed. New York: Free Press, 1967. Based on survey of 464 households in New York City housing projects.

Clark, Kenneth B. *Dark Ghetto: Dilemmas of Social Power.* New York: Harper & Row, 1965. Social psychological study of Negro ghetto dynamics.

Clinard, Marshall B. *Slums and Community Development: Experiments in Self-Help.* New York: Free Press, 1966. In Western and non-Western societies; offers program of planned social change.

Deutscher, Irwin, and Elizabeth J. Thompson, eds. *Among the People: Encounters with the Poor.* New York: Basic Books, 1968.

Elman, Richard M. *The Poorhouse State: The American Way of Life on Public Assistance.* New York: Dell, 1968. How welfare system often perpetuates poverty.

Ferman, Louis A., Joyce L. Kornbluh, and Alan Haber, eds. Intro. by Michael Harrington. *Poverty in America,* rev. ed. Ann Arbor: University of Michigan Press, 1965. Symposium.

Hunter, David R. *The Slums: Challenge and Response,* new ed. New York: Free Press, 1968. Assessment of programs.

Lyford, Joseph P. *The Airtight Cage: A Study of New York's West Side.* New York: Harper, 1966. Impotence of the urban poor.

Miller, Herman P. *Poverty: American Style.* Belmont, Calif.: Wadsworth, 1966.

Miller, Herman P. *Rich Man, Poor Man.* New York: New American Library, 1964. Interpretation of Census income statistics.

Seligman, Ben B. *Permanent Poverty.* Chicago: Quadrangle, 1968.

Seligman, Ben B., ed. *Poverty as a Public Issue.* New York: Free Press, 1965. Poverty and U.S. anti-poverty program.

Wallace, Samuel E. *Skid Row as a Way of Life.* New York: Harper, 1965. Participant observer's study of homeless men.

Wilensky, Harold L., and Charles N. Lebeaux. *Industrial Society and Social Welfare: The Impact of Industrialization on the Supply and Organization of Social Welfare Services in the United States,* new ed. New York: Free Press, 1965.

Will, Robert E., and Harold G. Vatter. *Poverty in Affluence: The Social, Political, and Economic Dimensions of Poverty in the United States.* New York: Harcourt, Brace and World, 1965. Nature, causes, forms, results.

Chapter 31: Problem Families I: Child and Youth

1. Procreation

Butcher, Ruth L., and Marion O. Robinson, "The Unmarried Mother." *Public Affairs Pamphlet* No. 282. New York: 1959. Unwed pregnancy as a personal, family, and social problem,

Cady, Ernest and Frances. *How to Adopt a Child.* New York: William Morrow, 1956. Helpful discussion of each step.

Freedman, Ronald, Pascal K. Whelpton, and Arthur A. Campbell. *Family Planning, Sterility, and Population Growth.* New York: McGraw-Hill, 1959. Relation to planning to family size.

Gebhard, P.H., W.B. Pomeroy, C.E. Martin, and C.V. Christenson. *Pregnancy, Birth and Abortion.* New York: Hoeber-Harper, 1958. Based upon detailed interviews.

Rainwater, Lee. *Family Design: Marital Sexuality, Family Size, and Contraception.* Chicago: Aldine, 1965. Comprehensive survey of factors determining family size.

Smith, David T., ed. *Abortion and the Law.* Cleveland: Press of Case Western Reserve University, 1967.

Smith, I. Evelyn, ed. *Readings in Adoption.* New York: Philosophical Library, 1963.

Vincent, Clark E. *Unmarried Mothers.* New York: Free Press, 1962. Careful survey and analysis.

2. Problem Homes

Bernard, Jessie. *Marriage and Family Among Negroes.* Englewood Cliffs, N.J.: Prentice-Hall, 1966.

Bloom, Benjamin S., Allison Davis, and Robert D. Hess. *Compensatory Education for Cultural Deprivation.* New York: Holt, Rinehart and Winston, 1965.

Christensen, Harold T., ed. *Handbook of Marriage and the Family.* Chicago: Rand McNally, 1964. Comprehensive symposium.

Elmer, Elizabeth. *Children in Jeopardy: A Study of Abused Minors and Their Families.* Pittsburgh: University of Pittsburgh Press, 1967.

Feldman, Frances L., and Frances H. Scherz. *Family Social Welfare: Helping Troubled Families.* New York: Atherton Press, 1967.

Fink, Arthur E., C. Wilson Anderson, and Merrill B. Conover. *The Field of Social Work,* 5th ed. New York: Holt, Rinehart and Winston, 1968. Current practice of social casework, social group work, and community welfare organization.

Frazier, E. Franklin. *The Negro Family in the United States,* rev. ed. New York: Macmillan, 1957. A standard work.

Goldstein, Bernard. *Low Income Youth in Urban Areas: A Critical Review of the Literature.* New York: Holt, Rinehart and Winston, 1967. Synthesis of recent and significant research.

Helfer, Ray E., and C. Henry Kempe, eds. *The Battered Child.* Chicago: University of Chicago Press, 1968. About thousands of children severely injured or killed each year in the U.S.

Howard, Donald S. *Values and Social Welfare: Ends and Means.* New York: Random House, 1968. Historical and international perspective.

Kadushin, Alfred. *Child Welfare Services.* New York: Macmillan, 1967. Kinds of social problems child welfare services are designed to meet.

Nye, F. Ivan, and Lois Wladis Hoffman. *The Employed Mother in America.* Chicago: Rand McNally, 1963. Includes discussion of effects of her employment on her family.

Rogler, Lloyd H., and A. B. Hollingshead. *Trapped: Families and Schizophrenia.* New York: Wiley, 1965.

Sussman, Marvin B., ed. *Sourcebook in Marriage and the Family,* 3rd ed. Boston: Houghton Mifflin, 1968.

Winch, Robert F., and Louis Wolf Goodman, eds. *Selected Studies in Marriage and the Family,* 3rd ed. New York: Holt, Rinehart and Winston, 1968.

3. *Juvenile Delinquency*

Barron, Milton L. *The Juvenile in Delinquent Society.* New York: Knopf, 1964. Sociological study of juvenile delinquency with interdisciplinary interpretations.

Cicourel, Aaron V. *The Social Organization of Juvenile Justice.* New York: Wiley, 1968. Challenges the conventional view that delinquents are "natural" social types.

Cloward, Richard A., and Lloyd E. Ohlin. *Delinquency and Opportunity,* new ed. New York: Free Press, 1966. To control problem, changes are recommended in the existing social setting of delinquency.

Cressey, Donald R., and David A. Ward. *Delinquency, Crime, and Social Process.* New York: Harper & Row, 1969. Analysis of major assumptions, concerns, and theories of those involved in the "crime problem."

Eldefonso, Edward. *Law Enforcement and the Youthful Offender: Juvenile Procedures.* New York: Wiley, 1967. Topics of immediate concern to the police officer in his work with juveniles.

Ferdinand, Theodore N. *Typologies of Delinquency: A Critical Analysis.* New York: Random House, 1966.

Giallombardo, Rose, ed. *Juvenile Delinquency: A Book of Readings.* New York: Wiley, 1966. 52 selections from contemporary literature.

Glueck, Sheldon and Eleanor. *Delinquents and Nondelinquents in Perspective.* Cambridge: Harvard University Press, 1968.

Klein, Malcolm W., ed. *Juvenile Gangs in Context: Theory, Research, and Action*. Englewood Cliffs, N.J.: Prentice-Hall, 1967. Recent articles and research studies.

Matza, David. *Delinquency and Drift*. New York: Wiley, 1964. Analysis of adolescent motivation.

Rainwater, Lee, and William L. Yancey. *The Moynihan Report and the Politics of Controversy: Including the Full Text of: The Negro Family: The Case for National Action, by Daniel Patrick Moynihan*. Cambridge: M.I.T. Press, 1967.

Short, James F., Jr., and Fred L. Strodtbeck. *Group Process and Gang Delinquency*. Chicago: University of Chicago Press, 1965. Self-conception, status within the gang, and group process.

Stratton, John R., and Robert M. Terry, eds. *Prevention of Delinquency: Problems and Programs*. New York: Macmillan, 1968. Anthology: theoretical, empirical, evaluative aspects of delinquency control.

Vaz, Edmund W., ed. *Middle-Class Juvenile Delinquency*. New York: Harper & Row, 1967. Series of theoretical and research articles.

Wheeler, Stanton, ed. *Controlling Delinquents*. New York: Wiley, 1967. Relations of delinquents with those charged with their detection, adjudication, and rehabilitation.

4. Sex

Brown, Helen Gurley. *Sex and the Single Girl*. New York: Random House, 1962. Frank treatment.

Gagnon, John H., and William Simon, eds. *Sexual Deviance*. New York: Harper & Row, 1967. Articles deal with general problems and especially with prostitution and homosexuality.

Gebhard, Paul H., John H. Gagnon, Wardell B. Pomeroy, and Cornelia V. Christenson. *Sex Offenders: An Analysis of Types*. New York: Harper & Row, 1965. Study of 1500 male sex offenders of 14 types.

Group for the Advancement of Psychiatry, *Sex and the College Student*. New York: Mental Health Materials Center, 1965.

Murtagh, John M., and Sara Harris. *Cast the First Stone*. New York: McGraw-Hill, 1957. History of organized prostitution and of efforts at its reform in New York City.

Reiss, Ira L. *The Social Context of Premarital Sexual Permissiveness*. New York: Holt, Rinehart & Winston, 1967. Sample study of five schools and of nation.

Schofield, Michael. *Sociological Aspects of Homosexuality: A Comparative Study of Three Types of Homosexuals*. Boston: Little, Brown, 1965. Study of 150 English homosexuals.

Schur, Edwin M. *Crimes Without Victims*. Englewood Cliffs, N.J.: Prentice-Hall, 1965. Comprehensive discussion of homosexual behavior.

Weinberg, S. Kirson. *Incest Behavior*. New York: Citadel, 1963.

Chapter 32: Problem Families II: Adults

5. Occupation

Blau, Peter M., and Otis Dudley Duncan, with Andrea Tyree. *The American Occupational Structure*. New York: Wiley, 1967. Reassessment of "land of opportunity."

Dubin, Robert. *The World of Work: Industrial Society and Human Rela-*

tions. Englewood Cliffs, N.J.: Prentice-Hall, 1958. Organization of work in contemporary industrial society.

Leggett, John C. *Class, Race, and Labor: Working-Class Consciousness in Detroit.* New York: Oxford University Press, 1968. Detailed sociological study of social setting of work.

Mason, Edward S., ed. *The Corporation in Modern Society.* Cambridge: Harvard University Press, 1959. Organization of work through corporate structure, impact on other organizations.

May, Edgar. *The Wasted Americans.* New York: Harper & Row, 1964. Why do millions of Americans subsist on welfare in the midst of an affluent society.

Moore, Wilbert E. *The Conduct of the Corporation.* New York: Random House, 1963. Functions and policies of the corporation.

Ross, Arthur M., and Herbert Hill, eds. *Employment, Race and Poverty.* New York: Harcourt, Brace & World, 1967. Examination of racial biases in U.S. employment practices.

Rostow, W. W. *The Stages of Economic Growth: A Non-Communist Manifesto.* Cambridge, England: Cambridge University Press, 1960. Development and nature of mass-consumption society.

Slocum, Walter. *Occupational Careers: A Sociological Perspective.* Chicago: Aldine, 1966. Careers in work organizations of our "employee society."

Taylor, Lee. *Occupational Sociology.* New York: Oxford University Press, 1968. Occupations, occupational structures, and their meaning.

6. Health

Anderson, Odin W. *The Uneasy Equilibrium: Private and Public Financing of Health Services in the United States, 1875–1965.* New Haven: College & University Press, 1968.

Apple, Dorrian, ed. *Sociological Studies of Health and Sickness.* New York: McGraw-Hill, 1960.

Folta, Jeannette R., and E. S. Deck, eds. *Sociological Framework for Patient Care.* New York: Wiley, 1966.

Freeman, Howard E., and others, eds. *Handbook of Medical Sociology.* Englewood Cliffs, N.J.: Prentice-Hall, 1963.

Kellner, Robert. *Family Ill Health: An Investigation in General Practice.* Philadelphia: Lippincott, 1963.

King, Stanley H. *Perceptions of Illness and Medical Practice.* New York: Russell Sage Foundation, 1962.

Knutson, Andie. *Individual, Society, and Health Behavior.* New York: Russell Sage Foundation, 1965.

Luchterhand, Elmer, and Daniel Sydiaha. *Choice in Human Affairs: An Application to Aging-Accident-Illness Problems.* New Haven: College & University Press, 1966.

Mechanic, David. *Medical Sociology.* New York: Free Press, 1968.

Scott, W. Richard, and E. H. Volkart. *Medical Care.* New York: Wiley, 1966.

Skipper, James K., Jr., and Robert C. Leonard, eds. *Social Interaction and Patient Care.* Philadelphia: Lippincott, 1965. Psychosocial aspects of the care of hospital patients.

Suchman, Edward A. *Sociology and the Field of Public Health.* New York: Russell Sage Foundation, 1963.

Susser, Mervyn W., and William Watson. *Sociology in Medicine.* New York: Oxford University Press, 1962.

7. Crime

Bedau, Hugo Adam, ed. *The Death Penalty in America: An Anthology,* rev. ed. Chicago: Aldine, 1968.

Blumberg, Abraham S. *Criminal Justice.* Chicago: Quadrangle, 1967. "Inside" examination of criminal courts.

Bordua, David J., ed. *The Police: Six Sociological Essays.* New York: Wiley, 1967.

Cameron, Mary Owen. *The Booster and the Snitch: Department Store Shoplifting.* New York: Free Press, 1964.

Dinitz, Simon, and Walter C. Reckless, eds. *Critical Issues in the Study of Crime: A Book of Readings.* Boston: Little, Brown, 1968.

Geis, Gilbert, ed. *White-Collar Criminal: The Offender in Business and the Professions.* New York: Atherton Press, 1968. Origins and manifestations, descriptive and theoretical.

Giallombardo, Rose. *Society of Women: A Study of a Woman's Prison.* New York: Wiley, 1966.

Gibbons, Don C. *Society, Crime, and Criminal Careers.* Englewood Cliffs, N.J.: Prentice-Hall, 1968. Review and critical analysis of theories of crime causation and of correctional handling of offenders.

Johnson, Elmer H. *Crime, Correction, and Society,* rev. ed. Homewood, Ill.: Dorsey Press, 1968. Popular text within framework of social control.

Knudten, Richard D., ed. *Criminological Controversies.* New York: Appleton-Century-Crofts, 1968. Probes 12 major problems pro and con.

Polsky, Ned. *Hustlers, Beats, and Others.* Chicago: Aldine, 1967.

Savitz, Leonard. *Dilemmas in Criminology.* New York: McGraw-Hill, 1967.

Sellin, Thorsten, ed. *Capital Punishment.* New York: Harper & Row, 1967.

Skolnick, Jerome H. *Justice Without Trial: Law Enforcement in a Democratic Society.* New York: Wiley, 1966. Aspects of administration of criminal justice.

Sutherland, Edwin H., and Donald R. Cressey. *Principles of Criminology,* 7th ed. Philadelphia: Lippincott, 1966. A leading text again revised.

Sykes, Gresham. *Crime and Society,* 2nd ed. New York: Random House, 1967. Examines crime as a normal feature of society.

Taft, Donald R., and Ralph W. England, Jr. *Criminology,* 4th ed. New York: Macmillan, 1964. Crime as an outgrowth of our culture, review of competing theories.

8. Old Age

Barron, Milton L. *The Aging American: An Introduction to Social Gerontology and Geriatrics.* New York: T. Y. Crowell Co., 1961. Indicates merits of "whole life" planning in community, region, nation.

Clark, Margaret, and Barbara Gallatin Anderson. *Culture and Aging: An Anthropological Study of Older Americans.* Springfield, Ill.: C. C. Thomas, 1967.

Koller, Marvin R. *Social Gerontology.* New York: Random House, 1968. Aging process in individual and its social significance.

Rose, Arnold M., and W. A. Peterson. *Older People and Their Social World.* Philadelphia: F. A. Davis Co., 1965.

Rosow, Irving. *Social Integration of the Aged.* New York: Free Press, 1967.

Shanas, Ethel, and others. *Old People in Three Industrial Societies.* New York: Atherton Press, 1968. In United States, Britain, and Denmark.

Vedder, C. D., ed. *Problems of the Middle Aged.* Springfield, Ill.: C. C. Thomas, 1965.

Williams, Richard H., Clark Tibbits, and Wilma Donahue. *Processes of Aging: Social and Psychological Perspectives.* New York: Atherton Press, 1963. Interdisciplinary description of current worldwide research.

Williams, Richard H., and Claudine G. Wirths. *Lives Through the Years: Styles of Life and Successful Aging.* New York: Atherton Press, 1965.

9. Death

Bowman, LeRoy. *The American Funeral: A Study in Guilt, Extravagance, and Sublimity.* Washington: Public Affairs Press, 1959. Competent survey and analysis of funeral business.

Choron, J. *Death and Western Thought.* New York: Collier Books, 1963.

Douglas, Jack D. *The Social Meanings of Suicide.* Princeton: Princeton University Press, 1967.

Dublin, Louis. *Suicide: A Sociological and Statistical Study.* New York: Ronald Press, 1963.

Durkheim, Emile. *Suicide.* Transl. by J. A. Spaulding and George Simpson. Glencoe, Ill.: Free Press, 1951. A sociological landmark study.

Fulton, Robert, ed. *Death and Identity.* New York: Wiley, 1965.

Glaser, Barney G., and Anselm L. Strauss. *Awareness of Dying.* 1965. *Time for Dying.* 1968. Chicago: Aldine.

Sudnow, David. *Passing On: The Social Organization of Dying.* Englewood Cliffs, N.J.: Prentice-Hall, 1967.

Chapter 33: Problems of Minorities: Racial, Ethnic, Class

For bibliographies on racial and ethnic minorities and their interrelations, see selected readings above for Part Four.

1. Class

Bendix, Reinhard, and S. M. Lipset, eds. *Class, Status, and Power: Social Stratification in Comparative Perspective,* 2nd ed. New York: Free Press, 1966. Power, class behavior, mobility, pending issue. Comprehensive reader.

Domhoff, G. William. *Who Rules America?* Englewood Cliffs, N.J.: Spectrum Books, Prentice-Hall, 1967. Nature and perpetuation of the "power elite" in American society.

Lasswell, Thomas E. *Class and Stratum: An Introduction to Concepts and Research.* Boston: Houghton Mifflin, 1965. Fresh re-thinking of data and theory.

Lenski, Gerhard. *Power and Privilege: A Theory of Stratification.* New York: McGraw-Hill, 1966.

Miller, S. M., and Frank Riessman. *Social Class and Social Policy.* New York: Basic Books, 1968.

Mizruchi, Ephraim Harold. *Success and Opportunity: Class Values and Anomie in American Life.* New York: Free Press, 1964.

Tumin, Melvin M. *Social Stratification: The Forms and Functions of Inequality.* Englewood Cliffs, N.J.: Prentice-Hall, 1967.

Chapter 34: Problems of Community and Society

1. Local Community Conditions

Bensman, Joseph, and Arthur J. Vidich. *Small Town in Mass Society.* Garden City, N.Y.: Doubleday, 1958.

Bernard, Jessie. *American Community Behavior,* rev. ed. New York: Holt, Rinehart & Winston, 1962.

Stein, Maurice R. *The Eclipse of Community.* New York: Harper & Row, 1964. Problems and prospects of American community life.

Warren, Roland L. *The Community in America.* Chicago: Rand McNally, 1963.

2. Mass Manipulation

Berelson, Bernard, and Morris Janowitz, eds. *Reader in Public Opinion and Communication,* 2nd ed. New York: Free Press, 1966. Comprehensive handbook.

Cutlip, Scott M., and Allen H. Center. *Effective Public Relations,* 3rd ed. Englewood Cliffs, N.J.: Prentice-Hall, 1964. Leading text on how to do mass communications.

Doob, Leonard W. *Public Opinion and Propaganda,* 2nd ed. New York: Holt, Rinehart & Winston, 1956. A basic text.

Duncan, Hugh D. *Communication and the Social Order.* New York: Bedminister Press, 1962. Symbolic interactionist theory.

Katz, Daniel, Dorwin Cartwright, Samuel Eldersveld, and Alfred McClung Lee, eds. *Public Opinion and Propaganda: A Book of Readings.* New York: Holt, Rinehart & Winston, 1954. Sponsored by the Society for the Psychological Study of Social Issues.

Lee, Alfred McClung. *How to Understand Propaganda.* New York: Rinehart, 1952. Analysis of mass manipulation in terms of communication content, personnel, media, organizations, opinions, and strategies.

MacDougall, Curtis D. *Understanding Public Opinion: A Guide for Newspapermen and Newspaper Readers.* New York: Macmillan, 1952. Written by experienced newspaperman and sociologist.

3. Natural Catastrophes

Fritz, Charles E., "Disaster," chap. 14 in Robert K. Merton and Robert A. Nisbet, *Contemporary Social Problems,* 1st ed. New York: Harcourt, Brace & World, 1961, pp. 651–694. Useful survey of disasters and of disaster research.

Grosser, George H., Henry Wechsler, and Milton Greenblatt, eds. *The Threat of Impending Disaster: Contributions to the Psychology of Stress.* Cambridge: M.I.T. Press, 1964. Responses of individual and group to a variety of impending disasters.

Moore, Harry Estill. *Tornadoes Over Texas.* Austin: University of Texas Press, 1958.

Prince, S. H. *Catastrophe and Social Change.* New York: Columbia University Press, 1920. Study of Halifax disaster.

Sorokin, Pitirim A. *Man and Society in Calamity.* New York: Dutton, 1942. Reactions of societies to crises.

Tannehill, Ivan R. *Hurricanes.* Princeton: Princeton University Press, 1937.

Wallace, Anthony F. C. *Human Behavior in Extreme Situations: A Survey of the Literature and Suggestions for Further Research.* Committee on Disaster Studies Report No. 1, Publication 390. Washington: National Academy of Sciences and National Research Council, 1956.

4. Depressions, Inflations

Angell, Robert C. *The Family Encounters the Depression.* New York: Scribner's, 1936.
Cavan, Ruth S., and Katherine H. Ranck. *The Family and the Depression.* Chicago: University of Chicago Press, 1938.

5. Pollution and Waste

Carson, Rachel. *Silent Spring.* Boston: Houghton Mifflin, 1962. Destructive influence of irresponsible use of insecticides.
Dasmann, Raymond F. *A Different Kind of Country.* New York: Macmillan, 1967. On conservation of an environment fit for human habitation.
Fraser Darling, F., and John P. Milton. *The Future Environments of North America.* New York: Doubleday and Natural History Press, 1966.
Udall, Stewart. *The Quiet Crisis.* New York: Holt, Rinehart & Winston, 1963. Case for conservation presented by the U.S. Secretary of the Interior.

6. Overpopulation

Freedman, R. *Population: The Vital Revolution.* Chicago: Aldine, 1965. A detailed study.
Stewart, Maxwell S., "A New Look at Our Crowded World." *Public Affairs Pamphlet* no. 393. New York: 1966. A compact summary of data and issues.
Studies in Family Planning, a serial report on population control programs issued by the Population Council.
Thompson, Warren S., and David T. Lewis. *Population Problems,* 5th ed. New York: McGraw-Hill, 1965. A standard reference work.

7. Wars, Cold and Hot

American Friends Service Committee. *The Draft?* New York: Hill & Wang, 1968. A consideration of the evidence pro and con by a special panel of specialists.
Cochran, Bert. *The War System.* New York: Macmillan, 1965. Pessimistic view of current international relations policies.
Coser, Lewis A. *The Functions of Social Conflict.* 1956. *Continuities in the Study of Social Conflict.* 1967. New York: Free Press.
Heath, Robert C., ed. *Statements of Religious Bodies on the Conscientious Objector,* 5th ed. Washington: National Service Board for Religious Objectors, 1966.
Iklé, Fred C. *The Social Impact of Bomb Destruction.* Norman: University of Oklahoma Press, 1958. Comparative study of reactions to major bombings.
Janis, I. L. *Air War and Emotional Stress.* New York: McGraw-Hill, 1951. Review of reactions to atomic and other bombing.
Tatum, Arlo, ed. *Handbook for Conscientious Objectors,* 9th ed. Philadelphia: Central Committee for Conscientious Objectors, 1968.

Tax, Sol, ed. *The Draft*. Chicago: University of Chicago Press, 1967. University of Chicago symposium.

Waller, Willard, ed. *War in the Twentieth Century*. New York: Dryden Press, 1940. Interdisciplinary symposium.

Chapter 35: Social Research, Planning, and Action

Bauer, Raymond A., and Kenneth J. Gergen, eds. *The Study of Policy Formation*. New York: Free Press, 1968. Symposium on past and new approaches.

Clark, Terry N. *Community Structure and Decision-Making: Comparative Analyses*. Chicago: Science Research Associates, 1968.

Freeman, Linton C. *Patterns of Local Community Leadership*. Indianapolis: Bobbs-Merrill, 1968.

Lowry, Ritchie P. *Who's Running This Town? Community Leadership and Social Change*. New York: Harper, 1968.

McCord, William. *The Springtime of Freedom: The Evolution of Developing Societies*. New York: Oxford University Press, 1965.

INDEX

Abortion, 46, 318
Academic freedom, 294
Accident, 293-294, 342
Accommodation, in marriage, 42–43; to new culture, 220, 276
Action research, 298; structure, 133
Adaptation, 132, 353
Addict, 337
Addiction, 299, 322, 336
Administrator, 103, 149, 166
Adolescence, 35, 37, 293; "little," 35
Adoption, 293, 318, 320
Adults, 328–342
Adulteration, 338
Adultery, 48–49, 326–327
Advertising, 88, 131, 158, 177, 264, 305, 330, 353–354
Affluent society, 316
Ageing, 293, 332–334, 339–341
Aggregation, 82
Agitation, 103, 117, 311
Agitator, 25, 62, 149, 305; types of, 104–105
Agriculture, 145, 256, 283, 292, 329, 356
Alcohol, 315, 328, 336, 342
Alcoholic, 293, 337
Alcoholics Anonymous, 337
Alcoholism, 53, 309–310, 349
Alienation, 106, 328, 331
Alihan, Milla Aissa, 237
Alimony, 49
Allee, W. C., 236
Amalgamation, 276
Ambivalence, 14, 19
Amentia, 52
American Cancer Society, 336
Americanization, 349
Ancestor, 345
Annulment, 47, 49, 50
Anomy, 298, 299, 302
Anthropology, 126, 249
Antisocial, 321; behavior, 302
Applied sociology, 298, 306
Apprenticeship, 330

Area, as ecological factor, 236; of transition, 282
Army, as total institution, 133
Art, 211
Artisan, 21, 295, 329, 331
Artist, 56, 295
Assault, 326
Assembly-line, 329, 331
Assimilation, 27, 276, 282, 310, 348
Association, 11, 107, 130, 131, 133, 151, 161, 252
Asylum, 133
Attention, 75, 76, 82, 104, 297
Attitude, 3, 11–14, 16, 107, 206, 210, 212, 222, 309
Attorney, 338, 339
Audience, 138
Authority, 181, 184, 212, 309, 324
Automobile revolution, 352
Autonomy, 325

Babyhood, 293
Backlash, 348
Bakwin, Harry, 34
Bandana Curtain, 21
Behavior, collective, 66–121; basis of, 67–68; defined, 69; field of, 67–69; crowd, 70; group, 6; pattern, 212; random, 73
Belief, 110, 174–176, 191, 206, 207, 213, 236
Bellicosity, 359
Bereavement, 47, 293, 328, 341–342
Bernard, L. L., 5
Bestiality, 326
Betrothal, 44
Bigamy, 49
Bigotry, 313
Biological intermixture, 218; process, 192
Biosphere, 242
Biotic balance, 241, 270, 283; community, 235, 276
Birth, 46, 275; control, 45, 182, 293, 318, 319, 357–358; rate, 192, 213, 357